Using Social Media for Global Security

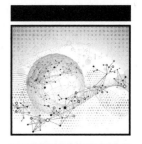

Using Social Media for Global Security

Ravi Gupta
Hugh Brooks

John Wiley & Sons, Inc.

Using Social Media for Global Security

Published by
John Wiley & Sons, Inc.
10475 Crosspoint Boulevard
Indianapolis, IN 46256
www.wiley.com

Copyright © 2013 by John Wiley & Sons, Inc., Indianapolis, Indiana

Published simultaneously in Canada

ISBN: 978-1-118-44231-9

ISBN: 978-1-118-44221-0 (ebk)

ISBN: 978-1-118-63185-0 (ebk)

ISBN: 978-1-118-63191-1 (ebk)

Manufactured in the United States of America

10 9 8 7 6 5 4 3 2 1

For general information on our other products and services please contact our Customer Care Department within the United States at (877) 762-2974, outside the United States at (317) 572-3993 or fax (317) 572-4002.

Wiley publishes in a variety of print and electronic formats and by print-on-demand. Some material included with standard print versions of this book may not be included in e-books or in print-on-demand. If this book refers to media such as a CD or DVD that is not included in the version you purchased, you may download this material at http://booksupport.wiley.com. For more information about Wiley products, visit www.wiley.com.

Library of Congress Control Number: 2012954402

Anything that is in the world when you're born is normal and ordinary and is just a natural part of the way the world works. Anything that's invented between when you're fifteen and thirty-five is new and exciting and revolutionary and you can probably get a career in it. Anything invented after you're thirty-five is against the natural order of things.

— Douglas Adams

Man verdirbt einen Jüngling am sichersten, wenn man ihn anleitet, den Gleichdenkenden höher zu achten, als den Andersdenkenden.

One degrades a youth with surety, when one directs him to appreciate the like-minded thinkers more than those who think differently.

— Friedrich Nietzsche

About the Authors

Ravi Gupta is an entrepreneur who specializes in commercializing technologies that use biological principles to solve a variety of problems. He has designed and built social media platforms, data processing algorithms, and crowdsourcing techniques to help governments and commercial clients bolster disaster relief, improve medical diagnostics, and model crowd behavior in emergency situations. He currently focuses on exploring how insects, neural networks, immune systems, and microorganisms solve coordination and security problems. He then uses the insights from the natural world to tackle human issues ranging from reconceiving cyber security to understanding financial markets to increasing medical access in denied areas. He holds a B.S. in Brain and Cognitive Sciences and a B.S. in Political Science from MIT, and a Masters in Security Studies from Georgetown University. He is available for stalking on Twitter under the user name—@ravistalking—which features sarcastic tweets about science, technology, metal music, and foreign affairs.

Hugh Brooks is a security consultant with clients in the government and private sectors. Hugh's passion is for finding creative and unique solutions for security problems. To this end, he has helped envision, design, and create innovative solutions for crowd-driven applications, poly-agent based modeling, mobile health and education, and cyber security. A frequent world-traveler, bibliophile, and persistent student of many subjects, he has worked extensively on the confluence of social media, terrorism, and illicit activity, and designed social media solutions for a variety of security problems. A former enlisted U.S. Marine Corps Reservist, he received a B.A. in Political Science and African Studies from the University of Florida, and a Masters in Security Studies from Georgetown University. Hugh tweets under the moniker—@Sefu_Africa—where he futilely tries to monitor and address security and technological innovations and issues across the African continent and throughout the globe.

About the Technical Editor

Russell D. Vines (CISSP, CEH, CISM, SECURITY+. PCI QSA, NSA IAM), is the Chief Security Advisor for the Gotham Technology Group, and is an expert in Information Systems Security, focusing on the prevention, detection, and remediation of security vulnerabilities of international corporations, government, military, and financial organizations.

He is the author or co-author of eleven books on InfoSec published by John S. Wiley and Sons and is a frequent contributor to web and trade publications and a frequent speaker at industry events.

Russ also teaches CISSP and Certified Ethical Hacking (CEH) for Gotham Technology Group. Russ' blog can be found here: `http://blog.gothamtg.com/author/rdvines/`. Links to his books can be found here: `http://www.amazon.com/Russell-Dean-Vines/e/B001H6GO56/`

Credits

Executive Editor
Carol Long

Project Editor
Ed Connor

Technical Editor
Russell Dean Vines

Production Editor
Kathleen Wisor

Copy Editor
Kim Cofer

Editorial Manager
Mary Beth Wakefield

Freelancer Editorial Manager
Rosemarie Graham

Associate Director of Marketing
David Mayhew

Marketing Manager
Ashley Zurcher

Business Manager
Amy Knies

Production Manager
Tim Tate

Vice President and Executive Group Publisher
Richard Swadley

Vice President and Executive Publisher
Neil Edde

Associate Publisher
Jim Minatel

Project Coordinator, Cover
Katie Crocker

Proofreader
Nancy Carrasco

Indexer
Robert Swanson

Cover Image
© Aleksandar Velasevic / iStockphoto

Cover Designer
Ryan Sneed

Acknowledgments

We live in two worlds that do not usually meet. The first is the defense and security world made up of police officers, soldiers, analysts, and diplomats, the most capable of whom anonymously strive to secure our communities. Over the course of our careers, they have posed to us thousands of questions and challenges, which motivated us to write this book. They are too many to list and we wish to protect their anonymity, but the most prominent are John Sims and Donald Codling. Also, we thank Steve Anson for giving us the opportunity that directly led to this book's publication.

The second is the new media technology world made up of hundreds of entrepreneurs, technology companies, non-governmental organizations, thinkers, and geeks, many of whom we mention throughout the book. They are the ones who invent the technologies and deploy them innovatively. This book primarily catalogs their exploits, tweaks them, and introduces them to a different audience. We would list their names in detail, but the list would be quite long, and, understandably, some of them are hesitant to be associated with the security world for various reasons.

Of course, we would not be able to connect the two worlds if it were not for yet another world that has supported and sustained us throughout this process. We thank everyone at Wiley, especially, Carol Long and Edward Connor, for patiently guiding us through our first book. We also thank the Georgetown University Security Studies Program staff and faculty for fostering a community comprising a unique blend of people and subject matter that led us to collaborate and think creatively about security issues. Lastly, writing this book quickly was quite an endeavor for us and it generated its fair share of anxiety and sleepless nights. We thank our friends for making sure the book did not consume our lives completely by distracting us with parties, trips, and stupid but fun ideas.

We do not have the room to include everyone, but for those who put up with us the most during the book's writing, we thank: Dominic, Steph, Mariko, Holly, Daniel, Mike, Bernd, the Walkers, Ramses, Pleepleus, and the Reyes fiesteros.

Contents at a Glance

Contents

Introduction

We wrote this book because the United States Department of Homeland Security (DHS) once ruined an Irish tourist's vacation because of a tweet. In 2012, before embarking on a vacation to the U.S., Leigh Van Bryan excitedly tweeted that he was going to "destroy America." When he landed in the US, the DHS detained him in a cell with Mexican drug dealers for 12 hours. With the best of intentions, the DHS confronted him with his tweet, not realizing that "destroy America" was not a threat but slang indicating he was going to have fun on his vacation. Seemingly, the DHS was using a fairly rudimentary method of social media monitoring to recognize threats without understanding the nuances of social media use and data analysis, leading to a misguided arrest and a waste of investigative resources. The DHS also apparently did not realize that terrorists are not very likely to tweet their operational plans right before they attack.

This and other similar episodes illustrate the knowledge gap in government and security circles regarding social media data analysis and technology use. Although there are many exceptions, too many well-intentioned security professionals use social media ineffectively and irresponsibly. Misguided use of social media wastes time and money, erodes people's civil liberties and privacy, and jeopardizes security.

We have also noticed that some people tasked with providing or analyzing security either think social media is the greatest thing ever created or the most useless. In reality, it is neither. It is indeed something that young people waste time using, but it is also a potent tool and a reservoir of data for helping solve security problems concerning irregular warfare challenges, discrete intelligence collection, intelligence analysis, covert operations, risk analysis influence operations, and much more. The sooner policymakers, military and law enforcement personnel, diplomats, and other security professionals realize this, the safer our world will be for it. Social media will not solve all of your problems but it can definitely help solve some.

What This Book Is About

Most books about social media and security are concerned with personal security. They deal with important issues about identity theft and, for example, how to set privacy settings on Facebook. Although we briefly address the topic, this book is *not* about personal security. This book is also not about conducting marketing and creating brand awareness through social media; however, some of the approaches we discuss are related and applicable in those areas as well.

This book is about how to use social media data and technologies to improve and positively influence matters of global security. Specifically, this book will teach you the following seven skills:

1. Collection, aggregation, and filtering of social media data and other related data

2. Analysis of social media data to map social networks; identify the networks' key agents and relationships, and track the ideas propagating through the networks

3. Analysis of social media and other data in real time to understand and forecast crises, events, and behaviors

4. Incentivizing populations globally, including in hard-to-reach areas, to provide intelligence

5. Incentivizing populations globally to help you solve complex problems related to security

6. Persuading populations globally to adopt viewpoints and perform actions that help your mission

7. Using social media data and technologies intelligently, cost-effectively, realistically, and with regards to privacy norms and ethics

Our intent is not to dictate how you should use social media, but to reveal the opportunities that social media presents. We provide you with the basic information, skills, and ideas to get started. We hope you will expand, critique, and build on the knowledge contained herein. We also hope this book encourages you to seek out and learn more about the relationship between social media and security issues. Throughout the book, we regularly reference controversial stories and issues, but we do not dictate how you should think about them. Our focus is on detailing how to use social media to improve and conduct specialized operations, not on debating the future of social media and estimating its influence. We are standing on new ground and we leave it to you to measure its fertility.

Before we outline the approaches and methods discussed in the forthcoming chapters, we want to briefly address what we mean by global security.

What Constitutes Global Security

We encourage you to, for the most part; forget what you know about global security. Terms such as global security and international security are constantly evolving and often subject to intense academic discussion. Traditionally, the terms have dealt with states and issues of interstate war and power. Practitioners were encouraged to apply theories such as Realism and Liberalism to assessing how states react to security issues. As the World Wars and Cold War wound down and the number of major interstate conflicts dwindled, the focus then shifted to encompassing international organizations and intrastate issues like civil wars.

Due to globalization and major terrorist attacks, the focus has shifted again to assessing the effects of non-state actors. The spread of inexpensive and powerful technologies such as computers and biotechnology has increased the ability of non-state actors including terrorists, criminals, and rioters to impact international security. We now live in a globally connected world, where partly due to emerging and widespread social media technology, a self-immolating distraught young man can spark events that affect the lives of billions and foil the foreign policies of the most powerful countries in the world. Simply put, power is constantly shifting and diluting from states to groups and individuals.

So when we say global security or international security, we mean everything that affects the safety and lives of people around you. Global security now encompasses great power politics, civil wars, terrorist groups, transnational narcotics, human trafficking, irregular warfare, cyber criminals, violent rioters, lone-wolf serial murderers, disease epidemics, and much more. Traditional Realism considered states as rational actors that performed cost-benefit analyses before committing action. This mode of thinking is not relevant to our needs. Now, especially when using social media technologies, you have to take into account the emotions, fears, and hopes of small groups and individuals. As the definition of international security has expanded, so have the theories and heuristics that help you understand it. Beyond this book and the usual foreign policy and security books, we encourage you to read up on disparate fields such as cognitive science, behavioral economics, statistical modeling, biology, and physics. Using social media effectively demands a familiarity with unfamiliarity and unconventional ways of thinking.

Who Should Read This Book

Since the definition of global security has expanded, so has the number and type of people concerned with it. This book is intended for the emerging international security workforce—those who have to plan, execute, and manage everything from counterterrorism operations to risk analysis projects. We are writing for the analyst and operator, examples of which appear in Table I.1.

Table I.1: Examples of Intended Audience

PERSONNEL	ORGANIZATION	MISSION
Military operators	Department of Defense, NATO, UN Peacekeepers	Plan and conduct military operations in hard-to-reach areas
Law enforcement officials	FBI, LAPD, NYPD, Interpol	Preempt and stop criminal attacks; disrupt narcotics and trafficking networks
Counterterrorism officials	Department of Defense, FBI, Mossad	Analyze and disrupt terror networks
Foreign service officials	State Department, Embassy officials worldwide	Conduct outreach in hostile areas
Disaster responders	U.S. Navy, Doctors Without Borders, Red Cross, Red Crescent	Forecast and respond to humanitarian crises
Intelligence analysts	CIA, Department of Defense, MI-5	Collect intelligence using discrete methods
Policy makers	U.S. Congress staff	Guide the assessment and adoption of technologies
Chief Security Officers	Multinational corporations	Protect assets and assess risk in supply chains
Contractor analysts and operators	Government contractors	Complete intelligence and security tasks

Table I.1 is not exhaustive. Even if you are not directly involved with global security issues, or are not a practitioner, we hope this book will provide you with another perspective to assess, report, and understand the emerging, interconnected world.

How This Book Is Organized

To aid understanding, this book is split into the following four parts:

- Part I provides you with the necessary background knowledge about social media to use the methods detailed in the book.

- Chapter 1 illustrates how social media is impacting global security issues. If you doubt social media's influence, capabilities, and relevance, you need to read this chapter.

- Chapter 2 defines social media, introduces pertinent existing and emerging technologies, and describes their use globally. Understanding the different technologies and patterns of usage around the world will help you take into account contextual factors when analyzing social media data and focus your efforts when building crowdsourcing platforms. Even if you are generally familiar with social media, we encourage you to read the chapter so you do not miss key relevant facts.

- Part II describes how to conduct social media data analytics to solve specific problems.

  - Chapter 3 introduces key analytical terms, methodologies, and definitions. If you have little experience using quantitative methodologies and conducting data analytics, this chapter will prove especially helpful. You can also apply the methodologies to problems not related to social media data. You need only a general knowledge of basic math and scientific principles, and we do our best to ensure it does not put you to sleep.

  - Chapter 4 details best practices for collecting and managing social media and other relevant data. It explains several processes for collecting, filtering, and storing data, and discusses when to use which process. It also addresses technical and legal issues concerning data collection, and what you should look out for when building or purchasing data collection tools.

  - Chapter 5 focuses on social network analysis, and explains how to do social network analysis using social media data to map networks, identify key people and relationships in networks, and track the spread of ideas.

  - Chapter 6 explores different methods of using social media data and other data to understand and forecast a variety of security events, behaviors, and issues. Methods include intelligence monitoring of real-time social media data, language and sentiment analysis, correlation and regression analysis, and volumetric analysis.

- Part III shows how to design, build, and maintain crowdsourcing platforms, which enable you to communicate with and collect information and solutions from the crowds using social media.

  - Chapter 7 introduces the concept of crowdsourcing, its relationship to social media technologies, and its advantages and limitations. It also covers when it is appropriate to crowdsourcing and provides numerous examples of relevant crowdsourcing projects.

- Chapter 8 covers the general rules and steps for designing, building, and managing crowdsourcing platforms regardless of their objective.

- Chapter 9 illustrates how to design, build, and maintain crowdsourcing platforms to incentivize populations in a variety of situations and areas to provide intelligence about a range of security issues,

- Chapter 10 illustrates how to design, build, and maintain crowdsourcing platforms to incentivize populations to solve security and related technical problems.

- Chapter 11 illustrates how to design, build, and maintain crowdsourcing platforms to discreetly influence populations and encourage them to adopt certain viewpoints and behaviors.

- Part IV introduces more complex ways of using social media data, and using social media to solve issues tangentially related to social media. It also addresses critical issues regarding privacy and the ethics of social media use.

  - Chapter 12 summarizes more complex analytical methodologies and their increasing relevance to social media. The methodologies are cluster analysis, geo-spatial network analysis, and agent modeling.

  - Chapter 13 describes how to use social media technologies and crowdsourcing to improve provision of education and health services in denied areas, so as to improve security in those areas.

  - Chapter 14 discusses current and arriving laws and norms concerning privacy and use of social media data that may impact your ability to use social media effectively, safely, and lawfully. It also teaches those of you concerned about privacy or those who fear abuse of social media use by oppressive regimes, how to protect your identity, privacy, and free speech.

The chapters feature numerous examples, walkthroughs, and case studies regarding real-world issues and events. We reference many major news events that came up during the writing of this book, and bluntly call out contemporary misuse of social media data and technology. Our intention is not to be controversial or disrespectful but to be intellectually honest and straightforward.

All the information in this book is available in the public domain or based on examining publically viewable websites and platforms. Our intention is not to divulge secrets or sensitive information. We only pulled together publically available information from disparate fields and converted them into a digestible format. To this purpose, we reference numerous websites and publications throughout the book. Go through them for more information. Also refer to the Appendix if you want more information about existing social media platforms and software solutions.

Conventions

To help you get the most from the text and keep track of what is happening, we have used a number of conventions throughout the book.

WARNING Boxes like this one hold important, not-to-be forgotten information that is directly relevant to the surrounding text.

NOTE Notes, tips, hints, tricks, and asides to the current discussion are off-set and placed in bold like this.

As for styles in the text:

- We *highlight* new terms and important words when we introduce them.
- We show keyboard strokes like this: Ctrl+A.
- We show filenames, URLs, and code within the text like so: `persistence.properties`.

Tools You Will Need

You need a decent computer, a simple cell phone, and regular access to the Internet to accomplish the walkthroughs. Familiarity with cell phones and mainstream social media platforms such as Twitter will help.

You will need certain software and services to complete the walkthroughs. We recommend you use the ones listed in Table I.2. We picked them because they are simple, easy-to-use, and relatively inexpensive. However, many other open-source and commercial software solutions and services can replace the ones we listed and you should feel free to use them if you are more comfortable with them. A good example of a relevant open-source program is the U.S. Naval Postgraduate School's Lighthouse program (`http://lhproject.info/about-lighthouse/`).

Table I.2: Recommended Software Tools and Services

SOFTWARE TOOL	LICENSE	URL
UCINET	Commercial (with free trials)	`https://sites.google.com/site/ucinetsoftware/home`
NodeXL	Open-Source	`http://nodexl.codeplex.com`
Microsoft Excel	Commercial	`http://office.microsoft.com/en-us/excel/`
Ushahidi Crowdmaps	Open-Source	`http://www.ushahidi.com/products/crowdmap`
FrontlineSMS	Open-Source	`http://www.frontlinesms.com`
Clickatell	Commercial (as a service)	`https://www.clickatell.com`

NOTE   The organizations that made the software tools in Table I.2 in no way sponsor, condone, or encourage the use of their software to complete the tasks in this book. They do not have a relationship with us.

What's on the Website

Social media technologies become obsolete and replaced at a rapid rate, and so will your knowledge about social media if you do not actively seek out new information. The companion website helps you keep up-to-date by providing updates about the most cutting-edge and relevant technologies, analytical methods, software solutions, and news stories and issues. The website also hosts several data files including ones we use and reference in the walkthroughs and examples throughout the book. Lastly, visit our website if you are interested in learning more about the DHS episode we referenced earlier.

A Note on Using Social Media Ethically

We dedicated a chapter to the human rights and privacy issues concerning social media. However, because the topic is so pivotal and controversial, we also wanted to briefly say a few things about it now. Doing so will help you understand where we are coming from and our expectations for how you should use the knowledge in this book.

Our goal is to impart you with knowledge that will help you curb terrorist attacks, stop criminals, ensure peace in communities, give a voice and freedom to the oppressed, and save victims of humanitarian disasters. We encourage everyone to use the tools and information we discuss lawfully, ethically, responsibly, and to achieve positive goals. Where possible we have minimized the ability of antagonistic actors to exploit this knowledge for their end.

Still, risk exists that some may use the knowledge here to imperil security and harm populations. We feel, however, that the risks are smaller than expected and far outweighed by the benefits of sharing knowledge. Many antagonistic actors already use social media data and technologies, and in some cases, very effectively. Many governments, private organizations, and humanitarian organizations need to desperately catch up. Besides, most of the techniques we discuss do not deal with uncovering people's identities and seeking them out, which is what antagonistic actors largely care about. We instead focus on how you can use aggregate, non-personal data to solve problems. Additionally, we teach how you can use social media to benefit and work with populations who knowingly consent and want to work with you, so as to reduce the risk that they feel exploited or used. This book will also reduce the chance that governments and other organizations misuse or abuse social media. It will instead help them use social media safely, lawfully, and effectively with concern for people's privacy and civil liberties. Lastly, proper use of the knowledge will greatly improve the quality of life in many areas around the world. For example, proper use of crowdsourcing techniques can spur delivery of health services and mobile technologies in the poorest areas, while improving stability and security in those areas.

Note that privacy and ethical issues concerning social media are hotly debated, complex, and nascent. In the coming months and years, governments will likely begin outlining rules and policies for using social media data and technologies. Eventually, countries and groups will establish norms concerning social media privacy and the ethics of using social media technologies to solve security issues. We strongly urge you to recognize and adopt new policies and guidelines as they emerge to avoid breaking the law, upsetting your community, and chilling the free speech and anonymity that makes the Internet and social media so great. As of this writing, we are in the Wild West of social media use. Be aware that this situation will not last for long, and then adapt and be creative—because the "bad guys" certainly will.

Summary

We hope governments and law enforcement globally begin to use social media data and technologies to understand and counter emerging security problems. Like other technologies, social media is not inherently good or evil, a panacea, or a catastrophe—it is a way to connect with each other, a reflection of the changes society is undergoing, a buzzword, and a tool that in the right hands can make the world a freer and safer place.

Using Social Media for Global Security

Understanding the Influence of Social Media Globally

In This Part

Before you can use social media for global security, you have to understand exactly what social media is, why it matters, how it works, and how people around the world use it. In Part I, we explore how social media is impacting global security for both good and ill, and the role it plays in pivotal security issues ranging from revolutions to gang violence. We also examine the various technologies that comprise social media and how they are spreading to every part of the world, whether they be fast-emerging cities or desolate conflict zones.

CHAPTER 1

Understanding Social Media's Impact on Global Security

In December 2010, a Facebook status update sparked a chain of events that led to the downfall of three governments. Meanwhile, YouTube videos helped convince and motivate an isolated young man to gun down American servicemen. A few months later, tweets and BlackBerry messages helped rioters loot with precision and spread chaos in one of the most powerful and monitored cities in the world. Meanwhile, gangs in the West used Facebook to glorify their acts of violence and inflame vicious cycles of violence. These events shared common factors—the most apparent being the unique role of social media technology. This chapter illustrates social media's impact on global security, comprising international, national, and local security issues. Specifically, it describes how social media has helped people globally organize revolutions and riots, terrorists recruit and encourage attacks, and gangs glorify and spread violence. It ends with a discussion highlighting the need to appreciate social media's impact on security and sets you on a journey to discovering how you can use social media technologies and crowdsourcing methods to secure your community, country, and planet.

NOTE If you already appreciate how social media is impacting global security and do not need to be persuaded, feel free to skip to Chapter 2.

Organizing Revolutions and Riots

To most, social media conjures up thoughts of celebrities tweeting embarrassing pictures, long-forgotten friends connecting with each other on Facebook, and aspiring performers posting videos of their antics on YouTube. But in recent years, thoughts and discussions surrounding social media have led to heavy subjects such as revolutions in the Middle East and riots in the West. The 2011 Arab Spring and 2011 London riots are controversial yet powerful examples of how social media is impacting matters of security. Activists and individuals globally have begun using social media as a way to connect with each other, amplify their voices, coordinate actions against government and law enforcement, and publicize their side of the story—actions that have changed the world. To begin appreciating why it is important to understand and use social media's influence on security, we will start in Tunisia.

Arab Spring

In late 2010, a 26-year-old Tunisian man named Mouhamed Bouazizi decided to kill himself. Unable to find a job, he became an unlicensed street vendor, but faced constant harassment and humiliation from the local police. One day, a policewoman confiscated his goods and slapped him, driving him to post a status update on Facebook, available at this link: `http://arabcrunch.com/2011/01` `/the-last-facebook-status-update-of-bouazizi-who-set-him-self-on-fire` `-marking-starting-the-tunisian-revolution.html`. Roughly translated and paraphrased, the status said, "I am lost and don't know what to do."

He then complained to the local governor, who ignored him. Incensed, he doused himself with gasoline and set himself on fire. A few days later, another unemployed and distraught Tunisian man jumped off a building. Soon the news of the deaths spread throughout the country, igniting protests leading to the overthrow of the Tunisian government.

In this and the following cases, do not lose yourself in identifying the myriad factors such as skyrocketing food prices, corruption, and lack of political rights that motivated people to protest. What is important is appreciating how Tunisians (and eventually other people) used social media to share with each other and the world the news about their country's problems, to help organize protests, and to help delegitimize and fight back against government and security forces.

Official Tunisian media including the local newspapers and radio stations did not discuss the suicides. Tunisians, a young, literate, and computer-savvy people, used mainstream social media sites such as Facebook and Twitter and blogs to share their thoughts about how they can improve their situation—specifically, overthrowing the government. Indeed, from late December 2010 to early January 2011, Tunisian membership of Facebook jumped from a steady 1.8 million users to more than 2 million almost overnight.[1] Figure 1.1 shows a graphical representation of the growth in Facebook in Tunisia in late 2010-early 2011.

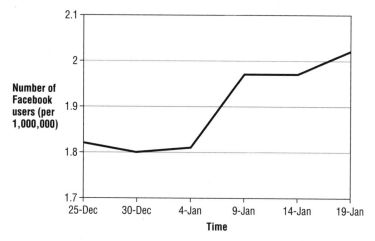

Source: Socialbakers.com (2012) "Tunisia: Country Reports: Twitter/Facebook." Accessed: 25 April 2012. http://www.socialbakers.com/facebook-statistics/tunisia

Figure 1.1: Tunisian Facebook growth in late 2010–early 2011

When the government started to crack down on the ensuing protests, Tunisians started posting videos and pictures on social media sites such as YouTube and Flickr about oppressive government action, which further incensed the population and motivated more people to join in the protests. Videos of government forces committing violence against protestors proved especially motivating. Meanwhile, Tunisian diaspora groups used social media to publicize the plight of their relatives back home. International monitoring groups and news organizations like Al-Jazeera and the BBC started noticing the tweets and YouTube videos pouring out of Tunisia and the diaspora. They began running stories on the protests, which caught the world's attention and much of its support. Eventually, the government cracked under the pressure and the autocratic ruler, Ben Ali, gave up power and fled. Figure 1.2 shows a timeline of the initial events of the Arab Spring.

People in neighboring countries took notice, and motivated by similar factors, they also began protesting. In many cases, people in neighboring countries employed more sophisticated social media techniques. Young Egyptian activists spearheaded the aggressive use of Twitter to share logistical information concerning the times and locations of protests, whereabouts of government forces, and even methods to protect protestors from tear gas and other police action. Allegedly, these same activists had helped the Tunisians use social media to organize protests and win the public relations war. Some reports indicate that the international human rights organizations and the U.S. government had helped train and equip these activists with technology.[2]

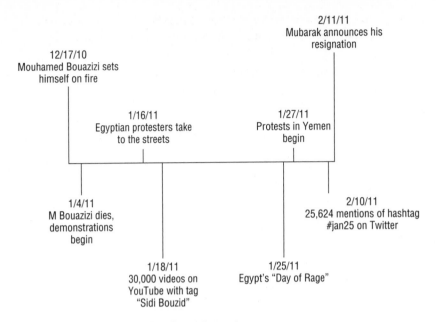

Note: Not a detailed timeline, includes only some key events
Sources: Council on Foreign Relations. (2011) *The New Arab Revolt: What Happened,*
What it Means, and What Comes Next. CFR, New York; Wright, R. (2011) *Rock the*
Casbah: Rage and Rebellion Across the Islamic World. Simon & Shuster, New York.

Figure 1.2: Early Arab Spring timeline

Sympathetic and curious people outside of Egypt were also able to use social media to publicize the protests. Many non-Egyptians created crowdmaps (explained in Chapter 7) and other social media platforms that geo-spatially displayed the locations and outcomes of protests in Cairo. News organizations including Al-Jazeera created intuitive and aesthetic websites that featured real-time feeds of tweets from protestors. As Figure 1.3 shows, the Arab Spring and specifically, the Egyptian protests were some of the most popular topics on Twitter. Other topics typically receive significantly fewer mentions. According to Twitter, the hashtags #egypt and #jan25, which refer to the Egyptian protests, were respectively the most and eight most popular hashtags on Twitter in 2011.[3] Such growing global interest eventually pushed Western governments to encourage Mubarak to step down.

NOTE If some of the terms are confusing and unfamiliar, do not worry. We define them in the forthcoming chapters.

The Egyptians often used more advanced methods to disseminate information because the Mubarak government was more vigilant and aggressive than the Ali government. To ensure government forces did not monitor social media sites to determine the locations and timings of protests, the Egyptian protestors tweeted to secretive hashtags made up of nonsense words. Only activists and protestors in the know understood what tweets to these hashtags meant, so only they knew where protests were going to happen. Many Egyptian activists noticed that during the 2009 Iranian Green Revolution protests, the Iranian government monitored social media sites to identify activists, and then capture and torture them. So the Egyptians also used secretive hashtags and other anonymization techniques, such as the creation of multiple Twitter accounts, to make it difficult for government forces to identify and capture them. Eventually, the protests in Egypt led to Mubarak's overthrow. Soon Libya and Syria also became engulfed in protests. Libyan protests led to a bitter conflict, and the eventual overthrow and death of Gaddafi. Weeks later, a bloody civil war broke out in Syria. Even far-flung countries like Malaysia (Beshir 2.0 rally) and the United States (Occupy Wall Street protests) saw protests partly inspired by the ideals, revolutionary fervor, and the social media organizing and publicizing techniques of the Arab Spring.

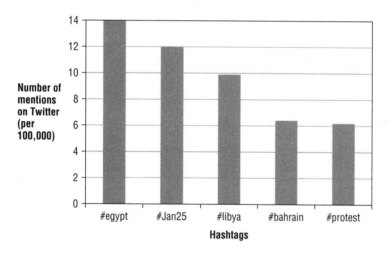

Source: Huang, C. (2011) "Facebook and Twitter Key to Arab Spring Uprisings: Report." The National. Accessed: 15 August 2012. http://www.thenational.ae/news/use-news/facebook-and-twitter-key-to-arab-spring-uprisings-report

Figure 1.3: Arab Spring mentions on Twitter from January–March 2011

Quantifying to what extent social media launched and sustained the Arab Spring is difficult. Several articles, books, and blog posts have described the role of social media during the Arab Spring and debated its contribution to the protests.[4, 5, 6, 7] We encourage you to read them to develop a better understanding of social media's power and limitations. However, what is undeniable and the most relevant for our case is the fact that during the Arab Spring, social media technologies:

- Helped people directly involved in the Arab Spring and those sympathetic to the protestors' plight publicize their message to the international community;

- Undermined the legitimacy of government forces by showcasing vivid examples of government oppression and violence through shared videos and pictures;

- Helped protestors mobilize and coordinate action against government forces.

Even if social media use was simply one of many driving factors of the most captivating international security issues of 2011, it was a unique and significant one that cannot be ignored.

London Riots

The Arab Spring took place successfully in developing countries with an enormous population of tech-savvy and frustrated youth. However, social media's impact on security is not limited to a single part of the world. Young people have also used social media to destabilize governments and create security problems in stable Western countries. The most prominent example took place barely months after the Arab Spring, in London. While many tout the Arab Spring as the evidence of the positive impact that social media can have, most see the London riots as the evidence of the negative.

Protests and demonstrations broke out in London after the police controversially killed a young man and were not reprimanded. When police attempted to disperse a demonstration concerning the killing, violence broke out, culminating in riots and copycat riots that lasted for several days across the United Kingdom and cost hundreds of millions of pounds in damage. For now, do not focus on the economic, racial, and cultural factors that led to the riots, but on the role social media technologies, especially location-specific technologies, played in helping rioters organize and outmaneuver police forces. Also, take note of how even the police forces and the public started to use social media technologies to capture rioters and secure their communities.

Rioters used a variety of mainstream and location-specific social media technologies to communicate about the protests. They posted pictures of themselves next to stolen goods on Flickr, used a smartphone application named Sukey to identify the physical location of police forces in real time, and used BlackBerry Messenger to coordinate attacks. News organizations in Britain suggested that extensive coverage of the riots on Twitter by rioters and witnesses encouraged others to join in and prolong the rioting. During the riots, on the 8th and 9th of August 2011, Internet traffic to UK websites increased by 14 percent, and there was a staggering 2.57 million relevant tweets. Nearly 3.4 million people from the UK visited Twitter's homepage.[8, 9, 10] Figure 1.4 shows a timeline of the 2011 London riots.

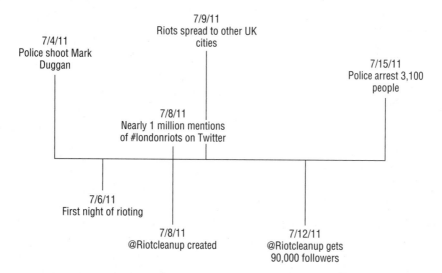

Note: Not a detailed timeline, includes only some key events
Sources: Guardian (2011) "Datablog: Data Journalism During the Riots: What We Know. What We Don't."
Accessed 25 April 2012.
http://www.guardian.co.uk/news/datablog/2011/dec/09/data-journalism-reading-riots;
Mashable.com (2011) "London Riots and Twitter." Accessed 25 April 2012.
http://mashable.com/2011/08/09/london-riots-twitter/ ; Stone, Z. (2011) "Retweet to Rebuild:
Social Media Helps Clean Up London Post-Riots." Good Culture. Accessed: 14 August 2012.
http://www.good.is/post/retweet-to-rebuild-social-media-is-helping-cleanup-london-
post-riots/

Figure 1.4: 2011 London riots timeline

Location-specific technologies such as BlackBerry Messenger, that allowed messages to be private and specific to physical space or an individual's contact list, technologically prohibited police forces and the public at large to eavesdrop on the rioters' conversations. Rioters were thus able to quickly and confidentially discuss logistics concerning rioting. The UK government found it legally and technologically difficult to gain access to those confidential messages or shut down those technologies, some of which were also being used by emergency and law enforcement personnel responding to the riots.

Again, quantifying the role social media played in prolonging and intensifying the London riots is difficult. However, the riots showed that social media technologies:

- Can help create and exacerbate security problems in even the most secure and stable parts of the world;

- Become even more complicated for security forces to deal with when they involve location-specific technologies. In Chapter 4, we look more closely at issues regarding location-specific social media technologies, but the gist is that they will make social media data analytics and event forecasting that much more difficult, and their use has only just begun.

Only a few months after the Arab Spring, groups developed even more advanced methods to use social media technologies to positively and negatively impact security.

Recruiting Terrorists and Encouraging Attacks

Populations revolting for freedom and young people lashing out at their communities are not the only ones who use social media to create domestic and international security problems. Although some "analysts" go overboard with terrorists' ability to use social media, terrorists do use social media to recruit, plan attacks, and spread terror. Their methods are numerous and often ingenious.[11] In fact, terrorists seem much more knowledgeable than law enforcement and government about social media and how to exploit it. Assessing how much social media helps terrorists is difficult, but social media has clearly amplified their abilities and opportunities. The case of Arid Uka's recruitment and terrorist operation exemplifies the emerging threats governments face.[12]

While the Arab Spring was capturing the world's imagination and attention, a 21-year-old man spent days poring over jihadi propaganda on the Internet. He eventually shot and killed several American servicemen at the Frankfurt airport. Again, our focus is not on the social and psychological factors that motivate a young man to become a jihadist-motivated terrorist, but on how social media helped terrorists convince and motivate a person to commit murder.

Terrorists affiliated with al-Qaeda, extreme right-wing organizations, and otherwise, have long used the Internet to spread propaganda about their ideology and attacks, distribute training guides, and recruit others. They host forums where they discuss how to create bombs, post videos to YouTube demonizing their enemies, and ingratiate themselves with possible recruits by chatting with them over Twitter, Facebook, and even video game worlds like the World of Warcraft. As Table 1.1 shows, groups like the Taliban, Hamas, Hezbollah, and al-Shabaab even have official Twitter accounts and they are well versed in the modern practices of online brand management and interactive public relations. The marketing departments of companies could learn a thing or two from them.

Most often, virtual interactions between terrorist recruiters and curious, at-risk youth are followed up with physical meetings. What makes Arid Uka's case so interesting is that he allegedly never physically met any of his compatriots. He was radicalized virtually. He routinely read jihadi literature on blogs, talked with jihadists on Facebook, and even performed quests with them on World of Warcraft. The online conversations and quests helped cement Uka's relationship with jihadists and in turn helped convince him to commit an act of terror.

In fact, according to Uka, a Facebook post prompted him to launch the attack. The night before the attack, Uka saw a video on Facebook showing American soldiers supposedly raping a Muslim girl. Uka did not realize the video was from a fictional movie.

Table 1.1: Terrorist Groups on Twitter, as of May 2012

TWITTER USERNAME	GROUP AFFILIATION	NUMBER OF FOLLOWERS
@HSMPress	al-Shabaab	12,533
@almanarnews	Hezbollah	11,396
@AlqassamBrigade	Hamas	2,316
@ABalkhi	Taliban	4,975
@alsomood	Taliban	939
@MYC_Press	al-Shabaab	685

Terrorists have been recruiting and carrying out attacks without social media technologies for centuries. However, social media has enabled them to:

- Amplify their voice and reach more potential recruits globally;
- Publicize and glorify their cause and side of the story;
- Streamline information operations before, during, and after operations.

Glorifying and Promoting Gang Culture and Violence

The ubiquity and democratic nature of social media means that antagonistic actors at every level of society can and will use it, including members of gangs and criminal organizations. Gangs use social media to fight virtual turf wars, glorify gang culture and violence, and recruit others. Their acts may not be as sensational as those of protestors and terrorists, but they still can seriously harm communities.

Gang members primarily use social media as an avenue for spreading propaganda, allegedly replacing the traditional mode of spraying graffiti on buildings. They post pictures of their logos on Facebook walls, tweet pictures of themselves doing drugs, and even post videos of them attacking innocent bystanders. Comments denouncing and threatening rival gangs often run alongside the pictures and videos. Often, gang use of social media is creative and aimed at setting traps for their enemies. Irish gang members have allegedly sent their rivals messages from fake girls, enticing them to appear at a certain location at a specific time. The gang members then ambush the tricked rival and attack him. [13, 14] Suggesting that social media motivates gang members to commit crimes and violence is stretching social media's influence. However, social media does make it easier for gangs to further inflame gang feuds. The killing of 5-year old Nizzel George in Minneapolis illustrates how inflamed gang feuds result in serious harm to communities.[15]

The feud started in August 2010, when 16-year old Scarface gang member Juwon "Skitz" Osborn allegedly shot and killed a Y.N.T. gang member. A month later, the Y.N.T. gang seemingly retaliated and shot Osborn twice, eventually killing him. Osborn's friends started a group called the "Skitz Squad" and vowed to seek revenge. Skitz Squad and Y.N.T. traded barbs, eventually using Facebook to threaten each other. They memorialized Osborn and reminded each other of his death, and posted pictures of gang members flashing gang hand signs that promoted their gang and that denounced the opposing gang. The threats and trash talk online grew at a rapid rate, eventually culminating in a hail of bullets at a house where Nizzel George lived.

Over the last few years, gang use of social media has grown considerably and will likely continue to grow. Generally, the size of a gang's social media presence correlates with their international fame and longevity. Table 1.2, derived from a 2011 study[13], provides an idea of the extent to which gangs and criminal organizations are active on social media. Often, they have multiple accounts on the same social media site.[13]

Table 1.2: Criminal Organizations and Gangs on Social Media, as of 2011

ORGANIZATION NAME	NUMBER OF FACEBOOK FOLLOWERS	NUMBER OF TWITTER FOLLOWERS
Hell's Angels	42,811	13,411
Crips	5,457	3,657
Bloods	3,497	47,171
Mara Salvatrucha (MS-13)	1,454	3,303
Latin Kings	1,003	6,823

Gangs and criminal organizations use social media to the same ends as terrorists. They use it to bolster their status and efforts, and specifically, to:

- Spread propaganda about their lives and increase its attractiveness to young people;
- Trash talk each other and inflame already tense situations;
- Plan and use it to carry out attacks.

Acknowledging Social Media's Impact

Social media will increasingly affect global security in positive, negative, and ambiguous ways. Setting aside the case of the Arab Spring and related protests, when it comes to security issues, social media is usually seen as a threat to stability and peace. However, apart from the Arab Spring, some examples of people using social media effectively to combat violence and secure communities exist. For example, during the London riots, the police and the public-at-large used social media to fight back against the rioters and improve security. The London police scanned through CCTV images to find pictures of rioters. They then posted the pictures on the popular photo-sharing site Flickr and asked people to contact them if they identified the person in the picture.[16] Also, British citizens used Twitter hashtags such as #riotcleanup to help organize public cleaning crews and neighborhood watches.[17]

Although, such effective and beneficial use of social media is increasing, it is still rare. We have researched and dealt with actors on both sides of the security arena concerning their use of social media, and the gap between the "bad" and "good" guys is frankly appalling. Simply, the bad guys have been far more adaptive and creative with new media technology. You can find many cases of how terrorists, criminals, rioters, and others are using social media data and technologies to increase their effectiveness and create unique security problems that governments today do not even understand, let alone address. Governments and security officials are trying to catch up but they sometimes do it in questionable ways that ends up setting back the case for using social media for global security. The introduction described one such case involving the U.S. Department of Homeland Security. This book is an attempt to level the field and put social media data and technologies in the hands of individuals and groups vying for peace, security, and liberty.

If you are not yet persuaded that social media is impacting global security, for good and ill, then we encourage you to look through cited articles and books. If you still are not convinced, use the book as a shovel and commence burying your head in the sand. If you are adequately convinced, let us start discussing how you can also use social media data and technologies to improve global security and solve your relevant problems. However, before you can use social media, you need to understand what it is. Chapter 2 will kick off the journey by explaining exactly what social media is, why it is so popular, and how people use it.

Summary

- Criminals, terrorists, and rioters are using social media to amplify their voices, recruit, and plan their operations.
- During the Arab Spring, protestors throughout the Middle East used social media to organize and help overthrow their governments.
- During the London riots, young people used localized social media platforms to coordinate looting and defy the police.
- Terrorists use social media to spread propaganda about their case, demonize their targets, and recruit others to carry out attacks.
- Gangs use social media to threaten each other, recruit members, and plan violence and other criminal activities.
- Due to rioter, terrorist, and criminal use of social media, governments everywhere are facing new, more robust non-state threats that they increasingly do not understand.
- Some groups and governments are using social media effectively to overthrow oppressive governments and secure communities. However, most are largely unaware of the potential social media offers and how they can and should use it.

Notes

1. Socialbakers.com. (2012) "Tunisia: Country Reports: Twitter/Facebook." Accessed: 25 April 2012. http://www.socialbakers.com/facebook-statistics/tunisia

2. Twitter. (2011) "Year in Review." Accessed: 15 August 2012. http://yearinreview.twitter.com/en/hottopics.html

3. Nixon, R. (2011) "U.S. Groups Helped Nurture Arab Uprisings." New York Times. Accessed: 14 August 2012. http://www.nytimes.com/2011/04/15/world/15aid.html?pagewanted=all

4. Ghonim, W. (2012) *Revolution 2.0: The Power of the People is Greater Than the People in Power*. Houghton Mifflin Harcourt, Boston.

5. Council on Foreign Relations. (2011) *The New Arab Revolt: What Happened, What it Means, and What Comes Next*. CFR, New York.

6. Pollack, K.M., et al. (2011) *The Arab Awakening: America and the Transformation of the Middle East*. Brookings Institution Press, Washington, DC.

7. Wright, R. (2011) *Rock the Casbah*: *Rage and Rebellion Across the Islamic World*. Simon & Shuster, New York.

8. The Guardian (2011) "Datablog: Data Journalism During the Riots: What We Know. What We Don't." Accessed: 25 April 2012. http://www.guardian .co.uk/news/datablog/2011/dec/09/data-journalism-reading-riots

9. Mashable.com (2011) "London Riots and Twitter." Accessed: 25 April 2012. http://mashable.com/2011/08/09/london-riots-twitter/

10. Gold, J. (2011) "UK Riots: An Infographic." Accessed: 6 May 2012. http://visual.ly/uk-riots-infographic

11. Cilluffo, F.J., Cozzens, J.B., and Ranstorp, M. (2010) *Foreign Fighters*: *Trends, Trajectories, and Conflicts Zones*. George Washington University: Homeland Security Policy Institute. Accessed 25 April 2012. http://www.gwumc.edu/ hspi/policy/report_foreignfighters501.cfm

12. Bartsch, M., et al. (2011) "Radical Islamic Roots of the Frankfurt Attack." Der Spiegel Online. Accessed 25 April 2012. http://www.spiegel.de/ international/germany/0,1518,748910,00.html

13. Decary-Hetu, D. and Morselli, C. (2011) "Gang Presence in Social Network Sites." International Journal of Cyber Criminology. Accessed 14 August 2012. http://www.cybercrimejournal.com/davidcarlo2011julyijcc.pdf

14. Finger, S. (2012) "Police: Street Gangs Embrace Social Media, Too." Wichita Eagle. Accessed: 14 August 2012. http://www.kansas .com/2012/06/10/2366765/police-street-gangs-embrace-social.html

15. McKinney, M. (2012) "Gangs Sometimes Fire First Shots Online." Star Tribune. Accessed: 14 August 2012. http://www.startribune.com/local/ minneapolis/162483976.html?refer=y

16. Couts, A. (2011) "London Riots: Police Use Flickr to Help Catch Looters." Digital Trends. Accessed: 14 August 2012. http://www.digitaltrends .com/international/london-riots-police-use-flickr-to-help-catch -looters/

17. Stone, Z. (2011) "Retweet to Rebuild: Social Media Helps Clean Up London Post-Riots." Good Culture. Accessed: 14 August 2012. http://www.good .is/post/retweet-to-rebuild-social-media-is-helping-cleanup -london-post-riots/

CHAPTER 2

Understanding Global Social Media Use

You cannot effectively use something that you do not understand. Using social media to solve complex security problems requires understanding exactly what social media is and how people use it, especially in the developing world. This chapter should serve as a reference guide for all things social media as you think about how to construct and apply various analytical methods and crowdsourcing platforms. It defines social media technologies, explains its growth and appeal, shows the different types of social media technologies, and illustrates how they are used in every part of the world. We also sprinkle various tips and advice applicable to any relevant social media and security project throughout the chapter.

NOTE We will periodically update the information in this chapter on the companion website.

Defining Social Media

Social media is fast becoming a term that means everything to everyone, and thus does not really mean anything anymore. By defining social media, we want to focus the scope of this book and the resulting efforts, and to ensure you use only the most relevant and appropriate technologies. Also, the term "social media" tends to have a Western bias that should be overcome. News articles and books about social media likely discuss Facebook, Twitter, LinkedIn, and other platforms that Western users use heavily. However, they ignore social media platforms, such as Orkut, that are popular in only certain parts of the world, and platforms built around texting technology, such as South Africa's Motribe or MXit.

Social media is all the devices and platforms that allow users globally to virtually create and share information with each other. *Platforms* are the virtual spaces that allow users to come together, and create and share information. *Devices* are the computing technologies that enable users to access the platform.

Social media differs from traditional media such as newspapers in its ability to allow for spontaneous and easy two-way or multiple-way interaction. Using social media such as Twitter, the president of the United States can talk to you and you can talk back to him. When the president is on television, he can talk to you but you cannot talk back to him. You can try, but people around you will think you are crazy.

Based on the definition, social media technologies encompass a variety of devices and websites—everything from YouTube to cell phones to Twitter to the PlayStation 3. Also, all crowdsourcing platforms are by definition social media platforms. We discuss crowdsourcing in much greater detail in Part III of the book, but for now you should know that *crowdsourcing* is the act of influencing, incentivizing, and leveraging crowds through social media to provide you with information and help you solve problems. For now, references to building and running crowdsourcing platforms are comparable to building and running social media platforms. We explain why we do not consider all social media platforms to be crowdsourcing platforms when we discuss the different types of platforms.

> **NOTE** You should begin to realize that using social media technologies involves using literally hundreds of websites and devices, many of which you have access to at a moment's notice. Later in the chapter, we look in detail at the menu of technologies available for your use.

Another big component inherent in the definition of social media involves the creation and sharing of information. Information on social media is meant to be promiscuous—it can be and often is created by numerous people at different times, and consumed by numerous people at different times. Some social media platforms such as Flickr, a picture-sharing site, broaden the scope of sharing. Users posting pictures on Flickr usually want others, which can include anyone on the Internet, to consume their pictures. Other social media platforms such as Pair focus the scope of sharing. Pair is a smartphone application that enables couples to share messages, pictures, videos, and sketches only with each other. Regardless of whether sharing is broadened or focused, every social media technology allows for the spontaneous creation and sharing of information. This ability has led to the creation and sharing of petabytes of data—more digital information is now created in a day than existed in the entire written works of mankind from the beginning of recorded history. See Figure 2.1 for a graphical representation of the definition of social media.

> **NOTE** You should begin to realize that using and analyzing social media data involves gleaning insights from an incomprehensible amount of information about almost anything from every part of the world. Later in the chapter, we look in detail at the types of data available for your use.

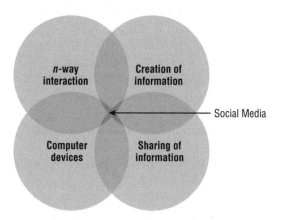

Figure 2.1: Definition of social media

Grasping Social Media's Popularity and Appeal

Social media's ability to enable people to communicate and share information with each other instantly and easily is the source of its rapid appeal and adoption. Grasping the source of this appeal will help you design crowdsourcing platforms that achieve similar adoption success, and help you identify key insights when analyzing social media data.

Growth of Social Media

Social media emerged out of the Web 2.0 revolution, which was a set of features and applications that promoted interoperability, sharing, and multiple-way communication. Social media existed before Facebook in the form of MySpace and other platforms, but it took off in a big way after 2004 when Facebook was launched. Since then, one out of every five people on earth has started using some form of social media regularly.[1]

Statistics for major social media platform use testify to social media's popularity. YouTube receives half a billion visits every month. Half a million new users join Twitter every day. Almost 10 percent of the world's population uses Facebook, resulting in Facebook's membership being larger than the populations of every country except China and India.[2] Social media's popularity is especially pronounced among the youth, the under–30-year-olds. Young people, who tend to be more open to adopting new technologies, use social media more regularly. Considering that nearly 50 percent of the world's population is under 30, social media use will only continue to boom.[3] In some places, social media is so popular that generations of youth do not realize other parts of the Internet exist. While launching a crowdsourcing platform in East Africa, we learned that many young people thought Facebook was synonymous with the Internet. We had to teach them that there was more to the Internet and even how to type in a URL, an unexpected obstacle.

NOTE When designing social media platforms or analyzing social media data, do it from the perspective of young people. That does not mean you need to listen to annoying music and stay up all night. Simply recruit some smart 20-year-olds to help you do relevant work—but make sure they actually are smart.

Philosophy Behind Social Media

The reason social media's communication and sharing aspects are so appealing is because they tap into the fundamentals of human nature. They help humans be human. We are social animals and attracted to fostering relationships, communicating, and sharing with others.[4] Tools that allow us to do that with more people and more easily will naturally be attractive to us.

NOTE As you design your own crowdsourcing platforms, ask yourself whether your platforms will help others communicate and share, and essentially be human.

The fundamental human tendency to share and communicate also helps us organize in a creative and spontaneous way. Two general modes of organization exist—top-down and bottom-up. Each way has its advantages and disadvantages. The top-down or centralized method, analogous to traditional media such as newspapers and television, involves a central authority providing rules, information, and norms that stipulate the behavior of individuals. The resulting behavior is reliable and easy to produce; however, it is rarely creative and truly influential. Many traditional information operations are designed with the top-down method in mind. For instance, news websites such as www.magharebia.com provide a limited set of information to a limited audience. The website creators are in total control of the information provided to visitors, but their ability to creatively engage with and influence visitors is limited. In an age where media consumers are increasingly becoming familiar with and expecting to help create and share media, the top-down method seems increasingly dull and outdated.

The bottom-up or decentralized method, analogous to social media, involves providing individuals with the ability and/or space to come together and organically generate and spread rules, information, and norms. Because no central authority is stipulating limits to individual behaviors, the individuals are free to come up with creative solutions and information at a rapid rate. The resulting behavior is thus risky and to an extent uncontrollable, but usually leads to groundbreaking insights. Social media platforms are the perfect avenue for allowing individuals to come together organically and adopt the bottom-up method. Crowdsourcing, explored in detail in Part III, taps into the ability of individuals to have the freedom to provide information and solutions at a flexible pace. Many of the most successful social media platforms such as LinkedIn use moderators to exercise some centralized control over their users' behaviors, but users still take the lead. When users feel empowered, they are more open to engagement. Applying the bottom-up method to conduct information and other types of operations requires giving up the mentality that you can control everything. You have to take on some risk, but you will receive great rewards for it. See Figure 2.2 for a graphical summary of top-down and bottom-up methods.

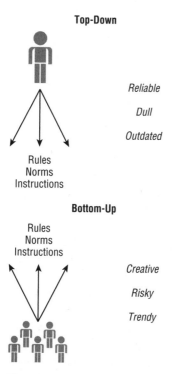

Top-Down

Reliable

Dull

Outdated

Rules
Norms
Instructions

Bottom-Up

Rules
Norms
Instructions

Creative

Risky

Trendy

Figure 2.2: Top-down and bottom-up methods

Providing your users with freedom allows you to tap into their cognitive surplus, another concept underlying the success of social media. *Cognitive surplus* relates to the idea that as people globally gain more free time in their daily lives, they will use the time to not only consume but also create.[5] Due to the spread and adoption of various technologies, people around the world spend less time toiling in fields and working in factories. They use their increased free time to watch television and surf the Internet, but to also create and share information using social media. As globalization continues to spread technologies that create free time, more people than ever before will have the time, energy, and desire to create and share things using social media. You have the opportunity to use social media to tap into people's free time and use the increasing cognitive surplus to solve your most pressing problems. For you, the cognitive surplus could result in your platform users creating discrete intelligence, solutions, and insights relevant to security issues. Also, the existing cognitive surplus harnessed by other platforms could provide you with the data to complete your analysis of countless issues.

Social Media Technologies

The decentralized, creative engine powering the spread and growth of social media has resulted in a proliferation of social media technologies. Understanding the different types of technologies will help you appreciate which type of technology is most relevant to your needs. This section explores the different types of platforms and devices. We provide many more examples in the Appendix.

Platform Types

A platform, as defined earlier, is a virtual meeting ground for social media users. They exist in physical and cloud servers, and may also include a website. A platform provides the ability to create information, process, manage, and store the information, and display all or some of the information. Currently, hundreds of active social media platforms exist, some of which have millions of users, many of which have thousands, and a few of which have hundreds. We have many ways of categorizing and exploring the different types. We have chosen the way that is most relevant to an operator and thus categorized platforms by their main feature and functionality. Most successful platforms combine numerous features and functionalities, and span the categories.

Social Networking

Social networking platforms emphasize and enable users to create relationships and foster their personal and/or business networks—to meet and get to know others. They put the social in social media. Table 2.1 lists examples of social networking platforms and their name for the functionality that allows users to network with others. The most popular social media platforms employ some sort of social networking functionality because, as discussed, humans crave the ability to network with others. This craving and tendency to maintain relationships seduces users and keeps them coming back regularly over a long period of time.

Table 2.1: Social Networking Examples

NAME	FUNCTIONALITY
Facebook	Friends, Groups
Twitter	Followers
Google+	Circles
LinkedIn	Connections
hi5	Friends
Orkut	Friends, Crush List, Communities
youKawan	Contacts

In many cases, such as Facebook and Google+, the social networks built on the platform reflect the social networks of people offline. In a few cases, such as Second Life, users build largely virtual social networks that do not reflect their social networks offline. Such platforms allow users to remain anonymous and indulge in behaviors they may find embarrassing or lacking in the physical space around them. However, they still allow users to build meaningful virtual relationships with other anonymous users. Social media platforms that do not employ or emphasize a social networking functionality usually focus on acquiring discrete data from populations at irregular intervals.

NOTE The widespread use and success of social networking functionalities in social media testifies to their usefulness and power. If you want to collect data about the social networks of key individuals or understand how certain groups behave online, tap into the data provided by social networking sites. If you want to build a platform that has a sustained and committed user base over a long-term period, integrate some sort of social networking functionality.

Twitter is one of the most popular social networking sites in the world and a great source of data. We will rely on it heavily to provide data for social media analysis. If you are not already, you should become familiar with Twitter. See Figure 2.3 for a screenshot of one of our Twitter accounts.

Figure 2.3: Screenshot of Twitter account

Media Platforms

Media platforms emphasize and enable users to create (including upload) and share media with others. Media includes video, pictures, audio, and text. Due to the widespread use of substantial computing power in even the most simple social media devices, multimedia creation and sharing has become commonplace and expected. Table 2.2 lists examples of media platforms and the type(s) of media they allow users to create and/or share. All social media platforms employ some sort of media creation and sharing—it is inherent in the definition of social media. Media is information and social media requires the sharing of information. Many platforms enable users to create and share different types of media simultaneously. The most popular social media platforms employ a mix of media creation and sharing because individuals on the Internet like to engage with different types of media. A variety of media provides users with different types of entertainment and keeps their attention.

Many popular media platforms, such as Flickr, enable users to both create and share media. Some platforms, such as Digg, enable both but emphasize the re-creation of media. The re-creation of media is where the line between creating and sharing a product breaks down and involves mostly informing others about an existing media product. In Digg, users can share with others online news articles, pictures, and videos they find on the Internet. The media these users create are mostly the textual comments that accompany the sharing of the product. News aggregators such as the Huffington Post are also examples of such platforms.

Table 2.2: Media Platforms Examples

NAME	MEDIA TYPE(S)
YouTube	Video
Flickr	Photos
Instagram	Mobile Photos
SocialCam	Video
Vimeo	Edited "High-End" Video
Pinterest	Various content

Many media platforms enable users to interact with different types of media but become known primarily for one type. For example, YouTube is known for its video-sharing feature but users can also create and share textual information through video comments and profile pages. Some media platforms feature a specific form of one type of media. For example, blogs are generally known to feature the creation and sharing of text. Blogs can feature large textual entries or small textual entries. The former are colloquially called blogs and hosted by services such as WordPress and Blogger, whereas the latter are called microblogs and hosted by services such as Twitter and Tumblr. Some blogs such as Adam Curtis' BBC blog feature essay-length textual entries about complex political issues, whereas Kim Kardashian's Twitter page features 140-character-length textual entries about topics that are definitely not complex political issues.

WARNING   Expect to deal with different types of media when analyzing social media data. Also, when designing platforms, factor in the ability for users to engage with different types of media, especially video and pictures. The widespread popularity of televisions and the relatively lower popularity of books indicate that humans like to look at things rather than read about them. However, people also like to express their opinion about media and the easiest way to do so currently on social media is by allowing users to write short textual comments. Design platforms that feature videos, pictures, and/or relatively short pieces of text, and you will likely attract users.

Location-Based

Location-based platforms emphasize and provide users with various features and functions based on their location in physical, real-world space. Such platforms, popular on smartphones, usually use GPS technology to triangulate a user's approximate physical location. They then either share the location with others openly, use it to provide the user with specific media, and/or use it to geo-tag the media the user shares with others. Table 2.3 lists examples of location-based platforms and why they use your location. Due to the proliferation of smartphones globally and demand for social media that increasingly blends our virtual and real worlds, location-based functionalities are becoming more widespread.

Table 2.3: Location-Based Platform Examples

NAME	LOCATION FUNCTION
Foursquare	Check-in
Google Latitude	Location of Circles
Find My Friends	Location of Friends
Yelp	Local Reviews and Check-ins
GroupOn	Check-in, Local Deals
Facebook Places	Check-in, Friend Location

Currently, location-based platforms are used primarily to help users share their location with their social networks and local businesses. Foursquare is the most prominent example of such a platform. Increasingly, location-based features are being integrated into other social media platforms for the sake of the platform owners. Any interaction users have with these platforms is geo-tagged with their physical location, which allows the platform owners to collect more detailed and sensitive data about their user base. They then sell the data to third parties or use it to tweak the services they deliver to the platform users so it is more relevant and useful to them.

Greater reliance on location-based platforms and features is generating privacy concerns. Some users are concerned that their privacy is being invaded for unscrupulous reasons, and they are wary of further combining their virtual and physical worlds. However, the popularity of location-based platforms and features suggest that privacy concerns are not yet a major issue. Still, remain cautious when implementing location-based features into your platform in case privacy policies and/or norms concerning collecting and leveraging the physical location of users change.

NOTE Geo-tagged information collected through location-based platforms especially bolsters the ability to glean insights from social media data. As further described in Part II of the book, the ability to tell where information is coming from greatly helps perform a variety of analyses and answer several important questions relevant to security issues. Using social media to solve global security problems is about marrying the virtual and real world, and nothing does that more prominently than location-based platforms.

Crowdsourcing is the act of sourcing media from the crowd. It involves incentivizing users through a variety of means to provide the platform owners and others with intelligence and solutions. Whereas other social media platforms focus on enriching the experience of the user, crowdsourcing platforms focus on enriching the collective user base, other individuals, and/or the platform owners by distributing knowledge from one user to others. Crowdsourcing platforms are used to solve a variety of problems, from helping organizations design T-shirts to collecting information from hard-to-reach areas. Table 2.4 lists a few examples of crowdsourcing platforms and what they crowdsource.

Table 2.4: Crowdsourcing Platform Examples

NAMES	INFORMATION CROWDSOURCED
Amara	Translations
Amazon's M-Turk	Labor
Crisismappers	Geo-location labor, Verification
Crowdflower	Labor
Threadless	T-Shirts
DARPA's Grand Challenge	Technology Innovation

Through a platform and given the right incentive structure, you can crowdsource any and all types of media and knowledge. Most crowdsourcing platforms collect information from users in a variety of formats and also display it and share it in a variety of formats. For instance, Ushahidi's crowdmaps collect textual reports and pictures, and display the information on an interactive map interface.

Crowdsourcing platforms are relative newcomers to the social media world, yet the concept has existed since social media's inception. For instance, Facebook crowdsources information about you and your network and then shares that knowledge with others on Facebook and with advertisers. Increasingly, platforms are making crowdsourcing a specific solution or information set the distinct feature of their platform. For example, the U.S. government's `challenge` `.gov` website specifically crowdsources solutions to U.S. government problems, and largely lacks other social media features. Indeed, one of the most popular websites on the Internet, Wikipedia, is simply a giant crowdsourcing platform.

Crowdsourcing platforms are popular because they are explicit in leveraging user expertise and knowledge to solve problems. Many users like feeling important and/or contributing to a cause or someone. They will gladly let others tap into their free time and cognitive surplus. The spread of crowdsourcing platforms to all parts of the world offers exciting opportunities to utilize a diversity of expertise and voices. The applications of crowdsourcing are endless, but can be roughly broken down into eight areas: collective knowledge, collective creativity, community building, open innovation, crowdfunding, crowd tools, cloud labor, and crowd civic engagement.

NOTE Crowdsourcing is a major topic of this book and we offer several suggestions regarding creating and running different types of crowdsourcing platforms later.

Combination Platforms

Combination platforms provide users with various combinations of the features available in the aforementioned social media platforms. The most popular social media platforms are combination platforms, and offer users numerous functionalities. It is rare to find a social media platform that is not a combination platform. Some, however, emphasize the combination more than others. Additionally, numerous social media platforms are inter-connected and share information with each other. The content a user creates on one platform can often be found on other platforms. Table 2.5 lists examples of combination platforms and the features they provide.

Table 2.5: Combination Platform Examples

NAME	FEATURES
Reddit	Social networking, Media, Crowdsourcing
Facebook	Social networking, Media, Location-based, Crowdsourcing
Path	Social networking, Media
Pinterest	Media, Social networking, Crowdsourcing
Pair	Media, Social networking, Location-based
Meebo	Media, Social networking, Location-based

NOTE Users used to social media platforms expect a combination of features. Users new to social media platforms or using social media to meet a specific need likely do not require a combination. When designing a platform, ensure that the platform offers some mix of features. The widespread popularity and success of combination platforms should be convincing enough.

Device Types

People use numerous devices to access social media platforms. Powerful computer devices that can access the Internet have proliferated due to Moore's law. The law is named after Intel co-founder Gordon Moore and is the observation that the number of transistors on integrated circuits or simply computer power seems to double roughly every 18-24 months. Figure 2.4 shows Moore's law in graph form.

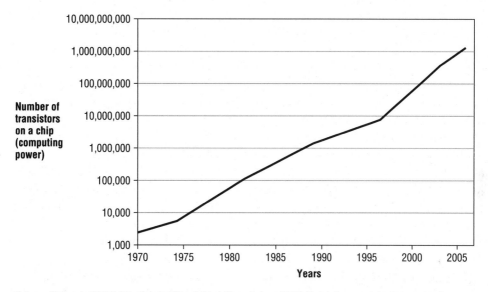

Source: Fildes, J. (2007) "Meeting the Man Behind Moore's Law." BBC News. Accessed: 19 August, 2012. http://news.bbc.co.uk/2/hi/technology/7080646.stm

Figure 2.4: Moore's Law

Increasingly, every single device has a powerful computer built in, and increasingly that device can talk to the Internet and connect to a social media platform. We will briefly explore the various devices populations use to access social media platforms. You should be familiar with most of the devices we mention, but a few may surprise you.

> **NOTE** Understanding device use will help you understand the fidelity and validity of social media data, and design platforms geared toward specific devices. Some devices are better for accessing certain types of platforms and more geared toward specific platform features.

Desktop Computers and Laptops

The most obvious and traditional computing devices, desktop computers and laptops are the primary means in Western countries to access social media platforms. Traditional computer devices offer increased functionality, which has spurred platform providers to offer more features and integrate their services across software platforms. For example, the Google suite of software platforms enables the user to use his or her Google account to connect to numerous social networking platforms automatically, share connections across the platforms, and share and coordinate media. Laptops have long since beat out desktops as the most commonly used and sold devices.[6] They increase the appeal of the mobile nature of social media, and therefore encourage social media platforms to focus on offering location-based features and audio-video chatting over wireless. Users favor laptops and desktops for lengthy content creation, suggesting that users in parts of the world where laptop and desktop use is large are more likely to engage in social media platforms that encourage the creation of complex or lengthy content.

The popularity of these devices is limited in the developing world where the relatively high cost of a desktop or laptop is a prohibitive barrier to use. Thus, social media platforms targeted toward the developing world focus more offering access and features that leverage mobile phone technologies. Many developing countries currently make access to desktops available through Internet cafés where access is cheap. However, the prevalence of more powerful mobile technologies will likely stunt the growth and use of Internet cafés.

> **WARNING** Keep the Western bias of desktops and laptops in mind when creating a crowdsourcing platform. Do not expect farmers in rural Colombia, who do not have regular access to laptops, to submit lengthy and complex intelligence reports through your crowdsourcing platforms.

Gaming Devices and Smart Televisions

In Western countries and in wealthier parts of the developing world, young people are increasingly using gaming consoles with Internet connectivity, such as the X-Box 360, PlayStation 3, and Nintendo Wii, to access social media platforms. Apart from providing access to third-party social media platforms such as Facebook, the creators of these platforms are also increasingly offering some form of in-house social networking platform for their users. However, these social networking platforms are not very popular. They tend to be overwhelmingly focused on helping gamers connect with each other to play games together, and often lack common features available on mainstream social networking platforms, such as the ability to share pictures with others. Additionally, accessing these platforms is difficult. Gaming devices come with controllers that are designed for mimicking virtual guns and not for typing.

However, the rapid advancements and spread of wireless keyboard, voice recognition and dictation, and movement recognition technology may make it easier to use gaming devices to access game-centric social networking platforms and eventually increase their popularity. Also, smart televisions are emerging and may eventually replace all televisions. They are devices that enable users to easily access the Internet using voice control and motion sensor devices such as the X-Box 360's Kinect system. Because practically every household in the Western world and increasingly in the developing world has a television, the eventual adoption of smart televisions will increase overall connectivity to the Internet. The growth in access, not only in numbers but also in terms of overall time spent connected to the Internet, increases the opportunities to tap into the emerging cognitive surplus.

NOTE The combination of gaming, television watching, and social media platforms will increase the levels and types of content shared on social media, providing greater social media data to analyze. The devices in question also often track usage behavior, such as when a person turns on his or her smart television, which offers correlative behavioral data with which to bolster the analysis of social media data.

Tablets

Tablet computers, including the iPad, Samsung's Galaxy Tab, Barnes and Noble's Nook Tablets, Kindle, and a number of other devices have rocked the computing world in recent years. These devices feature elegant touch interfaces, impressive computing power, wireless Internet connectivity, often some kind of 3G or 4G connectivity, and are incredibly light and portable. Most of these devices enable users to access third-party social media platforms such as Twitter through integrated applications. Due to their popularity and portability, they are rapidly becoming the primary means of connecting to social media and the Internet. The tablet revolution is not limited to the Western world. Low-cost and durable tablets such as the Ubi-Slate and Aakash Tablet (manufactured in India and sold at a price of $35–$60 USD) are enabling poor people in rural areas to participate in the wider social media world. The cheap tablets are creating a leveling effect where children and youth in rural Indonesia will be able to connect and share at the same level as a spoiled teenager in the suburbs of Beverly Hills.

NOTE The tablets provide content and two-way access to the world's poorest. In the coming years, the data shared among and collected from these populations will be extremely valuable to those interested in security, and any crowdsourcing platform created for security purposes should consider making it accessible through tablets. We cannot emphasize enough the impact tablets will have in the developing world in the coming years. If you want to make change, start handing out cheap tablets to groups of kids and watch them astound you.

Smartphones

Ever since Steve Jobs unveiled the iPhone in 2007, the smartphone has revolutionized mobile technology and made people ever more dependent on computers. Smartphones are the powerful, feature-rich cell phones that enable users to access the Internet, make phone calls, and play games. In the Western world, the smartphone is becoming the main access point to the Internet, especially to social media. Because of reduced design and manufacturing costs, the smartphone is quickly finding a foothold in even the poorest areas of the world, and in about a decade will likely be ubiquitous globally. Google is currently dedicated to creating a smartphone specifically for the developing world.[7]

Due to the popularity and spread of smartphones and of other cell phones, many developing countries are leap-frogging traditional land-line infrastructure and wired connectivity, and going directly to mobile technology. Some parts of the developing world have powerful 4G wireless networks that put the United States' mobile networks to shame. Mobile networks in the developing world will soon host much of the world's social media traffic. In the developing world, the youngest generation today will likely grow up using smartphones, and will use them to access social media at unprecedented rates. Most will not own a smart television or gaming system, nor will they have the inclination to do so. They will be mobile, active, and opinionated—and ready to express themselves through their phones. Additionally, they will primarily use their phones to access and share imagery and text. Voice data plans will likely remain expensive but data and texting plans will remain inexpensive. Increasingly, the social media data you collect and analyze will come from smartphones, and will likely consist of various types of media and contain location information, because smartphone users are more likely to share their location with others.

The number and variety of smartphones and corresponding operation systems will continue to grow. Although the interfaces and applications will vary, access to social media platforms including messaging systems will be omnipresent and device agnostic.

WARNING   Needless to say, in a few years' time, a social media or crowd-sourcing platform that does not include easy and intuitive smartphone access will fail.

"Dumb phones"

"Dumb phones" are cell phones that have less computing power, memory, functionality, and Internet accessibility than smartphones. Before the iPhone and Android phones came along, you were probably using a dumb phone. Dumb phones are arguably the most widely used device globally. They are more popular than other devices because they are inexpensive, easy to use, require access to only mobile networks and not the Internet, and are widely available.

Dumb phones are extremely popular in the non-Western world, and in some cases essential for people to do everything from keeping in touch with friends to banking. People primarily use dumb phones for texting (sending short messages to either other individuals or organizations), also known as SMS (short messaging service). Many service providers provide inexpensive texting plans that include group messaging and social network messaging. GroupOn is an example of a popular group texting platform. Organizations are also creating forms and polls for dumb phones that users can fill out using only texts. Some countries such as Kenya use dumb phones to make mobile payments (M-Pesa) or provide and collect data on market prices (M-Farm).

CAUTION   It is essential that you do not write off dumb phones as irrelevant. They may not be popular in the Western world anymore but they are still extremely popular in the rest of the world. Leveraging dumb phone and texting technology to gather intelligence from and pushing information through texting en masse to populations in hard-to-reach areas is key to using social media to improve global security. Additionally, understanding how to analyze texting data with its slang and abbreviations, and making your crowdsourcing platform accessible via texting and dumb phones is essential.

Vehicles and Augmented Reality Devices

Predicting which technology will be widespread in the future is difficult, but we can say with some certainty that social media will become integrated with motor vehicles and augmented reality devices. Many new cars contain impressive internal computers that enable users to control the cars through mobile devices such as smartphones, and connect to the Internet through an interface built into the car's dashboard. Despite the dangers, people like to text and surf the Internet while driving. To minimize the danger, automakers have started building in systems that enable drivers to post to social media platforms or have their Facebook and Twitter feeds and incoming text messages read to them and accessed hands-free. Airlines have also realized that they can keep their passengers docile and the kid behind you from kicking your seat by offering Internet access during flights, which increases overall social media connectivity.

Augmented reality devices are an indication that emerging technologies will continue to alter the way in which the virtual world and reality intersect. Augmented reality devices generally overlay the virtual world over reality, and enable users to access information in virtual space while still fully engaging in physical space. One of the most buzz-worthy prototypes thus far, Google's Glasses, enables users to access and interact with their social networks and the rest of the virtual world through a small screen positioned close to the eye, which is partially controlled through eye movement or brain waves. The screen, the lens of the glasses, is also one-way transparent, which keeps others from seeing what the user is seeing. This device and similar objects push information to users based on their location and many pre-programmable cues (for example, they can read reviews of stores and restaurants as they walk by), or even potentially identify passersby through face recognition software that connects to Facebook.[8] Augmented reality will be a game changer for social media in the future, and should be watched carefully. Apple hired a pioneer of the heads-up display only to have him poached by Google, so we can expect some competition to drive this area forward.[9]

NOTE The security implications of such emerging technology are enormous and frankly scary. Let your imagination run wild when considering what a complete intersection of the virtual and real words will create.

Social Media Use Differences Globally

Social media platforms differ in terms of access and popularity globally. Because we intend to use social media to solve security problems around the world, it is imperative to look beyond Western-dominated uses of social media and corresponding social media platforms. Many existing and emerging security problems arise out of parts of the world that are very different from the West such as Somalia, where prevalence and use of social media is unique. Therefore, to adequately analyze social media data coming from disparate parts of the world and to build platforms that appeal to disparate population sets, understanding how different regions use social media is essential. For instance, although Facebook has more than half a billion users worldwide and is popular throughout, some social media platforms such as Odnoklassniki are far more popular than even Facebook in certain regions of the world. Additionally, in many parts of Africa and the Middle East, the rapid rise of sophisticated 3G and 4G networks has disproportionately spurred the growth of SMS-based social media networks as opposed to those that rely on laptops.

This section provides a small slice of the global differences concerning social media use. Technologies and adoption rates will change, probably rapidly, so refer to our website to get the most updated information. Regardless, keep this section in mind when analyzing data or deploying a crowdsourcing platform. Look past your natural and biased way of using social media and find ways to integrate local information and platforms into your efforts.

NOTE We do not provide detailed demographic information about social media use. Generally, younger people (under the age of 30) and women are more active on social media platforms. However, accurate estimates of such information are difficult to acquire.

North America (U.S. and Canada)

The launching pad of social media, North America is home to the most famous and feature-rich social media platforms. Most users access the platforms through laptops, smartphones, and tablets. Facebook and Twitter dominate, and new platforms pop up rapidly. Numerous platforms are competing for users, so do not expect users to flock to your crowdsourcing platform. However, the widespread social media use produces enormous data for analysis. Privacy issues are also a major concern, although most users do not hesitate to post private information. While many are concerned about privacy, few actually exercise their concern. As the U.S. and Canadian governments increase oversight of social media, privacy rules and norms surrounding social media will likely change in the future. (See Table 2.6 for the top three platforms in the region. Estimates for this and subsequent tables come from a variety of sources, which are detailed in the Appendix are listed on the companion website.)

Table 2.6: Top Platforms in North America as of May 2012

POPULARITY	CANADA	USA
1	Facebook (18 million estimated users)	Facebook (157 mil)
2	LinkedIn (5 mil)	Twitter (108 mil)
3	Twitter (6 mil)	LinkedIn (58 mil)

Latin America

Latin American countries rank among the top countries most engaged in social networking platforms. In fact, Latin American countries are adopting social media at the fastest rates. Most Latin American users access the platforms through computers. Orkut, a feature-rich social media platform created by a Google employee, is very popular in Latin America, and is surpassed in popularity only by Facebook. Other popular platforms include hi5, a feature-rich social networking platform, Badoo, an online dating/flirting platform, and Skyrock, a blogging platform. Twitter is becoming more popular because it is easy to post to (tweet) using SMS and dumb phones, a popular technology in Latin America. (See Table 2.7 for the top three platforms in the region.)

Table 2.7: Top Platforms in Latin America as of May 2012

POPULARITY	ARGENTINA	BRAZIL
1	Facebook (18 million estimated users)	Facebook (47 mil)
2	Twitter (7 mil)	Orkut (34 mil)
3	Badoo (5 mil)	Badoo (15 mil)

Europe

Europe has the most social media users in the world. The social media activity of Europeans is generally similar to their North American counterparts. Overall Facebook, blogs, and Twitter are very popular in Europe, but some country differences within Europe are discernible.

Germans are very interested in social networking sites focused on connecting with classmates. Examples include Wer-Kennt-Wen (translates to "who knows whom"), Stayfriends, and Studivz, a Facebook-clone for college students. The North American counterpart to such sites is classmates.com.

Russians and former Soviets are far more interested in Odnoklassniki, also a classmate networking site, and V Kontakte, a Facebook clone (including similar layout, color scheme, and usability). Russia has a "hacker culture," and they look for ways to distinguish themselves and replace Western sites.

The Francophones prefer Facebook but also frequent sites popular in Latin America including Badoo and Skyrock. Their Anglophone neighbors to the north prefer Facebook and Twitter. Due to heavy use, London is considered the Twitter capital of the world. The British also use location-based platforms such as BlackBerry Messenger heavily, which the youth used extensively during the London riots.

The Spanish and Portuguese have more in common with their Latin American counterparts and favor Orkut, Badoo, and Tuenti, an invitation-only private social networking site. (See Table 2.8 for the top three platforms in the region.)

Table 2.8: Top Platforms in Europe as of May 2012

POPULARITY	BELGIUM	GERMANY	POLAND	RUSSIA
1	Facebook (4 million estimated users)	Facebook (23 mil)	Nasza-klasa (13 mil)	V Kontakte (23 mil)
2	Badoo (1 mil)	We-kennt-wen (9 mil)	Facebook (8 mil)	Odnoklassniki (16 mil)
3	LinkedIn (1 mil)	Stayfriends (6 mil)	Badoo (4 mil)	Facebook (5 mil)

East Asia

Asians are tech-savvy and heavy users of social media, primarily through computers in Internet cafés and mobile devices. The Chinese government censors Internet use, actively filters content on major platforms such as Twitter and YouTube, and encourages its citizens to use home-grown social media platforms. Qzone, a feature-rich platform, allegedly has 500 million users, whereas an instant message or a more private Twitter-like service known as QQ allegedly has more than 700 million users. Other sites include the Facebook-like RenRen, with 100 million mostly student users, and Sina-Weibo, a microblogging platform with more than 300 million users. The government, platform managers, and users censor much of the content on these sites.

The Japanese prefer Twitter over Facebook, with each having 30 million and 8.5 million users, respectively. During the Japanese tsunami, many Japanese used Twitter and SMS capabilities to ask for help and share disaster information. Other popular platforms include Gree, a gaming and social networking platform that is popular among the youth.

The Taiwanese and South Koreans prefer Facebook and blogging sites such as Plurk (Taiwanese) and Cyworld (South Korean). (See Table 2.9 for the top three platforms in the region.)

Table 2.9: Top Platforms in East Asia as of May 2012

POPULARITY	CHINA	JAPAN	SOUTH KOREA	TAIWAN
1	QQ (700 million estimated users)	Twitter (29 mil)	Cyworld (19 mil)	Facebook (11 mil)
2	QZone (500 mil)	Gree (23 mil)	Facebook (7 mil)	Plurk
3	Sina-Weibo (250 mil)	Facebook (8 mil)	Twitter (3 mil)	Twitter

Southeast Asia

Due to the growth of mobile networks and the spread of dumb phones, many Southeast Asians prefer to use Twitter. Instant messaging applications such as Whatsapp are popular throughout Southeast Asia, whereas in Vietnam, Zing Me and Go.vn are far more popular among youth with dumb phones. In some countries such as Malaysia and Thailand, citizens are using social media to organize protests and rallies. Therefore, Southeast Asian governments are increasingly monitoring social media use. (See Table 2.10 for the top three platforms in the region.)

Table 2.10: Top Platforms in Southeast Asia as of May 2012

POPULARITY	INDONESIA	VIETNAM
1	Twitter (19 million estimated users)	Zing Me (8 mil)
2	Whatsapp	Facebook (4 mil)
3	-	Go.vn (2 mil)

South Asia

Like the rest of the world, India and Pakistan have enthusiastically jumped on the Facebook bandwagon, upsetting previous giant Orkut. LinkedIn is increasingly popular among the rising professional and middle class. Due to the widespread use of dumb phones, microblogging and Twitter are also gaining a foothold. (See Table 2.11 for the top three platforms in the region.)

Table 2.11: Top Platforms in South Asia as of May 2012

POPULARITY	INDIA	PAKISTAN
1	Facebook (45 million estimated users)	Facebook (6 mil)
2	LinkedIn (13 mil)	LinkedIn (0.1 mil)
3	Orkut (15 mil)	Twitter

Middle East

Facebook and Twitter use is fairly common throughout the Middle East, and helped sparked the Arab Spring. Middle Easterners access social media via computers in Internet cafés and mobile devices. As in China, censorship is a critical issue in much of the Middle East. Governments often filter content and harshly prosecute those who post offensive material. Governments are cracking down on dating/flirting platforms such as Badoo. The Iranian government is going further and developing its own platforms, likely leading to a ban of Western platforms. Despite the encroaching censorship, Facebook and Twitter remain popular. Other popular platforms include Cloob and Velayatmadaran, a virtual meeting point for supporters of the Ayatollah. To get around restrictions, the youth increasingly use BlackBerry Messenger to communicate secretly among themselves. (See Table 2.12 for the top three platforms in the region.)

Table 2.12: Top Platforms in the Middle East as of May 2012

POPULARITY	BAHRAIN	EGYPT	IRAN	IRAQ	SAUDI ARABIA
1	Facebook (0.3 million estimated users)	Facebook (10 mil)	Cloob (0.8 mil)	Facebook (1 mil)	Facebook (5 mil)
2	Twitter (.06 mil)	Twitter (0.1 mil)	Twitter (0.06 mil)	Twitter (0.02 mil)	Badoo (1.5 mil)
3	LinkedIn (0.08 mil)	LinkedIn (0.5 mil)	Velayatmadaran (0.004 mil)	-	Twitter (0.1 mil)

Africa

Due to widespread cell phone use and the availability of numerous inexpensive SMS plans, social media platforms accessible by smartphones and dumb phones, also known as mobile apps, are very popular across Africa. Popular mobile apps include Whatsapp, Motribe, and Mxit. Other methods of accessing social media include Internet cafés. As described before, in many places, Facebook is synonymous with the Internet.

Several non-governmental organizations are building crowdsourcing platforms across Africa to collect via dumb phones information concerning health, agriculture, conflict, and education. Examples include M-Farm, Ushahidi, and Esoko. As smartphones become cheaper and more widely available, and fiber optic cables connect more African countries, social media use will become more and more popular. Africa holds many exciting opportunities for collecting data and engaging with populations using social media. This book came about largely in part due to what we have learned doing social media projects in Africa. (See Table 2.13 for the top three platforms in the region.)

We realize that we have thrown a lot of information at you. However, knowing it is essential to analyzing data on social media. Chapter 3 will begin teaching you how to analyze social media data by detailing what analysis is and how you can use it.

Table 2.13: Top Platforms in Africa as of May 2012

POPULARITY	KENYA	SOUTH AFRICA
1	Facebook (1 million estimated users)	Facebook (4 mil)
2	WhatsApp	LinkedIn (1 mil)
3	Twitter (0.1 mil)	Twitter

Summary

- Social media are the virtual platforms that enable multiple people to spontaneously create and share information with each other through a variety of computer devices.

- Social media use is growing rapidly around the world, especially among those under 30 years old.

- Social media allows for bottom-up organization, which is unreliable but creative and engaging.

- Five types of social media platforms exist: social networking, media, location-based, crowdsourcing, and combination.

- Six major device categories are used to access social media platforms: desktop computers and laptops, gaming devices and smart televisions, tablets, smartphones, dumb phones, and vehicles and augmented reality devices.

- Social media use differs globally. Although Facebook is generally popular everywhere, specific platforms are more popular in certain regions primarily because of cultural reasons and the type of device technology available in those areas.

- Recognizing and appreciating how social media is used globally will help you improve your analysis and build more attractive crowdsourcing platforms.

Notes

1. eMarketer (2012) "Worldwide Social Network Usage: Market Size and Growth Forecast." Accessed 14 May 2012. http://www.emarketer.com/Mobile/Article.aspx?R=1008903

2. Henrikson, J.U. (2011) "The Growth of Social Media: An Infographic." Search Engine Journal.com. Accessed: 13 May 2012. http://www.searchenginejournal.com/the-growth-of-social-media-an-infographic/32788/

3. Qualman, E. (2010) "Over 50% of the World's Population is Under 30 —Social Media on the Rise." Socialnomics.net. Accessed: 13 May 2012. `http://www.socialnomics.net/2010/04/13/over-50-of-the-worlds-population-is-under-30-social-media-on-the-rise/`

4. Brooks, D. (2011) *The Social Animal: The Hidden Sources of Love, Character, and Achievement*. Random House, New York.

5. Shirky, C. (2010) *Cognitive Surplus: Creativity and Generosity in a Connected Age*. Penguin, New York.

6. Eddy, N. (2008) "Notebook Sales Outpace Desktop Sales." eWeek .com. Accessed: 13 May 2012. `http://www.eweek.com/c/a/Midmarket/Notebook-Sales-Outpace-Desktop-Sales/`

7. Lee, T.B. (2011) "Android Poised to Dominate the Developing World." Forbes.com. Accessed: 13 May 2012. `http://www.forbes.com/sites/timothylee/2011/08/16/android-poised-to-dominate-the-developing-world/`

8. Freeman, K. (2012) "Facial Recognition App IDs Your Friends Using Facebook." Mashable.com. Accessed: 12 May 2012. `http://mashable.com/2012/05/10/facial-recognition-app/`

9. Weintraub, S. (2010) "Apple Hires 'Senior Prototype Engineer' for work on wearable computing." Computerworld.com. Accessed: 13 May 2012. `http://blogs.computerworld.com/15750/apple_hires_senior_prototype_engineer_for_work_on_wearable_computers?source=rss_weintraub`

Analyzing Social Media Data to Solve Security Problems

In This Part

Social media use throughout the world generates a cornucopia of data that is unmatched in its size and breadth. Intelligent analysis of social media and other types of data can help you understand and solve various security problems, including uncovering the online networks of violent terrorists and forecasting the emergence of famines. In Part II, we will describe the fundamentals of conducting social media intelligence analysis and the process of collecting social media and other types of data. We will then illustrate how you can analyze social media and other data to map social networks, identify key influencers and topics in social networks, and understand and forecast various security events.

CHAPTER 3

Introduction to Social Media Analytics

Analyzing social media data improves operational planning and execution. It can help you understand social networks and what they are discussing, identify key people and relationships, and understand and forecast events. However, analysis offers benefits only if it is conducted accurately and honestly. This chapter lays the foundation for learning social media analytics by defining what analysis is, what it is not, and how it can help, providing an analysis overview, and introducing the analytical methodologies this book covers.

Defining Analysis

Conducting any type of analysis requires knowing what it is and how it differs from other ways of making sense of the world. However, it has limitations and can easily fall prey to corrupt practices. Only by understanding the powers and limitations of analysis can you start to learn how to analyze social media to solve various problem sets. The subsequent sections may seem academic and dry at times, but unless you are comfortable with doing quantitative analysis, you should go through them. It will help you analyze social media and other types of data, and appreciate and critique the analyses of others.

What Is Analysis

Analysis is the systematic study of relevant data to gain insights about a topic. Analysis involves carrying out a variety of objective methodologies on evidence to find answers to specific problems. The methodologies are a series of steps, derived from past analytical studies and theories that if applied correctly to data will likely lead to accurate answers. This part of the book is dedicated to learning about the different methodologies and the proper ways of applying them.

Analytical methodologies can be applied to virtually any problem set, but we are focused on solving a few security-related sets. Table 3.1 shows the relevant problem sets, their descriptions, and specific examples. Occasionally we also touch on how social media analysis can help solve other problem sets.

CROSS-REFERENCE Chapter 5 details using specific analytical methodologies to study social network structures, identify key people and relationships, and determine the ideas and topics of discussions of the networks. Chapter 6 details using methodologies to understand and forecast behavior and events.

The outputs of the analyses are concrete answers to sample problems. They are the Twitter handles of the most influential people in networks, the probability that violence will break out in a certain area, the name of the social media platform that played the most pivotal role in helping rioters organize, and much more.

Limits of Analysis

As you read this chapter, keep in mind that analysis has limits. If used correctly, it offers tremendous insight into the most complicated subjects. However, analysis rarely results in certain predictions, precise rules describing human behavior regardless of environment, or perfect understanding. Analytical methodologies are tools that help you discover, describe, and forecast human behavior in the context of security. Due to the complexity of human behavior and the incomplete nature of the data in question, the relevant analytical methodologies are somewhat flawed and imprecise. The best way to push against the limits of analysis is to adopt analytical tools from other unrelated fields and to be intellectually honest at all times.

NOTE We are not teaching all the nuances and complexities involved with conducting analytical studies. Our focus is on preparing the operator to quickly understand complex events and behavior, not to publish research studies in academic journals. We are knowingly sacrificing some academic rigor for practicality, but not enough to tarnish the accuracy and honesty of the analysis.

Table 3.1: Relevant Problems for Analysis

PROBLEM SET	DESCRIPTION	SPECIFIC PROBLEM EXAMPLES
Understand the structure of social networks	Track the development of relationships between people online and offline, and understand how people use social media to maintain online and offline relationships.	To what extent and why are human traffickers using social media to communicate with each other?
Identify key people and relationships	Determine who in social networks wields influence over people in the networks, and has the ability to affect their behavior and relationships.	Which online violent extremist recruiters are the most effective at recruiting at-risk youth?
Determine the proliferation of ideas in networks	Understand which topics and ideas individuals and groups are discussing and sharing.	What type of violent extremist literature, rhetoric, and ideals disseminate through online social media?
Understand and forecast behavior	Understand the relationship between behavior, environmental constraints, and discussions and networks on social media. Also, use the understanding and real-time data to determine how likely individuals or groups are to undertake a specific behavior in the future.	How are gangs using social media to inflame tensions with rival gangs, and is their use changing?
Understand and forecast events	Understand the relationship between events, environmental constraints, and discussions and networks on social media. Also, use the understanding and real-time data to determine the likelihood of specific events occurring in the future.	What is the likelihood that there will be a famine?

What Is Not Analysis

Analysis comes naturally to humans as the basis of critical thought, but it is often riddled with cognitive fallacies and pitfalls that lead to incomplete or incorrect answers. Also, a meaningful portion of the security and defense world is staffed with people with no formal training in applying objective analytics to complex problems. What often passes for "analysis" is the subjective opinion of a biased individual with little real-world experience and/or no grounding in the scientific method. The process for such "analysis" is usually simplistic, and consists of the following steps:

1. Based on unexamined biases or your "gut," determine the point you want to prove or the prediction you are certain will come true.

2. Pick out data that supports your starting point.

3. Discredit conflicting data or, even better, simply ignore it.

4. Write a mostly qualitative piece full of anecdotes and quotes from self-proclaimed "experts" supporting your point.

5. Realize that you need some quantitative material, and insert the result of a survey you conducted. The survey usually involves asking three people what they think about a topic they do not know much about.

6. Focus a lot on formatting your "analysis" and ensure it contains lots of shiny graphics.

This faulty analytical process has resulted in misleading predictions about major foreign policy events and wastes of taxpayer money. The faulty analytical process is especially harmful when it comes to the business of forecasting and discovering the causal effects that produce security events. The United States government and other organizations often fund "analysts" who claim to forecast events but have no idea how to conduct analysis and routinely engage in the analysis don'ts, as described later. If you are native to the foreign policy or defense world, learn to disregard the "analysis" of pundits and so-called experts. Ignore those who proudly call themselves experts or claim they can "predict" something with 100 percent certainty. "Experts" are more likely than randomly generated results to be incorrect about major security and foreign policy issues. Chimpanzees randomly throwing darts at a board plastered with predictions are almost as likely to choose the right answer as "experts."[1] Unless you have a strong interest or background in quantitative methods, statistics, or science, forget what you know about "analysis."

Analysis Overview

The overall analytical processes and methodologies described herein are similar to what is taught in sophisticated political science and social science courses. One process uses a set of methodologies to create theories that aid understanding of security events and relevant behavior, and the second process uses another set of methodologies to apply those and other theories to other cases. Doing so will help us answer the types of problem sets described in Table 3.1. Specifically, the theories we develop and use will help describe rules of individual and group behavior in relevant contexts, determine the probability that a future event or action will take place, and identify relationships and causal effects between people, objects, and environments.

Unlike the "hard sciences" such as physics and chemistry, few hard-and-fast universal laws or strong theories exist in political and social science. We are primarily studying humans, not large static objects (although a lot of humans are increasingly behaving as large, static objects). The complexity of our subject makes determining laws for individuals and groups very difficult. Compared to the axiomatic laws of physics that describe the behavior of objects, determining the theories that describe humans and their "rational behavior" is incredibly complex and requires accounting for a dizzying array of factors.

Therefore, focus more on the data and allow the data to tell you about how humans are behaving in specific contexts. Then use what the data has said to help understand how humans are behaving in other similar contexts. This process or type of reasoning is known as *inductive reasoning*. In some cases, use existing proven and tested theories about how humans or other similar beings and objects behave individually and in groups. This process or type of reasoning is known as *deductive reasoning*. Of the analytical methodologies we describe, some are primarily inductive and others are primarily deductive, but all involve both types of reasoning. In reality, the two processes are often mixed and intertwined. We separate the two to aid understanding.

The following sections detail the overall analysis process as follows. First, we describe the preliminary procedure to formulate the problem you are trying to solve. Second, we explore each of the two processes or types of reasoning and the method of choosing the appropriate one for the problem. Third, we list the analysis dos and don'ts. Fourth, we introduce several methodologies and describe when they are most useful.

Preliminary Procedure

The preliminary procedure helps lay the foundation of the analysis and mitigates the likelihood you will waste time and resources later. The procedure consists of four steps that we describe next and also summarize in Figure 3.1.

The very first step when conducting analysis involves figuring out what you want to analyze and why; in other words, formulating a problem of interest. In most cases involving security operations and analysis, formulating your problem of interest is not difficult. Based on your mission and role, a third party, commander, or boss has probably tasked you with either discovering more about something or someone and/or forecasting what they might do in the future. See Table 3.1 for sample problems.

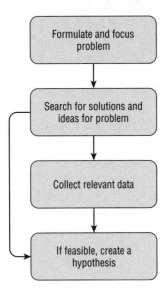

Figure 3.1: The preliminary procedure for analysis

The key is ensuring that your problem of interest is narrow and specific enough to generate an analysis that is feasible and results that are accurate. The following guidelines will help you narrow the problem:

- Examine the behavior of only specific individuals and/or groups. The fewer individuals or groups examined, the better. For example, consider that you are attempting to study the behavior of people in violent protests, and how the violence comes about. Narrow your problem to identify the groups and individuals who participate in the more violent parts of a protest.

- Limit the size of the relevant physical and/or virtual space. If you know that an event is taking place, most protests must get permits that designate location. Look for the groups operating in that location and focus on them. Additionally, look at online social networks most frequently used or visited in the past and concentrate on a few key individuals (we discuss how to recognize who to look at later).

- Specify the type of behavior examined. If you are looking specifically for those engaging in violence, look at which are using the angriest or most profane language in the spaces you have designated.

- Identify the time period in which the behavior and/or event takes place. If you know that the protest takes place over a weekend, but preparations are being made well in advance, start collecting data a few weeks or months out depending on the size of events, and collect for a brief time afterward.

After adequately formulating and focusing the problem, check the Internet to see if others have tackled a similar problem (`scholar.google.com` is a good resource). Being smart and lazy is the way to go. If others have paved the way intelligently and honestly, feel free to learn from their journey. You might stumble upon a methodology or a ready solution that will save you time and resources. Of course, do not outright steal or plagiarize the work of others. Check with the corresponding author to see how much you can borrow—he or she may be flattered and happy to help.

> **NOTE** When adopting the work of others, use the lists in the section titled "Analysis Dos and Don'ts" to evaluate their analysis.

If your Internet search did not turn up the solution, begin assembling relevant data, which includes social media data and even other data such as weather information, stock market indices, and demographic information. Chapter 4 is dedicated to determining what constitutes relevant data and collecting and managing social media data. Due to the inconsistent nature of social media data, the type and amount of available data will vary considerably. Collecting and thus getting a sense of the data available this early in the analytical procedure may drive the choice of analytical process and methodology.

Formal and academic guides to analysis usually suggest that you formulate the hypothesis before you start assembling data. A *hypothesis* is an educated guess about the likely solution to the problem. This advice should not go unheeded because a hypothesis can help focus your study. If you can formulate a strong hypothesis based on existing studies and theories, you have a better sense of the type of data you need to collect and the types of analytical methodologies you need to apply. Do understand that this is a much more effortful and different process than formulating a hypothesis based on your unexamined biases or "gut." Later paragraphs explain how and why.

However, first you should understand that in the emerging field of social media analytics and based on the complex and unique problems you are likely trying to solve, the advice is not always practical and in some cases even harmful. A misguided hypothesis can introduce bias into your analysis and lead you to ignore certain data. You may then miss out on a range of solutions you could not even have imagined. Consider that you want to identify the most influential person on Twitter in regards to spreading violent neo-Nazi propaganda. You select to study only one group of neo-Nazis, because the group is routinely mentioned in the news media as an example of a neo-Nazi group. Keep in mind that popularity in the news media is not necessarily equal to influence within the specific population. You then miss out on the influence of other groups and how individuals in those groups may be influencing the group you choose to study.

Generally, you should formulate a hypothesis if three criteria are fulfilled. One, the problem is not that unique and others have successfully attacked it or similar ones. Your hypothesis will then likely be a version of their solution. Two, established and tested theories exist that help describe the types of human behaviors in question. For instance, social networks tend to follow certain rules regardless of the context. Apply the theory to the problem to create a hypothesis that is grounded in experimental evidence. Three, the physical, virtual, and temporal factors constituting the problem's environment are so limited that the menu of likely solutions is small. For example, environmental factors may make it so that an event will certainly take place either tomorrow or next week. Based on your experience, knowledge of similar past events, and cues, you can then reasonably guess when the event may happen.

We caution against using hypothesis in our case for several reasons. One, few people have published rigorous studies assessing the types of security problems and social media data most relevant to you. Two, social media analytics is far from formalized and few proven theories exist that adequately and reliably explain behavior involving social media. Behaviors that describe human interaction and behavior offline may not always translate to interaction and behavior on social media. Three, the likely relevant environmental factors are not limiting enough to limit the menu of likely solutions. In fact, the environmental factors are probably relatively more numerous because the data and problems likely involve the behavior of many individuals that live in many different parts of the world, and use many different social media platforms.

After formulating or bypassing the hypothesis and collecting the data, the preliminary procedure winds to a close. The next step is determining the type of reasoning or process most appropriate for conducting the analysis. In reality, the line between the preliminary procedure and determining the appropriate analytical process is blurry. Well into your own analysis, you may stumble onto evidence or theories that provide you with an adequate solution quickly or further focus your problem. Or, you start out with a hypothesis and then ignore it if the analysis leads you down unimagined roads. Or, you will likely need to collect more data to complete the analysis. Be intellectually honest with yourself and flexible, and the blurry line will cease to be an issue.

The Analytical Processes

Determining which process is most adequate for your needs depends on the problem, other available work on the problem, and the amount of available data. Each process has different requirements, and provides distinct advantages and disadvantages. Understanding the concepts underlying each reasoning process will help you determine the ideal process and methodology. The most realistic option is to combine the different types of reasoning and modify the combination of processes to fit your needs.

Inductive Reasoning

Inductive reasoning or *induction* is a bottom-up, data-driven approach that involves identifying patterns in data and then codifying the patterns into theories that can also explain other data.

Inductive reasoning is an exploratory process that provides you with insights when you have little idea about possible solutions to your problem. When you fail to generate a hypothesis according to the aforementioned criteria, you need to use the inductive process. Analyzing social media data entails using a lot of induction. As we mentioned before, the study of social media data, and the effect of social media on behavior and vice versa is fairly new. The study of social media and its relationship with security-relevant behavior is even more nascent. You will likely find few established theories that will give you an idea about the solution to your problem. Figure 3.2 outlines the induction process.

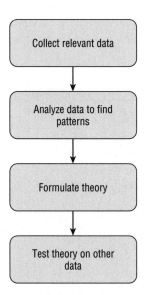

Figure 3.2: The inductive process

First, gather a substantial sample of data or observations concerning the problem of interest. Try to collect a large enough sample size of observations. However, do not become obsessed with collecting data. More data does not always give you more knowledge. Chapter 4 briefly covers how to determine the correct size of an adequate data set using statistical tools. However, do not worry if you cannot meet all statistical requirements. Usually, external factors will limit the size of your data set. The likely issue will be the lack of data, not its overabundance. Also, you may not have the time and resources to collect data and meet all the statistical requirements.

After you have the sample, use a number of statistical tools to apply the methodologies. We describe this process and the relevant tools in detail later. The methodologies and tools will help you pick out patterns in the data that, if strong enough, you can develop into rules that describe past, present, and future human behavior.

Lastly, codify the rules into a theory that elegantly describes a solution to your problem and general behavioral rules that could help solve other similar problems. Test the theory on other data sets and on other problems to make sure your theory is sound and applicable. Even if the theory holds true only for your data set and problem, do not despair. You may have discovered something unique about that data, which is a theory in its own right.

There is nothing inherently bad about induction. However, misguided or overzealous use of induction can lead you down the wrong path. Incorrectly applying inductive methodologies to data will reveal incorrect patterns that lead to the development of incorrect theories and solutions. Also, induction will not work if you do not have an adequate amount of data. If your data consists of only a few samples, many of which may be outliers or unrepresentative data points, then induction will hurt more than help.

INDUCTION EXAMPLE: SOCIAL MEDIA USE DURING RIOTS

Consider that the problem is determining how young people use location-based smartphone applications such as BlackBerry Messenger (BBM) to organize violence during riots in major cities. The solution involves detailing the extent to which young people use the application, when they use it, why they use it, and how it affects the violence. The following steps describe the ensuing overall analytical process and the use of induction:

1. **Narrow the problem and limit the people, behaviors, event, and time period involved. Rephrase the problem as: How did the British rioters use BBM during the 2011 London riots to organize acts of violence at specific locations?**

2. **Check around for similar work and solutions. Many reports examine the London riots but few do in-depth analytics measuring the effects of BBM messages, mainly because the messages are very difficult to come by.**

3. **Collect relevant data including the messages (perhaps by contacting the UK government and the makers of BBM, Research in Motion), news reports detailing the locations of rioters at given moments, openly available social media data such as tweets about the riots, and police reports about damaged stores.**

4. **Stop and take account of what you know so far. You have a well-defined problem and data, but few hints telling you what the data might suggest. For example, the data could suggest that only certain groups of rioters used BBM to organize the targeting of very specific stores, or that messages on Twitter and not BBM were used to organize the violence.**

5. Apply inductive reasoning and corresponding methodologies to see if noticeable patterns correlate BBM use and violence. Perhaps you discover that moments before a store was attacked, there was a spike of BBM messages mentioning the store's location. You may also uncover that the creators of those BBM messages were almost always males aged 20+. BBM messages from teenagers or females never mentioned the locations that suffered violence. Finally, you can discover that the only stores BBM users mentioned and thus targeted were sports stores.

6. Codify your discoveries into a theory. The theory could say that during riots, males in their twenties are very likely to use location-based social media platforms to target violence against stores that carry goods they find appealing, such as sports equipment and clothing.

7. Test your theory on other data sets. Examine the data from riots in the U.S., Latin American cities, and European cities to see if the behavior your theory describes is universal.

8. Use the tests' findings to refine your theory and its scope of application.

WARNING   We fabricated this example. We have no idea if males aged 20+ really did use BBM to loot sports stores in London.

Deductive Reasoning

We already introduced deductive reasoning in the induction case study. Step 7 in the case study is an example of deduction.

Deductive reasoning or *deduction* is a top-down, theory-driven approach that involves applying established theories and well-developed hypotheses on data to test the validity of the theory and hypothesis.

Deductive reasoning is a more formal and focused process that helps you confirm if your educated guess about the likely solution to the problem is valid. When you can generate a hypothesis according to the aforementioned criteria, you should use the deductive process. You may still use induction, but deduction will save you time and effort by focusing your analysis on examining only a few possible solutions. In a few cases, deduction will be applicable. For example, many new studies confirm that theories that govern how the social networks of humans develop offline can in some specific cases explain how social networks develop on social media. Other studies confirm that how ideas spread through social networks is partly independent of the mode of communication. Assembling a comprehensive list of existing theories that apply to social media is difficult. You will have to do your own research, especially because it is heavily dependent on your problem. Figure 3.3 outlines the deductive process.

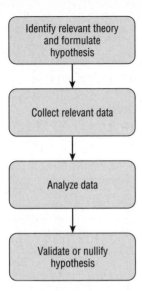

Figure 3.3: The deductive process

First, determine which existing theories, studies, and solutions to similar problems are the most relevant to your problem. Evaluate them to ensure they are analytically sound and applicable. They are applicable if they consider populations, behaviors, and environmental factors similar to those in your problem, and they suggest their rules and results are applicable to other problems and data sets. Compare competing theories if applicable, and formulate a hypothesis.

Next, gather data necessary to prove or nullify your hypothesis. In some cases, deduction requires gathering less data than induction. If substantial literature and evidence backs up your hypothesis, you can be reasonably confident that you only need to collect data about items and factors your hypothesis considers. However, if you have the time and resources, collect other data. Later, you can apply the inductive process and corresponding methodologies to the extra data to ensure you did not miss anything.

After you have enough data, use a number of statistical and other tools to apply the methodologies. We describe this process and the relevant tools in detail later. The methodologies and tools will help you evaluate whether the theories that inspired your hypothesis are applicable, and the extent to which your hypothesis is valid.

Lastly, determine the solution to your problem by refining or junking the hypothesis and applicable theories on the basis of the analysis' results. You may discover that only parts of the hypothesis are valid as a solution. Likely, you will find that special conditions related only to the items and factors in your problem are required to validate the hypothesis. You may also discover that the hypothesis is completely wrong and what you thought was the solution is not valid, in which case you will need to either apply other hypotheses or apply the inductive process. You may also refine existing theories and make them more elegant and simple, which you may further validate through other analyses or leave others to do it.

Deduction is most appropriate when you can generate a well-informed and specific hypothesis. However, executing a deductive process with a poorly developed or weak hypothesis will lead to an invalidation of the hypothesis and frustration, and a waste of time and effort. You will then have to start all over again. As a general rule, use deduction only when your hypothesis is strong, or when you cannot collect enough data to do induction.

DEDUCTION EXAMPLE: KEY TERRORISM PROMOTERS ON SOCIAL NETWORKS

Consider that the problem is determining which individuals promoting terrorism on social media networks are the most influential at spreading propaganda and appealing to at-risk youth. The solution involves detailing how terrorist recruiters and sympathizers use social media, and determining the effectiveness of recruiters and their ability to influence the behaviors of others through social media communication. The following steps describe the ensuing overall analytical process and the use of deduction:

1. Narrow the problem and limit the people, behaviors, time, and communication tools involved. Rephrase the problem as: Which known recruiters sympathetic to al-Shabaab were the most influential on Twitter during al-Qaeda's merger with al-Shabaab in terms of spreading positive propaganda about the merger to American youth?

2. Examine and evaluate other similar work and solutions. Several studies describe methods to quantitatively measure the influence of specific people in online social networks, and their ability to propagate messages through online social networks.

3. Collect relevant data including the tweets of known al-Shabaab sympathizers, al-Shabaab affiliates, al-Qaeda affiliates, and American youth that al-Shabaab routinely target for recruitment. Also collect the statements that al-Shabaab and al-Qaeda propagated about their merger in news stories.

4. Stop and take account of what you know so far. You have a well-defined problem, data, and several theories that have successfully solved problems similar to yours.

5. Compare the theories, and formulate a specific hypothesis that states a likely solution to your problem. The hypothesis could say that the known recruiters sympathetic to al-Shabaab most effective at spreading positive propaganda on Twitter are the recruiters who have at least a 5 to 1 ratio of followers to following.

continued

DEDUCTION EXAMPLE: KEY TERRORISM PROMOTERS ON SOCIAL NETWORKS (*continued*)

6. Apply deductive reasoning and corresponding methodologies to see if your hypothesis is valid. Perhaps you discover that the hypothesis is indeed valid. You may find that at-risk American youth tend to read, retweet, and discuss (as one methodology describes influence) more messages spread by recruiters with a 5 to 1 ratio than by recruiters with a less than 5 to 1 ratio. You may also discover, perhaps by happenstance or because you applied some inductive processing, that recruiters with a 10 to 1 ratio have far more influence.

7. Refine the theory to say that Twitter accounts with a 10 to 1 ratio of followers to following are far more influential on Twitter than those with a 5 to 1 ratio, who are in turn more influential than those with a smaller ratio.

8. Test your theory on other data sets. Examine the data from the Twitter recruitment and propaganda efforts of Hezbollah, non-Jihadi groups, and even non-terrorists such as celebrities marketing a product, to see if the behavior your theory describes is universal.

WARNING   We fabricated the theory about measuring influence on Twitter. Later, we discuss actual methodologies for defining and measuring influence on social networks.

Combining Reasoning Processes

You probably noticed that the final steps of each reasoning process involve applying parts of the other reasoning process. Few social media and security analyses are clearly defined as requiring either induction or deduction. Most require variants of both, sometimes in the middle of the analytical process and often at the end. As you conduct more analyses, you will learn when to utilize a reasoning process. There is no right answer because it is a cyclical process. Given time and resources, use induction constantly to discover insights and deduction to test them. Your analysis will be much stronger for it and you will develop your own analytical tools that you can deploy quickly in the future or use to educate others. Figure 3.4 graphically illustrates this process.

Analysis Dos and Don'ts

Before learning the different methodologies, it is necessary to adopt good analysis habits. Many of you are conducting analyses to support sensitive and dangerous operations. Adopting good habits and taking care to avoid pitfalls will drastically improve the reliability and integrity of your analysis. Think of abiding by the analysis dos and don'ts as insurance against charges of incompetence or sloppiness. Also, you will help develop the field of social media analytics by creating and sharing well-done analyses.

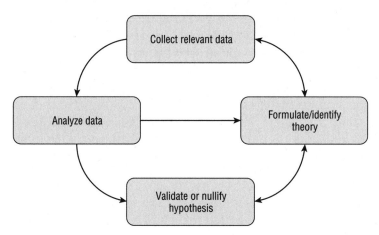

Figure 3.4: Combining induction and deduction

The following is a list of analysis dos. In an ideal world, you should abide by all of them, but in the real world where resources and time are limited, we encourage you to at least try. The act of trying will put the quality of your analysis head-and-shoulders over much of existing "analysis."

- Ensure to the best of your ability that the methodology you undertake is repeatable. Given the same data and a description of your analytical process, another person whom you have not worked with should be able to reach similar conclusions. This rule is the cornerstone of the scientific process and of real analytics. Some of you may be working in classified environments where realistically few others will look at your analysis. Still, as you go through your analysis, imagine that someone else will be looking at your work and trying to repeat what you did.

- Abide by *Occam's razor*, which states that a theory explaining a behavior, prediction, or conclusion that is simpler and has fewer assumptions is more precise and accurate than a more complicated theory. In other words—keep it simple, stupid. If a theory that uses social media data to forecast famine requires hundreds of variables and lots of assumptions—such as "This theory applies only if the price of wheat is exactly USD $5.76/bushel in the area"—then it is not very useful for future purposes. It might still tell you something about that particular event, but your goal should always be to uncover the underlying rules governing human behavior concerning security so you can quickly analyze other similar problems.

- Make any theory you develop falsifiable, which means that a specific data point or observation should be able to disprove your theory. For example, the statement, "It will rain tomorrow" is falsifiable. A specific data point, in this case measuring whether it rains tomorrow, can disprove or prove the conclusion. The point is to keep you from producing solutions to problems that do not hold up to analysis or scrutiny, and thus do not help your mission. Consider the induction case study about social media use in riots. In the case study, we came up with a falsifiable conclusion, that during riots only males aged 20+ use location-based social media to organize violence against stores carrying goods they like. If examination of other riots shows that it was mostly females aged 40+ organizing violence, the theory is falsified. This allows you to then limit your theory to only the 2011 London riots or to redo your analysis. Also, if others can test your conclusions, they can validate them and you can pat yourself on the back for a job well done.

As is often the case, the list of ways to do something wrong is a lot longer than the ways to do something right. The following is a list of analysis don'ts. Do your best to avoid them to ensure your analysis is intellectually honest, stands up to scrutiny, and provides you with accurate insights. Resource and data constraints may compel you to fall prey to an analysis mistake. Still, being aware of your analysis' faults will help you prepare for possible eventualities and negative fallout.

- Do not discard or ignore data because it does not support your hypothesis or because it goes against any patterns you discover in the overall data. You are primarily analyzing humans—subjects that are complicated and rarely do what you want them to do. Finding data that goes against established theories about human behavior is the norm. Often unusual data or outliers are clues to more expansive solutions, or special exceptions for solutions. Sometimes, the outliers are not outliers but representatives of a much larger data set that will completely invalidate your analysis. Also, if you consciously leave out conflicting data, you leave yourself open to criticism. We discuss how to deal with outliers later. Humans are especially susceptible to discarding data that clashes with our beliefs due to cognitive bias. We naturally tune out information that challenges the theories we develop about how the world works. Take extra care to ensure you are not ignoring conflicting data.

- Do not confuse anecdotes with indicators of real patterns, also known as the *exception fallacy*. You cannot generalize based on a few qualitative examples or the thoughts of a few people because your generalizations could be completely incorrect. For example, you may be investigating if drug dealers use certain code words on Twitter to indicate different kinds of drug dealing activity. You may then look at the tweets of a few known drug dealers and recognize they use the word "wedding" to indicate a drug drop. You cannot then generalize that all drug dealers use the word "wedding" to also indicate drug drops. If you do, you will likely miss out on other code words. Also, some drug dealers might actually be going to, and so discussing, a wedding. To conduct induction properly, you need to collect a much larger set of examples to ensure you are not only citing outliers. The exception fallacy is the basis for racial stereotyping. Simply because you see a few people of a race commit crime, does not mean that everyone of that race commits crimes.

- Do not overstate the strengths of your forecasts. Predicting complex events such as humanitarian crises and drug trafficking activity with certainty is extremely difficult. Be up front or at least aware that there is a chance that your forecasts may not come true. Generally, the fewer the number of things, people, and conditions you are dealing with, the greater the accuracy of your forecast.

We provide only the most relevant dos and don'ts. Several more are available and we encourage you to read the book we cite in the notes and other books and articles on analysis so you can continue to improve your analysis.

Analysis Methodologies

Methodologies are the series of steps that will allow you to apply the two reasoning processes on the data. In this section, we introduce four methodologies that are the most pertinent for social media analysis and ones we use the most. Chapters 5 and 6 describe them in greater detail and illustrate how to use them to solve security-related problem sets. To solve complex problems, you will need to combine the methodologies. Keep in mind that social media analysis is in no way limited to only these four methodologies. Therefore, we also briefly touch on other methodologies and recommend you adopt various other methodologies as you see fit. Be creative and flexible.

> **WARNING**   Again, our focus is on helping you conduct quick and accurate analysis to support operations, not to publish in academic journals. Therefore, in the name of clarity and ease of understanding we have taken liberties with definitions and the use of various concepts. If you are a professor of statistics or quantitative methods, please do not send us hate mail or hate tweets.

So far, the information we have covered, such as the preliminary procedure and dos and don'ts, applies regardless of the type of methodologies you employ. Information from now on will apply only to specific methodologies with the exception of a brief overview of variables, a key component of all methodologies. If you are familiar with conducting analyses you can skip the Variables section.

Variables

Variables are symbols that represent a variety of quantitative or qualitative values. Anything that varies can be a variable. For example, the various types of illegal drugs can be variables, or the age of the top Facebook users in Africa. Analysis involves manipulating and comparing variables at different times in different situations to tease out patterns, causal effects, and insights. Understanding variables and how they differ will help you formulate meaningful analyses. Every robust analysis has the following three types of variables:

- **Dependent**—The variable that you will measure and that other factors affect.

- **Independent**—The variable that varies during the analysis and directly or indirectly affects or is correlated with the dependent variable.

- **Controlled**—The variable that you hold constant during the analysis so you can isolate the effects of particular independent variables and eliminate the possibility that other variables are affecting the dependent variable.

If the variable types are new or confusing, then consider the following example.

DETERMINING VARIABLES EXAMPLE: VIOLENT FLASH MOBS

Say you want a method to tell if a violent flash mob is likely to happen at a certain location. A *flash mob* is when people assemble suddenly in a place at a specific time. Flash mob organizers and participants usually use social media to spread word about the flash mob and help organize it. Imagine that prior analyses indicate that a violent flash mob is likely to happen at a specific location if a significant number of tweets mention the name of the location within 20 minutes, regardless of who is tweeting. Your analysis then needs to determine the value of the significant number. Restate the problem as "What number of tweets must mention the name of the location within the 20-minute time period?" Your hypothesis could be that more than 100,000 tweets need to mention the name of the location within the 20-minute time period. Notice that to get this far you used deduction—looking at prior analyses and theories to determine your hypothesis.

For now, do not worry about the methodology you will use to verify the hypothesis. Focus on determining the variables you need to conduct the analysis. The dependent variable in this case is the appearance of a violent flash mob. The independent variable is the number of tweets. The number of tweets affects the appearance of the violent flash mob.

Unfortunately, security-related analyses are rarely this simplistic. The variables are usually a number of things. In this case, the dependent variable can be anything that indicates the appearance of the violent flash mob. Possible dependent variables include news reports about mobs, police reports about mobs, or a certain number of people committing violence in a specific area of physical space.

> To make things more complicated, perhaps prior analyses are not certain about the time period within which the tweets need to appear. Now you have two independent variables. One is the number of tweets and the other is the time period. Perhaps as an indicator of a violent flash mob, the number of tweets does not matter as much as tweets with mentions of a location that appear within three minutes of each other. The analysis then needs to determine whether one or both independent variables affect the dependent variable and to what extent. In one part of the analysis, one of the independent variables will become a controlled variable. In another part, the other independent variable will become the controlled variable and vice versa. In other words, hold one independent variable constant while measuring the effect of the other independent variable. In the third part of the analysis, measure the combined effect of or relationship between the independent variables on one or all of the dependent variables.

Methodologies in this Book

The following sections briefly introduce the methodologies you will learn to use to analyze social media and related data.

Social Network Analysis

Social network analysis (SNA), a type of network analysis, is the study of the social structure known as social networks comprised of individuals and their relationships. A social network can consist of the relationship between two people or of the relationships between everyone on Earth. See Figure 3.5 for an example of a social network. Because social media is all about creating and sustaining social networks and relationships between people, understanding SNA is essential to understanding social media.

SNA emerged from the interaction of disparate fields including psychology, graph theory, and statistics, and forms part of the emerging field of network science. Several network science theories, some of which contradict each other, describe how social networks behave. They sacrifice the importance of a specific individual and the attributes that describe the individual to generalize about how typical human relationships function. The theories exist as algorithms that conduct specialized mathematics on social network data and output specific answers. Therefore, you can consider SNA to be a somewhat deductive process, yet one that also draws from induction.

SNA enables you to map, measure, and describe almost anything about a social network and its components. SNA can provide information about individuals, a few relationships, or large-scale networks. You can use SNA to understand the ideas of interest of social networks, how individuals gain influence in social networks, how individuals form relationships with others, how the relationships evolve over time, and how the relationships affect the behavior of individuals in the social network. You can also use SNA to determine which individuals are the most influential, which individuals are the most vocal, which relationships are the most influential, and which relationships are necessary to sustain the structure of the network. SNA also enables you to measure the relationships between different types of social networks. For example, with SNA you can measure whether and how an individual's social network on Badoo influences his or her social network in the physical world (friends, family, and so on) and vice versa. SNA is very useful for understanding how violent extremists use social media to develop relationships with at-risk populations, forecasting how the social networks of human traffickers and narcotics smugglers evolve over time, identifying the key individuals and relationships in drug trafficking networks, and much more.

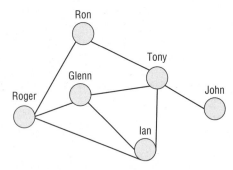

Figure 3.5: Social network example

The rise of social media and especially social networking platforms has produced gargantuan amounts of data about social networks. Now, it is easy to find sample social network data on the Internet, which researchers usually derive from Facebook, to test network science theories. The explosion of readily available social network data and sophisticated SNA software preloaded with algorithms is producing the golden age of network science. Many theories underlying SNA are now being put to the test like never before, and several companies are creating automated tools to analyze social networks exhibited on social media platforms.

Chapter 5 delineates how to conduct SNA. However, the following describes the overall SNA process:

1. Formulate the problem.

2. Collect related data about social networks, specifically information about the structure, strength, and type of relationships between individuals.

3. Input the data into SNA software to map or draw the social network.

4. Use the SNA software to run specific algorithms on the data.

5. Compare and contrast the algorithm outputs to answer the problem.

Language and Sentiment Analysis

Language and sentiment analysis (LSA) is the study of patterns in linguistic content, such as Facebook status updates and text messages. It is the application of theories and tools from fields including text analytics, computational linguistics, statistics, and natural language processing (NLP). LSA is actually an umbrella term we use to address a variety of language processing tools and analyses. The various language tools and analyses help identify what individuals and groups are saying, why they are saying it, who is saying it, what they mean exactly by what they are saying, and how they feel about what they are talking about. As with SNA, the explosion of social media data consisting of billions of tweets, status updates, private messages, and texts from people globally has significantly bolstered the use of LSA. Because social media is all about communication, and much of the communication is text-based, understanding LSA is essential to understanding the meaning of communication. LSA is very useful for geolocating and understanding texts from victims of humanitarian crises, determining the identity and likely location of a suspicious blog's author, forecasting the coordination of criminal activity such as planning of violent riots, and much more.

LSA involves both inductive and deductive processes. Many existing LSA theories and algorithms process language and output answers with varying reliability. While most LSA tools focus on processing the English language, few process non-Western and less mainstream languages such as Swahili. Existing LSA tools also have difficulty processing unstructured data with lots of slang, idioms, and sarcasm such as the tweets of teenagers, although advances are being made rapidly. You will use both existing LSA tools and algorithms and create your own through deduction and induction.

Chapter 6 delineates how to conduct LSA. However, the following describes the overall LSA process:

1. Formulate the problem.

2. Collect related data consisting of massive amounts of textual content.

3. Evaluate existing LSA tools for relevance. If relevant, input data into the LSA tool (usually available as commercial or open source software).

4. If no relevant LSA tool is found, create your own LSA tool and algorithm either by adapting existing LSA tools, creating entirely new LSA theories through deduction, and/or by conducting correlative analyses (described later) on the textual data.

5. Compare and contrast the LSA tools' outputs to answer the problem.

Correlation and Regression Analysis

Correlation and regression analysis (CRA) is the study of correlations and/or relationships between anything, or more accurately, between a dependent variable and one or more independent variables. CRA uncovers correlations between seemingly separate things and enables you to determine whether and to what extent the two things either directly or indirectly affect each other, or whether a third thing affects both simultaneously or concurrently. CRA is usually the first type of analysis one learns in a basic statistics course and is used in virtually every field.

To be more precise, correlation and regression analysis are different types of analyses. You use correlation analysis when you simply want to find associative relationships between distinct things, regardless of if they affect each other. For example, there is a correlation between the sale of winter coats and gloves. When there is a spike in sales of winter coats, there tends to be a spike in the sale of gloves. Note that correlation does not imply causation. It is not that the purchase of a winter coat causes or affects a buyer to purchase gloves or vice versa. It is that a third thing, cold weather, causes the buyer to purchase both a winter coat and gloves.

You use regression analysis when you want to uncover predictive relationships between two things, regardless if they cause each other. By a predictive relationship, we mean that the change in value of one variable can help you forecast how the other variable will change. For example, you can do regression analyses on data about the sales of winter coats and gloves. You can then create an equation that tells you that a 15% increase in the sale of winter gloves tends to be associated with a 20% increase in coats. Regression analysis also tells you about the accuracy of your predictive equation.

WARNING   Use common sense when using CRA, and understand the direction of causal relationships. You have to use experience and knowledge to figure out that it is cold weather that causes humans to purchase more winter coats and gloves, and not the sale of winter coats that causes the sale of gloves.

CRA is an essential tool for understanding social media data and insights hidden therein. Expect to regularly use CRA to support other methodologies and to uncover correlations and causal relationships between various things. In the case of CRA, think of social media primarily as the vehicle for delivering data that enables you to uncover the intuitive and counterintuitive correlations and relationships between disparate things. CRA is very useful for establishing correlation relationships between microeconomic indicators and weather data to forecast famines, establishing causal relationships between specific messages on social media and violent acts on the ground, determining the existence of causal relationships between drug smuggling activity in rural areas and the momentary sentiment of rural populations, and much more.

Chapter 6 delineates how to conduct CRA and further discusses how correlation analysis is different from regression analysis. However, the following describes the overall CRA process:

1. Formulate the problem.

2. Collect related data. Generally, the more data the better.

3. Input data into an appropriate CRA tool (tools are usually available as commercial or open source).

4. Analyze the CRA tool output and establish whether a correlation exists.

5. Conduct regression analysis using CRA tool to determine whether the variables share a predictive relationship.

6. In the case of associative and predictive relationships, use a priori knowledge to determine the existence and direction of causality.

Volumetric Analysis

Volumetric analysis (VA) is a type of CRA that focuses only on discovering associative and predictive relationships between events or behavior and changes in the volume of traffic or activity on social media platforms. Data traffic and activity on social media platforms, hereafter known as data volume, includes the number of tweets in a day that mention a specific word to the number of texts from a specific location. Information about data volume is often easier to collect than content data. Social media platforms like to make such data available to showcase their popularity and success.

We separate out VA from CRA because of the powerful insights that analyzing data traffic and activity can reveal about security-related issues. Examining changes in data volume and focusing on unique spikes or drops in data volume often reveal the presence of unique events. In the security world, unique events are the most important events because civil wars, terrorist bombings, and natural disasters are not everyday occurrences. VA is very useful for identifying sharp drops in social media activity from a specific location to uncover security threats in the area, correlating spikes in communication between two countries with a spike in drug smuggling activity in the countries, and much more.

Chapter 6 delineates how to conduct VA. However, the following describes the overall VA process:

1. Formulate the problem.

2. Collect related data including data volume over numerous periods of time, including periods that do and do not include the scope of time relevant to the problem.

3. Use data volume collected from all periods of time to establish a baseline data volume that describes "normal" data volume. Factor in normal growth or decline in data volume, as needed.

4. Use VA tools to compare data volume from the period of time of interest with baseline data volume. Identify atypical changes in data volume.

5. If atypical changes exist, use a priori knowledge to correlate changes in data volume with event or behavior.

6. Use CRA tools to determine the existence of an associative or predictive relationship between changes in data volume and event or behavior.

Methodologies Not in this Book

We encourage you to frequently discover and use other types of analyses on social media data. A great way to discover interesting and powerful analytical methodologies is to explore other fields such as physics, biology, and ecology. In fact, we started using VA after reading about how ecologists measured changes in population volumes to uncover unique ecological events. VA is actually a term we borrowed from chemistry. Researchers studying the presence of alien life are using VA to determine changes in the composition of chemicals to identify the presence of life.

To gain a better understanding of SNA and to come across more powerful SNA algorithms, read about the application of network science on other fields. We stumbled onto SNA after reading about neural networks and how network science helps explain the influence of relationships on neurons and vice versa. Likewise, we started to appreciate the power of CRA by reading about complexity science, an emerging field that involves examining the behavior and structure of complex systems. Geoffrey West, a prominent physicist and complexity scientist, has used variations of CRA to uncover startling and interesting rules between population size, gross domestic product (GDP), income, patents filed, and crime rates for any city, be it in the U.S., China, Europe, or elsewhere.[2] Simply put, West found that if you double the size of a city, you get a 15 percent increase in any of the aforementioned areas, as well as many others. West's findings highlight the underlying strength and influence of citywide social networks.

If your time to study other fields is limited, fear not. Chapter 12 briefly explores exciting but more complex analytical methodologies and tools that you can apply to social media data. They include:

- **Agent modeling**—Create virtual avatars of individuals and social networks to model their behavior in various situations and environments, and responses to changes in their environments. Social media data provides information about individuals and social networks to program the avatars.

- **Geo-spatial network analysis**—Uncover how the structure of towns and cities, and the distribution of resources such as waterholes, can help forecast the likelihood of criminal or violent activity in specific areas. Social media data and crowdsourcing platforms provide information about the location and distributions of relevant items.

- **Cluster analysis**—Group millions of social media users by various attributes to focus SNA and targeting efforts.

But before you start exploring more advanced methodologies, you need to learn the more basic ones. Chapter 5 continues your education in analysis by teaching you how to conduct social network analysis.

Summary

- Analysis is a systematic process that reveals solutions to many, but not all, concrete problems.

- This book focuses on helping you do analysis quickly to support operations, not publish in academic journals.

- Analyzing precisely and honestly is essential to getting correct solutions. Follow the dos and don'ts.

- All analysis starts with the preliminary procedure, which involves formulating a focused and narrow problem, exploring existing solutions and theories, collecting related data, and generating a hypothesis only if existing solutions and theories back up your hypothesis.

- After the preliminary procedure, select a methodology based on the reasoning you want to employ.

- Inductive reasoning is data-driven and involves identifying patterns in data and then codifying the patterns into theories that can also explain other data.

- Deductive reasoning is theory-driven and involves applying established theories and hypotheses on data to test the validity of the theory and hypothesis.

- Most analyses will involve a mix of the two types of reasoning processes.

- This book focuses on applying four types of analytical methodologies:

  - Social network analysis involves studying social networks online and offline, and the relationships and individuals that make up the social networks.

- Language and sentiment analysis involves identifying patterns in linguistic content on social media platforms that reveal insight about events and behavior.

- Correlation and regression analysis involves determining correlative and direct and indirect causal relationships between various factors and things.

- Volumetric analysis involves determining correlative and direct and indirect causal relationships between behavior and events, and data traffic and activity on social media platforms.

Notes

1. Tetlock, P. (2006) *Expert Political Judgment: How Good Is It? How Can We Know?* Princeton University Press, Princeton, NJ.

2. West, G. (2011) "The Surprising Math of Cities and Corporations." TED. Accessed: 24 May 2012. `http://www.ted.com/talks/geoffrey_west_the_surprising_math_of_cities_and_corporations.html`

CHAPTER

4

Collecting and Managing Social Media Data

Analyzing social media first requires collecting and managing enormous amounts of social media and other types of data. The widespread use of social media globally has produced petabytes of data, most of which is not relevant to your purpose and analysis. The most important part of conducting social media analysis is adequately and intelligently finding and manipulating relevant data without becoming overwhelmed. To this end, this chapter explains what constitutes social media and related data; details the process to determine your data needs; and describes how to collect the data, filter the data, and store and manage the data. The chapter also discusses the benefits and drawbacks of building your own data management system and buying a commercially available one. We do not expect you to have the technical acumen to actually build the data collection apparatus. However, knowing the technical concepts behind data collection will greatly inform your analysis and expectations, and help you select and use the appropriate data collection technologies.

Understanding Social Media Data

Social media data is all the user-generated content and corresponding metadata on social media platforms.

User-generated content includes the pictures on Facebook, the diaries on Qzone, the videos on YouTube, the tweets on Twitter, and much more. Most of it is unstructured, which means that for the most part it does not follow predefined rules. A 15-year-old in Malaysia can tweet something in Malay that is full of local slang and does not follow grammatical rules, and a 60-year-old in the United Kingdom can tweet the Queen's English using perfect grammar. Apart from both being text and containing less than 140 characters, each tweet will probably look completely different. The unstructured data concept also takes into account that content on different platforms can have very little in common. A picture on Orkut is very different than an invite on LinkedIn.

Metadata is information about the user and the content they post or, in other words, data about the data.

Social media data includes not only the content you see, but also metadata that includes the location where the picture on Facebook was taken, the date and time when the diary was uploaded on Qzone, the countries where people watched the video on YouTube, the number of people who retweeted a tweet on Twitter, the number of friends a person has on hi5, and much more.

The amount of user-generated content and metadata is enormous and growing every day at a rapid rate. Consider that two years ago, Twitter was generating 8 terabytes of data per day.[1] This amount grows significantly when you take into account current-day use, all the other data on social media platforms, and then the metadata. Finally, the amount grows even larger when you include any relevant data you might need to complete your analysis. Such data can include information about weather and climate, geospatial maps, terrorist attacks, maritime piracy incidents, demographic statistics, and much more. As you can infer, maritime piracy data looks very different and is thus structured very differently than data on hi5. "Big data" is the buzzword people use to describe all this complex and unstructured data that standard database solutions cannot solve.

Using and making sense of big data is necessary for analysis and a difficult task, but not an impossible one. In fact, dealing with big data will soon cease to be a problem and people will go back to calling it simply "data." Numerous organizations are making rapid advances in data-related technologies, many of which we will explore. You should start to get a sense of how to deal with big data now before these technologies become ubiquitous and you are left behind. Overall, dealing with big data requires executing the following process:

1. **Determine collection needs**—Figure out what data you need and how much of it, who has it, and if it is possible to even get it.

2. **Collect the data**—Download publically and commercially available data using a variety of methods.

3. **Filter the data**—Eliminate noise from the data you collected, and validate it to ensure its usefulness and legitimacy.

4. **Store and manage the data**—Keep the filtered data in a secure and flexible database that you and others can add to and access as needed.

5. **Analyze the data**—Either manually analyze the data or create automated algorithms and analytical tools that use the analytical methodologies we explore in Chapters 5 and 6 to output solutions to your problems.

The following sections further describe the steps. Figure 4.1 illustrates the overall process. Many commercially available social media data and analysis software can complete steps 2 through 5 without you lifting a finger. We go over evaluating and choosing software later. But first we want to go through the steps as if you were going to do them yourself or with the help of technical staff, so you understand the overarching technical concepts behind data collection and management. Keep in mind that this book is not for programmers and technical developers who are coding and building the systems. We expect you to be the person who will work or manage the developers, or make the decision to purchase the relevant commercially available software. Understanding what goes into creating such systems will improve your ability to evaluate your developers and software purchases.

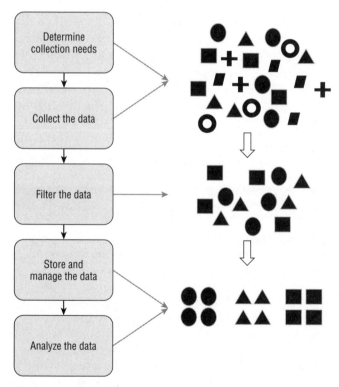

Figure 4.1: Overall data process

CROSS-REFERENCE If you would like to try coding some quick and relatively painless ways to download data autonomously, watch for points where the following sections refer you to the website and further instructions.

Determining Collection Needs

Before you can deal with big data, you need to establish what constitutes big data for you. In some cases, a small amount of data will do the trick, but in others you will need a lot. In some cases, one type of data will be enough, but in others you will need numerous types. It depends on the problem you are trying to solve, the analytical methodology you want to use, the time and resources you have, the accuracy you require or desire, and the environmental constraints you face including access to data. Overall, to determine your data collection needs, you need to answer the following questions:

- What data will solve the problem?
- How much data is enough?
- Who has the data?
- Will they give the data?

This section explains how to answer each of these questions. You should not expect to answer the questions sequentially. Answer the questions in the order in which they are easy for you to answer. The answer to one may significantly influence the answer to another one, and compel you to come up with another answer to the question. For example, if you know about the types of data available in or about a specific area of interest, that will greatly inform and limit your answer to the question, "What data will solve the problem?" An answer to one question may even completely disrupt your approach to the problem and force you to come up with another approach. Consider the following example.

DETERMINING DATA COLLECTION NEEDS EXAMPLE: CONFLICT IN RURAL COLOMBIA

Imagine you want to use what people are saying on social media to determine if there is conflict occurring in specific areas of rural Colombia. You are aware of several non-governmental organizations (NGOs) running social media platforms for different reasons in the area, and determine one way to answer the question is through volumetric analysis. Based on past studies, you conclude that sudden changes in the price of crops in one area compared to the price of crops in nearby areas can tell you if something is happening in that one area. You can then infer that that something is probably related to security and conflict, because the area is known for having lots of conflict and because nearby areas have the same weather, proclivity to natural disasters, and health.

You first ask the question: What data will solve the problem?

You determine that you need data about the price of crops in certain areas over a long period of time.

You then ask: How much data is enough?

You determine that you need to collect 100 daily reports of a specific crop's price from five areas, from the past five months till today.

You then ask: Who has the data?

You identify an existing social media platform, run by a local NGO called mPrice that incentivizes Colombian farmers to text the price at which they sell their crops. In response, the Colombian farmers receive the average crop prices in their area, so they know what the market looks like and if their price is too high or too low. You look at mPrice's platform more closely and find out that they only started two months ago. You then need to go back and refine the answer to the first question. Again you ask, How much data is enough?

You can only get data from the past two months till today. You decide to make up for lack of data over time by collecting more daily reports. Luckily, mPrice collects 1000 daily reports of a specific crop's price from five areas. You then ask, Will they give the data?

You politely ask mPrice, but they refuse. They say they do not like to work with your government, and besides, they make some data available publically. You look at their public data, but it only gives you the average weekly crop price in an area. You decide that is not nearly enough data to conduct volumetric analysis. You have no choice but to start over.

You then decide to determine if security problems exist in specific areas through analysis of other types of data. You identify an NGO called mDisease that queries rural Colombians about health problems. The NGO then uses the information to provide diagnostic services to its users. You reason that by analyzing changes in health problems, you can identify whether the rural Colombians are suffering through extreme conditions such as security problems in their areas. You have already answered the first question—you know you need information about the health status of the rural Colombians. Again, you go through the process of asking the remaining three questions.

What Data Will Solve the Problem?

Expect to require several different types of data to solve one problem. Security events and related behavior are complex, and numerous factors influence them. The data that solves the problem has to take into account at least some of those factors. Use your creativity and knowledge of the problem topic to determine which data will account for the factors or variables in your problem. Additionally, thinking about the data you need reduces the chance that you unwittingly become overwhelmed with irrelevant data.

For example, consider forecasting if peaceful protests in a Middle Eastern country will erupt into violence and revolution. At first glance, the following factors could play a role in this forecasting behavior problem: the authority and power of the government, the demographics of the protestors, the entire population's view of the government, the protestors' view of the government, the intensity of the protests, government response to protest, and many more. Fortunately, numerous studies exist that posit theories about crowd behavior and the birth of revolutions. They allow you to then reduce the number of factors that affect your problem and solution. Imagine that the theories reduce the number of factors to the demographics of the protests and the protestors' perception of the government response to the protest. Then you only need to collect data on those two factors or variables. Data that can provide information about those factors could include census data the government routinely collects and mentions on Twitter about the government response arising from the location. You now know exactly what type of data to collect. If the Twitter data is not available, you can look at videos protestors post on YouTube about the protests. If they are posting many videos showing government violence against the protests, you can infer their perception of the government response.

Over time, you will develop an intuition for quickly identifying the types of data that will help you solve your problem. Prior knowledge about the people, the location, and the issues involved will go a long way toward developing your intuition. We have developed our own intuition about what types of data are most relevant to solving security-related problem sets. See Table 4.1 for a list of data types you will most need to solve the five problem sets.

Table 4.1: Example Data Types for Problem Sets

PROBLEM SET	DATA TYPE
Understand the structure of social networks	Lists of user accounts, the user's followers or friends, the user's groups
Identify key people and relationships	The user's followers or friends, the user's groups, how many times a user messages someone else, who reads the user's messages
Determine the spread of ideas	Retweets, reposts, "Likes", number of times content has been favorited or shared
Understand and forecast behavior	Past behavior of people involved, demographic statistics, geospatial constraints, political and sociological factors, real-time social media feeds of people involved
Understand and forecast events	Past event information, behavior of people involved, demographic statistics, geospatial constraints, political and sociological factors, real-time social media feeds of people involved

How Much Data Is Enough?

Determining the size and amount of adequate data is far from an exact science, especially when it comes to social media data. Frankly, statisticians are not sure what to make of social media data. Ideally, in a traditional statistical analysis, you want to assemble a random assortment or sample of data. A random sample ensures you do not have biased data, which can lead to misleading conclusions. However, social media data is not random, and hence is inherently biased. Despite its popularity, only certain types of people use social media, and those people may have distinct behavioral patterns. Acknowledge this bias and take it into account when considering the strength of conclusions or theories you infer from your analyses.

In many cases, social media data is also lacking or limited. The realities on the ground limit the amount of data you can collect and what you consider enough data. Billions of people use social media in urban areas, but only a few hundred may use social media in specific rural areas. In other cases, such as for specific events, only a certain amount of social media may be available. Perhaps, only a few hundred people tweeted about an event, and that will limit what you consider enough data. Also, you may not realize that you are missing out on enormous amounts of social media data. During the Arab Spring, the protestors used secret hashtags made up of nonsense words to share logistical information among protestors. If you did not know about the hashtags, you would have missed out on a lot of critical data you need to understand how protestors organize protests using social media.

Despite the difficulties of dealing with social media data, you can use a few guidelines to determine what constitutes enough data. The guidelines also depend on the type of analysis. Generally, collect as much data as you possibly can, given time and resources. Contemporary computers and statistical software can handle millions of data points. The more data you have, and the more diverse it is (data about tangential topics or from many sources), the less likely your analyses will suffer from bias. Collecting all the data you can is much more important for social network analysis than the other statistical analyses in this book. If you want to analyze the social network of human traffickers in Eastern Europe who use cell phones, you need to know who all those people are and how they are connected with each other. If you do not know about certain people and relationships, you may miss out on key components of the social network, leading to a junk analysis.

If collecting as much as possible is out of the question, you should collect at least a large enough sample of the population you want to analyze. Determining the exact percentage that constitutes a large enough sample is difficult and depends on the population size. However, a good rule of thumb to maintain confidence in your analysis and reduce errors is to collect at least a high single-digit percent of the population you want to analyze, somewhere around 10 percent. The concept behind increasing confidence and decreasing error levels is simple. For example, consider that you want to determine what percentage of the global population is male and female. To do your analysis, you will ask people what gender they are and keep track of what they say. You then ask the next 10 people you see for their gender—eight of them say male, and two say female. Based on your observations, you conclude that 80 percent of the world's population is male, and 20 percent is female. Of course, that conclusion is wrong. About 50 percent of the population is male, and the other 50 percent is female. The world's population is 6 billion people, but you only asked 10 people, or 0.0000000017 percent of the total population size. You should ask at least 600 million people, or 10 percent of the total population size. That is still a lot of data to collect. Fortunately, you do not need to always collect 10 percent of the total population size if the population size is extremely large. Statistical theories and tests show that collecting 500–1000 data points per population is usually enough. If you ask only 500–1000 people about their gender, you can be fairly confident in your analysis. Technically, with 500–1000 data points, you will get a confidence level of 95 percent, which says that there is a margin of error of about +/– 5 percent, or your numbers are off by 5 percent. In other words, there may be 55 percent males and 45 percent females, or 47 percent males and 53 percent females. A margin of error of only +/– 5 percent is usually very good. Cases where you have much less data points, or where the total population size is tiny, such as 10, will result in high error rates. You cannot be confident in cases where the population size is so low.

WARNING In reality, determining sample sizes and confidence levels is more complicated than what we posit, but we assume you are not doing academic studies. Also, we would fall asleep while writing out all the caveats.

Analyzing social media data is of course more difficult than the simple polling study about genders. The following short example describes the process and challenges.

SOCIAL MEDIA DATA ANALYSIS EXAMPLE: ADEQUATE POPULATION SIZE FOR ANALYSIS

Consider that you want to conduct volumetric analysis and correlate suicide bomber activity in a certain country last year with online activity. You may have a theory that right before a suicide bomb, there is a spike in activity on extremist forums, probably because sympathizers post supportive messages. You do not care about who posted what. You only want to see if a few days before a suicide bomb, there was a spike in forum postings. You have a comprehensive list of all the suicide bombs that occurred in the country last year, and detailed data about some of them (time, location, motive). You also have data from extremist forums including forum data logs (posting times), user logs (who, from where, what time, how long), and other usage statistics from last year.

You have data and now you need to determine if you have enough, and how much of it you need to do your analysis. The less you need to use to get an accurate result, the better, because that will reduce the time and resources you need to spend on acquiring more.

> To see if you have enough data, you need to identify the total population size of the various variables you are considering. According to your findings, there were a total of 100 suicide bombings and 100,000 forum posts.
>
> Now, you check to see how much detailed data you have about each population set. In this case, detail is the date and time of each bombing and posting. You find that you have detailed data for 50 bombings and 80,000 postings.
>
> Because the total population size of suicide bombings is relatively low, the more data you have about the entire population size, the better. In this case, you have 50 percent of the total population size, resulting in 50 data points. The total number of data points is low, which reduces your confidence level. However, you have a substantial portion of the total population size, which increases the confidence level.
>
> You have enough data about forum postings. You have 80 percent of the total population size, which is quite large. Overall, you can be reasonably confident in your analysis and should continue doing the correlation.

To conclude, for most statistical analyses, collect at least 10 percent of the total population size. If that is not possible, collect at least 500–1000 data points from each population you want to analyze. For social network analysis, collect as much as you can.

CROSS-REFERENCE The website has calculators that will help you calculate the confidence and error levels in your analysis, based on how much data you use.

Who Has the Data?

Identifying who has the data is usually the easiest step of the data collection process. In most cases, the answer to the question is obvious. If you are after specific social media data, the owner of the social media platform will have the data. Facebook owns and has all the data users create and share on Facebook. Twitter owns and has all the data users create and share on Twitter. Some companies run platforms that do not share the company name. For instance, Google runs Orkut. Click the About Us or Contact page on social media platform sites and, in most cases, you will find out the identity of the ultimate owner of the platform and the data. In some cases, informal groups, individuals, non-profit organizations, or governments will run social media platforms. You will likely have to contact the individuals or members of the informal groups, non-profits, or of the governments. In a few cases, the owner of the social media platform will provide the data and requests for the data to third-party organizations. Twitter allows a few companies such as Gnip to sell data users create and share on Twitter. Often, the data you request will exist on several different social media platforms, and numerous people or organizations will own the data.

Many people in the West link together their Twitter, LinkedIn, and Facebook accounts. A posting on one platform is then available on another platform. Either platform can then be the source of the data.

Collecting related, non-social media data is somewhat more difficult. If you are working in this field, you likely already have a list of data sources. See Table 4.2 for a list of non-social media data sources that we find useful when solving security analytical challenges. Part III of the book covers collecting non-social media data using crowdsourcing.

Table 4.2: Useful Non-Social Media Data Sources

SOURCE NAME	DATA TYPE	URL
U.S. Census	Census and demographics	`www.census.gov`
World Bank	Various country statistics and indicators	`data.worldbank.org`
World Bank Worldwide Governance Indicators	Various country governance indicators	`info.worldbank.org/governance/wgi/sc_country.asp`
Reddit	Miscellaneous	`www.reddit.com/r/opendata`
University of Maryland START GTD	Terrorist attacks	`www.start.umd.edu/start/data_collections/`
Harvard Institute for Quantitative Social Science	Miscellaneous social science related	`dvn.iq.harvard.edu/dvn/`
MIT DSpace	Miscellaneous science and social science related	`dspace.mit.edu`
RAND Data	Miscellaneous political and social science related	`www.rand.org`
National Counterterrorism Center	Terrorist incidents	`www.nctc.gov/site/other/wits.html`
Open Data Initiative	Miscellaneous	`www.opendatainitiative.org`

SOURCE NAME	DATA TYPE	URL
Jane's IHS	Miscellaneous security related	`www.janes.com/products/janes/index.aspx`
Google Correlate	Miscellaneous	`www.google.com/trends/correlate`
Google Public Data	Miscellaneous social science related	`www.google.com/publicdata/directory`
New America Foundation	Drone strikes in Pakistan	`counterterrorism.newamerica.net/drones`
UN Open Data	Various country statistics	`data.un.org`

When evaluating non-social media data sources, keep the following questions in mind. These questions also can apply to social media data sources.

- Does the data source provide enough data? If you are trying to find a causal relationship between insurgent attacks in Baghdad and Iraqi conversations on social media, make sure that the source for the insurgent attacks lists an appropriate amount of attacks. A list consisting of only two attacks will not get you anywhere.

- Can other sources appropriately validate or make up for missing data? Often, several organizations keep track of and make data available about the same topic. In our case, combining and cross-referencing data sources is fine, as long as the data looks similar, and the organizations collect the data using similar methodologies. If one organization uses on-the-ground researchers to collect data about insurgent attacks, and the other uses what they heard on Facebook, the methodologies are dissimilar and combining them may cause problems. However, you can use dissimilar data sets to cross-reference and validate the data.

- Do reputable organizations or individuals use or collect the data? University programs routinely collect data about specific topics using sound methodologies. For example, the University of Maryland's START Global Terrorism Database collects information about terrorist attacks around the world and other related activities. Other reputable organizations include think tanks and government departments (depending on the government). Increasingly, individuals are starting blogs and websites where they collect data about niche topics. These individuals are often not connected with a university or think tank, and are often located in places such as rural Africa and Latin America. However, do not let the lack of organizational affiliation dissuade you from using the data. Some unaffiliated blogs and websites are great sources for data, especially where the authors live in the region they are blogging about. See if reputable organizations and individuals use the data source. If they do, then you can trust the data. If they do not, contact the website's owners and ask questions about their intentions and how they go about data collection. You never know when you might stumble on a hidden data source gem. Generally, keep away from websites that are openly biased or partisan. They likely scrub away data that does not support their biases.

■ How much of the data is already cleaned and filtered? Before they make the data available, many organizations use their own methodologies to filter the data and eliminate incorrect and redundant information. Some go further, and structure the data so they meet a specific format. Consumers of the data then know what to expect each time they download the data, improving overall efficiency. However, sometimes organizations delete information that, although irrelevant for 99 percent of their consumers, is relevant to you. Look through the source's filtering methodologies so you know exactly what is in the data and what is not, and how much resources you will need to devote to further filter the data. In some cases, especially if the source of the data is an academic organization, you can ask and get access to the raw, unfiltered data.

Will They Give the Data?

Identifying the data source is only half the battle. The real challenge lies in actually getting the data, and in some cases persuading the data owner to give you the data. Persuasion may take the form of asking nicely or paying money. Overall, you will face one of the following four situations when trying to get the data.

The Data Is Publically Available

Three categories of organizations own publically available data that you can download for free at any time. The first category involves nonprofit organizations and transnational nonprofit organizations collecting the data, including the African Development Bank, the United Nations, the World Health Organization, Amnesty International, and university-sponsored initiatives. They are collecting the data as a public service, and in most cases make the data available in a variety of formats openly on the web. They often want people to consume the data and will go to great lengths to make sure their data collection methods are sound and routine, and that you can download the data from them in an easy and reliable manner, such as through monthly XLS file data sets. Getting data from them is easy. If they have data they have not made publically available, you can usually ask.

The second category involves nonprofit organizations running social media (most likely crowdsourcing) platforms that are free to users and focus on sharing specialized data, including Wikipedia and Ushahidi's Crowdmaps. In some rare cases, for-profit organizations run similar types of platforms, including IBM's Many Eyes (`http://www-958.ibm.com/`) data visualization platform, where users can upload and share data sets. As in the first category, the organizations expect and encourage the users to download the data from these sites. However, unlike in the first category, the organizations usually do not filter and validate the data.

The third category involves for-profit organizations running social media platforms that are free to users, including Twitter, Facebook, and Orkut. Organizations in the third category differ from those in the first two, primarily by their intention. Organizations such as Twitter do want you to openly and freely share some data with each other, but they do not care if you can download the data in an easy and reliable manner. Thus, they do not make available most of the data through easily accessible methods such as XLS file data sets. They will usually allow you to access part of the data through their application programming interfaces (APIs). We discuss APIs later. Getting data from organizations in the third category is more difficult than getting it from organizations in the first two categories. Also, third category organizations will limit the amount and type of data you can get. Asking them nicely will usually not do the trick, but you could pay for it.

The Data Is Privately Available

As big data grows in importance, more organizations are realizing that they can sell data. Two categories of organizations own privately available data that you can purchase. The first category is relatively new and involves social media platforms like Twitter indirectly selling primarily social media data. They are starting to realize that they need to generate revenue and so are looking toward selling the data users create on their platforms. They still make some of the data publically available through APIs, but make the majority of it only privately available. Because this category is nascent, buying social media platform data is not as easy. You will likely have to go through third-party companies such as Gnip that manage the data sales for the social media platforms. Online marketing companies are also getting into the game and striking special deals with social media platforms to sell the data. Expect the data to be expensive.

The second category is more established and involves for-profit organizations such as Western Union and IHS Jane's selling primarily non-social media data. In some cases, they openly advertise the sale of the data, but in other cases, they will only sell data if you ask. For the latter, prices will vary, especially if the data is unique and exclusive.

The Data Is Classified

Governments including intelligence agencies and law enforcement agencies have access to enormous amounts of data that is usually not available to the public. Governments may have special relationships with social media platform owners that allow them to access much of the platform data. To access government data, you likely need a clearance and you need to convince the government to sponsor your project. The rules for using sensitive but fundamentally open source information are complex and highly dependent on the project, and we wish you the best of luck figuring them out.

People Who Do Not Like You Own the Data

You will face this situation more than you expect, especially if you work on areas that are not friendly to your government. If you are working on behalf of the U.S. Department of Defense, do not expect Chinese platforms such as QZone to provide you with data, no matter how nicely you ask. Many non-profit organizations, especially those in the developing world, are also skeptical of sharing data with people working for or with governments and militaries. The best way around this is to get someone else to ask for you. In our experience, organizations are more open and willing to work with graduate students. Much of society considers them harmless and insignificant. Partner with universities, dust off your old college e-mail, or hire students to do the data sourcing for you. When asking for data, you can then only say you are working on a project that requires the data. You do not want to lie about your identity, project, or intentions, but you do not have to tell them the whole truth.

Collecting the Data

After determining what data you need, and where and if you can get it, you can start collecting or downloading the data. Expect to download data from numerous sources simultaneously and over a substantial period of time. Automate the collection and routinely download the data so you can focus on other tasks. You have numerous manual and automated ways to collect the data, and they depend on the type of data you are trying to collect and the format in which it is available. We explore the ways that are easiest and quickest to implement and will serve most of your needs.

> **NOTE** We wrote this section assuming you will desire some sort of automated data collection system. However, the information is also relevant if you want to only manually collect data for a one-off project.

Data Framework

The first step for creating an automated data collection system is building a data-gathering framework. The framework will house the technologies that go out into the world, download data, and bring it back to you. The framework can be as simple as a Google Document, which you can learn how to create on our website, or as a robust Django-based application, which you should hire developers to create. The technical details of a robust framework are beyond the scope of this book, and generally not something you should worry about. Commission trusted developers to create the framework, and communicate to them the importance of making the framework light, adaptive, and fast.

APIs

The second step is creating a technology that collects data from web APIs and housing it in the framework. Dealing with online data requires understanding what APIs are and how they work. They are one of the most important ways to share information and processes on the Internet among different organizations. Most of the websites you regularly use either offer an API or use several APIs. In simple terms, a typical web API enables you to query an online service using a small bit of code. Essentially, you ping an API or send it some information about what you want through the Internet, and the API outputs other information or modifies your inputted information in response. See Figure 4.2 for a visual description of the API process.

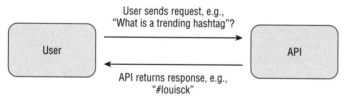

Figure 4.2: API process

Table 4.3 lists examples of a few relevant APIs. They range from APIs that tell you what your friends are tweeting to APIs that spell-check a sentence for you. Services that combine various APIs to create a whole new application are known as *mashups*. You are learning how to create a mashup. More and more of the Internet is populated with websites and platforms that are mashups.

Table 4.3: Examples of Relevant APIs

NAME	DESCRIPTION	URL
Yahoo! Term Extractor	Extracts significant words or phrases from content	`developer.yahoo.com/search/content/V1/termExtraction.html`
Yahoo! Geo Technologies	Collection of various APIs that help identify, extract, and share locations from content	`developer.yahoo.com/geo/`
Facebook Graph API	Get various information about a Facebook page or profile	`developers.facebook.com/docs/reference/api/`
OpenStreetMap Editing API	Fetch data from the crowdsourced OpenStreetMap database about the locations of places	`wiki.openstreetmap.org/wiki/API`
TwitterCounter API	Retrieve information about a Twitter username such as number of followers	`twittercounter.com/pages/api`
Face API	Detect, recognize, and tag faces in any photo	`developers.face.com/docs/`
Wolfram Alpha API	Return information about anything—similar to a smart search engine	`products.wolframalpha.com/api/`
Cadmus API	Receive various popular social media feeds	`thecadmus.com/api/docs`

Several free and payment-based APIs offer specific data that you can then download and use as you please. Free APIs allow anyone to ping them with some restrictions. Payment-based APIs, a burgeoning industry, allow subscribers who are making some sort of monetary payments to ping them with usually fewer restrictions. Some charge a flat monthly fee or even per ping.

We prefer collecting data through APIs. Because the platform host or data source is usually the one offering the API, you can trust the data. Most social media platforms have some sort of APIs, and they are usually technologically reliable. They are also legal and safe to use. Twitter may sue you if you use other ways to get data from Twitter. But they will not sue you if you are using their APIs and following their API rules. Using APIs has a few downsides, especially free ones. Most free APIs have rate limits where they limit the number of times you can ping them over the course of a time period. They often change the rate limits and institute other confusing restrictions. Also, because APIs are a relatively new phenomenon, standardized rules are only now emerging about how data is shared across different APIs and which coding language the APIs should process. Social media platforms are leading the charge on APIs, and other data websites have only recently started to catch up. Most APIs you will run into are known as REST APIs that you ping using HTTP code and that output information in JSON, XML, RSS, or ATOM code. Because Twitter is a pioneer in offering data through APIs, we will explore its APIs as an example. The details of the Twitter APIs will help you understand the boundaries of data collection using APIs, and keep you from making impossible demands of your developers or software. The details will also illustrate how the technologies of data collection can change your analysis. Later, we discuss using APIs to analyze, and not only collect, data.

Twitter's APIs

Twitter offers several APIs and it encourages the public to use them to create mashups. The more mashups that use Twitter, the more ubiquitous Twitter becomes. Twitter and other social media platforms have created websites that teach people how to use their APIs. You only need a basic understanding of coding to get started.

NOTE See `http://dev.twitter.com/` **for Twitter's API website. To get access to other platform API sites, Google the name of the platform and the word "API" and click the first link that pops up. Most API sites are labeled "[Name of social media platform] for Developers."**

By using Twitter's APIs, you can in near real-time get information about what specific people are tweeting, who is retweeting a specific tweet, what tweets contain a specific word, how many followers a person has, the profile pictures of specific people, and much more. Different APIs or portions of the APIs provide different types of information, and so you should expect to create a technology that pings several APIs simultaneously, sometimes using data queried from one API to query another API. To use some of the APIs you may need your own Twitter account; an API key that lets Twitter track who is pinging its APIs; and OAuth authorization, which is the emerging standard for authenticating API requests. Visit Twitter's website to learn how to acquire the authentications.

The Search and Streaming APIs are two of the most popular Twitter APIs. To use the Search API, you send a search query to the API; in other words, ping the API with a keyword. The API then returns the most recent tweets at that time that contain the keyword. So if you ping the API with the word "President," it will return a list of the most recent tweets containing the word "President." You can also send more complicated queries. You can ask for tweets containing some keywords and/or missing certain keywords, tweets created in a certain time period, tweets in specific languages, and more. You also do not need to provide authentication—anyone can ping the Search API.

WARNING   Twitter and other social media companies frequently change the requirements for accessing their APIs. As of this writing, rumors are swirling that Twitter may require authentication to use any of its APIs. Always check their website to find out about their newest policies regarding APIs before you begin a data collection project.

However, the Search API has limits. It only gives you tweets going back about a week, and it limits the number of times you can ping it per hour but does not tell you the limit. To be safe, ping it only once per hour. It also does not provide all the tweets containing the keywords, but only an unknown percentage. The Streaming API, in contrast, does not have a time-based rate limit. However, it requires authentication and only provides you about 1 percent of tweets that contain your search query at the moment you ping the Streaming API. It also does not return tweets from the past.

CROSS-REFERENCE   The website teaches how to create a Google Document that pings the Search and Search API routinely using your search criteria. It requires a basic understanding of programming to build from scratch. The website also provides a pre-constructed Search API application that you can customize without any coding knowledge.

You should start to appreciate how the boundaries of the free Twitter APIs can influence your data collection and thus analysis efforts. If you can only get data from the free Twitter APIs, you cannot do analysis on all the tweets, but only a tiny percentage of all tweets. You are missing out on enormous amounts of data, regardless if the vast majority of tweets are irrelevant to you. You can try getting around the rate limits by having numerous different accounts ping the API, and then incorporating the data later. However, if Twitter catches you, it will shut off your access to it APIs completely. Thus, we do not recommend you do so. Also, you will not be able to do analysis on tweets older than a week, unless you keep pinging the APIs for a long time and actively store the tweets.

RSS Feeds

The third step for creating a data aggregation system is creating technology that downloads data from RSS (Resource Description Framework Site Summary or Really Simple Syndication) feeds. An RSS feed of a website is basically a URL where the website regularly spits out the content and associated metadata of the website in XML (eXtensible Markup Language) format. XML is a language that allows someone to deliver data using a customized structure so humans and computers can easily make sense of it. RSS feeds are sort of like APIs, except you do not ping an RSS feed with a search query. Instead, the RSS feed spits out the data and you simply hook into it at any time and download the data to your heart's content, like a hose hooking into an open fire hydrant.

RSS feeds are commonplace, easy to use, and popular. Many news sites and blogs deliver textual data, pictures, and podcasts through both their websites and their RSS feeds, so you can trust the data. Popular applications like Google Reader and Flipboard aggregate numerous RSS feeds from sites like the New York Times, Wired, and the Atlantic, and use the data to deliver news. Downloading data from RSS feeds is ideal for us, because the analysis of many security issues requires assessing data from news sites and blogs.

> **NOTE** To find the RSS feed of a website, click on links on the website that say "RSS," "Feed," or "ATOM," which is a cousin of RSS feeds. The RSS feed's URL is the URL of that link.

Several RSS feed readers exist either as standalones or integrated with other data aggregators. You should never pay for a standalone RSS feed reader because numerous high-quality free ones exist. The only downside to RSS feeds is that the data you can get from an RSS feed including content, metadata, and the time span of historical data is limited to what the owner of the RSS feed wants to provide.

> **CROSS-REFERENCE** The website teaches how to create a simple RSS feed reader and aggregator, and integrate it with the Google Doc Twitter API aggregator.

Crawlers

The fourth step is creating technologies called *crawlers* to download data from websites and platforms that do not offer APIs or RSS feeds. Crawlers are a relatively old technology that browse or crawl through specified parts of the Internet in a systematic fashion looking for specified data. A specific crawler can, for example, collect all URLs mentioned on a specific website, download all textual data and pictures on a specific page of a website, or download data from large offline XLS or CSV data set files. Search engines use crawlers to go through the Internet and collect information about websites that they then index and organize. The crawlers usually jump from link to link, scouring the Internet for information like spiders crawling through their spider webs hunting for mosquitoes. Crawlers are useful for collecting data from older websites that do not have APIs or RSS feeds, forums, websites that are trying to prohibit data collection, and websites that routinely provide large data sets.

Programming a crawler requires minimal coding knowledge, usually of the language Python. Several free crawlers are available that you can download and greatly modify. Crawlers come in the following five types:

- **Link**—Identify, collect, and index all URLs on a website
- **Content**—Identify, collect, and index all content on a website
- **Search**—Identify and index the relationships between several websites and collect information about them like a search engine
- **Focused**—Identify, collect, and index specific data from specific websites
- **Non-web**—Identify, collect, and index specific data from existing data sets and other offline files

Regardless of the crawler you use, you have to tell it four things:

- Which websites or pages to target
- How to interact and communicate with other crawlers
- When to check for changes to the targeted pages so that it knows when to crawl through them again
- How to avoid being banned from the targeted page by, for example, crawling it only once every few days. Major websites will usually make a page specific for crawlers that tell it how to behave.

CROSS-REFERENCE The website lists several open source and proprietary crawlers that you can use and modify.

The flexibility and modifiability of crawlers confer several advantages. They are easy to create and modify, can crawl through virtually any website, and can download almost any type of data. However, their strengths are also their greatest weakness, because much of the Internet dislikes crawlers and thwarts them. Many popular platforms like Twitter identify and block crawlers. They allow the crawlers of search engines like Google and Bing to crawl through websites but not yours. Also, websites are increasingly incorporating human verification checkpoints on their pages, the most popular of which is CAPTCHA (or RE-CAPTCHA), which most crawlers have difficulty getting past. See Figure 4.3 for a picture of a CAPTCHA. Although most crawlers are easy to implement, the strongest ones require creative developers. Using crawlers to download information from Neo-Nazi or Jihadi forums that are often password-protected requires ingenuity that you cannot get for free. You may also need developers on hand if your targeted sites change in look and structure. You then have to reprogram your crawler and teach it to navigate the changed site, which can be tedious and frustrating.

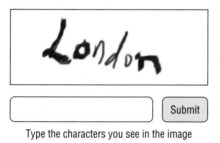

Type the characters you see in the image

Figure 4.3: CAPTCHA example

Filtering the Data

After downloading data through APIs, RSS feeds, and crawlers, you need to filter the data and eliminate parts of it that are irrelevant. Unless you have stumbled onto some amazing hidden relationship between the international drug trade and Justin Bieber, most of the data generated on social media platforms is irrelevant to you, and is thus noise. A significant portion of activity and information on social media platforms, especially those that are Western-centric, are about popular culture events or mundane topics, and are at best entertaining and at worst self-aggrandizing. One study found that people consider nearly a third of all tweets to be completely useless to them.[2] Sifting through social media data to delete irrelevant data is difficult but necessary. You will not face a similar problem with non-social media data, because most non-social media data is already filtered. The University of Maryland's START databases will not likely start mixing lists of terrorist attacks with pictures of bunnies with pancakes on their heads (unless maybe terrorists start putting pancakes on the bunnies' heads).

We have already covered the first step in eliminating noise—determine and focus your data needs. If you are not pinging Twitter's Streaming API with the keyword "Justin Bieber," you will likely not receive tweets containing only "Justin Bieber" in them. Similarly, do not download the RSS feed of the gossip site TMZ, and do not crawl websites dedicated to Justin Bieber. Focus your search queries and target websites that are tangential, if not directly relevant.

We expect the furrowing of your brow and the criticism that you are about to put forth. Indeed, we have heard it numerous times before. The criticism is that by focusing your search queries, you may miss something. Maybe Mexican drug cartels are impersonating 15-year-old girls on the Internet and coordinating drug activity under the guise of talking about Justin Bieber, and you need to crawl through Bieber fan sites and tweets. That could absolutely be true. Drug cartels could also be impersonating fans of *Twilight* or the New York Yankees. The possibilities are endless and a black swan may pop up anywhere. In our field, the lookout for ever more intelligence and information in fear of missing something has understandably become more intense since the attacks of September 11th, 2001. Our response is:

1. Studies on data analysis and human intelligence have shown that more information does not equal more knowledge. In fact, in some situations, more information causes us to either become paralyzed or even make the wrong decision.[3]

2. We are not teaching forensic analytics or data mining. We are not teaching you how to discover the ultimate source of a tweet, or spot the critical text message between terrorists. Our focus is on uncovering answers by looking at aggregate data and behavior.

3. However, some of our tools will help you conduct forensic analytics, but in indirect ways. For example, through volumetric analysis, you can uncover whether unusual changes in the virtual traffic of Bieber fan sites in correlation with increasing real-world drug activity can tell you something about whether Mexican drug cartels really are impersonating Bieber fans online. After identifying a relationship, you can refocus your data needs.

4. To uncover unusual relationships, and to keep your analysis innovative, it helps to periodically shift your data collection needs and modify your search queries, sometimes without an educated guess as to why. Introducing randomness into data collection may help.

5. Come to grips with the fact that you will never be able to deal with all the data the Internet and other sources generate. As database technologies proliferate and improve, so do the technologies to create and share data. Chasing after every last piece of data will leave you exhausted and seriously tax your resources. You likely will never catch up, and that is okay. It helps to focus on what you know best and let someone else chase doubtful connections.

NOTE Mexican drug cartels might read this book and decide to shift their communication to Justin Bieber forums. So maybe you do want to focus on the Bieber forums.

After focusing your searches, delete duplicates and spam from your collected data. Much of the content on Twitter is simply people retweeting what others have tweeted. Unless you are interested in the popularity of certain messages in a network, you can consider retweets to be duplicates and thus noise. Spam bots, which post nonsense, pornography, and malware, are pervasive on social media sites, especially Twitter. If an event is really popular, and a hashtag becomes associated with it, expect the spam bots to quickly inundate the hashtag with spam.

Creating a noise-eliminating tool from scratch is difficult and a waste of time and resources. The easiest route is to purchase access to an API that filters social media data for you (the APIs usually do more than just eliminate noise) or to use a free collection of data aggregation and analysis tools called SwiftRiver that we again mention in the last section of this chapter. In some cases, the APIs of social media platforms will build in options to remove noise and spam. Twitter, for example, allows you to query its API in such a way that it does not return retweets.

Filtering the data often goes beyond simply eliminating noise and spam. Filtering can also involve validating the data to ensure only correct information is stored and that misinformation is removed. Currently, the technology to do so is nascent and very difficult to implement. Many companies claim their commercial APIs can validate data, but for the most part their claims are more fantasy than reality. You will have to manually validate data by looking at some of the data at random and asking:

- Are other people saying the same thing? If only one person claims to see something while people around him do not, he may be lying.

- Is the source trustworthy? You may have a list of certain Facebook or Twitter accounts that you know post incorrect information. You can easily program the Twitter API and other data aggregation tools so you do not receive data from sources you do not want.

Storing and Managing the Data

Deciding how to store and manage the data is one of the most important decisions you will make. The type of storage you use, its size, and complexity, will affect how you integrate, access, and use your data. It will also affect the cost of storing the data, which may affect the scope of your analysis. Conversely, the type of analysis you want to do will affect the type of storage you use. Conducting a one-time analysis with a small amount of data does not require as complex or as much storage as repeat analyses that involve ingesting massive amounts of social media data over a long period of time. We will cover the span of data storage requirements from the most minimalist project to the most multifaceted. Unless you are doing a simple analysis, you will need the help of technical database developers to help you formulate and manage your database. Still, understanding the two relevant database management system types will help you appreciate how you can use the data for analysis and choose an appropriate database technology. You may use each of the two types or only one. Some projects will be more appropriate for one and some more for the other. Other types of database management systems exist, but they are not as relevant and are more obscure and thus more difficult to implement.

Relational Databases

The most popular database management system type is known as relational databases. Currently, they are the most widely used, although their popularity is waning because they are not appropriate for dealing with lots of complex data.

What Are They?

Simply put, *relational databases* organize data into linked tables of rows and columns. In the table, the rows represent an object (known as a *tuple*) and the columns represent attributes of the object. Anytime you use Microsoft Excel to create a spreadsheet, you are in essence creating a relational database. Programming languages such as Structured Query Language (SQL) enable users to conduct queries on the table. They are colloquially known as SQL databases because programmers prefer using SQL to access them. Using SQL you can, for example, access all the objects that have a certain attribute or access certain objects but not others. In the context of social media data, relational databases enable you to store instances of a content created on social media platforms as an object and the metadata about the content as attributes. See Figure 4.4 for an illustrated example of a relational database. Relational databases are the most established and traditional ways of storing and managing data.

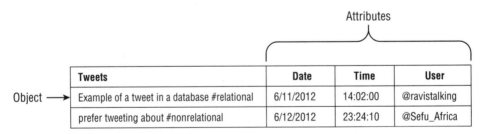

Tweets	Date	Time	User
Example of a tweet in a database #relational	6/11/2012	14:02:00	@ravistalking
prefer tweeting about #nonrelational	6/12/2012	23:24:10	@Sefu_Africa

Figure 4.4: Relational Database Example

Advantages and Disadvantages

The advantages of relational databases derive from their ubiquity. Governments and corporations prefer using them because of their longevity and reliability. Due to this widespread use, you can easily find personnel to implement and manage relational databases. Also, they have gone through numerous iterations and are user-friendly and secure. Major companies such as Oracle and Microsoft support relational databases, and numerous free, open source versions also exist, the most famous of which is MySQL.

In terms of managing and representing social media data, relational databases have numerous disadvantages. The most significant is that they cannot handle enormous amounts of data and do not scale easily. Imagine storing millions of tweets, Facebook updates, and text messages in countless tables. Add to that video, pictures, and audio. Every time you query the database for a particular piece of data, the computer will have to go through an enormous amount of data, which will significantly slow the database down. Relational databases were meant to keep track of the inventory of stores, not what most people on the planet are saying. Programmers have come up with clever ways to quickly query data from large relational databases, but they are reaching their limits. Also, the tables in the database are difficult to modify on the fly. In other words, it is difficult to add attributes (columns) after you have already defined the tables. If you are running a store and need to keep track of objects, you will have a set amount of attributes for each object. The attributes may include quantity and price. You will likely not need to add new attributes to all or some of the objects. However, because social media data is so unstructured and differs wildly, you may need the flexibility to add or subtract attributes depending on the content. One tweet may have five attributes, but a text message may only have two. The second most significant disadvantage is that, despite their name, relational databases do not tell you anything about relationships. Social media data is all about how people use different media to communicate and create relationships with each other. Knowing how one piece of content is related to another piece of content is essential. Relational databases cannot easily tell you how, for example, one Twitter account is connected to another Twitter account. You cannot easily link seemingly disparate content together, which causes you to miss out on querying information about relationships and connections between content.

Due to these crippling disadvantages, do not use relational databases if you expect to use massive amounts of social media data. The only time you should consider using relational databases is when you have a small or one-time analysis. For example, if want to use regression analysis to find the strength of the relationship between an increase in Craigslist ads in the adult section and police reports of kidnapping in one city, you can most likely use a Microsoft Excel–based relational database. The rows could be something as simple as each instance of kidnapping. One column could be whether an adult listing appeared within five days of the kidnapping, and the second column could be how many listings appeared.

Non-Relational Databases

The second most popular database management system type is known as non-relational databases. They are gaining in popularity and power because they are ideally suited for handling social media data.

What Are They?

Non-relational databases are basically databases that are in no way similar to relational databases. Colloquially they are called NoSQL databases because they either do not use SQL or use another language along with SQL. Numerous types of non-relational databases exist, but the ones most relevant for us are document-oriented and graph databases. Not all document-oriented databases are graph databases, but some more or less can function as graph databases. The most cutting-edge technology companies including Facebook, Google, Amazon, and Twitter are leading the charge in adopting non-relational databases.

Document-oriented databases store information about an object as a document, similar to a Microsoft Word document. The document can hold numerous attributes, other types of media, and any other data associated with the object. Because each document is standalone, you can easily add attributes later to specific documents. Programming languages such as JSON then enable you to query the document or part of the document however you wish. If you need to add more information to the document, you can always replace the document with an updated version. In most document-oriented databases, the documents are not linked together in any meaningful way. They look like a stack of documents in a file cabinet. So when you query a document, the computer has to rummage through the cabinet. Programmers have come up with ingenious ways to speed up this process. Due to their flexibility, document-oriented databases such as MongoDB are fast becoming popular. See Figure 4.5 for an illustrated example of a document-oriented database

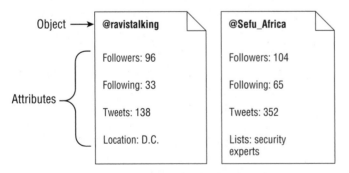

Figure 4.5: Document-oriented database example

A graph database goes a step further than document-oriented databases and stores information about the objects and their relationships with each other in a network. As in social networks, each object is a node and it can have as many attributes as desired, similar to documents. Each object is then connected to other objects. You can then link different content or objects together, or in more advanced cases allow the objects to find and create links themselves. Queries can then find information about each object and its attributes, and/or information about how they are connected to other objects. Graph databases such as neo4j are a new and emerging technology. See Figure 4.6 for an illustrated example of a graph database.

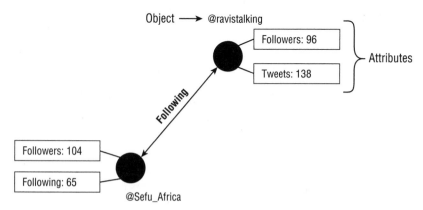

Figure 4.6: Graph database example

Before discussing the advantages and disadvantages of non-relational databases, we need to discuss what we consider the object in those databases. In relational databases, the object is usually the content. It is the tweet, the text message, or the YouTube video. The content can also be the object in non-relational databases, however it is better for an entity to be the object.

Entity Extraction

An *entity* is a name, place, organization, or date that a piece of content refers to or mentions. For example, in the text message, "Michael is going to Malaysia," the entities are Michael and Malaysia. By extracting entities and classifying them as objects in non-relational databases, you are going beyond simply storing tweets and text messages. Instead, you are representing all the people, places, things, and times mentioned on social media virtually, and storing information about them and how they relate to each other. Thus, when you query information from the database, you are querying information about specific things, thereby allowing you to analyze things and how they relate to each other. Entities can also be the objects in relational databases, although it is difficult to update information about them later because of the static nature of relational databases.

You can still store the content or the actual text message about the entity if you desire. In the preceding example, the entity Michael would have as an attribute, the text message "Michael is going to Malaysia." If someone else then texts "Michael is married to Mandy," you can then update the Michael entity with that additional information. You can then not only associate Michael with the new text message, but also derive the entity from the new text message and relate it to Michael as an attribute. So the entity of Michael is now connected to the entity Malaysia (because that is where he is going), and the entity Mandy (because that is his wife). This method of representing entities as objects in a graph database then allows you to create an impressive dossier on all things and how they are related, and it works like the human brain, which is phenomenal for storing lots of linked information and manipulating it quickly.

To do entity extraction, you usually take the content and send it to an entity extractor API. The API then returns the entities. A few open source entity extractors exist, although they are limited in how many times you can use them, how well they can detect entities given misspellings and slang, and how many entities they can detect. A commercial entity extractor such as Basis Technology's is more robust and smarter. A free entity extractor will likely not realize that "Ravi" is a name, but a commercial one probably will. If you are serious about collecting social media data long-term to tease out the relationships between disparate things, you must integrate entity extraction technology into your data system.

Advantages and Disadvantages

Non-relational databases confer numerous advantages when it comes to dealing with social media data. As mentioned before, the hottest technology companies are investing in and adopting non-relational databases, which makes it likely that they will grow in popularity, power, and appeal. One reason why companies such as Facebook like non-relational databases is because they can scale and handle enormous amounts of data easily. You can add as many documents and nodes to the network as you want, whereas modifying existing tables can be difficult. Many non-relational databases exist on cloud or localized cloud servers that can easily take on more data without you having to go out and purchase physical servers. Cloud servers, which are becoming more secure, also allow users who are not at a specific location or on a specific device to access the data through the Internet at any time. Also, other technologies such as Hadoop make it easier to query non-relational databases and make them more resilient and reliable. Such technologies also allow you to run algorithms through the data and query the results of those algorithms in ways that you cannot do with tables and relational databases. Another big advantage is that non-relational databases model social networks much better than relational databases. They are designed to manage social media data because they focus on managing information about relationships and objects whose attributes can change frequently. If need be, after extracting entities and their attributes, you can delete irrelevant information, thereby saving on data costs. Hence, major social media companies like Facebook and Twitter are funding their development.

The disadvantages stem from the novelty of the technologies supporting non-relational databases. Non-relational databases have only recently become popular and are still very much in development. Kinks and security problems exist and need to be worked out. Also, programmers that can work with non-relational databases are few and expensive. However, as the technology flourishes, the disadvantages will dissipate.

Due to the overwhelming advantages and the diminishing disadvantages, we highly recommend implementing some sort of non-relational database, preferably a graph database, to store and manage social media data. They are suited for social media data and linking them together as they naturally are linked. If you expect to ingest a large amount of data or do numerous or long-term projects, you should use a non-relational database.

Third-Party Solutions

Some of you may have headaches or may have thrown your hands up in exasperation. Collecting, filtering, and storing social media and other data requires a lot of effort and resources. Implementing it for large or long-term projects from scratch necessitates the employment of technical developers, program managers, and subject matter experts. The process becomes even more cumbersome and expensive if you desire automated analytics that can further filter the data for you and deliver it to you in fancy visualizations. Creating your own automated analytics is beyond the scope of this book, although Chapters 5 and 6 briefly cover how you can create manual analysis into automated analysis.

CROSS-REFERENCE   Chapter 5 describes how to use a free software known as NodeXL to download various types of social media data quickly and without much human involvement.

Fortunately, many third-party organizations offer all of the above and more. From our count, nearly 240 software solutions offer either a part or all of the overarching collecting, filtering, storing, and analyzing process. Some only do data collection, some only do a type of filtering, and some do everything and more. They vary in their reliability, usefulness, and price. Some are absolutely awful, some are great at one thing and terrible at other things, some are reasonable at everything, and some are even free. Some offer great customer service and even allow you to customize part of their software offering. Some offer parts of their software as commercial APIs that can help you collect data or do entity extraction.

Choosing the right software solution is difficult, and you will have to make trade-offs. Recognize that few software solutions are appropriate for security purposes. They are more focused on helping companies and ad agencies do brand management and measure popularity, not identify sex traffickers or detect violence. Many major companies that traditionally offer social media solutions to commercial clients, such as Radian6 and IBM, are increasingly focusing on the government and security sector, but they have a long way to go. Unfortunately, social media literacy is low in government and military sectors, and commercial entities exploit this fact to sell subpar and outdated products. We partly wrote this book so that our government officials do not waste money on subpar social media analytical products. Use what you have gained from the book so far and the following questions to evaluate potential third-party products:

- Can it deal with various types of unstructured data? Twitter is popular now, but another social media platform may replace it tomorrow. Any software that collects data must be able to deal with all types of unstructured data, not just Twitter or Facebook.

- How much data does it download? Systems that only ping free APIs for data will not have nearly enough data as systems that purchase the firehose, or all of the data. Based on your requirements, you may need some or all of the data. Ask how it collects the data.

- How does it filter the data? The system should eliminate duplicates and spam, but you should be suspicious if it goes much further. Some use machine translation to translate foreign language messages. However, machine translators do not pick up slang, code words, and sarcasm. Key information may be lost in translation. Also, you may need to know how many times a tweet has been retweeted. Inquire exactly how the filtering algorithms work and what they do.

- What exactly do the analyses do? Many companies claim their systems can do automated analyses on the data they collect. Most of the time, the analysis is very simplistic and results in aesthetically pleasing graphics that do not help your mission at all. Do not get swayed by shiny things. Insist on knowing exactly how the system does the analyses and what assumptions it makes when doing them. Very few companies actually do social network analysis using social media data, but many claim they can. Many also claim they can identify influencers, but their algorithms to do so are rubbish. Some companies create analytical tools based on absolute nonsense and you should call them out on it. We explore some in Chapters 5 and 6. We are not saying that companies that offer sophisticated automated analytics do not exist. It is just that they are usually smaller, focused on a niche area, and harder to find.

▪ How do they store and share the data? Most host the data and the software on a cloud server and allow you to access it as a web application. However, for security reasons, many government customers need software that sits behind a firewall on local servers. Ask if this sort of enterprise solution is possible, and who else gets to access the data you are accessing.

▪ Do they provide support? The major social media solution companies are great at providing customer service. However, small or open source organizations are doing some of the most cutting-edge work in this field and cannot afford to provide service. Determine what level of service you need. If you have the resources, skill, time, and audacity to take on more for yourself, then explore open source products. The SwiftRiver platform is a free yet powerful social media aggregation and analysis system that requires only some technical skill to set up and deploy. Check it out at `http://ushahidi.com/products/swiftriver-platform`.

▪ How much does it cost? Because the social media solution market is only now emerging, prices vary considerably. Compare prices and know that most of what you want is probably available for free. Government clients get ripped off a lot. Be aggressive on the price. Oftentimes, hiring developers to build a system for you that is made up of free and commercial APIs will be cheaper.

▪ Does it claim that it will solve all your problems? Ignore anyone who says they have solved it all. Social media data collection, management, and analysis are at their primitive, fetal stage. The solutions that exist today will be embarrassing compared to what will emerge five years from now.

▪ Can you access it on mobile devices? You probably own a tablet or smartphone, and there is no reason why you should not be able to access software using those devices. Ask if you can access the system using mobile devices, and if the company says no, ask why not. Most likely, they will say they are working on it. The reality is that it is because they are older companies that are desperately trying to stay relevant and tweaking their software to become mobile-accessible. Stay away from such outdated technology.

▪ What kind of database does it use? If it does not use non-relational databases, be wary. As explained before, solutions that use relational databases will not deliver the data and flexibility you need quickly and reliably, especially as social media use grows.

Now that you know how to collect data, you can begin conducting analysis. Chapter 5 will describe the process for conducting social network analysis.

Summary

- Social media analysis consists of intelligently finding and manipulating social media content, associated metadata, and related non-social media data.

- To determine collection needs, you need to ask:

  - What data will solve the problem? You will likely need a diverse set of data including social media, metadata, and sociological data.

  - How much data is enough? A Ten percent sample of the population size or 500–1000 data points per population is enough to give you a reasonably error-free answer.

  - Who has the data? Social media companies, non-profit organizations, governmental departments, universities, think tanks, unaffiliated but trusted bloggers, and private companies will likely have the data you need.

  - Will they give the data? Public data is easy to get, and you can buy private data but it is usually expensive. Commission a graduate student to get data from unfriendly sources.

- Data collection will likely require incorporating API queries, RSS feed readers, and customized crawlers together in a framework.

- Filter the data using focused search queries and commercial and open source APIs to eliminate noise, spam, and duplicates.

- Use relational databases to store and manage your data for one-time analyses or small projects. For large or long-term projects that involve lots of data, use non-relational databases such as the graph database. They are better suited to handle social media data and can handle lots of data easily.

- Entity extraction allows you to keep track of all the people, places, things, and times mentioned in social media content and how they relate to each other, and reduce the amount of data you need to store.

- Use what you read to evaluate third-party software applications, which can offer impressive and awful solutions across the social media data process.

Notes

1. Rao, L. (2010) "Twitter Seeing 6 Billion API Calls Per Day, 70K Per Second." Accessed: 14 June 2012. `http://techcrunch.com/2010/09/17/twitter-seeing-6-billion-api-calls-per-day-70k-per-second/`

2. The Telegraph (2012) "130 Million Tweets Everyday Are Not Worth Reading, Researchers Find." Accessed: 14 June 2012. `http://www.telegraph.co.uk/technology/twitter/9057314/130-million-Tweets-everyday-are-not-worth-reading-researchers-find.html`

3. Hall, C., Arissa, L., and Todorov, A. (2007) *The Illusion of Knowledge: When More Information Reduces Accuracy and Increases Confidence.* Accessed: 14 June 2012. `http://webscript.princeton.edu/~tlab/wp-content/publications/Hall_Ariss_Todorov_OBHDP2007.pdf`

Mapping and Analyzing Social Networks

Mapping and analyzing social networks can reveal the identity of key people and relationships, and track the spread of ideas. This chapter details the steps to conduct social network analysis to map and analyze social networks primarily exhibited on social media. It introduces key concepts and definitions, reviews and selects appropriate software tools to conduct the analysis, and teaches you how to use the tools to map social networks, identify influencers, and determine the proliferation of and relationship between ideas. Although this chapter focuses only on using data from social media to conduct analysis on standalone social networks, you can use the same processes and tools to conduct social network analysis on data from other sources such as financial records, and compare and combine different networks.

Key Concepts and Definitions

Social network analysis (*SNA*) seeks to discover the underlying rules governing the behavior of people in a social network through the use of specialized algorithms. It involves studying the relationships between people and how those relationships affect everyone in the network, and even in other networks. SNA is ideal for understanding how people use social media to form and sustain social networks, and influence people in their online networks and beyond. It can also help explain how relationships formed offline can influence relationships formed online and vice versa. Specifically, SNA can help you answer questions such as:

- Which individuals on social media have the most influence and reach with their message?

- What clusters of online groups have the most influence over others?

- If a positive message were injected into the debate, who should help propagate the message?

- Do major influential individuals for either side of a problem set appear inactive or not important?

- If you know the network structure, what nodes, when eliminated, will best cause the breakdown or hinder the network?

SNA comes in many forms and can reveal a variety of insights about social networks and the people in them. This chapter focuses on how SNA can help you:

- Map social networks by creating a visual representation of social networks sustained on social media. In other words, visually grasp who talks to who and how much.

- Identify influencers by using specialized algorithms to identify people and relationships that wield the greatest influence over other people in the network. The algorithms you choose to employ depend on the characteristics of the network.

- Identify the topics and ideas that the most people are discussing together at a specific moment in time.

CROSS-REFERENCE You, in your role as a private law-abiding citizen or a dissenter against an oppressive regime, may be understandably worried that governments and others are using sensitive information about you available on social media to conduct SNA and other types of analyses without you knowing about it or being comfortable with it. In the wrong hands, such analyses could be potentially harmful. Check out Chapter 14 for tips on how you can protect your privacy and yourself.

Before you can start employing SNA tools to solve problems, you need to understand each of the elements that make up social networks, the role of influence, and how algorithms can help uncover influence.

Elements of Social Networks

Each social network consists of numerous elements, the most important of which are nodes and links.

A *node* is a person. When constructing social networks on social media, a node can be a Twitter account, a forum user, or a blogger, because in the social media world, social media accounts represent people. In some cases, numerous people can use one account and they would act as one node. However, we will not worry about such cases because they are rare, and, for the most part, one social media account usually only represents one person. Technically, anything can be a node. A piece of social media content such as a text message can be a node and the links can be anyone who reads or receives the text message. But for simplicity's sake and to ease understanding, we will only consider persons as nodes. We will use the words individuals and persons interchangeably with nodes.

A *link* is the relationship between two nodes. Links are also known as ties or edges. In our case, a link is the indication of a communication channel between two people on social media. A link can exist between two people on Twitter if they follow each other or if one follows the other. It can exist between two people on a blog if one comments on another's article and the blogger comments back. We will use the word relationships interchangeably with links.

Each link can contain many different attributes, the most relevant of which is reciprocity or symmetry. A link is said to be reciprocal or bidirectional if the communication channel between two people flows both ways, or if both people communicate with each other. If only one person communicates with the other, the link is not reciprocal or unidirectional. For example, if Ahmed follows Kim on Twitter, but Kim does not follow Ahmed back, there is a one-way link between Ahmed and Kim. If Kim followed Ahmed back, the link is reciprocal because there is a two-way link between them. Other attributes can include strength. For example, consider a social network consisting of Felipe, Anne, and Michal. Each person in the network communicates with every other person in the network. Thus, all links are reciprocal. However, each person can differ in the extent to which they communicate with each other. Felipe and Anne send a text message to each other once a week, Felipe and Michal send a text message to each other three times a week, and Anne and Michal send a text message to each other ten times a week. See Figure 5.1 for a visual representation of the network under consideration. Because Anne and Michal communicate with each other more often than Felipe and Anne do, or Felipe and Michal do, the link between Anne and Michal is stronger than it is between Anne and

Felipe, or Felipe and Michal. Additionally, the link between Felipe and Michal is stronger than it is between Felipe and Anne. For the sake of simplicity and to ease understanding, we will not analyze attributes apart from reciprocity, such as strength, when conducting SNA.

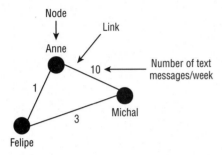

Figure 5.1: Social network with link attributes

You may have noticed that reading written descriptions of social networks can be confusing and tedious. Mapping social networks visually as in Figure 5.1 is an easy way to bolster comprehension of social networks. Figure 5.2 maps a social network with unidirectional and bidirectional links. Arrowheads indicate the direction in which the link flows. In the network in Figure 5.2, Francisco talks to Zane but Zane does not talk back to him, whereas Zane talks to Emi but Emi does not talk back to him. The links between Francisco and Zane, and Zane and Emi are unidirectional. However, Arturo and Zane talk to each other and have a bidirectional link.

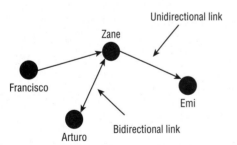

Figure 5.2: Unidirectional and bidirectional networks visualized

Another way that will also help you prepare data for SNA is through matrices or a square array. Figure 5.3 represents the network described before in a matrix; refer to it as you read the subsequent sentences. Reading a matrix is very simple, because they are similar to spreadsheets. We numbered the columns and rows to ease explanation. The names in Column A represent the nodes who choose who they should communicate with and to what extent. The names in Row V represent the nodes who the nodes in Column A choose with whom to communicate. In other words, the nodes in Row V receive the link from the nodes in

Column A. Start with Row X, and the first name in Column A, which is Felipe. Then go right, across the other columns, and read who he communicates with and to what extent. For example, in Column C, under the heading of Anne, you will see the number 1. That is because Felipe sends Anne one text message a week. In Column D, under the heading of Michal, you will see the number 3, because Felipe sends Michal three text messages a week. In Row X, Column B, under the heading of Felipe, you will see a 0. The 0 represents lack of a link and non-applicability because Felipe cannot choose to communicate with himself. Similarly, pick Row Y, which represents who Anne has chosen with whom to speak. Going across Row Y, under Column B and under the heading of Felipe, you see the number 1 because Felipe and Anne text each other once a week. And so on.

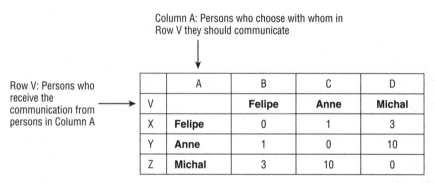

Column A: Persons who choose with whom in Row V they should communicate

Row V: Persons who receive the communication from persons in Column A

		A	B	C	D
V			Felipe	Anne	Michal
X	Felipe	0	1	3	
Y	Anne	1	0	10	
Z	Michal	3	10	0	

Figure 5.3: Social network as a matrix

This matrix communicated not only the presence of links but also the strength of the links, by the number of text messages sent by each person. We, however, will not consider other attributes, including strength. Thus, we will only represent the links using a binary code of 1 or 0. In other words, if Felipe texts Anne, you will see a 1 in Row X, Column C. If Felipe never texted Anne, you will see a 0. See Figure 5.4 for this binary representation of the social network. If you are still confused about matrices, do not worry. Later you learn how to create such matrices to prepare the data for SNA.

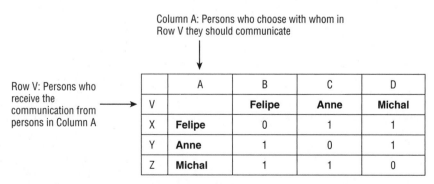

Column A: Persons who choose with whom in Row V they should communicate

Row V: Persons who receive the communication from persons in Column A

		A	B	C	D
V			Felipe	Anne	Michal
X	Felipe	0	1	1	
Y	Anne	1	0	1	
Z	Michal	1	1	0	

Figure 5.4: Social network as a binary matrix

Influence and Memes in Social Networks

Apart from cataloguing who speaks to whom, SNA's true power lies in identifying the nodes and relationships that drive the behavior of all other nodes in the social network. Identifying key influencers in social networks exhibited on social media enables you to focus your research, investigation, and targeting efforts concerning people on social media.

Influence is changing how an individual or group perceives the world and their relationship to the world. A key influencer is a node in the social network whose behavior and content influences the behavior of others in the network. When a key influencer speaks, his followers and even others outside his immediate network listen and eventually respond. For example, the terrorist Anwar Al-Awlaki was a key influencer because others consumed the messages and content he created on social media, and consequently changed their viewpoints and behavior.

Memes are the ideas, concepts, and beliefs present in messages and content that spread from person to person, and spurs influence. Two competing theories describe exactly who can be a key influencer on a social network, or in other words, spread memes most effectively and widely. One theory says that key influencers are prominent individuals such as celebrities who can influence people in a variety of social networks, sometimes regardless of the context, by virtue of their persona. The competing theory says that the identity of the key influencer is fluid and highly dependent on the social network and context. Anyone can become a key influencer, regardless of how famous or prominent they are, by virtue of their message and their position in the network.[1] An individual's position in a network is a function largely of how many people they talk to and how many people those people talk to. It is also a function of how easy it is for the individual to talk to numerous people directly and indirectly, and how many constraints they face. A constraint appears when an individual has to go through another individual to speak to the rest of the network.

Real-world evidence suggests that for the issues you will face, the latter theory is correct. A person who appears at the right time with the right message and has the right amount of people listening to them can become a key influencer within a social network. As social networks and context change, that person may, after some time, cease to be a key influencer in the network, and another person may take their spot as the key influencer. This theory focuses the definition of the key influencer.

A *key influencer* is the person who spreads memes to the most people directly and indirectly in a social network with the least amount of constraints. SNA provides the ability to identify the key influencer in any network largely by virtue of her position in the network, regardless of the context or whether the individual was an influencer before. As mentioned in Chapter 3, conducting SNA on a network and identifying a key influencer involves picking a specific algorithm and then applying that algorithm to the network data. The algorithm then outputs a list of the most influential nodes. Similarly, algorithms can help you identify the memes that are propagating through networks at a certain moment of time.

Algorithms in SNA

Because SNA is an emerging field, there is no scientific consensus that states which algorithm is the best at identifying a key influencer in a network. Numerous algorithms exist and some are specific to only niche problem sets and network types. The algorithms usually have the name of the mathematician or scientist who came up with it. A typical SNA software package (that we describe later) provides the option to apply numerous algorithms to a given data set. We will not list the various algorithms that exist or explain the math behind them because they will only induce headaches and confusion. Instead, we will only conceptually explain the three most relevant algorithms that you will learn to use. Comparing the results of the three algorithms will bolster your analysis and increase confidence in your result. The algorithms approach the problem differently, and it is difficult to say which approach is more correct. Using and comparing the three algorithms ensures that one algorithm does not skew the analysis too much. However, in some cases, one algorithm is significantly better than the others, and we identify those cases. Ideally, you would want to create your own special algorithm for your own special cases, but that is a complicated venture beyond the scope of this book and largely unnecessary. The three algorithms we will concern ourselves with here measure centrality, closeness, and betweenness.[2]

Algorithm 1: Bonacich's Approach to Degree Centrality

Centrality is a simple concept that says an individual's influence is measured by how many direct links he has with other individuals. The more links an individual has, the more central he is or the more centrality he has. However, centrality does not always equal more influence. Consider the examples of Connie and Paul, who go to the same school and have five different friends each but do not know each other. They both have the same amount of centrality because they both have five direct links. However, Connie's friends are friends with a lot more people, but Paul's friends do not have any other friends except for Paul. See Figure 5.5 for a visual representation of Connie and Paul's networks.

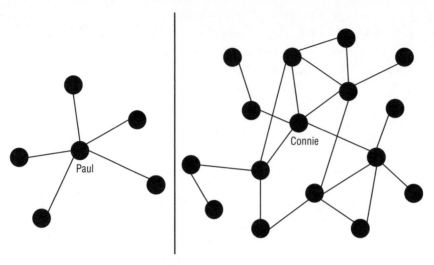

Figure 5.5: Networks with different Bonacich centralities

Connie's social network is thus much larger than Paul's. Consequently, Connie's friends can talk to plenty of other people but Paul's friends can only talk to Paul. In such a case, Paul could actually turn out to have more influence, because his friends only really have Paul to communicate with. On the other hand, Connie's message can reach a lot more people. In this case, who is more influential— Connie or Paul? The answer depends on the nature of the social network, the individuals in the network, and the environment in which everyone is located. Phillip Bonacich tweaked the standard Degree Centrality algorithm to take this social insight into account. The algorithm enables you to determine whether in a specific scenario, an individual is more influential if he can talk to a lot of people or if he can monopolize communication within a small group. Bonacich's approach enables you to choose which scenario is appropriate by selecting a positive or a negative attenuation factor called the Beta number. If you think an individual is more influential if he can talk to more people, choose a positive Beta number. If you think an individual is more influential if he can monopolize communication within a small group, choose a negative Beta number. Use your judgment to figure out which scenario is more appropriate. Do not worry if you are a little lost. We go over in detail how to use this and other algorithms later in the chapter.

Algorithm 2: Eigenvector of Geodesic Distances

Closeness goes one step beyond centrality and takes into account the indirect links that an individual can make to all other individuals in his social network. In other words, closeness takes into account the fact that if Connie says something to her friends, her friends might tell their friends, who might tell their friends, and so on. Connie may then be able to influence someone who she has never directly communicated with, simply because her friends are so popular and close with others. Thus, Connie has high closeness. In Paul's case, whose friends are largely disconnected from the rest of the school, Paul is not very close to others in the school, and has low closeness. The eigenvector approach calculates how close an individual is to everyone else in his network. The closer Connie is to people in her network by virtue of her friends being so popular, the easier it will be for her to influence a greater number of people in the network. This algorithm is more appropriate for larger, more complex networks.

Algorithm 3: Freeman's Betweenness Centrality

Betweenness considers the social fact that the individual who controls access to the network and decides if the network gets to hear a message wields immense influence over the network. In other words, the more people who depend on an individual to help them communicate and make connections with other people, the more influential is the individual and the more betweenness he has. Such individuals are often known as gatekeepers, because they control the flow of information. People have to go through them if they want to speak to other members of the network. Removing them from the network would cripple the network. In Paul's network, Paul is the gatekeeper because if his friends want to speak to each other, they have to send their message to Paul first, who then relays it to others. Freeman's Betweenness Centrality measures how much betweenness an individual has, by essentially counting how many times the individual falls between two people in a network. The algorithm works only in cases with binary link data, which is when links are coded as only 0 and 1, and not by an attribute.

Choosing SNA Software Program

The final step before conducting SNA is choosing the right software program with which to do it. You can always manually map and apply the algorithms to your data sets. However, for those who are not masochists, we highly recommend choosing an SNA software program. At least a hundred SNA software programs are available and they range in cost, features, algorithms available, and usability. Some software suites bundle two or more software programs together, and many allow for interoperability—you can use the same data set in different software without reformatting it. The following three types of SNA software exist:

- **Visualization**—Maps the social network or graph in 2-D and 3-D graphics, and allows you to edit and export it
- **Analytical**—Applies various SNA algorithms to data sets
- **Combined Packages**—Combine the functionality of visualization and analytical software and enable you to do both with the same data set

Unless you need to create nice looking graphics of social networks, do not use strictly visualization software. We highly recommend using software that combines visualization and analytical capabilities. Increasingly, more and more software programs are combining both capabilities so the list of choices is immense. They are available open source and commercially, and range in prices. Some are free, some are affordable, some are expensive and worth it, and some are expensive but not worth it. The commercial ones usually have more features and algorithms, are more reliable, and offer some sort of trial period. The open source ones are free and actually fairly powerful and have a lot of features, but they are hard to use. We recommend using a combination of commercially available and free SNA software programs, depending on your needs. In the remaining sections, we will describe how to use one commercially available software program and one free software program.

The commercially available software program we teach you to use is called UCINET. Unless you have a large budget and require hundreds of features that go beyond SNA, we recommend you get UCINET, which comes packaged with a visualization software program called NetDraw. It is relatively cheap (only $150 for a license), is widely used in academic circles, is easy to use, has the algorithms you will use, and has a free 90-day trial period. We use UCINET in our case studies. On its website, UCINET also features free data sets to play around with, user guides, and a free online textbook that goes more in-depth into SNA. UCINET is available as a download at `www.analytictech.com/UCINET/`.

UCINET does not work on Apple and Linux computers. However, you can run UCINET and other Windows-only programs on Apple and Linux computers by purchasing an easy-to-use and relatively cheap Windows emulation software program called Parallels Desktop, which is available for download at `www.parallels.com/products/desktop/`. You can also use a free, open source Windows emulation software program known as WineHQ, which is harder to set up but generally works well with UCINET. It is available for free download at `www.winehq.org`.

If you want free software or do not want to use Windows emulation software, we recommend getting a software program called R, which is available at `www.r-project.org`. R is more difficult to use and requires some familiarity with coding; however, many user guides and wiki pages detail how to use R in laymen's terms. R also enables you to apply many more algorithms, although finding and integrating those algorithms can be tedious. You can also use R for other types of analyses including advanced statistical analyses. Many other free software solutions exist, and we encourage you to try them out. A list of SNA software is available at `www.wikipedia.org/wiki/Social_network_analysis_software`.

Although not necessary, you should also expect to use a program like Microsoft Excel that enables you to input data into spreadsheets. The added benefit of using Microsoft Excel is that you need it to run the second software program we teach you how to use. The second program is not exactly a software program but instead is a template file for Excel. It is known as NodeXL and is available for free at `nodexl.codeplex.com`. NodeXL is similar to UCINET in many ways and provides some unique features geared for users interested in analyzing social media data. Specifically, NodeXL enables you to easily and automatically download social media data whereas with other SNA software such as UCINET, you will need to download the social media data manually. In other words, NodeXL comes with a free data aggregation and filtering system. NodeXL also enables you to identify the memes in a network. Like UCINET, NodeXL does not work on Apple and Linux computers and requires that you use the Windows operating system. You also need Microsoft Excel versions 2007 or 2010.

SNA requires completing three steps:

1. Creating and formatting a data set based on downloaded social media data

2. Visually mapping the social network using a visualization tool

3. Applying algorithms to the network data, and then comparing the results of the algorithms to find the key influencer(s)

The remainder of this chapter details the three steps through three real-world examples or walkthroughs. For the first two examples, we will teach you how to use UCINET. For the third example, we will teach you how to use NodeXL. The first two examples will teach you how to identify influencers. The third final example will teach you how to identify the memes being discussed together by people on Twitter. As you read through the examples, notice the differences between the two software programs and develop an understanding of when to use which type of software. Overall, use UCINET when you need to identify influencers using the specific algorithms mentioned before. Use NodeXL when you want to automatically download and format social media data, and determine what topics people are talking about online. As we describe later, you can also transfer files between the two programs.

First Example—Identify Influencers

The example is the social network of people likely in Pakistan and on Twitter who regularly tweet anti-Taliban content. Identifying the key influencers in such a network can help you to, for example:

- Contact and incentivize influential people to amplify their tweets of anti-Taliban information

- Understand the most influential anti-Taliban messages, trends, and themes, and configure information operations to mimic them

- Guide those at risk of recruitment by the Taliban or extremists to connect with the most influential and persuasive anti-Taliban communicators

We then go through the steps again, albeit with less detail, with a second example. We are focusing on Twitter data for both examples because Twitter data is readily available, it translates easily to social networking data, and a lot of people in the government are interested in seeing how they can use it.

Creating the Data Set

Preparing the data set involves creating the matrices we referred to earlier. We will then input the matrices into the UCINET software, so the software can use it to map and analyze the networks. Unfortunately, most contemporary SNA software programs do not automatically download social media data and format it into a data set that you can readily use. For now you will have to manually code the data set using steps detailed in the subsequent sections. Of course, you can use NodeXL for this example and save yourself some time because NodeXL enables you to automatically download social media data and format it properly. However, manually downloading social media data and mapping networks will help you understand and appreciate the complexity of SNA. Thus, we recommend you use UCINET for now. Have UCINET installed and ready as you follow along.

CROSS-REFERENCE **To follow along, download the files**
`anti-taliban.##h` **and** `anti-taliban.xls` **from the website. You can either use the files or create a relevant data set on your own.**

Collect the Twitter Data

First, follow these steps to build the list of relevant Twitter users:

1. Formulate the data collection need. We are searching for the Twitter accounts of people on Twitter who are saying anti-Taliban things and are likely in Pakistan.

2. Identify a few popular, appropriate Twitter users. You have two ways to go about this, depending on your knowledge of the topic. If you know some

Twitter users that match your criteria, start with them. Otherwise, ping the Twitter Search API with English and Arabic translations of words an anti-Taliban person might use, such as "Taliban," "evil," "behead(ings)," "killings," and "immoral." Read through some tweets and make a list of a few users with a lot of followers and tweets that seem to match your criteria. Identify users who do not seem to be linked with each other; that is, are not following, followed by, and retweeting each other. Check the users' location status to see if they are from Pakistan. If their location is not available, then read through their tweets to see if they mention participating in activities or being in places that suggest they are in Pakistan. Because anti-Taliban rhetoric originating from Pakistan is a fairly niche topic, the number of users you will find will be limited. We used both ways to make our initial list.

3. Build off the initial list of users. Catalog who the initial users are following, followed by, and retweeting—these are the second-degree users. Keep track of how they are linked to the initial user; that is, if the links are unidirectional or bidirectional. If the second-degree user follows or retweets the initial user but the initial user does not follow or retweet the second-degree user, the link is unidirectional from the second-degree user to the initial user. If the initial user also follows or retweets the second-degree user, the link is bidirectional. Read through the tweets of second-degree users to see if they tweet about issues related to the topic. Discard the ones who do not seem to be at all interested in the topic and are linked to only one initial user. They may be following the person for personal or other reasons. Do not discard users who have only a few tweets, have only a few followers, or are following only a few people. Remember that influence is not necessarily a function of how many followers or tweets a user has. Do ignore the Twitter accounts of major newspapers and international organizations. Thousands of followers can follow a major organization, and they may have nothing to do with your topic. Catalog the list in a rough network drawing. See Figure 5.6 for what our network looks like so far with 15 users.

4. Decide how many data points you need. In SNA, the more data, the better. However, theoretically the network you are cataloging can grow to include everyone on Twitter. Due to our time and resource constraints, we chose to limit the number of users to 32. Continue cataloging users until you see fit.

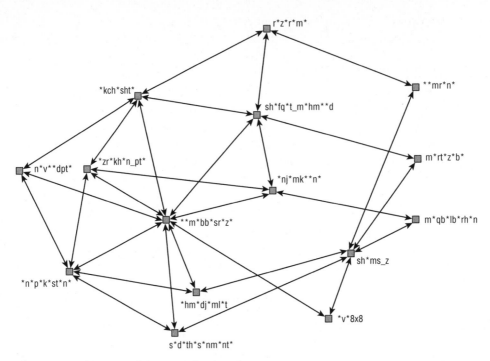

Figure 5.6: First example's network map of 15 users

> **NOTE** If you are following along by building your own data from scratch, it
> will probably look different from ours. This is due to the somewhat subjective
> nature of the data collection, and the time difference between us creating our
> data set and the publication of this book—some of the Twitter accounts may
> no longer exist or people may change their online behavior and stop following
> certain people.

The subjective nature of this type of data collection is a little frustrating. New
software solutions are in development that will help standardize this type of
data collection and reduce the subjectivity. However, some subjectivity will
always remain—the software solution will make the same assumptions that
you are making. Picking a niche topic and focusing your data collection needs
will reduce the overall amount of users involved, and thus make it less likely
that you ignore a big chunk of users.

> **NOTE** To protect the identity of Twitter users in the first two examples, we
> replaced the vowels in their user account names with asterisks.

Convert the Network Data into Matrix Format

You have multiple ways to perform the second step, including using network visualization software, which we describe later. You should go through this somewhat painful process at least once, so you understand what the underlying data looks like. Follow these steps to put the data into the appropriate format for SNA software:

1. Start a spreadsheet program. Open a program like Microsoft Excel. You can use other spreadsheet programs or you can bypass spreadsheet programs altogether and input your data directly into the SNA software. However, it is easier to manipulate data with programs like Excel and export it to different formats later.

2. Write the list of all users. In Excel, navigate to the cell at the first column, second row. Start inputting the names of the users, and work down the column till you exhaust all names. The order you put the names in is irrelevant. Leave out the "@" that is in front of Twitter usernames. You have now created the list of users.

3. Write the list of "link receiving users." Copy all the names in the first column. Navigate to the cell at the second column, first row. Either right-click with your mouse, or select Edit on the menu bar, and choose Paste Select. A menu should pop up. Select Transpose and click Paste. The column of names should now be pasted as a row in the first row. You have now created the list of link receiving users, who are the users that receive the link from the users in the first column.

4. Indicate links. Go through the matrix you have created and insert a 1 for every link that exists between a user and the linked user. To do so, start with the first name in Column 1. In our column, the first name is sh*ms_z and the corresponding row is numbered 2. On Row 2, move to the right through the columns, starting at Column 2, putting a 1 in the cell if sh*ms_z either follows or retweets the usernames heading the column. In our case, Column 2's name is also sh*ms_z. A user cannot have links with himself, so do not put anything in the cell. The user heading Column 3 is m*qb*lb*rh*n. The user sh*ms_z does follow or retweet m*qb*lb*rh*n, so put a 1 in the cell indicating a link between the two users. Continue through all the columns. Then move to Row 3, and so on. See Figure 5.7 for a screenshot of what our spreadsheet looks like.

5. Save the file. After going through all the rows and columns, save the file in CSV or XLS format. Go through the matrix again to ensure you entered everything correctly.

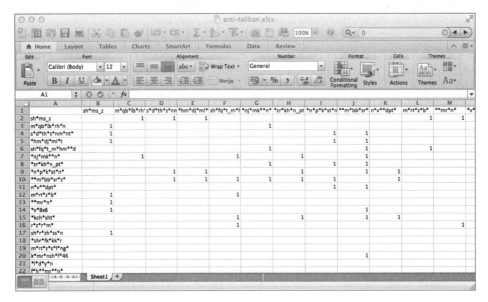

Figure 5.7: First example's network matrix

Enter the Data into the SNA Software

Third, follow these steps to copy the data into the SNA software:

1. Open UCINET. Install and start UCINET. You may use other software but most of our instructions will be specific to UCINET. SNA software, however, is usually fairly similar so you should be able to follow along with different software. When you start UCINET, you should see the home interface with a menu bar on the top. On the menu bar, select Data. In the menu, select the first choice of Data Editors, and then select Matrix Editor. Once you click Matrix Editor, a spreadsheet-type interface should pop up. You can also enter the Matrix editor by clicking the second graphic button on the home interface, directly underneath the menu bar.

2. Copy data into the Matrix editor. Open the CSV or XLS file you created using Excel. Highlight all the cells, including the names in the first column and first row and all the 1s indicating the links. Copy the cells. Go back to UCINET's Matrix editor. In the editor, make sure your cursor is at the first cell, which is the left-most, top-most cell. Usually when you start the editor, the cursor starts there as default. Otherwise, simply click the first cell to place your cursor there. Then go to Edit ≻ Paste, or use the standard hot key to paste the data. The data should populate the Matrix editor as it did the Excel spreadsheet. Finally, click Fill in the menu bar, and select Blanks w/ 0s. The number 0 should populate in all the cells that are empty, which should be any cells that do not have a 1. You can also click the graphic button underneath the menu bar that says the word Fill. See Figure 5.8 for a screenshot of the Matrix editor. Notice the options

on the right of the editor that say Mode. Make sure that under Mode, you select Normal. In networks where every link is bidirectional, select the option Symmetric. In a social media case, the network is rarely completely bidirectional or symmetric.

3. Save the file. Save the file by going to File ➢ Save or clicking the floppy disc graphic button. Name the file as something relevant and make sure to save it as a UCINET 4-6 file, and not UCINET 7 type or any other type. The extension of this type of file is .##h. Our file is saved as anti-taliban.##h. Once saved, close the Matrix editor and Excel, and return to the UCINET home interface.

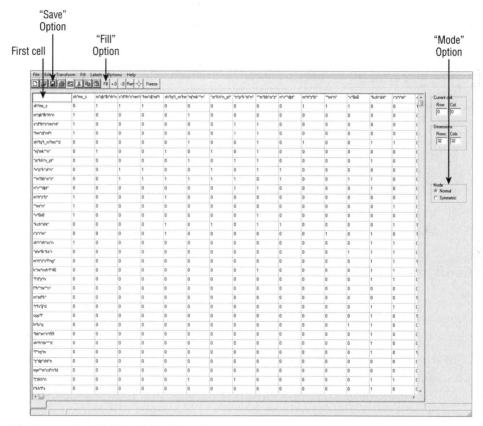

Figure 5.8: UCINET's Matrix editor

You have completed preparing the data set and can now move to visually mapping and analyzing the social network.

Visually Map the Network

Visually mapping the network is not necessary for analyzing the network and finding the key influencers. However, it can help you reason about the network and check your work and results. A network that looks extremely broken up or strange can be a clue that you need to double-check your data collection and coding, because most social networks are fairly integrated. Also, you can use the visual representations to explain your analysis to others. The process for visually mapping the network is fairly simple. However, making the network look good by configuring the features can be difficult. The subsequent sections show you the main steps for mapping and configuring the network. Refer to your SNA software user guide for more.

Create the Initial Map

First, follow these steps to create the initial visual representation of the network:

1. Open NetDraw. In UCINET's home interface, click Visualize on the top menu bar, and then select NetDraw. Alternatively, you can click the last graphic button beneath the menu bar. A new window should pop up, showing NetDraw's main interface.

2. Input the data set. On the menu bar at the top of NetDraw's interface, go to File ➢ Open ➢ Ucinet Dataset ➢ Network. In the pop-up, click the small button with an ellipsis next to the box. In the pop-up, select the .##h file you created or downloaded from our website. Click OK and open the file. On the NetDraw interface, you should see your network represented as a network map, as in Figure 5.9.

3. Save the map. Go to File ➢ Save Diagram As. In the subsequent menu, select how you want to export the image of the network.

Configure the Map

The extent to which you want to configure your map and make it look better depends on your needs. The following bullet points highlight a few features that may prove useful:

▪ **Move the nodes around**—Click on any node, represented as a colored shape, and drag it to move it around. The lines representing the links will move along with the dragged node. Use this feature to clean up the network map and make it less cluttered. The nodes with the fewest links should generally be away from the center of the map.

▪ **Resize the map to fit the area**—Critical to ensuring your map looks less cluttered, this option resizes your map to fit your screen. On the menu bar, go to Layout and select Resize. Alternatively, on the buttons under the menu bar, click the box that is fifth from the left.

▪ **Differentiate certain nodes by attributes**—You may want to call attention to certain nodes for a variety of reasons, perhaps because they are the key influencers. By assigning attributes to nodes, you can selectively change the look of specific nodes, or add more fidelity to the data set. Select Transform in the menu bar, and then Node Attribute Editor. In the pop-up, click Add Attrib at the top of the new window, and provide a name for the attribute. A new column should appear alongside the names. Put a 1 next to the name under your attribute column for nodes for which you want to assign that attribute.

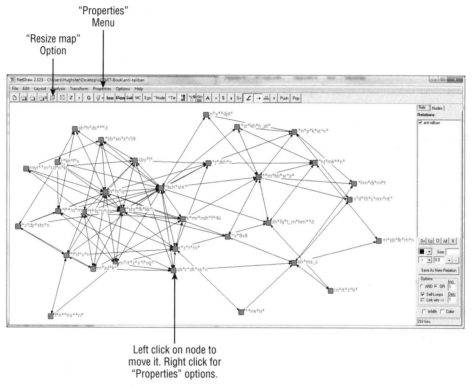

Figure 5.9: First example's complete network map

- **Change the look of nodes**—Click Properties on the menu bar and select Nodes. The subsequent menu options enable you to change the color, size, label, and shape of the nodes. You can choose to assign the properties to either all the nodes or by attribute. Alternatively, you can right-click any of the nodes in the NetDraw interface and change the properties of only the selected node. You can also use your mouse to draw a box around the nodes you want to change, and then right-click to change the properties of the selected nodes. The program tells you that a node is selected when it changes the node's look from a colored shape to that of a shape containing an X.

- **Change the look of links**—This is similar to changing the properties of links. Click Properties on the menu bar and select Lines. You can then change the color, size, label, and arrow head type of all or some links. You can also right-click specific links in the NetDraw interface and change the look of specific links.

- **Play with other options**—Notice that the Properties menu also enables you to change the background color and other properties of the map. Go through the Properties menu and other menus to see how else you can change the network map.

- **Edit the data set visually**—Right-clicking nodes and links also enables you to delete and add links and nodes. By adding and deleting nodes and links, you are editing the underlying data set. If you want to save the edited data set, go to File ➢ Save Data As ➢ Ucinet ➢ Binary Network. Give it a new filename and save it as a .##h file type. You will have created a whole new data set. This option can prove useful. Instead of cataloging a data set as a matrix or in a spreadsheet, you can build the data set in NetDraw and then save it. Be careful with adding attributes to nodes and then saving them. The algorithm operations we teach you may not work if the nodes have attributes assigned to them.

You have now completed visually mapping and editing the network, and can analyze it to find the key influencers.

Analyze the Network

Analyzing social networks involves running three algorithms through the data set and then comparing their results. Note that you can run many other algorithms also. Explore your SNA software to see what kinds of results you get with the other algorithms. The subsequent steps show you how to run the algorithms on UCINET, output the results in an exportable format, and compare them.

Run the Algorithms

First, follow these steps to apply the three algorithms to the data set:

1. Prepare UCINET. Close NetDraw and the Matrix editor, and return to UCINET's home interface.

2. Run the Bonacich Degree Centrality algorithm. On the menu bar, go to Network ➢ Centrality and Power, and select Bonacich Power (Beta centrality). In the pop-up, which is shown in Figure 5.10, click the graphic box with the ellipsis next to the box for Input Network Dataset. Select the appropriate .##h file. Then look at the bottom right of the window and find the options for setting the Beta value.

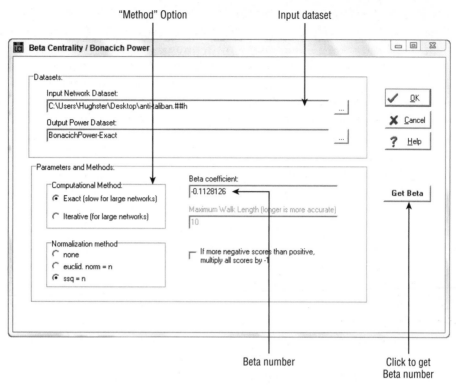

Figure 5.10: UCINET's Bonacich Centrality input pop-up

Our assumption is that, in this network, having your message heard by more people makes you more influential. The goal of the anti-Taliban people is to be heard so they can popularize their effort against the Taliban and make sure a lot of people know about the case against the Taliban. Thus, the Beta number must be positive. Click the Get Beta button to the right. Close the window that popped up. You should notice a number in the dialog box that says Beta Coefficient. Our number says 0.1128126. Unless specified otherwise, keep the default options for all algorithms. Finally, click OK and run the algorithm. A new window should pop up (most likely in the Notepad program), showing a text file with a list of the names and numbers next to them. The text file should say "Bonacich Power / Beta Centrality" near the top. These are the results of the algorithm. See Figure 5.11 for a screenshot. Save the text file with the name "Centrality_*name of file*.txt." Close the text file and return to the UCINET interface. We will return to the text file later.

3. Run the Eigenvector of Geodesic Distances algorithm. On the menu bar, go to Network ➤ Centrality and Power, and select Eigenvector. In the pop-up, click the graphic box with the ellipsis next to the box for Input Network Dataset. Select the appropriate .##h file. The default value for Method should say "Slow & super accurate." If your data set is very large,

such as more than 10,000 nodes, and your computer is not very powerful, select Fast. Click OK and run the algorithm. A new window should pop up, showing a text file with a column of numbers next to another column of numbers, and when you scroll down, a column or list of the names and numbers next to them. The text file should say "Eigenvector" near the top. These are the results of the algorithm. Save the text file with the name **Closeness_***name of file***.txt**. Close the text file and return to the UCINET interface. We will return to the text file later.

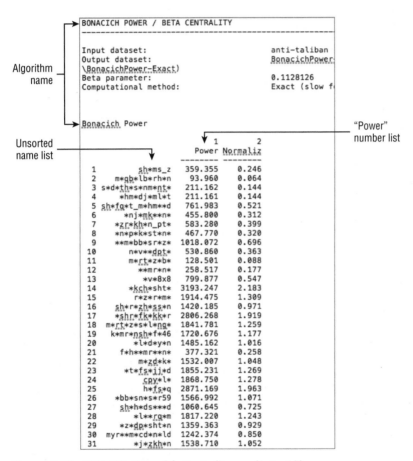

Figure 5.11: UCINET's Bonacich Centrality results text file

4. Run Freeman's Betweenness Centrality algorithm. On the menu bar, go to Network ➤ Centrality and Power ➤ Freeman Betweenness, and select Node Betweenness. In the pop-up, click on the graphic box with the ellipsis next to the box for Input Network Dataset. Select the appropriate .##h file. Click OK and run the algorithm. A new window should pop up, showing a text file with a list of the names and numbers next to them. The text file should say "Freeman Betweenness Centrality" near the top. These are the

results of the algorithm. Save the text file with the name **Betweenness_***name of file***.txt.** Close the text file and return to the UCINET interface. We will return to the text file later.

Compare the Results

Second, follow these steps to compare the results of the three algorithms to find the key influencers in the network:

1. Open the result text files. Open the three text files you saved before. Look at the top of the Closeness file, which is shown in Figure 5.12, and find the heading called "Eigenvalues," below which is a list of numbers. Find "Factor 1" and the "Percent" associated with Factor 1. If the percent value is less than 70, you should take the results of the Eigenvalue Closeness algorithm lightly. It means that the algorithm did not find enough differences in the network to produce an accurate enough result, probably because the network was too small. Our Factor 1's percent value is 15.8, so we will only slightly consider the results. In the same file, scroll down to the part that starts with the header "Bonacich Eigenvector Centralities" and lists the names with numbers next to them. You will notice that the names are listed in the order in which you entered the nodes in the Matrix editor. This ordering of list is considered unsorted. Look at the numbers next to the names under the heading of "Eigenvec," short for eigenvectors. You need the names sorted by the value of the eigenvectors, with the name with the highest eigenvec on top, because it is the most influential. Use Excel to re-sort the data in this way. Open the Centrality file. Find the list of names, and also realize that this list is also unsorted. You need it sorted by the "Power" numbers, with the name having the highest Power number on top because it is the most influential. Use Excel to re-sort this data as well. Open the Betweenness file and find the list of names. This list is already sorted by the "Betweenness" numbers, which is a good thing and saves you work. Line up the three sorted name lists next to each other. Table 5.1 lists the sorted list of names according to each algorithm. Finally, quickly skim through the numbers next to the column of names for each list. Within each list, if the numbers for some names vary significantly in value from the numbers for the other names, you can trust the output of the algorithm. The results are significant because there is some difference between the nodes. Within each list, if the numbers are all similar in value, you may not have enough data for that algorithm, and you should take those results less seriously.

2. Determine the number of key influencers. The number of influencers you want to find and focus on depends on what you want to do with the names and your resources. A good rule is that the number of influencers equals about 5–10 percent of the total number of nodes in the network. Our network has 32 nodes, so we are looking for three key influencers.

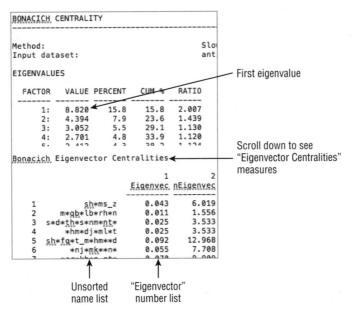

Figure 5.12: UCINET's Eigenvector Closeness results text file

3. Compare the names and their positions. Notice that the Closeness (Eigenvector algorithm) and the Centrality (Bonacich Centrality algorithm) result lists are identical. This will not always be the case, but it is in this network. The Betweenness list, however, is different from the other lists. Some names that appear at the top of the Closeness and Centrality lists do appear at the top of the Betweenness list. The user *kch*sht* tops all three lists, which indicates *kch*sht* is very likely a key influencer. In the case where the lists appear different, look at the top five names of the three lists and see if similar names appear in the top five. If you cannot find similar names in the top five, expand it to the top 10, and so on. In our case, the users h*fs*q and r*z*r*m* appear in the top five for all lists, alongside *kch*sht*. Go back to the result text files, and validate your results by comparing the value of the Power, eigenvec, and Betweenness numbers for each key influencer with the corresponding numbers for other nodes. Within each list, the greater the difference, the more likely your results are correct. Consider the numbers to be guidelines and not an objective measure.

4. Compare the algorithms. In some cases, you may have a bias against or with a certain algorithm. The algorithms define influence differently and you may prefer one definition to another. In such a case, give more weight to the output of one algorithm and less to the others.

5. Finalize your results. The key influencers for this network appear to be *kch*sht*, h*fs*q, and r*z*r*m*. Based on the numbers, *kch*sht* appears to be far more influential.

6. Compare results with the visual map. Look at the network map to see if the nodes you identified do appear to be more influential. Depending on your algorithm and influencer definition preference, the nodes you identify as influential should appear centrally located in the network, close to users, and between users. If you identify a node as influential and it looks isolated and only connected to one other node in a network of 100 nodes, you are likely incorrect. In our network map, the three key influencers appear central, close to other users, and between users. Therefore, our results appear correct. Note that looks can be deceiving. The user *shr*fk*kk*r appears well connected and indeed has high closeness and centrality, but *shr*fk*kk*r's lower position on the Betweenness lists indicates that *shr*fk*kk*r may not be as important as he or she visually appears.

Table 5.1: Influence Ranking of Users per Algorithm

CENTRALITY (BONACICH CENTRALITY)	CLOSENESS (EIGENVECTOR OF GEODESIC DISTANCES)	BETWEENNESS (FREEMAN'S BETWEENNESS)
*kch*sht*	*kch*sht*	*kch*sht*
h*fs*q	h*fs*q	**m*bb*sr*z*
*shr*fk*kk*r	*shr*fk*kk*r	sh*ms_z
r*z*r*m*	r*z*r*m*	h*fs*q
cpy*l*	cpy*l*	r*z*r*m*
*t*fs*jj*d	*t*fs*jj*d	*shr*fk*kk*r
m*rt*z*s*l*ng*	m*rt*z*s*l*ng*	*j*zkh*n
*l**rq*m	*l**rq*m	sh*r*zh*ss*n
k*mr*nsh*f*46	k*mr*nsh*f*46	sh*fq*t_m*hm**d
*bb*sn*s*r59	*bb*sn*s*r59	m*rt*z*s*l*ng*
*j*zkh*n	*j*zkh*n	*l*d*y*n
m*zd*k*	m*zd*k*	*nj*mk**n*
*l*d*y*n	*l*d*y*n	*v*8x8
t*kh*l*s	t*kh*l*s	*t*fs*jj*d
sh*r*zh*ss*n	sh*r*zh*ss*n	k*mr*nsh*f*46

Continued

Table 5-1 (continued)

CENTRALITY (BONACICH CENTRALITY)	CLOSENESS (EIGENVECTOR OF GEODESIC DISTANCES)	BETWEENNESS (FREEMAN'S BETWEENNESS)
*z*dp*sht*n	*z*dp*sht*n	*n*p*k*st*n*
myr**m*cd*n*ld	myr**m*cd*n*ld	cpy*l*
sh*h*ds***d	sh*h*ds***d	*l**rq*m
**m*bb*sr*z*	**m*bb*sr*z*	m*zd*k*
*v*8x8	*v*8x8	*zr*kh*n_pt*
sh*fq*t_m*hm**d	sh*fq*t_m*hm**d	*hm*dj*ml*t
*zr*kh*n_pt*	*zr*kh*n_pt*	s*d*th*s*nm*nt*
n*v**dpt*	n*v**dpt*	**mr*n*
*n*p*k*st*n*	*n*p*k*st*n*	m*qb*lb*rh*n
*nj*mk**n*	*nj*mk**n*	n*v**dpt*
f*h**mr**n*	f*h**mr**n*	t*kh*l*s
sh*ms_z	sh*ms_z	*z*dp*sht*n
**mr*n*	**mr*n*	*bb*sn*s*r59
s*d*th*s*nm*nt*	s*d*th*s*nm*nt*	m*rt*z*b*
*hm*dj*ml*t	*hm*dj*ml*t	myr**m*cd*n*ld
m*rt*z*b*	m*rt*z*b*	f*h**mr**n*
m*qb*lb*rh*n	m*qb*lb*rh*n	sh*h*ds***d

Second Example—Identify Influencers

The second real-world example is the social network of people likely in Pakistan and on Twitter who regularly tweet pro-Taliban content. Identifying the key influencers in such a network can help you to, for example:

- Focus investigation resources on the most influential communicators and recruiters
- Distance the most influential pro-Taliban messengers from the networks to cripple the network

- Understand the most influential pro-Taliban messages, and configure information operations to counter them

- Dissuade those at risk of recruitment by the Taliban or jihadists from connecting with the most influential pro-Taliban communicators

The objectives of analyzing the network in this example are different from those of the first network, thereby slightly affecting how we perform SNA and how we configure the algorithms. Because the first example contained all the explicit details on how to complete the steps and we do not want to be redundant, in this example, we will breeze through a truncated number of steps. Only use the following steps as guidelines and to check your results as you complete the SNA on your own.

> **CROSS-REFERENCE** To follow along, download the files
> `pro-taliban.##h` **and** `pro-taliban.xls` **from the website. You can either
> use the files or create a relevant data set on your own.**

Create the Data Set

The following steps summarize the process for assembling and coding the data:

1. Collect the Twitter data. Search for Twitter users that are pro-Taliban and likely from Pakistan. We use our existing knowledge to identify a few key users, and ping the Twitter Search API with English and Arabic translations of words such as "Taliban," "heroes," "martyr," and "sacrifice," and see who uses them regularly. Building out from our initial set of users, go a few degrees out from the initial list of users. Due to our time and resource constraints, we stopped at 91 users.

2. Convert the network data into matrix format. Catalog the names in Excel. Go through the spreadsheet, placing a 1 where links exist between the names in Column 1 and the names in Row 1. Save the file and review the work for corrections.

3. Enter the data into the SNA software. Copy the spreadsheet from Excel into UCINET's Matrix editor. Fill the blank cells with 0s and ensure the Mode type is Normal. Save the file as `pro-taliban.##h` and close Excel and the Matrix editor.

Visually Map the Network

The following steps summarize the process for visually representing and configuring the network map:

1. Create the initial map. Open NetDraw, and input the `pro-taliban.##h` data set.

2. Configure the map. Change the size, shape, color, and other properties of the nodes and links, as desired. Drag the nodes around to make the network map look less cluttered. Resize the network so it fits the screen properly. We decided to make the labels invisible because they were cluttering the map. See Figure 5.13 for our network map.

Figure 5.13: Second example's complete network map

Analyze the Network

The following steps summarize the process for running the algorithms through the data set and comparing their results to identify the top key influencers:

1. Run the algorithms. Input the data set into the three algorithm pop-up windows, select the right options, and run the algorithms. Our assumption is that in this network, because the message is somewhat unpopular on social media, having a small group of people repeatedly listen and absorb your message makes you more influential. The influencers in the network do not have to compete with other messages and can take time instilling their relatively less popular ideology into potential recruits and true believers. Thus, the Beta number for the Bonacich Degree Centrality

algorithm should be negative. Specifically, it is –0.0932322. Also, because the number of nodes is still fairly small, we select the Slow method for the Eigenvector algorithm. Save the output of the results, sort the list of the names by the Power, eigenvec, and Betweenness numbers (Betweenness comes pre-sorted), and create a list as in Table 5.2. To save space, Table 5.2 shows only the top 30 rankings for each algorithm. The complete list is available on the website. Notice that the Closeness and Centrality lists differ somewhat. Also notice that the Factor 1's percent value in the Eigenvector output is only 6.6, so give less credence to the eigenvector results. Otherwise, the numbers for the names seem to vary among each algorithm result list, which bolsters confidence in the overall results.

2. Compare the results. We estimate that about 5 percent of the network are influencers, resulting in five key influencers. Comparing the results, the key influencers appear to be: *bn_*lk*tt*b, *b*bd*sS*l**m, j*f*rh*ss**n1, *lm*s*f*r*q8, and *hm*dkh*n111. If you prefer one algorithm, for whatever reason, your results may look somewhat different. However, overall, *bn_*lk*tt*b does appear to be the most influential.

Table 5.2: Top 30 Influence Rankings of Users per Algorithm (Second Example)

CENTRALITY (BONACICH CENTRALITY)	CLOSENESS (EIGENVECTOR OF GEODESIC DISTANCES)	BETWEENNESS (FREEMAN'S BETWEENNESS)
*bn_*lk*tt*b	*bn_*lk*tt*b	*bn_*lk*tt*b
*lm*s*f*r*q8	n*rj*sk*ld*	*b**bd*sS*l**m
*b**bd*sS*l**m	J*h*d*l*mm*h	L*ND_D*F*ND*R
j*f*rh*ss**n1	*B*1433	*m*mb*nb*z
n*rj*sk*ld*	H***lj*h*d	*lm*s*f*r*q8
*b*lkh*	R*ckst*n*RC	j*f*rh*ss**n1
*B*1433	r*h*lc*h*d	*hm*dkh*n111
s*lt*n2277	*l_n*khb*	*lb*t*r2
HSMPr*ss	M*HH	B*nt**m**h
*hm*dkh*n111	*hm*dkh*n111	D**n*b*s*x
*b*Kh*d**j*hSP	*ls*m**d	yv*nn*r*dl*y
*lb*t*r2	L*ND_D*F*ND*R	*lr*sh*d_Kh*l*d
yv*nn*r*dl*y	*lb*t*r2	*b*lkh*

Continued

Table 5-2 (continued)

CENTRALITY (BONACICH CENTRALITY)	CLOSENESS (EIGENVECTOR OF GEODESIC DISTANCES)	BETWEENNESS (FREEMAN'S BETWEENNESS)
L*ND_D*F*ND*R	*s_*ns*r	*sl*m*cTh*nk*ng
J*h*d*l*mm*h	M*nb*rT*wh*d	J*h*d*l*mm*h
R*ckst*n*RC	*sm**_j*h*d	H***lj*h*d
Sh*r**lM*j*h*d	*b*lkh*	d*h*nt*d786
85W*l**D	*lv*z**r	st*ntr*d*r00
*b*H*k**mB*l*l	tvjh*d	n*rj*sk*ld*
M*HH	r*lg*h*d	*B*1433
MYC_Pr*ss	HSMPr*ss	G*t*Pr*t*19
sw*bzy	85W*l**D	*b*Kh*d**j*hSP
*ls*m**d	s***t*lj*h*d	HSMPr*ss
*hm*d*ss*ng	*b**_1986	M*HH
*b**_1986	d*h*nt*d786	85W*l**D
G*t*Pr*t*19	*lf*r*qm*d**	*ls*m**d
d*h*nt*d786	Sh*r**lM*j*h*d	sw*bzy
H***lj*h*d	st*ntr*d*r00	Tw**t_K*shm*r
*l_n*khb*	*lr*sh*d_Kh*l*d	Dr**s*lS*nn*h
st*ntr*d*r00	*m*mb*nb*z	*b**_1986

Third Example—Determine Top Memes

The third real-world example entails determining what topics and subjects people are currently discussing. Identifying the key memes in a network can help you to, for example:

- Understand how topics of discussion in a network change over time
- Understand which topics tend to be discussed together
- Identify the type of subjects you must anticipate discussing if you wish to join the network as a member

We will use NodeXL to conduct the analysis. We will determine what topics people are talking about in relation to a specific topic and who those people are. In our example, we will determine what other things most people talk about and mention in their tweets when they tweet about drugs, and we will determine the identity (usernames) of the people talking about drugs. Keep in mind that identifying current memes in a network is only one of NodeXL's abilities. The software can also download and format various types of social media data, draw network maps, conduct many of the same analyses we discussed in the UCINET examples, and do many other things. For ease of understanding, we will focus on only using NodeXL to download social media data and conduct the meme analysis. Check out the NodeXL website for instructions on doing other things with NodeXL. Install and ready Microsoft Excel 2007 or 2010 and NodeXL version 210 or above to follow along.

Create the Data Set

NodeXL makes it much easier to create a data set and download all the necessary data. You can use NodeXL to download all sorts of social media data such as the networks of certain Twitter accounts, YouTube searches, and Facebook profile information. For now, we will only download data about people talking about the topic of drugs on Twitter.

CROSS-REFERENCE To use our dataset, download the files `drugs_ NodeXL.xls` from the website. Note that if you decide to create a new file using the drug topic search, your analysis will look different because you will be analyzing tweets from a different time period. NodeXL only analyzes tweets from a 7-day period from the time of analysis. We are doing our analysis months before you do yours, so we are analyzing a very different set of tweets.

Feel free to download data about any other topic. Follow these instructions to start:

1. Find the "NodeXL Excel Template" file on your computer and install it. You should be able to find it by going to Start, then Programs, and then the NodeXL folder. The Microsoft Excel program will open with the NodeXL template pre-loaded. On older or less powerful computers, loading times may be long.

2. Save the opened file as a new Excel workbook file.

3. Notice the ribbon/Table Tools heading that says "NodeXL" on the top of the Excel window. Click on it to reveal the NodeXL ribbon of options. In the ribbon, on the top left side, click on "Import" and then select "From

Twitter Search Network." A small menu window will appear. Notice the other types of data in the menu that you can download quickly and easily.

4. Near the top of the window, type in the search or topic term you wish to analyze. We are analyzing the term "drugs."

5. Below the field where you entered the name, you need to select a number of options that determine what type of data you collect about the Twitter search term and how it is structured. Feel free to play around with the options. For now keep all the default options as is. Under the "Add an edge for each," we put a checkbox on all the options except for the "Follows relationship (slower)." We limited it to a hundred people. Make sure to check the box next to "Add a Tweet column to the Edges worksheet" and to "Expand URLs in tweets (slower)." For "Your Twitter account" option, we selected "I don't have a Twitter account."

6. After selecting the options, click "Ok." It may take some time but eventually you will see your Excel workbook fill up with information about your desired Twitter search term. A pop-up may appear asking you if it is ok to shut off text wrapping. In the pop-up, click "Yes" to continue with the data importing.

Analyze the Network

Analyzing the network to determine the top memes in this case involves identifying the terms associated with your search term. Associated terms refer to the words and phrases people mention in the Tweets that contain the desired search term. The number of times people mention a certain word in the same tweet that contains your search term determines that word's ranking. The following steps describe how to conduct the analysis:

1. After the workbook is filled with data, select the analysis you want to conduct. In the ribbon menu, near the top right of the Excel window, click on "Graph Metrics" and then select the similar looking "Graph Metrics" option in the drop-down menu. A new window should pop-up showing you a list of analyses you can conduct.

2. In the new window, deselect "Overall graph metrics" and select "Twitter search network top items." Then click on "Calculate Metrics."

3. A new worksheet should open showing all the results. Scroll through the worksheet to see the results. You should see the top ten people replied-to on Twitter from the people who tweeted the word "drugs." You will also see the top ten people mentioned, the top ten URLs, and the top ten hashtags (without the # character in front of the words). The top replied-to and people mentioned tell you about the people in the Twitter network that are tweeting the word "drugs." The top URLs and hashtags tell you what other things or memes people are talking about when they mention

the word "drugs" on Twitter. See Table 5.3 for the list of top ten hashtags that our analysis revealed.

Table 5.3: Top ten hashtags from analysis on Twitter search term "drugs"

RANK	HASHTAG (WITHOUT THE # IN FRONT)
1	myxfactorsobstory
2	imthepersonwho
3	drugs
4	bewhatiwannabe
5	cough
6	cold
7	shrugs
8	thanksmom
9	treasurehunting
10	real

Most of the hashtags found seem irrelevant to security and likely are. You will need to use NodeXL in a much more targeted way to acquire relevant information and analysis. We urge you to play around with NodeXL to see how you can better focus your analysis.

We now complete the social network analysis part of the book. We continue with other types of analyses in Chapter 6.

NOTE You can open the UCINET file in NodeXL by converting the UCINET .##h file into a DL file. First, in the UCINET home screen, select Data ➤ Export ➤ DL File, and then select the .##h file you want to convert. Next, in the NodeXL Excel file, select the NodeXL tab, choose Import ➤ From UCINET Full Matrix DL File, and select the appropriate DL file.

Summary

- Use social network analysis to map social networks exhibited on social media and other venues, and reveal the identity of key influencers.
- A social network is made up of links (relationships) between nodes (individuals).

- Links can be unidirectional, where person A talks to person B but person B does not talk back. Links can also be bidirectional or reciprocal, where person A and person B talk to each other.

- Social networks can be represented as a matrix, which looks like a spreadsheet, or graphically in a network map.

- A key influencer spreads memes, ideas, and concepts that spur changes in behavior, to the most people in a network with the least constraints.

- Three SNA algorithms are effective at finding key influencers in networks:

- Centrality (Bonacich's approach) assumes an individual's influence is a function of how many people he links to, and depending on the nature of the network, how many people his links link to. Sometimes it is better to have links with people who have no other links, so a person can monopolize communication with them. Sometimes it is better to have links with people who have other links, so your message can spread beyond your direct links.

- Closeness (Eigenvectors) assumes the more links that people in an individual's network have, the more likely it is for the individual's message and influence to spread to people beyond her networks, and thereby increase her influence.

- Betweenness (Freeman's) assumes that an individual has more influence if he is the ultimate middleman for the people he links to and controls what messages the people he links to get.

- SNA software enables you to visualize networks and analyze them. They vary widely in price and features. We recommend UCINET, which features lots of analytical algorithms and NodeXL, which features the ability to easily download and format social media data and determine what topics people are talking about online.

- Conducting SNA involves creating the data set, visually mapping the network, and analyzing the network.

- Creating the data set entails:

- Collecting Twitter data

  1. Converting network data into matrix format

  2. Entering the data into SNA software

- Visually mapping the network entails:

  1. Creating the initial map

  2. Configuring the map

- Analyzing the network entails:
  1. Running the algorithms
  2. Comparing the results

Notes

1. Thompson, C. (2008) "Is the Tipping Point Toast? Fast Company." Accessed: 29 June 2012. `http://www.fastcompany.com/magazine/122/is-the-tipping-point-toast.html`

2. Hanneman, R. and Riddle, M. (2005) *Introduction to Social Network Methods.* Riverside, CA: University of California, Riverside. Accessed: 29 June 2012. `http://www.faculty.ucr.edu/~hanneman/nettext/`

Understanding and Forecasting Events

Appropriate analytical methodologies can help you understand how security events and issues develop over time and identify the factors that influence the events. Some methodologies can also help you go beyond and manipulate the identified factors to forecast how the event will evolve in the future or whether similar events will take place. Specifically, language and sentiment analysis (LSA), correlation and regression analysis (CRA), and volumetric analysis (VA) can help you use social media and other data to understand and forecast a variety of security events, including famines and illicit behavior. The analyses can help you discover relationships between content on social media and events or actions on the ground, track the evolution of the relationships, and detect emerging security problems. This chapter begins by illustrating how simple monitoring of social media data can help you detect and understand events more quickly than traditional methods. It next defines forecasting, explains how it differs from predicting, and describes what it entails. The chapter ends by explaining how to conduct LSA, CRA, and VA through examples and walkthroughs.

Introduction to Analyzing Events

This chapter provides a few ways you can use formal and some informal methods to analyze security events so you can understand them and forecast their development and emergence in the near future. When we say security events, we also refer to corresponding behaviors, issues, problems, and actions. Events include terrorist attacks, natural disasters, homicides, riots, the act of drug smuggling, the act of sex trafficking, and much more. The majority of this chapter deals with using various analytical tools and formal methodologies to analyze social media and other data to understand and forecast security events. However, before we delve into how you can use the tools, we first want to discuss the role of social media data in intelligence analysis and how simple, informal monitoring of social media data can often help you anticipate and understand events better than traditional means.

Social Media Data as Intelligence

Publications about intelligence analysis discuss the intelligence cycle, which describes how intelligence is processed in a civilian or military intelligence agency.[1] You can formulate the cycle in many ways, and we are not all that interested in discussing the best way. We do, however, want to discuss the role of social media data in the intelligence cycle in general. This section helps you understand where social media data fits in the intelligence cycle and how you can integrate the rapid influx of social media data into your analysis.

Despite the type of intelligence cycle you prefer, it involves some variation of planning, collecting, processing, evaluation, analysis, and dissemination. It also involves the different intelligence collection disciplines that we list in Table 6.1. Assessing how social media data fits in with and compares to other collection disciplines can help you appreciate the role it plays in helping illuminate events and their causes.

Social media data is often superior to other collection disciplines because it cuts across and amalgamates the other disciplines. Social media is a form of OSINT because it is derived from publicly available sources. OSINT is a neglected collection discipline, and many people ignore it in lieu of data that is stamped "Secret" or "Top-Secret." However, because of the explosion of data available on the Internet and social media, OSINT can prove very valuable. If used correctly and in the right cases, OSINT can even outperform intelligence that is not publicly available.[2]

Although social media is often categorized as a form of OSINT, it also has elements of the other collection disciplines and combines them in powerful ways. Intercepting and collecting social media data entails, for example, collecting from phones (COMINT), from crowdmaps (GEOINT), lots of imagery data (IMINT), data about Internet traffic (ELINT), and can enable collection from humans through crowdsourcing (HUMINT). It also has its fair share of RUMINT, or rumor intelligence. Additionally, you can often collect social media data in real time, which you often cannot do with other forms of OSINT or the other INTs. The example in the subsequent section illustrates the utility of social media data as an intelligence collection discipline and the advantages it can confer over other traditional disciplines.

Table 6.1: Intelligence Collection Disciplines

COLLECTION DISCIPLINE	DESCRIPTION (INTERCEPTION AND/OR COLLECTION OF...)
SIGINT (SIGnals INTelligence)	Electronic signals
COMINT (COMmunications INTelligence)	A subset of SIGINT, involving electronic signals between people that are directly used in communication
ELINT (ELectronic INTelligence)	A subset of SIGINT, involving electronic signals not directly used in communication
MASINT (Measurement And Signals INTelligence)	Emissive bioproducts such as radiation or heat
IMINT (Imagery INTelligence)	Imagery via satellite and aerial photography
GEOINT (GEOspatial INTelligence)	Imagery and geospatial information that depicts physical features and geographically references activities
HUMINT (HUMan INTelligence)	Intelligence gathered via means of interpersonal contact as opposed to via technology
OSINT (Open Source INTelligence)	Publicly available information

Monitoring Attacks through Social Media

During the writing of this book, a tragic security event illustrated how simply monitoring social media can help you anticipate and understand events in real time better than the other disciplines, including traditional OSINT. On September 11, 2012, the U.S. consulate in Benghazi came under attack while several people were protesting across the Middle East against a video produced in the U.S. that mocked Islam. Four U.S. embassy personnel, including Ambassador Chris Stevens, subsequently died in the attack. Because of the attention drawn by the protests and possibly the lateness of the events, many mainstream news outlets failed to fully address the scale of the attack on the consulate and the death of the ambassador until the following day, September 12. However, information about the attack, including pictures, started to appear on social media almost immediately following the attack.

The Americans were allegedly attacked at around 2200 local Benghazi time (+3 GMT or 1600 EST) on September 11. At 1945 EST, the Associated Press reported the death of one American in the Benghazi attack. Other news outlets communicated this fact but failed to grasp and communicate the full extent of the attack or how it came about. The next day at 0721 EST, President Obama announced the death of Ambassador Stevens in the attack.[3] Five hours before the president's announcement at 0200 EST, we had already found gruesome pictures of Ambassador Stevens' body on social media.[4] The pictures were in fact hours old and had been posted soon after the attack. The pictures showed him being pulled from the building and carried by Libyans trying to save him, and showed close-ups of his injuries and face.

Meanwhile, reports quickly appeared stating that a group of Salafi Islamists had carried out the attacks. The reports did not appear on news media outlets, but from known anti-American Twitter accounts.[5] The involvement of the Salafis was initially denied, confirmed a week later, and is under investigation as of this writing.[6] News media outlets and others did not begin reporting on the full scale of the events in Benghazi till 0900 EST on September 12, until after President Obama's press conference. However, information depicting the full scale of the attack and the death of Ambassador Stevens had already appeared on Twitter two hours after the attack at 1800 EST on September 11.

Subsequent investigations revealed that the DoD operation centers around the region, aside from the one that retrieved the embassy personnel's bodies, were not fully aware of the attack till the day after. They were consuming information about the protests through the mainstream news outlets and were not monitoring social media for information about the attacks. This indicates that even American military personnel in the region had information that was several hours old compared to the information on social media, and so they had little to no clue or anticipation of the reality on the ground. The centers also did not push out information about the attack until well after the actual event because of the formalities and rigors involved with traditional intelligence collection and dissemination. They waited to collect information on the events, write reports on what was collected, submit it for release approval, and then submit it to their internal databases before releasing it to the community. By then, thanks to social media, we already knew who was being attacked and even had a clue about who may have carried out the attack.

Our intention is not to figure out exactly what happened when and who knew what when. The events are confusing and the politics surrounding the U.S. presidential campaigns were exacerbating the confusion. We only want to point out that simply monitoring and filtering social media data can help you figure out what is happening and anticipate hotspots and events. In this case, social media would not have helped anticipate a seemingly well-planned clandestine attack. However, it could have helped discover and validate essential facts earlier, mitigate confusion, and help with response.

Social media will not supplant traditional collection disciplines or overtake OSINT, but can augment them immensely. If you are sitting in an operational center that has the tools we discuss in this book deployed, you can use social media to help lift the fog. Social media data can serve as a first line of reporting for events that may otherwise go unnoticed and bring you closer to total information awareness. Traditional collecting disciplines and news outlets can then confirm the events. Through social media, you can gain a much quicker and fuller understanding of what is going on, and task other collection resources such as aerial vehicles and HUMINT assets to confirm or add to the information appearing on social media.

Of course, as we repeatedly mention throughout this book, you should not blindly trust anything you see on social media; hence, the need to always confirm using other intelligence sources. Fortunately, social media often regulates and validates itself. An example involving attacks in Somalia illustrates the intelligence validating and refining loop inherent in the social media environment.

In mid-later 2012, the Kenyan government launched an incursion against Somalia's al-Shabaab forces, which it claimed were becoming a threat to its country. On October 28, the Kenyans were involved in an amphibious assault on Kismayo, Somalia, which is an al-Shabaab stronghold in Southern Somalia. During the assault, the Kenyans began tweeting from their official accounts, including @KDFInfo, that they had taken the city. Al-Shabaab immediately countered by tweeting through its official account, @HSMPress, that it still controlled the city and that the Kenyans were not even in the city yet. The Kenyans later "adjusted" their statements to reflect a more accurate reality and were more forthcoming about the realities of their actions in Somalia.[7] During this episode, we saw two battles—one on the ground and one in social media. If you can watch and integrate information from both, you are much more likely to discern fact from fiction and do it at a much faster rate. You can then task your resources and organize responses more efficiently and effectively. You can also produce more robust and insightful intelligence analyses and forecasts. The following section focuses on how to use social media data to produce those analyses and forecasts.

Understanding Forecasting

Before you can start using tools to analyze social media data, and understand and forecast events, you need to have a firm grasp of what constitutes forecasting and the limitations it faces. Forecasting is the process of determining what will likely happen in the near future based on past experience and knowledge, and current trends of behavior. You cannot forecast an event if you do not understand it to some extent. To forecast, you typically complete the following steps:

1. Find relationships between one or numerous factors and an event.

2. Assess how accurately the factors indicate or cause the presence of an event by looking at past and current data.

3. Determine the presence of the factors in the future and changes in the relationships between them and future events.

4. Use the determinations to identify the likelihood of the event's presence in the future.

Simply put, you identify factors that have indicated an event in the past, and then determine the presence of those factors, and thus the event, in the future. For a forecast to be useful, it should ideally state what, when, and where an event will occur, and the likelihood that the forecast is correct.

Forecasting vs. Predicting

Forecasting is different from predicting, which also involves determining what will happen in the future based on a priori knowledge and behavioral trends. The difference between a forecast and a prediction is somewhat subjective. To us, the main difference is that a prediction has details and certainty, whereas in most cases a forecast lacks some details and is humble about its certainty. The determination that the sun will rise tomorrow at exactly 5:45 A.M. in Washington D.C. is a prediction. The determination that there is a 70 percent chance a famine will occur in Somalia in the next two weeks is a forecast.

Do not believe anyone who claims they can predict security events. They may get a few things right here and there, but their accuracy will not be very impressive. Prediction concerning security events, issues, and behaviors is difficult for three reasons. One, black swans—or seemingly random and unlikely events that have immense influence—can happen at any time and significantly impact security. By definition, past information cannot tell you when and where black swans will likely occur because they are so rare and so little information is available about them, so you cannot determine their trend of occurrence and predict them. The assassination of John F. Kennedy was a black swan—no one expected it and it changed American history. The uprising in Tunisia in 2011 was also a black swan. A few expected small protests and popular disgruntlement due to the poor economy in the area, but no one expected the populace to overthrow their autocratic government so quickly. No trend or event in recent Middle East history gave an indication that such a thing could or would occur. Ironically, people involved with security issues tend to be most interested in anticipating the black swans. Two, we do not know enough about human behavior to predict it. Security events are a function of human behavior, which is often complicated, confusing, lacking constraints, and difficult to comprehend. Three, security events also involve hundreds of other factors and variables, which we also often do not know much about. Accurately predicting a terrorist attack against a shopping mall involves assessing information about the terrorists, their capabilities and weapons, their willingness to commit an attack, the security in the mall, the behavior of shoppers at the mall, the counter-terrorism activities of local law enforcement and other agencies, and much more. Too many factors exist to account for, and predicting with certainty requires accounting for at least some of them.

Although predicting security issues with certainty is nearly impossible, forecasting them with some accuracy is possible and useful. In many cases, you have enough data and constraints to develop a robust hypothesis about if and/

or when something will happen. You also have enough computing power and tools to create analytical models that can use the data to forecast events. The Internet and social media have made more data available than ever before. Also, the popularity of quantitative analytics and widespread availability of analytical tools and methods has encouraged and enabled people in all sorts of fields to come up with different forecasting models that are impressive in their accuracy. For example, Princeton's Sam Wang (http://election.princeton.edu) and the *New York Times'* Nate Silver (http://fivethirtyeight.blogs.nytimes.com) have built distinct models that forecast American election results with impressive accuracy using somewhat different methods. Lastly, the Internet has provided a voice to people who think differently or process different information and come up with more accurate forecasts. What may appear to be a black swan to most people is not so for such people. The economic crisis in 2008 appeared to be a black swan, but many people saw it coming and warned others about it.[8] By listening to voices that are not in the mainstream concerning security issues and expanding your diet of information, you can also improve the chances that you are using appropriate information and ways of processing the information to come up with your forecasts.

Overall, forecasts are not always correct or precise, but they provide a good idea about what could happen and can spur preparations. In the security field, even a somewhat hazy forecast can save lives.

Forecasting Properly

Because forecasting is a function of available data, some events are more appropriate for forecasting with social media and related data. Generally, the best events to understand and forecast are the ones where more people use social media to talk about or organize them. Currently, such events include protests and riots, natural and other major disasters, disease epidemics, and to a lesser extent, terrorist attacks and gang or drug violence. As social media use expands globally, the list of events will likely grow. As discussed in Chapter 2, social media use differs by country and region, and so people in different areas use social media to talk about and organize events differently. Thus, you will be more likely to forecast certain events in certain areas.

Forecasting involves the following distinct process regardless of the type of analysis you use:

1. Determine the event you want to forecast. The more detailed the event, the less likely your forecast will be correct because you need to be much more precise. However, do not pick something that is too broad or vague, because it will not prove helpful. Conflict on a continent within the next few years is too broad; the time and location of the initial fight that sparks the conflict is too detailed; a clan conflict in a specific area within a range of days is just right.

2. Collect the appropriate data and refine the goal of your forecast based on the availability of the right data. You cannot forecast something you do not have data about. However, if you have a lot of data about a subject, you can either add details to your forecast and/or improve its accuracy, which is the likelihood that it comes true.

3. Deduce a theory from the data and then use the theory and induction to generate a forecast. Forecasting involves first coming up with a theory about when, where, and why certain events occur by discovering trends or factors that indicate the presence of the events in data. In some cases, the deduction process is not formal, and is based on experiences and knowledge instead of hard data. Next, if possible, check the theory on other unused past data to see if it is correct. Lastly, apply a correct theory to emerging data and extrapolate from it to uncover what will likely happen in the future. Identify how the relationship between an event and some factors or indicators is likely to develop or relate in the future, based on how it has developed or related in the past. The method of deduction and induction depends heavily on the type of data available:

   a. If the data consists of a lot of text or social media content, use LSA.

   b. If it contains a lot of statistics and details about variables over a long period of time, use CRA.

   c. If it contains data about the data, or changes in data or volume, use VA.

   d. If the data is mixed, which it likely will be, use a combination of analyses.

Other considerations also may affect the type of analysis you employ. Keep in mind the following guidelines that differentiate good and useful forecasts from poor and useless ones:

- Forecast only a little out temporally in advance. Forecasts that tell you what will happen in the next few hours, days, and weeks are more likely to be correct than forecasts that tell you what will happen years from now. The correct temporal range depends on what you are trying to forecast. If your event of concern involves lots of factors and is heavily dependent on individual human behavior, then forecast very little in advance. In such a case, the subject is too complex and it will be difficult to account for all of the factors months and years in advance.

- Use a variety of data types other than social media data. The more diverse the data, the more likely you are to find relationships and trends between events and other things, and indicators of future events.

- Always provide the likelihood that your forecast is correct. Be humble, and appreciate that you and no one else completely understands the world. Black swans can pop up anywhere at any time, and all sorts of weird things can happen that completely ruin your forecast. Either use a formal method or use your judgment to come up with a percentage that describes the probability that your forecast will come true. Do not bother issuing forecasts with low probabilities. If the probability an event will occur is 50 percent, that means the event is equally likely to occur and not occur. Such a forecast is useless. You might as well flip a coin and save yourself the hard work. A forecast that says an event is 75 percent or 25 percent likely to occur is far more useful. People can make decisions on such forecasts; they cannot make decisions on forecasts of 50 percent.

The next few sections detail how to conduct each of the three types of analyses to uncover relationships between disparate objects or behaviors, identify and track security issues, and forecast security issues. Some of the examples and analyses are more appropriate for illustrating how to understand events and others are more appropriate for forecasting.

Conducting Language and Sentiment Analysis

What a person says and how she says it can be very revealing at times. Understanding the overt and hidden meaning in linguistic content, whether it be written or spoken, can help you understand and anticipate numerous security events. Language and sentiment analysis is the process of analyzing linguistic content such as forum posts and text messages to reveal answers to a variety of questions, such as:

- Is the same person writing these two separate blogs?
- Are certain groups communicating using secretive hashtags on Twitter?
- Are certain groups using Facebook to plan an event?
- Are certain groups increasingly worried about an event occurring based on the sentiment of their text messages?
- What is the emotional state of the author of a forum post?
- Which topics do forum members tend to discuss together?

LSA, also known as natural language processing (NLP), is a burgeoning field that will only grow in strength as the Internet and social media make linguistic content more easily available for analysis. Numerous LSA tools exist and they differ in their accuracy, method of analysis, customizability, cost, usefulness, and output.

Some LSA tools tend to be more deductive. They analyze content based on assumptions about how people use language and output firm answers to your questions. Creators of the tools program them based on assumptions derived from a combination of past knowledge, experience, and scientific studies. Some such LSA tools are accurate and useful, but others fail to correctly analyze language and, thus, offer little benefit. LSA tools that detect sentiment are a popular example of tools that often fail. Sentiment detection tools analyze a piece of content, such as a person's status update on Facebook, and then try to determine the person's emotional state or intended emotional effect on the reader. In other words, the tools determine the emotional polarity of the content and the emotion the author of the content wishes to convey through it. Even more simply put, the tools tell you whether the author made a statement that most people would consider emotionally positive, negative, or neutral. For example, the statement "I dislike my neighbors and find them annoying" conveys negative emotion and sentiment. The statement "I really like the weather in October" conveys positive emotion and sentiment. The statement "I own a black guitar" conveys a lack of emotion and neutral sentiment. By using such a tool, you can discern the emotional state of lots of people at the same time on a social media platform, which can help you determine whether a positive or negative event is taking place.

Most people are naturally very good at detecting sentiment in the statements others make. They can instinctively discern whether the author of a statement is conveying positive, negative, or neutral sentiment by looking at the words in the statement, the author's tone, the context, the environment, and various other variables. Computers and LSA tools, however, are not as smart as people when it comes to figuring out sentiment. They tend to use theories and shortcuts that often fail because they cannot understand the nuances in language. Most sentiment detection tools focus only on the type of words in a statement to discern sentiment. The tools rely on the theory that some words are inherently emotionally charged and correlated with a statement's sentiment. For instance, people typically use the words "dislike," "hate," "angry," and "annoying" when they want to convey negative emotion and sentiment. The tools assume if a person uses such words then, in many cases, it is safe to assume the person is talking about something she sees negatively. However, that is not always the case. People often use such words sarcastically, atypically, or to describe what others have said. For example, most people would consider the statement "I hate it when I win!" to be sarcastic and conveying a positive emotion. Sentiment detection tools, however, would see that it contains the negatively charged word "hate" and classify it as conveying negative emotion. They fail to pick up on these nuances and so incorrectly classify statements as having negative sentiment when they really have positive or neutral sentiment.

> **WARNING** Always be wary of social media analysis systems or tools that claim to detect emotional sentiment. As of this writing, most sentiment detection tools are terrible at picking up on nuances, and so regularly fail at accurately detecting sentiment.

Despite their flaws, some deductive LSA tools are built on correct and tested assumptions and so are useful and accurate. We explore one such tool later in this section.

Other LSA tools tend to be more inductive. They find patterns of correlation and regression in large amounts of content and let you make sense of the patterns to answer your questions in your own way. Such tools usually only output various statistics about the content they analyze, and never direct answers to your questions. They will tell you how many times a certain word appeared in content, what other words a word appeared near in a statement, and how such statistics differed over time. You then use the outputted statistics to detect changes in behaviors that help you formulate a theory and answer your question. We explore this method of LSA later in this section.

As you probably noticed by now, most LSA tools and methods are both deductive and inductive. Many LSA tools keep track of how accurate they are over time and refine their assumptions and theories based on data to become smarter and more accurate. Many people create deductive LSA tools based on theories they induce after looking at large amounts of content and conducting scientific studies on language. The difference between the two types of LSA tools is somewhat artificial, but thinking about them in this way can help you discern which tool is more appropriate to answer your question. Neither type of tool is necessarily more useful than the other, but one is often more applicable for a particular problem depending on the kind of data you have, the time and resources you have, the accuracy of the LSA tool, and the answer you want. We now explore two ways you can use LSA tools and methods to understand and forecast security events and related behavior.

Determining Authorship

We are often asked about tools that can help identify the author of a blog post, document, tweet, or text message. In this section, we teach you how to use such a tool to identify authorship.

Correctly identifying the author of a piece of content can prove very valuable for a number of reasons. Knowing the identity of the author of the content you are analyzing to understand an event or behavior will only improve your analysis. For example, say you are analyzing posts on an online forum that violent extremists frequent to determine whether the extremists are planning violence against a specific target. You know that the majority of the forum members have no idea about operational plans and are merely followers of the violent ideology. They post misinformation about attacks that will never take place. You label them as the followers. However, you also know that a few members actually take part in operations and know about the future attacks. They post information on the forum that provides hints about future attacks. You label them as the operators. You also possess documents such as letters written by some of the operators that do not appear on the forum. However, you do not know which members of the forum are the operators and which ones are the followers. Because you do not know the identity of the forum members, you do not know which members' posts you should analyze and which posts you should ignore.

Authorship identification tools can help you compare the letters you possess with the posts of the forum members to identify the operator members. They help you figure out which of the individuals who wrote the letters are writing certain forum posts. They rely on the well-tested assumption that people have a distinct way of writing. The distinctions emerge in how people use words, spell certain words, structure sentences, and through many other traits. By comparing the letters with the forum posts, the tools can help you determine whether the authors of the letters also wrote some of the forum posts, and if so, which forum posts they wrote. You can then determine which of the forum members are the operators and analyze only their posts for intelligence about future attacks.

Numerous tools can help you determine authorship and, as you would expect, they differ in their features and abilities. In this section, we teach you how to use the Java Graphical Authorship Attribution Program (JGAAP), which is a free program available for download at `http://www.jgaap.com`. Throughout this section, we refer to JGAAP version 6.0.

Preparing for Authorship Analysis

The process of preparing for the analysis is fairly simple. Obviously, you first need to download and open the JGAAP program. Follow the instructions on the website to ensure you are opening the program correctly. Also make sure to download the program's user manual from the website, which shows you how to use the program with visuals and easy-to-understand instructions. Refer to the user manual as you go through this example.

Then you need to prepare all content for analysis. The content includes language whose authorship you do not know, which are known as the "test documents," and language whose authorship you do know, which are known as the "training documents." For our example, we will not use real social media content because of copyright issues, but instead use content and documents recovered from Osama Bin Laden's compound in Abbottabad and subsequently translated. The documents are available at Jihadica's website (`http://www.jihadica.com/abbottabad-documents/`). We also provide links to the exact documents we use on our website in Microsoft Word format. Feel free to use other content or follow along with the documents we use to make sure you are using JGAAP properly. We have had trouble using PDF documents with JGAAP, so you may need to convert PDF documents into Microsoft Word document format.

> **NOTE** Most LSA tools, including authorship identification tools, work mostly on content made up of the English language or other popular languages that use the Latin alphabet. Although analyzing translated documents is not ideal, it can still provide insights and answers as long as the translations are done consistently and carefully. JGAAP can analyze Arabic, but we have had trouble getting it to analyze Arabic in PDF documents.

In our example, we intend to discover whether Osama Bin Laden or his deputy "Atiyya" Abd al-Rahman is the author of a recovered and translated letter written to Nasi al-Wuhayshi, the leader of Al Qaeda in the Arabian Peninsula. The letter in question is the test document. The training documents are numerous lengthy letters written by Bin Laden and Atiyya to each other and others. If you do not have documents of your own, download the documents we use from this book's companion website. Make sure to save the documents in an easily accessible place on your computer.

Conducting the Analysis

Complete the following steps to conduct the authorship analysis:

1. Open and run the JGAAP. Notice the tabs across the top of the JGAAP window. When you first open the program, the tab labeled Documents should be selected.

2. In the JGAAP window, make sure English is selected as the language in the drop-down menu on the top. Under the section labeled Unknown Authors, click Add Document. Select the appropriate test document, which in our case is Test_Doc.docx. Next, under the section labeled Known Authors, click Add Author. In the pop-up window, type in **Bin Laden** for the author name and click Add Document. Add the appropriate training document, which in our case is Training_Doc_BinLaden.docx. Repeat the process to add Attiya as an author and add the training document labeled Training_Doc_Attiya.docx. After adding the documents, click Next to go to the next tab.

3. The Canonicizers tab provides the option to remove elements from the document that you believe are not related to the author's writing style, and so are not relevant to the analysis. Elements can include the amount of punctuation and cases of letters. Adding canonicizers is optional and will not make a big difference in our case, so we will not add any. Click Next to go to the next tab.

4. In the Event Drivers tab, you pick the elements of the documents that you want the program to analyze. Numerous event drivers are available for you to choose. Feel free to select whichever events you think are appropriate. You can read their description when you select them in the box labeled

Event Driver Description. We select Word NGrams and Sentences. By selecting these events, you can analyze how the authors use combinations of words and sentences. To select the events, click on them in the scroll menu labeled Event Drivers and then click the arrow pointing toward the right. When you have selected them, they will appear in the box labeled Selected. The Parameters section to the right of the Selected box for the Word NGrams event driver should indicate by default that N equals 2. If not, set N to 2 for the Word NGrams selection. Otherwise, you do not need to change the Parameters of your event driver selections. After selecting your event drivers, click Next.

5. The Event Culling tab provides the option to filter the event drivers you selected in the previous tab. Because the documents and the content being analyzed are not large, you do not need to worry about filtering. We will not add any event culling; click Next. Note that if the documents you use are large, then you may need to use event culling. Try the analysis with and without culling to see if the analysis differs. In many cases, the event culling will not make a big difference to the analysis.

6. The Analysis Methods tab provides numerous methodologies and algorithms with which to conduct your analysis. Getting into how the algorithms work is beyond the scope of this book, but feel free to try out different options. We will abide by the advice on JGAAP's website and select the Nearest Neighbor Driver method. To select the method, find it in the menu labeled Analysis Methods and click on it. Then, in the menu labeled Distance Functions, find and click on Cosine Distance. After making both selections, click the arrow pointing toward the right next to the Analysis Methods menu box. After making the selection, click Next.

7. The Review & Process tab gives you a summary of the options you selected in the previous tabs. You can go back through the other tabs and change the options if you want. After reviewing your options, click Process, which is in the bottom-right side of the Review & Process tab window.

8. A new window pops up with your results. Figure 6.1 shows the analysis results for our documents based on our options.

Reading the results is straightforward. The results indicate in order: the test document, the canonicizers, the event driver, the analysis method, a list of the training documents starting with the author most likely to have written the test document, and the numerical score outputted by the analysis next to the name of the training document. To understand the results, you need to look both at which author appeared first in the list and the numerical score. In the analysis for the event driver Sentences, the language in the test document was similar to the language in both documents. Both are ranked 1 and both have the score of 1.0. The Sentences event driver is not that helpful to our analysis.

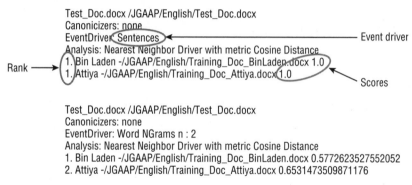

Test_Doc.docx /JGAAP/English/Test_Doc.docx
Canonicizers: none
EventDriver: Sentences ◄—————————————————— Event driver
Analysis: Nearest Neighbor Driver with metric Cosine Distance
1. Bin Laden -/JGAAP/English/Training_Doc_BinLaden.docx 1.0
1. Attiya -/JGAAP/English/Training_Doc_Attiya.docx 1.0
                                                          Scores

Rank ———►

Test_Doc.docx /JGAAP/English/Test_Doc.docx
Canonicizers: none
EventDriver: Word NGrams n : 2
Analysis: Nearest Neighbor Driver with metric Cosine Distance
1. Bin Laden -/JGAAP/English/Training_Doc_BinLaden.docx 0.5772623527552052
2. Attiya -/JGAAP/English/Training_Doc_Attiya.docx 0.6531473509871176

Figure 6.1: Authorship analysis results

In the analysis for the event driver Word NGrams, the language and words in the test document were more similar to the language and words in the Bin Laden training document than in the Attiya training document. Because we are measuring a form of distance between the test document and the training document, a lower score means the documents are closer and thus more similar. In our case, the Bin Laden training document had a score of 0.577 and a rank of 1, and the Attiya training document had a score of 0.653 and a rank of 2. The Bin Laden training document was closer and more similar to the test document. This result suggests that, based on the analysis, Bin Laden was more likely to be the author of the test document than Attiya.

You need to be aware of several caveats with this type of analysis. One, as we mentioned before, analyzing translated documents is not ideal. Translators can significantly change a document's language and structure. Two, the analysis and the results are not perfect. We recommend you run the analysis a few more times by selecting different combinations of event drivers and analysis methods. If you keep getting the same result, you can be more confident in the analysis. Three, you need a lot more content to do the analysis correctly. The more content the program can analyze, the more likely it will output a more precise answer. This fact poses a problem when analyzing social media content. Blog posts, forum posts, tweets, and status updates are not always lengthy. You need to collect lots of them to do a meaningful analysis. Four, some social media content may not be as useful for the analysis, and you have to be careful that you are comparing similar types of language together. For example, when tweeting, most people tend to use different types of words and grammar because of the 140-character limit that Twitter imposes. The way they write lengthy blog posts or letters is likely very different than how they write their tweets. You should compare tweets to tweets and blog posts to blog posts to make sure analysis is consistent.

By taking these caveats into account, you can significantly improve your ability to do authorship identification analysis and understand certain security events and behavior. Knowing who wrote what or even who did not write what can help you make better sense of intelligence critical to your understanding of a related event.

Tracking and Forecasting the Behavior of Rioting Violent Crowds

The authorship analysis tool gave you a straightforward answer about the likely identity of the author, and so answered your question. Other LSA tools do not outright answer your questions in such a way. Instead, they help you explore the data so you can create and test your theory about possible answers to your question. With LSA tools and some ingenuity, you can analyze language on social media to track and forecast the behavior of crowds. In this section, we do not detail how to use specific software tools. Instead, we focus on how you can structure a solution to a problem by using any one of a variety of LSA tools.

As discussed before, many individuals and groups use social media to organize events involving complex crowd behavior. By analyzing the content these individuals are posting on social media, you can figure out how and where the crowds are moving. Imagine you need to track and forecast the behavior of violent rioters in a city. The rioters are using Twitter and other forms of social media to organize attacks against specific targets in the city and share information about law enforcement. As is often the case, some individuals usually are taking the lead in directing the other rioters. They are posting information about where, when, and how other rioters should move. Through social network analysis you can identify these key individuals. You then simply need to track what the key individuals are saying to monitor the development of the riot. You can then create an early-warning system that gives you an idea of where the riot has been, where it is at the moment, and where it will likely be in the future.

Although this simple form of language analysis will help, it will not serve as a thorough and complete solution for several reasons. One, the list of key individuals may be long, and you may not have the resources to actively monitor all their messages. Two, others who are not on your list of key individuals may also be helping direct the riot. Three, people who are not involved with the riot may be posting information about the riot that can help you get a sense of the riot's behavior and evolution. To take these factors into account, you need to use methodologies and tools to build a system that can comprehensively track the riot's past, present, and future behavior. You can use the wide variety of methodologies and tools in numerous ways. Some of those ways are very complex and require sophisticated expertise in crowd behavior, linguistic and semantic processing, data processing, and cognitive science. We present one simpler way that you can use to understand the concept of LSA and get a head start on your own riot early-warning and tracking system. Research other ways and feel free to adapt and experiment with our way and those of others as you see fit.

Our way involves creating a system that rapidly analyzes enormous amounts of social media data to:

- Identify social media data relevant to the riot and filter out the rest.

- Analyze the relevant data to pinpoint key words and phrases that indicate past, present, or future riot behavior.

- Categorize the content based on the presence of key words and phrases, the author of the content, and other factors.

- Analyze the categories of content to reveal information about past riot behavior, flag present riot behavior, and provide useful early warnings of riot behavior.

Preparing for Riot Behavior Analysis

Preparing to build the comprehensive early-warning LSA system first entails figuring out what amount of relevant data is available to you and then getting it. The relevant data obviously involves the social media content that the rioters and key riot leaders are generating. For the sake of this case, let us assume that the people involved are predominantly using public social media platforms such as Twitter along with other platforms from which you cannot get data. In some cases, law enforcement can gain access to messages on private social media platforms, but we will not worry about that here. The other relevant data also involves social media content that people who are not involved with the riot, such as witnesses, are posting about the riot on public social media platforms. This amount of data can be quite large. Consider the data from the rioters and the witnesses to be the test data on which you will test your tools and do your analysis. Yet another type of data you need to collect and one that is not as obvious is social media content from past riots. This third type of data will serve as the training data with which you can train your tools. Your system needs to collect the data about the riot in question, and you should assemble the data about past riots. Do not combine the two data sets. In Chapter 4, we covered how you collect, filter, and store the relevant data.

Apart from the data, you also need to acquire the appropriate LSA tools and integrate them into your system. You need tools that can help you analyze the frequency with which certain words and phrases appear in content, what words and phrases tend to appear together, and keep track of the source or author of particular content. These tasks are simple, and most LSA tools can easily complete them. We will not focus on which tools you should use because numerous ones exist. New versions of popular analysis programs such as SPSS tend to already come with LSA tools. The website KDNuggets (http://www.kdnuggets.com/software/text.html) features a list of popular LSA tools. Most tools on that website present more features than you will need for this case. The Internet is full of free, open source LSA tools that provide you with all the features you need and that you can easily download, adapt, and use with minimal development skill. Apache's OpenNLP library (available at `http://opennlp.apache.org`) is one such repository of free and appropriate LSA tools. For now, do not worry about which LSA tool to use, but how you would use that type of LSA tool.

Designing the Riot Behavior Analysis Methodology

Acquiring the test and training data and the right LSA tools is the easy part of the analysis. The most difficult and critical part is formulating the analytical methodology that the system uses to make sense of the data and output appropriate warnings and indications. Formulating the methodology will be a primarily deductive process, and we will refine it through an inductive process using the training data.

Essentially, the methodology will determine which words and phrases in social media content are important and to what extent they tell you about the rioters' past, present, and future behavior. To do so, the system needs to be able to categorize various words and phrases according to their context and what they tell you about the rioters' behavior. The system then must apply weights to the content according to how important it is to the ultimate analysis. To help the system do this, you need to create an ontology, which describes how linguistic content should be categorized and what its relationships are to other content and behavior. The system's algorithms, which follow the ontology, process data and output early warnings and indications of the riot's movements and actions.

To create an ontology and methodology, take note of previous experience and knowledge to lay out the theories and assumptions that will underlie the methodology. First, categorize social media content based on what it tells you about the rioters' behavior. According to our experience and knowledge, we surmise that certain textual content on social media can tell you whether people are providing facts about events that are happening or have happened. Such content falls under the ontological category of Facts and indicates past or present behavior. We can also tell whether an event is about to take place, which falls under the ontological category of Possibilities and indicates future behavior. For example, the tweet "Three guys looting store on 15th" would fall under the Facts category. The tweet "Attack on 3rd at 1500, then wait for flare" falls under the Possibilities category. The categories of the tweets are self-evident to most people because they can easily figure out the meaning and intent of the tweet by looking at certain characteristics of the language used in the tweet. For example, in the Facts tweet, we realize that the verb "looting" is in its present form and indicates an action happening right now that is related to riots. The words "store on 15th" indicate the target and its location. The same type of quick linguistic analysis applies to the Possibilities tweet. The verb "Attack" indicates a future violent action that is about to take place and the words "3rd at 1500" indicate a location and future time concerning the action.

You need to train, or program algorithms into, the LSA tools that make up your system to also quickly analyze tweets and other social media content and put them in the Facts and Possibilities categories. Content that does not relate to either, such as "I'm sick of campaign commercials, make them end already," will be filtered out. Programming or training the LSA tools to filter out irrelevant content and categorize relevant content into Facts and Possibilities is much harder said than done. We address how to train tools to do this and other complicated tasks later.

Another part of the methodology is realizing that not all related content is as useful to you. We can surmise from experience that, for instance, a Possibilities tweet that comes from a key riot leader will have more influence on the behavior of the riot than a Possibilities tweet that comes from someone who is not at all involved with the riot. Also, a Facts tweet describing an event that is corroborated and validated by other Facts tweets is more trustworthy than a Facts tweet that addresses an event that no other Facts tweet does. Based on these considerations, you need to weigh the content you are analyzing. If you are not familiar with the concept of weights, think of it as if you are boosting the importance of certain content over other content. You and the system then pay more attention to what the boosted content says and give it more weight when making your decision. The weights of the content will then influence the outputs, which are the early warnings and indications of the riot behavior. You can and should analyze other parts of the content in other ways, such as figuring out location from language. For the sake of time and understanding, we stop here for now.

The system should look at the content in each category, assign weights to it, and then use that information to produce outputs. For example, it can look at the tweet "Consulate building on fire" and put it in the Facts category. It can then output to a crowdmap, indicating the location (the consulate) and the action taking place (on fire). This helps you track the behavior of the rioters. If the tweet contains temporal information, you can then also output that on a timeline so you can track the past versus present behavior of the rioters. Consider another example—the tweet "in 2 hours move west." The system puts the tweet in the Possibilities category and outputs a text warning to you indicating the action about to take place (riot moving west) and the time it will take place (2 hours). You then have an idea of how the riot may move in the near future. The system may also come across another tweet in the Possibilities category, but not output it to you because the system realizes that it came from someone who is not a key riot leader. To review, our methodology involves:

- Categorizing content into Facts and Possibilities
- Weighing Possibilities more if it comes from key riot leaders
- Weighing Facts more if it is repeated by multiple sources

You should now have an understanding of how even simply analyzing language and assigning it appropriate weights can provide you with important intelligence. However, to complete the system, you still need to program and train the LSA tools.

Program and Train LSA Tools

As mentioned before, numerous commercial and open source LSA tools can easily do the tasks required of them. Their capability rests on your ability to program and train them properly. By programming and training them, we mean teaching the LSA tools to follow specific algorithms so they know how to process the data and output the results you need. Unless you have a programming background, you will need a developer to help you program and train the LSA tools.

Programming an LSA tool is a two-step process (we refer to a single LSA tool but in reality your LSA tool may actually consist of a combination of numerous tools). The first step is to use your own knowledge and that of others to tell the LSA tool what content it should focus on and where it fits in the ontology. Part of that is telling it which sources to focus on, such as the list of key riot leaders and related hashtags. The other more significant part of it is telling it which language is the most revealing about the riots. In the riot scenario this language may include words and phrases that describe riotous action, the organization of logistics, times, dates, locations, and names of major landmarks. Many LSA tools and repositories contain lists that conveniently categorize words and phrases by the type of behavior or event they describe. You need to then program the LSA tool to correlate certain words and phrases that describe riot with the Facts and Possibilities categories. You literally tell the LSA tool that if it comes across the word "attack" and it is next to the word "tomorrow," it should categorize the content containing the words as Possibilities. You of course do not need to spell out exactly all the combinations, because LSA tools usually come with options to quickly correlate lots of words together.

You also need to program the LSA tool to look at the sources of the content and provide appropriate weight depending on the source. Looking at the source can also help the LSA tool categorize the content and verify if it really is related to the riot or is irrelevant. For example, the LSA tool may pick up and analyze the tweet "the #cloudatlas movie is going to #blowup tomorrow when it comes out" because it is looking at all content with "#blowup." The LSA tool can also download information about the source to see if he is on the list of key riot leaders, is tweeting other information related to riots, is following or followed by other people involved in the riot, or even located at the city where the riot is happening. After taking these factors into account, the LSA tool can then realize that the tweet is not relevant to the riots and discard it. In some cases, it may have trouble deciding. You can program the LSA tool to give scores to content based on how many of the criteria it meets (for example, its source, how many relevant words, and so on) and then classify the content based on its score. In the case where the aggregate score for the content is not high enough to categorize it but not low enough to discard it, you can program the LSA tool to create a separate category called Ambiguous. You as the user can then go into the system, read through the content in the Ambiguous category, and help the LSA tool properly categorize it. Lastly, you need to program the LSA tool to see if content in the Facts category is being repeated and validated by others and then giving that content more weight. This process is as simple as programming the LSA tool to scan how many times large phrases or sentences are repeated.

The second step is to train the LSA tool to work effectively and learn from its mistakes. This step is significantly harder to do, but it is necessary if you want to create a system that can handle the messy and complex data found in the real world. You need to test the LSA tool against the training data about past riots whose movements you know about. Act as if the past riot is happening at the present time, and input the appropriate data into the system. The LSA tool will go through it and report on the past, present, and future behavior of the riot. You can then assess how well the LSA tool did. Most likely, the first time you test the LSA tool, it will not do very well. You need to then implement machine learning algorithms into the LSA tool so that it can learn from the training data and refine its programming. In simplistic terms, the LSA tool looks at what kinds of words and phrases actually came up during the past riot and actually indicated real riot movement. It then goes back into its own programming and tweaks it because it then has a better idea of which words and phrases it should look for and what weights it should assign to them. Explaining this process in full is well beyond the scope of this book, but you can easily find resources online that explain it.[9] Over time, you should train the LSA tool on more training data so its efficacy constantly improves.

This section should have given you a good idea about what LSA is and how you can use it to make sense of social media data to understand and forecast security events. A better understanding and forecasting capability requires you to create and use more complex tools and algorithms. You will find that to use LSA effectively, you need to understand correlation and regression analysis.

Correlation and Regression Analysis

A large number of variables influence any event in the real world, and it is usually impossible to account for all of them. However, a few are usually more influential than the others. Understanding their relationship with the event and how they appear in the future can help you forecast the appearance of the event in the future. Correlation and regression analysis (CRA) is one of the simplest ways to identify and understand the relationship between the most important factors and the event.

You likely are already familiar with correlations and, to a lesser extent, regressions. Humans are very good at intuitively doing correlations. We keep track of a number of things and behaviors in the real world and try to figure out how they influence an event of concern. This natural ability is the reason superstitions exist. For example, you notice that on days you wear red socks, the Boston Red Sox baseball team wins and when you do not wear them, they lose. You correlate the wearing of your red socks with the record of the Red Sox. You then take it a step further and think that somehow you wearing red socks influences whether the Red Sox win. You then always wear your red socks on the day that the Red Sox play. From a rational perspective, this type of thinking is very wrong because correlation does not imply causation. It may only be a coincidence that your wearing of red socks correlates with the Red Sox winning. Most likely, you ignore the days when the correlation did not occur.

Statistical CRA helps us determine whether coincidences actually occur and whether they mean anything. Although you can do it relatively easily, you can also misinterpret its results easily. Another hard part about doing CRA is getting the right data to do it. In lab settings, getting the data to do it is not difficult. However, in the real world and when dealing with security events, you are not likely to get all the data you need. In this section, we address the concerns of interpreting results correctly and humbly, and in the next section we address dealing with incomplete and frustrating amounts of data. We first show you how to do CRA through an example concerning the issue of creating a system that provides early warnings of famines and uses data collected through social media. The example involves made-up data that illustrates the process of doing CRA. In the next section dealing with volumetric analysis, we use real-world data that shows that doing analyses for security events is not as easy as you may think.

WHEN TO USE REGRESSION ANALYSIS

You should use regression analysis when you want to determine the extent to which one variable can help you estimate the behavior (or value) of another variable. When doing regression, you assume that either:

- The independent variable directly affects the dependent variable.
- The independent variable indirectly affects the dependent variable through intermediate variables.
- An unknown variable affects both the independent and dependent variable.

In contrast, use correlation analysis when you want to determine simply whether two variables share some sort of associative relationship. You do not need to have any idea about the causality relationship between the variables when doing correlation analysis.

For example, say you collect data from children about their shoe sizes and their basketball ability. You analyze the data and find a correlation—the larger the shoe size, the better the child is at basketball. The correlation is only telling you about the association thus far. You need to use regression analysis to see how that association may look in the future.

You can easily reason that, clearly, shoe size does not directly or even indirectly cause a change in basketball ability, and vice versa. Shoe size and basketball ability share a correlation because a third variable, the height of children, affects both. The taller the child, the larger his shoe size and the better he is at basketball. You then conduct regression analysis and conclude:

> **"For every increase of X in shoe size, basketball ability tends to increase by Y."**

Note that this conclusion is very different from concluding:

> **"An increase of X in shoe size tends to cause an increase of Y on basketball ability."**

Concluding that shoe size causes change in basketball ability is absurd.

Think of the output of regression analysis as a tool. The tool uses the known behavior of one variable in the future to tell you the likely behavior of another variable in the future. The output of a correlation analysis is not a tool, but insight. The insight tells you that the behavior of two variables has an association such as when one variable always goes down the other always goes up. Simply put, regression analysis helps you forecast the future whereas correlation analysis helps you make sense of the past.

Creating Tools to Provide Early Warnings for Famines with Artificial Data

Imagine you want to build a system that provides warnings about famine conditions (and food insecurity) in different parts of the world. The system will need to collect data, analyze it to forecast possible famine conditions, and then output warnings to you about the possible famine conditions. To provide early warnings about famines in any part of the world entails collecting and analyzing information concerning a wide variety of factors, ranging from rainfall amounts, to market prices, to the state of the infrastructure in the region, to the needs of the affected population. Your system will need to do a lot of things and do them well. Indeed, the United States Agency for International Development's Famine Early Warning Network System known as FEWS NET works in a similar fashion (http://www.fews.net). This example is largely inspired by FEWS NET.

For now, we will focus on only part of the system and try to answer whether you can forecast famine conditions using only data about the price of grains in a region and the health status of the people in the region. Based on experience and knowledge, you deduce that the price and health status likely have a relationship to the famine. Rising grain prices indicates a lack of food and makes it less likely that people can buy food, which in turn increases the level of famine. A population's health status (people suffering through disease or not) obviously deteriorates when people are suffering through a major crisis like a famine. The analysis helps determine whether your deductions are correct. Social media plays a role in that it enables you to collect data about the grain prices and health status in near real time.

CROSS-REFERENCE In Chapter 4, we briefly discussed an example where we collected crop price and health data from Colombian farmers. In Chapter 7, we describe a social media platform known as M-Farm that collects African crop price data. Part III of the book discusses how to build social media platforms that crowdsource price and health data from hard-to-reach populations. Later, we address other ways that social media data can play a role.

Assume you have access to a social media platform that collects grain price and population health data from a region in Africa. The social media platform is SMS based and regularly queries participants for information. You also have data from a non-profit organization that indicates the level of famine that a region is suffering at any time. This famine indicator is calculated as a function of many variables, including the level of malnutrition and mortality. Note that the non-profit uses other health data, collected through in-field surveys, to calculate the famine indicator level. The health status data you use is collected through other means and so is different. In this case, the grain price and population health status are independent variables and the famine indicator is the dependent variable. You need to figure out whether the independent variables affect the dependent variable, how, and to what extent.

Conducting Correlation Analysis

To uncover the relationships between the variables, first conduct correlation analysis to determine whether there is some sort of an associative relationship between them. If the independent variables do not correlate with the dependent variable in any way, they likely do not affect it. Also, if they do not correlate, an intermediate or unknown variable also does not affect both of them.

To conduct the analyses in this section, you need basic statistical software. We describe the process by using Microsoft Excel to keep things simple, but you can use whatever software you want. We assume you are familiar with Microsoft Excel and know how to create basic line charts and use formulas to calculate things. If not, you can easily find numerous resources and videos online that show you how to use Excel. To do only correlations, you can also use the free web-based Google Correlate (available at http://www.google.com/trends/correlate).

CROSS-REFERENCE The data to do the analyses for the first example is available on our website as a comma-separated value (CSV) file with the name CRA_example.csv **and an XLS file with the name** CRA_exampe.xls. **The XLS file also contains the outputs of our analyses.**

The data file for the first example contains four columns. Column A, labeled Date, indicates the dates for which the data was collected. Each date point given corresponds to a week. In other words, assume the data is collected at the beginning of each week. Column B, labeled Health, contains data collected about the health status of people in the region. The value of the Health variable ranges from 0 to 10, where 0 indicates very poor health (suffering from lots of dangerous conditions and diseases) and 10 indicates good health. Column C, labeled Price, contains data collected about the price of grain in the region. The value of the Price variable is a numerical price that is equal to or greater than 0 (the currency is irrelevant). Column D, labeled Famine, contains data collected about the level of famine in the region. The value of the Famine variable ranges from 0 to 10, where 0 indicates very low levels of famine and 10 indicates very high levels. Twenty data points are given for each column. The amount of data is very small, but it serves instructive purposes. You need to determine whether the independent variables correlate with the dependent variable and to what extent. With your statistical software at hand, complete the following steps to conduct the analysis:

1. Open the data file in Excel.

2. Create time series line charts using all the variables. The line charts can help you visually assess whether the variables are correlated and if the relationship is linear. The X-axis variable for the line charts is the values from the Date column and the Y-axis variable is the values from the other columns. You need to create three line charts to see how the variables evolve over time. Ideally, you should chart the lines representing each variable in one chart. However, to do so you need to normalize the data so that the Y-axis range for each variable is the same. This process is unnecessary at this point because you can simply create three line charts and compare them visually. Create three line charts where one indicates how the health variable changes over time, the other the price variable, and the last the famine variable. The line charts are displayed in Figure 6.2. Notice that the Health line does not follow the same pattern as the Famine or Price line. That is, when the Famine or Price line spikes or drops, the Health

line does not. Also, notice that the Price and Famine lines do tend to follow the same pattern. This suggests that there is likely a correlation only between the Price and Famine variables.

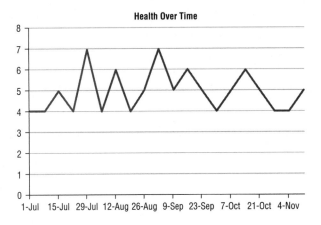

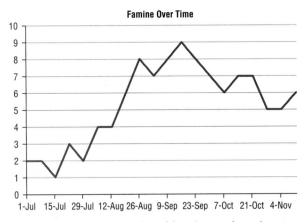

Figure 6.2: Line charts of Health, Price, and Famine

3. Compute the correlations for each variable with each other. Start with computing the correlation between the Health and Famine variables. Select an empty cell on the worksheet. In the cell, type the function `=CORREL(D2:D21,B2:B21)`. Press Enter and the cell should display 0.20615415, which is the correlation coefficient. Excel compares all the data points in the two stipulated columns in the function to compute the correlation.

4. Calculate the correlation between the Price and Famine variables. Select an empty cell on the worksheet and type `=CORREL(D2:D21,C2:C21)`. Press Enter and the cell should display 0.78758156.

5. Calculate the correlation between the Health and Price variables. Select an empty cell on the worksheet and type `=CORREL(C2:C21,B2:B21)`. Press Enter and the cell should display 0.13626333.

6. Consider the outputs or correlation coefficients for each variable pair. Two variables correlate if their coefficient is near 1 or –1, and they do not correlate if their coefficient is near 0. If the coefficient is near 1, the variables are said to positively correlate. That is, an increase in one variable produces an increase in the other variable. If the coefficient is near –1, the variables negatively correlate. An increase in one variable produces a decrease in the other variable. The only pair of variables that have a high correlation coefficient is the Price and Famine variables with a coefficient of about 0.78. This result makes sense from our cursory analysis of the line chart. When there is an increase in the Price variable, there is an increase in the Famine variable, and vice versa.

Conduct Regression Analysis

You know that there is an associative relationship between the Price and Famine variables and have some idea of how they have associated so far. You also know there is no relationship between health and the famine level. This finding is surprising because the health status of a person suffering through a famine usually deteriorates. The finding suggests that either your initial deduction was partially incorrect or that you collected faulty data. Most likely, the population did not understand exactly what you meant when you queried them for health status data, or they happened to be the lucky ones who survived the famine. This highlights the need to collect data from a large population and to compare different data sets.

You now need to use regression analysis to establish how well the Price variable can help you forecast the Famine variable in the future. In geek-speak, you need to identify the predictive or forecasting value of the independent variable.

In this case, we use a priori knowledge to determine that there likely is a causal and predictive relationship between prices and famine level. Spikes in prices can noticeably increase the level of famine. By knowing how much the prices contribute to the level of famine, you can figure out how future spikes or drops in prices will affect the future levels of famine in the region. Complete the following steps to find out this information:

1. Return to the same data file in Excel. Make sure the Analysis Toolpak and Data Analysis add-in is installed. Microsoft explains how to install the add-in at `http://office.microsoft.com/en-us/excel-help/load-the-analysis-toolpak-HP001127724.aspx`.

2. On the ribbon, select Data and at the far right of the ribbon options select Data Analysis.

3. In the pop-up window, select Regression.

4. In the new pop-up window, put a checkmark in the boxes next to Labels and Confidence Levels. Also, check the box next to New Worksheet Ply to output the results to a new sheet.

5. At the top of the pop-up window, for Input Y Range, select Column D with the famine level values. Make sure when selecting the column that you also select the row with the column label. For Input X Range, select Column C with the price values. After making your selections, click OK.

6. A new worksheet should appear with the results of the regression analysis. Figure 6.3 shows the results.

Regression Statistics

Multiple R	0.787581564
R Square	0.620284719
Adjusted R Square	0.599189426
Standard Error	1.513239602
Observations	20

ANOVA

	df	SS	MS	F	Significance F
Regression	1	67.3319063	67.3319063	29.40393901	3.75508E-05
Residual	18	41.2180937	2.28989409		
Total	19	108.55			

	Coefficients	Standard Error	t Stat	P-value	Lower 95%	Upper 95%	Lower 95.0%	Upper 95.0%
Intercept	−1.729806139	1.348759629	−1.28251625	0.215932408	−4.563444967	1.103832689	−4.563444967	1.103832689
PRICE	0.368739903	0.068001326	5.4225399	3.75508E-05	0.225874419	0.511605387	0.225874419	0.511605387

Figure 6.3: Regression analysis results for the first example

7. Reading the results consists of paying attention to three parts of the results. The first block of results at the top is labeled Regression Statistics and it tells you about the overall regression. The R Square value tells you how much the independent variable explains the variance of the dependent variable. In other words, it tells you to what extent the Price variable forecasts and informs the Famine variable. Think of it as the likelihood that

price forecasts the famine level. In our case, the R Square value is 0.62, which is not bad. The closer the R Square value is to 1, the better. This result says that the Price variable forecasts 62 percent of the value of the Famine variable. Other variables account for the other 38 percent of the forecast and effect.

8. Then pay attention to the block titled ANOVA. Take note of the number in the cell where the row labeled Regression meets the column labeled Significance F. The number in this case is 3.76E-05 or 3.76×10^{-5} or 0.0000376. The Significance F number denotes likelihood that the output appeared by random chance and not due to an actual pattern and relationship. In other words, it says that there is a likelihood of 0.00376 percent that the regression output was due to random chance. The smaller the number, the better.

9. Then look at the last block of results. First, look at the column labeled Coefficients. The coefficient for the row labeled Intercept indicates the value of the famine level if the price value is 0. In our case, the Intercept number is about –1.73, which does not make too much sense. You cannot have negative famine levels. However, you can also look at the number in another way. Consider it as an attenuation factor that decreases the amount of the effect that price has on the famine level. Next, look at the coefficient for the row labeled PRICE, which is about 0.3687. This says that for every increase of 1 in the value of the price, the value of the famine level goes up by about 0.3687. Essentially, it is the predictive value. These numbers allow you to write the equation:

Famine level = (Price x 0.3687) – 1.73

10. Second, look at the column labeled P-value. The P-values indicate how confident you should be in your coefficient values. Generally, you want a P-value of less than 0.05. The P-value for the row labeled Intercept is about 0.2159. This says that there is about a 21.59 percent likelihood that the Intercept number came about by chance and not due to any relationship. The P-value for the row labeled PRICE is 3.76E-05, which is the same as the Significance F-value. When you do regressions using only one independent variable, these numbers will match. However, when you do regressions using multiple independent variables, known as multiple regression analysis, these numbers may be different. In the multiple regression case, you have to look at the P-value of each independent variable's coefficient to see how confident you can be in their predictive value.

You have now completed the regression analysis and can use the equation given in step 9 as a way of forecasting how changes in price will affect changes in the famine level. We only went over a simple way of doing CRA. You can use a variety of statistical tools and methods to do more complex and, in some cases, more accurate, ways of doing CRA. No one way is necessarily better than the others—it all depends on context and the nature of the variables. Scour the Internet for more information on multiple and multivariate regressions to learn how to do more advanced CRA. Also, research more ways of testing the significance of your findings, such as t-tests. Lastly, compare different data sets and sources to ensure your results did not come about because of faulty data. The processes are basically the same, and once you understand how to do simple CRA, you can easily learn how to do the more advanced analyses.

Volumetric Analysis

Separating volumetric analysis (VA) from CRA is somewhat artificial. The tools and methodologies you use to do VA are the same as you would use to do CRA. The difference lies in the type of data you analyze. VA entails finding associative relationships and the strength of causal relationships in data dealing with volume of traffic. Traffic on the Internet includes the number of times someone searches a word on Twitter and the number of hits to a website. Traffic in the offline world includes the number of shipments between two countries and the number of transactions between two bank accounts. When doing VA, the focus is not on the nuances and make-up of the event or behavior. Instead, it is on how many times the event or behavior occurred and how such volume data corresponds to other events. Contrast that with LSA, where the nuances and make-up of the data and the text matter. In practice, when doing VA you will often need to use other types of data as well. Still, we separate VA out to highlight the importance of traffic volume data and how it can hold amazing insights in cases where you cannot get access to all the data you want.

In this section, we expand on the example given in the CRA section. We now consider the fact that in the real world, you do not always have access to all the data you want. Additionally, the data you do get is usually incomplete or incompatible with other data sets. We consider how you can use volume traffic data, which in many cases is easier to get than complete data sets. In the following example, we continue to consider ways you can create tools to provide early warnings for famine. This time, we use real-world data and Twitter data.

Creating Tools to Provide Early Warnings for Famines with Artificial Data

Imagine you are tasked with creating another tool for your famine early-warning system that is distinct from the one we discussed in the CRA section. This new tool should complement your other tools and work in conjunction with them to provide more robust early warnings that take into account a number of factors.

This tool should analyze different types of data and see if other behaviors can help you anticipate the onset and intensity of famine in a region.

One possibly useful data source is Twitter. Usually, when a major event happens, people take to Twitter to either report on it, as they did with the Benghazi consulate attack, or voice their opinion about it. Examining what people say on Twitter, when they say it, and how many people say it can tell you a lot about the event that is taking place. This view, however, does not always hold true, especially when dealing with events taking place in parts of the world that are not fully developed. Twitter is expanding into Latin America, Asia, and Africa aggressively and will likely be ubiquitous very soon. However, such widespread use of Twitter has not yet occurred. Information about events occurring in less developed areas such as Somalia may not appear on Twitter right away. You need to test whether you can use Twitter as a data source to analyze and provide early warnings about famines and food insecurity.

To test the viability of using Twitter as a valid data source, you need to examine how it has fared recently in anticipating famine and food insecurity events. The Somalia famine in mid-2011 serves as a good case study. It occurred relatively recently and you can easily find data about it. Overall, you need to assess whether information traffic related to the famine appeared on Twitter when famine conditions started to take place in Somalia, and whether the levels of the traffic matched the intensity of the famine level. If it did not, you need to determine the time lag between famine conditions taking place and information about it appearing on Twitter. If everything fails, you also need to find another data source that is more useful than Twitter.

Assemble Appropriate Data

We spent some time searching the Internet for relevant data. Apart from using the data sources we discussed in Chapter 4, we simply Googled together the terms "data" "Somalia" "famine" and sifted through the links. We found some that were useful and much that was incomplete, incorrect, or incompatible with other data sets.

CROSS-REFERENCE All the data that you need for this example is available on our website in the file VA_example.xls or VA_example.csv. The XLS file also contains the outputs of our analyses.

First, you need to obviously find the Twitter data. The British newspaper, the *Guardian*, has exactly the data you need on its website (the original raw data file is available on our website for download as a spreadsheet).[10] The Twitter data consists of the number of tweets per day over a 19-month period that mentioned "Somalia" and either "famine," "drought," or "food." The *Guardian* also provides data about the number of mentions in newspapers and total amount of aid flows by date.

> **NOTE** The *Guardian* is at the forefront of conducting social media analytics and using it to inform its reports. Check out `http://www.guardian.co.uk/data` for various data sets it makes available to the public. This example was largely inspired by the *Guardian*'s work concerning the Somalia famine.

You need data to do the analysis of Twitter data against. This data should indicate the level of famine over the time period that the famine took place. We found some United Nations data on malnutrition and other famine indicators for Somalia, but they are not broken down by clear time periods and so are not as useful for analysis. Other data needs to serve as the famine level indicator. The market price of red sorghum in Marka in Southern Somalia may do the trick. Red sorghum is a grain that is widely grown and consumed in Somalia. As discussed before, drastic increases in the market price of grains such as red sorghum can indicate food insecurity and famine conditions. It is not perfect, but a causal look at the data and comparisons to reports from the United Nations documenting the famine shows that it indeed is a good indicator for food insecurity and famine conditions. The market price data is made available by the Food Security and Nutrition Analysis Unit (`http://www.fsnau.org`) and is broken up by month over several years.

Conduct Analysis

Determining a correlation between the market prices and the Twitter mentions can help determine the utility of using Twitter data to anticipate famine conditions in Somalia. The correlation analysis will tell you not only whether they are correlated, but by how much Twitter data tends to lag behind the appearance of famine conditions.

First, you need to collapse the Twitter data into monthly periods. When doing CRA analysis, you should compare apples to apples. If one data set gives statistics by month, the other data set should also give statistics by month. You also need to make sure you are comparing months for when the data exists. Data for both price and Twitter mentions exists from August 2010 to January 2012. Then you draw two time series line charts, as depicted in Figure 6.4.

The line charts indicate that there indeed is a correlation between price and mentions, but the time lag is significant. When price spikes, the number of mentions also goes up. However, it takes a long time for the change in price to be reflected in the mentions. Notice that the price for sorghum started to go up in August 2010 at a fairly high and consistent rate till it reached a peak in May 2011. The price then started to go down after July 2011. The United Nations' considerations of the famine match this trend. It started to see signs of the famine in late-mid 2010 and officially declared famine in mid-2011.[10]

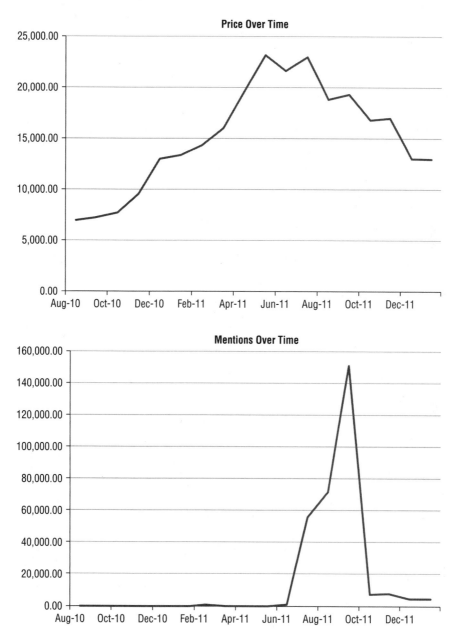

Figure 6.4: Line charts of Twitter mentions and sorghum prices

The number of Twitter mentions about the Somalia famine was few till June 2011. They started to spike thereafter, reaching a peak in September 2011, almost two months after the peak of the price surge and famine conditions. A closer look at the mentions data indicates that the number of mentions did start to go up slightly after September 2010. However, the numbers are very small and do not reach a significant amount until June-July 2011. The correlation coefficient backs up this finding. It is only 0.39, which is not very high.

Based on these findings, you can conclude that although Twitter mentions about the famine did go up during the famine, they are not very useful in regards to providing early warnings about the famine and food insecurity. People tweeted about the famine when they heard about it from newspapers and traditional media. They then responded to the news stories. By then, however, the famine was already well under way. You should conduct the same type of analyses on other famine cases to see if your conclusion about the lack of utility of using Twitter mentions as an early warning holds up.

You can also go back to the data provided by the *Guardian* to see if you can use other data sources as an indicator of famine conditions. Casually looking at the aid flow data suggests that it may actually correlate closely to the emergence of famine conditions. We leave the analysis to you.

We touched on only a few simple ways you can use simple statistical tools to analyze social media data to understand and forecast security events. We could write entire books about using only one of the ways. However, we hope you got the point so far about how social media data can help you and encourage you to explore other ways by yourself. We now move on to Chapter 7, where we begin discussing how you can use social media in other ways, namely to crowdsource.

Summary

- By using various analytical methodologies, you can uncover the relationships between events, behaviors, issues, problems, and actions concerning security.

- Social media intelligence is a superior type of open source intelligence that also shares features with other types of intelligence.

- Simply monitoring social media activity can help you recognize and anticipate security events, such as the attack on the Benghazi consulate, more quickly than consuming traditional media.

- Intelligence is often validated, challenged, and disseminated through social media.

- Apart from understanding events, social media data can also help you forecast the development of events.

- Forecasting entails being humble about what you think may happen in the near future. Anyone who says they can predict complex events in the future is either being dishonest or naïve.

- Language and sentiment analysis can help you discover the overt and hidden meaning in linguistic content, and its relationship to security events.

- Through language and sentiment analysis, you can determine the authorship of anonymous documents and track and forecast the behavior of rioting violent crowds.

- Correlation and regression analysis can help you understand and identify the associative and predictive relationships between different events and items.

- Through correlation and regression analysis, you can create tools to provide early warnings for famines and food insecurity.

- Volumetric analysis is a type of correlation and regression analysis that uses data concerning volume of activity and traffic on the Internet.

- Through volumetric analysis, you can further refine tools to provide early warnings for famines and food insecurity.

Notes

1. Directorate of Intelligence (2012) "Intelligence Cycle." U.S. Federal Bureau of Investigation. Accessed: 11 November 2012. `http://www.fbi.gov/about-us/intelligence/intelligence-cycle`; (2012) "How Intelligence Works" intelligence.gov. Accessed: 14 October 2012. `http://intelligence.gov/about-the-intelligence-community/how-intelligence-works/`

2. Scheuer, M. (2007) *Through Our Enemies' Eyes*. Potomac Books, Dulles.

3. Kelly, S. (2012) "Intelligence Official Offers New Timeline for Benghazi Attack." CNN. Accessed: 11 November 2012. `http://security.blogs.cnn.com/2012/11/01/intelligence-official-offers-new-timeline-for-benghazi-attack/`; (2012) "Timeline on Libya and Egypt: Attacks and Response." Washington Post. Accessed: 11 November 2012. `http://www.washingtonpost.com/politics/decision2012/timeline-on-libya-and-egypt-attacks-and-response/2012/09/12/85288638-fd03-11e1-a31e-804fccb658f9_story_1.html`

4. AKNN News (2012) "Timeline Photos." Facebook. Accessed: 11 November 2012. `https://www.facebook.com/photo.php?fbid=364777023602502&set=a.246675052079367.59435.246612585418947&type=1&theater`; @zaidbenjamin (2012) Twitter. "A picture believed to be for..." Accessed: 11 November 2012. `https://twitter.com/zaidbenjamin/status/245808824324333568/photo/1`

5. @syriancommando (2012) Twitter "American Embassy worker in...." "Accessed: 11 November 2012. `https://twitter.com/syriancommando/status/245753481649078272/photo/1`

6. Kiely, E. (2012) "Benghazi Timeline." Factcheck.org. Accessed: 11 November 2012. `http://factcheck.org/2012/10/benghazi-timeline/`

7. Check tweets of @Sefu_Africa on 28 September 2012, @kdfifno from 28 September 2012 to 31 October 2012, and @HSMPress on 28 September 2012.

8. Lewis, M. (2011) *The Big Short*: *Inside the Doomsday Machine*. W.W. Norton, New York.

9. Hastie, T., Tibshirani, R., and Friedman, J. (2009) *The Elements of Statistical Learning*: *Data Mining, Inference, and Prediction*. Springer, New York.

10. Provost, C., et al. (2012) "Somalia Famine: How the World Responded - Interactive." Factcheck.org. Accessed: 11 November 2012. `http://www.guardian.co.uk/global-development/interactive/2012/feb/22/somalia-famine-aid-media-interactive`

Crowdsourcing Intelligence, Solutions, and Influence

In This Part

Social media technologies not only provide you with data for analysis, they also provide you with the ability to engage and interact with people from all over the world. Focused and sustained engagement through social media enables you to crowdsource or tap into the cognitive surplus and resources of the crowds that use the Internet. In Part III, we explore the concept of crowdsourcing and how organizations have used it to solve various security and development problems. We then illustrate how you can use crowdsourcing to significantly bolster intelligence collection, solve complex problems, and influence populations.

CHAPTER 7

Introduction to Crowdsourcing

Although crowdsourcing is an old technique, social media technology enables you to crowdsource cheaper, faster, and better. This chapter lays the foundation of Part III of the book, which is dedicated to detailing how to build and run a variety of crowdsourcing platforms for different purposes. The chapter introduces and explores the concept of crowdsourcing and its relationship to social media, details the advantages of doing it, provides a few brief examples of relevant crowdsourcing applications, and explains when and when not to do it.

What Is Crowdsourcing?

So far the book has taught you how to take a more passive approach with regards to social media, namely to consume and analyze social media data. In this chapter you learn how to adopt a more active role, and build and run social media platforms for various purposes through the technique of crowdsourcing. Crowdsourcing via social media will help you do analysis, and the analysis you conduct will in turn help you crowdsource more effectively.

Crowdsourcing will soon replace social media as the hot new frontier of technology, because it offers tremendous, game-changing opportunities. Understanding crowdsourcing and how to do it will not only place you at the forefront of technology applications, but provide you with the tools to change how you accomplish a variety of missions, from getting community members to help local police identify thieves and murderers to encouraging Afghans to text you the locations of enemy combatants. Through crowdsourcing, you can accomplish previously unattainable objectives and accomplish existing objectives in a more efficient and inexpensive way. Also, building and running crowdsourcing platforms will help you bypass complicated ethical and privacy concerns surrounding using data collected on third-party social media platforms like Twitter. Instead, you can directly engage with and gain permission from the data source to use their data. Although crowdsourcing is difficult, doing it effectively can give you enormous leverage, insight, and influence.

Defining Crowdsourcing and Its Relevance

Chapter 2 briefly defined and introduced crowdsourcing as follows:

Crowdsourcing is the act of influencing, incentivizing, and leveraging crowds through social media to provide you with information and help you solve problems.

Expanding on the definition, crowdsourcing essentially involves taking a complex problem that is difficult and expensive to solve, splitting it up into smaller tasks, and then incentivizing people to solve the smaller tasks and, consequently, the larger complex problem. Crowdsourcing is similar to outsourcing but they differ somewhat. When you outsource something, you typically hand over the problem to an external entity that then coordinates its execution. When you crowdsource something, you hand over the problem to thousands of individuals and take the lead in managing and coordinating its execution. Outsourcing is also a lot more formal, and is backed up by contracts, whereas crowdsourcing is more informal and you may never even know the identity of the person who completes your task. You can use crowdsourcing to accomplish a variety of objectives, but in this book we concentrate on the three objectives described in Table 7.1 and further detailed in Chapters 9, 10, and 11. Note that you cannot crowdsource influence per se. However, you can use crowdsourcing platforms to foster engagement and interaction with populations, which can lead to influencing populations. The word "influence" here has the same meaning as it did in Chapter 5. Influence connotes delicately persuading people over a period of time to adopt your point of view or participate in a behavior that you desire. It does not connote brainwashing or spreading obvious misinformation. See Figure 7.1 for a visual summary of the objectives of crowdsourcing.

Table 7.1: Crowdsourcing Objectives

OBJECTIVE	DESCRIPTION	CORRESPONDING CHAPTER
Collect intelligence	Encourage the desired population to provide local intelligence on illicit drug and economic activity, criminal and gang activity, terrorist operational and recruitment activity, local perspectives, and various environmental conditions.	Chapter 9
Solve problems	Encourage the desired population to help solve complex problems or tasks ranging from the designing of promotional materials denouncing terrorism to creating sophisticated computer science algorithms that process signal intelligence.	Chapter 10
Influence populations	Encourage the desired population to adopt specific ideas and beliefs to, for example, coalesce support against terrorist groups, create and staff neighborhood watch programs, and help protestors overthrow autocratic rulers.	Chapter 11

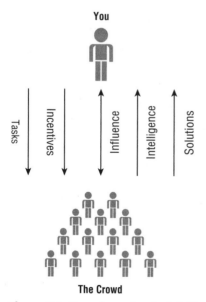

Figure 7.1: Crowdsourcing for Intelligence, solutions, and influence

Bolstering Crowdsourcing with Social Media

Crowdsourcing is not a new technique, but social media and the Internet have changed how it is done and amplified its advantages. Law enforcement and governments have used crowdsourcing to collect intelligence, solve problems, and influence people for decades. For example, police often place pictures of missing children on milk cartons, or have local TV networks show them on the news to crowdsource intelligence about the children. They then encourage thousands of local citizens to call in with tips, with extrinsic motivators like cash rewards or intrinsic motivators like the good feeling people get when they are helpful.

CROSS-REFERENCE Chapter 8 goes into detail about how you can use a variety of extrinsic and intrinsic motivators to encourage people to join your crowdsourcing efforts.

Many agencies and offices in the U.S. government contract out work to private entities and individuals, and ask the public to submit their opinions and recommendations concerning controversial policy—a way to crowdsource solutions. In the former, money is the clear motivator, whereas in the latter, it is the sense of civic duty. Government crowdsourcing efforts are also subtly influencing people. In 2010, the U.S. State Department, in partnership with several embassies, technology groups, and funding partners launched the "Apps4Africa: Civic Challenge." The contest allowed individuals from all over the world and especially from within East Africa, to submit ideas for technological solutions to everyday problems faced by Africans continent-wide. The problems spanned issues of governance, healthcare, education, and transparency. The contest offered prizes ranging from simply recognition to $15,000 for the best idea, but the real driving factor for many was the chance for individuals to vote on the problems they felt most necessary and feasible to address through technological solutions. For those voting and judging there was no reward other than civic duty. The challenge also implicitly encouraged populations in East Africa and elsewhere to use technology and entrepreneurship to solve their communities' problems.[1]

Social media is the ideal vehicle for crowdsourcing and has taken it to the next level. Due to social media, crowdsourcing has taken off in recent years and will only become more popular. Crowdsourcing via social media involves both building and maintaining dedicated websites and virtual platforms with social media feature integration such as the ability to talk to other people, and using existing social media platforms to advertise dedicated platforms or crowdsource tasks. Contemporary dedicated crowdsourcing platforms can include standalone websites, smartphone applications, and SMS-based communication networks. They generally fall into eight categories, many of them overlapping, which Table 7.2 describes. The crowdsourcing platforms you will learn to build and run fall into several of the categories. Explore the crowdsourcing efforts in each category to come up with ways you can use crowdsourcing to accomplish objectives we do not specifically address.

Table 7.2: Crowdsourcing Application Categories

CATEGORY	DESCRIPTION	EXAMPLES
Collective knowledge	Participants pool information about a certain topic, and then help distill and present it on the Internet.	OpenStreetMap, Wikipedia
Collective creativity	Participants upload ideas or artwork and distribute them for others to consume, adapt, enjoy, and critique.	Threadless, Zooppa, Crowdspring
Community building	Participants develop applications and devices to inexpensively and effectively help solve social problems such as improving health or fighting corruption.	Medstartr, Apps4Africa, NYC Big Apps
Open innovation	Participants innovate processes or products on behalf of companies and organizations that are looking for ways to do things better.	OpenIDEO, Google Hackathons, X-Prize Foundation
Crowdfunding	Participants help fund individuals or groups needing financial assistance for their project or startup.	Kickstarter, GoFundMe, Kiva.org, PleaseFund.Us
Crowd tools	Participants use websites, applications, or online tools to increase collaboration, idea generation, scheduling, and group learning.	Crowdcast, Basecamp, BrightIdea, ProjectSpaces. Reelapp, Crowdflare, Smartling
Crowd labor	Participants complete tasks and fill in manpower gaps for individuals or organizations.	Amazon's Mechanical Turk, Crowdflower
Crowd Civic Engagement	Participants who work through an online community on projects that do civic good such as election monitoring or crisis tracking.	Standby Task Force/ Ushahidi, Crowdmap, Reset SF, uReport, Map Mathare, Map Kibera, Women Under Siege Project

Social media significantly bolsters crowdsourcing primarily because of three reasons. One, social media enables you to reach more people. As explored later, crowdsourcing is more effective when you can reach a greater amount of people or a greater amount of types of people. Because social media use is nearly ubiquitous around the world, it assures you that more people will hear about your crowdsourcing effort and likely participate. Two, social media makes it easier for people to communicate and collaborate with each other. Many crowdsourcing efforts often require people who have never met to work together to solve complex tasks. Social media technologies integrated into dedicated crowdsourcing websites or existing social media platforms, such as hi5, provide numerous collaboration and communication tools that also make it easier for you to oversee and talk to the people to whom you are crowdsourcing. Three, social media can handle lots of multimedia and thus is more engaging and fun. No one wants to participate in something that is boring and dull. Through social media, you can use videos, pictures, audio, and lots of other ways of communications to entice and excite potential crowdsourcing users. The more interesting and fun your effort looks, the more people will likely participate.

Why Use Crowdsourcing?

Crowdsourcing via social media not only bolsters the act of crowdsourcing, but also your ability to accomplish the three aforementioned objectives. Specifically, it helps you solve more problems and get more information, more quickly, more discreetly, and for less money.

CROSS-REFERENCE If you do not need any more convincing about how crowdsourcing can help, then skip to the section with the heading, "Relevant Examples of Crowdsourcing." Otherwise, read on.

Solve More Problems and Get More Information

Solving more problems, completing more tasks, and solving seemingly unsolvable problems is a function of getting more people to help, trying out new creative approaches, and leveraging the wisdom of the crowds. Crowdsourcing via social media enables you to engage with more people than ever before, and more types of people than ever before. This greater reach increases the likelihood that you will engage with the person who has the solution to your problem or the piece of information you need. Often, complex problems are made up of so many diverse smaller technical and scientific niche problems that it is difficult to assemble all the experts who can solve the larger complex problem. Crowdsourcing enables you to tap into experts in niche areas living around the world that otherwise you may not be able to find or incentivize using traditional outsourcing or employment methods. For example, Amazon's Mechanical Turk platform enables you to hire individuals who can translate texts in obscure languages such as Somali at relatively cheap rates.[2] Additionally, researchers who are sitting in their offices thousands of miles away from the country they are researching may not have the same insights into what is happening on the ground as locals, despite how good the researchers are at using Google. If you want an accurate picture about local conditions, sourcing intelligence from local inhabitants is the best way. Finally, to influence and co-opt populations in denied areas, you have to engage with the population. They will react more favorably to you and your efforts if you talk with them on the Internet through crowdsourcing platforms than by dropping flyers on their head.

Tapping into more people and different types of people also increases the overall creativity involved and provides alternative perspectives with which to approach and solve problems. You may find it shocking to learn that the Washington D.C. metro area hosts security analysts and policy-makers who have largely gone to the same schools and read the same blogs. Thus, they largely share the same ways of approaching and solving problems. Such groupthink corrodes the ability to get things done competently and intelligently. People alien to D.C. and similar cities and organizations can bring to bear new perspectives and help develop effective and creative solutions to problems. They can also provide new viewpoints with which to acquire and process intelligence. If they are the populations you are interested in co-opting and engaging with, they also are probably the best at evaluating and correcting your efforts.

Apart from niche experts and fresh perspectives, crowdsourcing also enables you to solve more problems through the wisdom of crowds. James Surowiecki popularized the term, which posits that the average of the responses of many people to a question is often more accurate than the response of a few experts.[3] If you want to guess the weight of an object, it is better to ask a hundred people what they think and then average their responses than ask the alleged weight-guessing champion of the world. The phenomenon is valid partly because more people means more perspectives are included, and also that more people bring to bear more information and insights to a problem that an expert may have missed. Keep in mind that in some cases the wisdom of the crowd will fail you—specifically, when the problem requires extremely specialized and technical knowledge, or when the crowd is not diverse enough. Crowdsourcing via social media is perfect for leveraging the wisdom of the crowd, because on the Internet you can tap into lots of people from all sorts of backgrounds, including very specialized and technical ones.

Work Quickly

Solving a problem traditionally is arduous work. You have to hire employees or contractors, and hope they are as good as they claim. Doing so usually involves lots of paperwork and bureaucracy. When unforeseen problems appear or more nuanced information and expertise is required, projects can go into a tailspin and fall behind schedule. Crowdsourcing can bypass bureaucracy and make it easy for experts to find you, instead of you finding them. Lots of people doing small tasks or giving you little bits of information simultaneously means your project gets done faster, and that you are never lacking for manpower. As long as you set up your crowdsourcing effort properly, you can let people on the Internet and social media take care of most of the problems you would face traditionally. They free up your time for other things, and their constant interaction with you and each other means things get done at a constant, quick rate.

Work Discreetly

Organizations in the security field often need to work discreetly. For instance, they need to collect intelligence from denied areas and hostile populations who are suspicious of them or hesitant to talk to them for fear of reprisal. Social media allows people to communicate with each other while hiding their identity, and even hide the fact that they are communicating at all. A person can create anonymous profiles and fake identities, or private message or text others and then delete the messages. Crowdsourcing platforms are ideal for collecting intelligence without compromising the identity and lives of the people who are providing you with information. You can also hide your identity and intentions when creating a platform, although as you learn in Chapter 8, that is not always a good idea.

Organizations conducting information operations on populations also need to work discreetly and subtly. People are more likely to agree with you and adopt your way of thinking if you can make them believe that they came up with the idea or perspective. Doing so requires subtlety and discretion, and not making it obvious you are trying to convince someone of something. Crowdsourcing platforms enable you to subtly communicate and encourage people to adopt your ideas and influence, while maintaining deniability and face. Through incentives on crowdsourcing platforms, you can discreetly nudge populations to think and do how you wish them to, and make it seem as if they are convincing each other.

Save Money

Crowdsourcing can provide enormous cash savings. Setting up a crowdsourcing platform and then running it with monetary incentives is much cheaper than contracting out work or hiring employees. Creating a web page, smartphone application, or mass texting people is cheap because the technology is widespread. After your project is finished or changes in focus, you can easily shut down and adapt your platform to other needs. You cannot as easily get rid of subpar employees or retrain them. Threadless (www.threadless.com) is a pioneering crowdsourcing company that encapsulates how crowdsourcing lowers costs. Threadless is a website that crowdsources T-shirt designs. Every week users submit T-shirt designs, and vote and comment on each other's designs. At the end of the week, Threadless founders pick the design with the most votes and positive feedback, and print T-shirts with the design. The user with the chosen design gets about $2000 as a reward. Threadless then sells the T-shirts for a lot more money. Threadless does not reveal its annual revenue but it is estimated to be in the tens of millions of U.S. dollars. Threadless makes so much money from just printing T-shirts because its profit margins are large and its costs are low. Instead of hiring T-shirt designers, it crowdsources designs and provides cash rewards that are small when you consider the company's revenues, but large for amateur T-shirt designers.[4] Due to crowdsourcing, Threadless saves a lot of money and, thus, makes a lot of money.

Depending on the population and your skills, you can even motivate people to provide you with information and solutions without providing monetary incentives. You will be surprised at how many people will help you out for free or in return for things such as market information. We provide examples of non-monetary incentives in Chapter 8 and in the subsequent examples.

Relevant Examples of Crowdsourcing

To illustrate how crowdsourcing is relevant to the problems you face, this section briefly reviews four popular crowdsourcing platforms. The platforms span solving collecting intelligence, humanitarian and military problems, and influencing populations. In practice, all social media platforms are influence platforms because they promote communication between people. The greater the communication between people, the more likely they are to influence each other. Lots more examples are available throughout Part III.

OpenIDEO

IDEO, a California-based design consulting firm, founded OpenIDEO (www .openideo.com) as a way of galvanizing organizations and people globally to come together and solve humanitarian challenges. OpenIDEO is a website where governments, corporations, individuals, and large non-profits work with OpenIDEO to come up with challenges that usually focus on solving a health or environmental problem in developing countries. See Table 7.3 for a list of relevant challenges. OpenIDEO then posts the challenges on its websites and invites users from around the world, who sign up for free, to come up with solutions to the challenges. The users often collaborate on solutions using social networking and messaging tools built into the OpenIDEO website. Users then vote on solutions and incrementally improve them as the challenge continues. At the end of the challenge period, the organization sponsoring the challenge may then adopt and implement one of the solutions, sometimes with the users who came up with it.[5]

Table 7.3: OpenIDEO Challenge Examples

CHALLENGE	SPONSORS	URL
How might we design an accessible election experience for everyone?	Information Technology and Innovation Foundation	`www.openideo.com/open/voting/brief.html`
How might we improve maternal health with mobile technologies for low-income countries?	Oxfam and Nokia	`www.openideo.com/open/maternal-health/brief.html`
How might we increase the availability of affordable learning tools and services for students in the developing world?	Enterprising Schools	`www.openideo.com/open/how-might-we-increase-the-availability-of-affordable-learning-tools-educational-for-children-in-the-developing-world/brief.html`
How can we manage e-waste and discarded electronics to safeguard human health and protect our environment?	Itaú Unibanco, U.S. Department of State, and U.S. Environmental Protection Agency	`www.openideo.com/open/e-waste/brief.html`
How can technology help people working to uphold human rights in the face of unlawful detention?	Amnesty International	`www.openideo.com/open/amnesty/brief.html`

What makes OpenIDEO unique is that OpenIDEO users do not receive any type of concrete reward such as cash or prizes. The users participate because they want to work with others, play a role in solving an important societal challenge, be helpful, or simply have fun working on something that is not their normal job. Keep OpenIDEO in mind when considering how to incentivize participants to join and stay with your crowdsourcing efforts.

DARPA Shredder Challenge

Apart from development, health, and environmental problems, crowdsourcing can also help solve military and intelligence problems. The U.S. Defense Advanced Research Projects Agency (DARPA) frequently launches crowdsourcing challenges. In late 2011, DARPA launched the Shredder Challenge with the objective of acquiring computer algorithms that could reassemble and make sense of shredded documents. While collecting intelligence, law enforcement, intelligence, and military agencies frequently come by shredded documents that hold valuable information. An algorithm that could help reassemble the documents would significantly help intelligence collection. With the goal of creating such an algorithm, DARPA launched a crowdsourcing website where it hosted pictures of five shredded documents and then invited teams and individuals from all over the world to use the pictures to reassemble the documents. DARPA pledged a cash prize of $50,000 to the first team that could reassemble the documents. It used social media to advertise the challenge, which also got coverage in popular science magazines and websites. In only 33 days, the challenge was solved. Nearly 9000 teams competed, and the "All Your Shreds Are Belong to U.S." team, based in San Francisco and made up of computer programmers, was the first to succeed and win. Lots of experts were skeptical that the challenge would work, but they were clearly proven wrong.[6]

By crowdsourcing, DARPA saved time and money because it did not have to contract the work out. It also tapped into the creativity and different perspectives of people on the Internet that led to an ingenious solution in record time. DARPA will likely build on the algorithms and solutions it received through more traditional means and move forward toward completing its objective. Crowdsourcing how to reassemble five shredded documents gave DARPA an immense head start to creating an algorithm that could reassemble hundreds of shredded documents. Expect DARPA and other U.S. government agencies to launch more crowdsourcing challenges, and keep track of them at www .challenge.gov.

If you research DARPA's history of crowdsourcing, you will likely come across one of its most popular crowdsourcing projects known as the "Red Balloon Challenge" or the "Network Challenge." In the challenge, DARPA deployed ten red weather balloons throughout the United States. They then asked teams to identify the physical location of each balloon. The first team to submit correct location information for each balloon would receive a cash reward of $40,000. A team from MIT solved the challenge by incentivizing people on social media platforms to help them identify and locate the balloons. In other words, the MIT team crowdsourced the location of the balloons. Essentially, the DARPA crowdsourcing challenge was solved by a crowdsourcing technique. The Red Balloon Challenge illustrated the power of crowdsourcing and specifically of social media networks to coalesce people to collect intelligence and solve seemingly complicated problems.[7]

GCHQ Spy Recruitment Challenge

U.S. governments are in no way the only governments experimenting with crowdsourcing. In some ways, British authorities are leading the way with crowdsourcing. In late 2011, the British intelligence service, the Government Communications Headquarters (GCHQ), launched a crowdsourcing platform with the objective of recruiting potential employees who are good at cracking codes and thus ideal for analyzing signal intelligence.

For the challenge, GCHQ posted a code at `www.canyoucrackit.co.uk` and invited British citizens to solve it. The code consisted of 160 letters and numbers arranged in a rectangular display. Those who decrypted the code would find a keyword that, if entered, would lead to another website. The website congratulated the solvers and asked if they were interested in applying their skills to combating terrorism and cyberthreats. Interested solvers could then submit a job application for 35 open jobs. At least 50 people have since solved the code.[8]

GCHQ employed a relatively simple and straightforward crowdsourcing approach. The website itself was interactive and allowed for two-way communication, and popular social media platforms such as Facebook only played a role in marketing the effort. Still, the GCHQ example illustrates how crowdsourcing through the Internet can even be used for something as banal as hiring intelligence analysts. Subsequent chapters reveal how the British government and the London Metropolitan Police are using other crowdsourcing efforts to solve security problems, especially those that are most relevant to city police officers.

M-Farm

Crowdsourcing can also help intelligence collection via the more straightforward task of incentivizing people to submit data about their lives and environment through social media. M-Farm is an organization based in Kenya that is dedicated to providing farmers in East Africa with information about crop prices in their area. It hopes that farmers will use the price information to make more informed decisions about how they should set their own crop prices, thereby increasing market transparency and profits in East Africa.

Crop buyers and sellers in Kenya register with M-Farm and, in return, get access to a truncated phone number known as a *shortcode*. They then send a free text to the shortcode providing the price of a commodity in a certain location. M-Farm agents at local markets also text the price of various commodities. M-Farm's central database then aggregates and analyzes the price information. Crop buyers and sellers can also send a free text to the shortcode asking for the price of a commodity in a certain location. M-Farm's database responds with the desired information through a text. M-Farm has now evolved to helping farmers sell their crops using SMS and the Internet. It has also apparently realized its data is valuable and has started selling it in various formats.[9] Because Kenya is one of the few African countries with a stock exchange, the future implications for such a service could be huge in driving country, region, or global prices based on micro-level inputs from the crowd.

M-Farm illustrates how an organization can collect critical economic and other (security, health) information from areas and populations in seemingly denied areas using dumb phones. M-Farm created a virtual crowdsourcing platform on the SMS communication network and incentivized people to participate simply by providing them with information. Because more information increased the ability of the farmers to make better decisions, they in turn became more likely to volunteer information. Also, because correct information is critical, the farmers are also more likely to volunteer correct information. Note that the overhead costs for running such a crowdsourcing platform are very low because dumb phones and SMS are relatively inexpensive. They are much cheaper than hiring and deploying numerous in-field data gatherers.

Knowing When to Crowdsource

The preceding examples illustrate only a few potential applications of crowdsourcing via social media. We review several more examples and applications in the subsequent chapters, and we hope you recognize that the applications are numerous. However, numerous applications do not result in ubiquitous applications. Some cases are appropriate for crowdsourcing and a few are not.

When to Crowdsource

When you should crowdsource depends on what you are trying to accomplish. If your objective is to collect intelligence, you should crowdsource when you need to:

- **Be independent of existing but uncooperative social media platforms**— Some social media platforms share data but some do not for various reasons, including because they do not like you. Or, the country you are interested in has banned its populace from using Western-based social media platforms, which are usually more open about sharing data. Launching and maintaining your own crowdsourcing platform ensures that you do not have to deal with unfriendly platforms or get around bans of popular platforms. Countries are unlikely to ban platforms that are used by a small portion of their population or are built under benign auspices, such as providing economic data to farmers.

- **Collect intelligence discreetly from certain areas**—Some population somewhere distrusts you and will not provide you with intelligence. However, a few individuals in that population may if you can protect their identity and compensate them. To communicate with such individuals, you can build discreet crowdsourcing platforms, most likely through SMS. The platforms would allow sympathetic individuals to provide you with intelligence without compromising their safety.

- **Control the type and rate of data**— Popular social media platforms are currently willing to share data, but that may not always be the case. Also, social media platforms typically limit what kind of data you can get and how much of it you can get in a time period. Maintaining your own platform frees you of dependency and limitations on platforms, which understandably are hesitant about sharing too much data about their users.

- **Create and maintain an exclusive data source**—Many of you likely come across information that you would rather other governments and organizations do not acquire. Limiting whom Facebook or M-Farm shares their data with is difficult. If you have your platform that is collecting the type of data you need, you can control who else gets access to the data.

If your objective is to solve problems, you should crowdsource when you need to:

- **Solve problems that require expertise in lots of areas**—As discussed, crowdsourcing enables you to quickly reach and employ experts in all sorts of niche subjects.

- **Solve problems cheaply**—In an age of dwindling budgets, crowdsourcing done well can significantly lessen the cost of solving some problems.

- **Solve tedious tasks efficiently**—Some problems are easy to solve, but hiring the people to solve them can be difficult and arduous. Crowdsourcing platforms enable you to quickly farm out simple tasks and get them solved without the hassle of dealing with a slow bureaucracy.

- **Generate creativity and new insights**—Allowing people from around the world to work on your problem will broaden the information and viewpoints brought to bear on the problem. A dose of new data and perspective usually leads to creative solutions.

If your objective is to influence populations, you should crowdsource when you need to:

- **Influence people subtly**—The worst way to convince people of believing or doing something is making it obvious that you are trying to convince them. Crowdsourcing platforms enable you to subtly engage with populations and seed ideas. You can then work with the target population to develop the idea so they feel a sense of ownership about the idea, and come around to your perspective.

- **Be discreet about your objective**—Obvious convincing and co-opting tactics will likely draw the attention of adversaries. Virtual platforms are usually safer and more discreet for everyone involved.

When Not to Crowdsource

Regardless of your objective, you should not crowdsource when:

- **Confidentiality and secrecy is very important**—Crowdsourcing requires putting things out on social media and the Internet, which anyone can access. Obviously, if you think a piece of information or a problem is confidential and valuable, you should not post it on the Internet.

- **Your tolerance for risk is very low**—Anytime you engage with populations over social media, you are giving up some control to the population. Loosening the grips on what the population can say and do is essential to fostering participation and creativity. If you are terrified of what a population may do or say on your website, you should not run certain types of platforms where open interaction is allowed. We teach you how to manage the population and manage the risk, but some risk will always be there. The risk is what makes the Internet and social media so great.

Now that you are familiar with crowdsourcing and how it has proven useful in the security world, you can begin crafting and deploying your own crowdsourcing platforms. Chapter 8 will show you the ingredients that go into building a crowdsourcing platform, regardless of your ultimate objective.

Summary

- Crowdsourcing represents the frontier of social media technology application.

- Crowdsourcing involves harnessing people on the Internet and social media to solve a series of simple tasks that result in the completion of a complex problem.

- Use crowdsourcing to collect intelligence from denied areas, solve various problems, and influence populations globally.

- Governments and law enforcement have used traditional modes of crowd-sourcing for decades. Crowdsourcing is not a new technique; social media has simply bolstered it and amplified its abilities. Crowdsourcing through social media enables you to reach more people, foster communication and collaboration between participants, and use multimedia to attract participants.

- Today, crowdsourcing on the Internet is done through standalone web-sites, smartphone applications, SMS-based networks, and existing social media platforms.

- Through crowdsourcing, you can solve more problems and get more information. Also, you can do it all much more quickly, discreetly, and inexpensively.

- Several examples exist of crowdsourcing efforts that are relevant to security and development issues. Some include OpenIDEO, the DARPA Shredder Challenge, the U.K. GCHQ Spy Recruitment Challenge, and M-Farm.

- Crowdsourcing is most effective and appropriate for collecting intelligence when you need to:
  - Be independent of existing but uncooperative social media platforms.
  - Collect intelligence discreetly from certain areas.
  - Control the type and rate of data.
  - Create and maintain an exclusive data source.

- Crowdsourcing is most effective and appropriate for solving problems when you need to:
  - Solve problems that require expertise in lots of areas.
  - Solve problems cheaply.
  - Solve tedious tasks efficiently.
  - Generate creativity and new insights.

- Crowdsourcing is most effective and appropriate for influencing populations when you need to:
    - Influence people subtly.
    - Be discreet about your objective.
- Do not crowdsource when:
    - Confidentiality and secrecy is very important.
    - Your tolerance for risk is very low.

Notes

1. U.S. Department of State (2012) "Apps4Africa:About." Accessed: 16 July 2012. http://apps4africa.org

2. Amazon MTurk (2012) "Introduction." Accessed: 15 July 2012. https://www.mturk.com/mturk/welcome

3. Surowiecki, J. (2005) *The Wisdom of Crowds*. Anchor, New York.

4. Chafkin, M. (2008) The Customer is the Company. Inc. Magazine. Accessed: 11 June 2012. http://www.inc.com/magazine/20080601/the-customer-is-the-company.html

5. OpenIDEO (2012) "How It Works." Accessed: 11 June 2012. http://www.openideo.com/faq

6. DARPA (2011) "DARPA's Shredder Challenge Solved." Accessed: 11 June 2012. http://www.darpa.mil/NewsEvents/Releases/2011/12/02_.aspx

7. Greenemeier, L. (2009) "Inflated Expectations: Crowd-Sourcing Comes of Age in the DARPA Network Challenge." Scientific American. Accessed: 24 September 2012. http://www.scientificamerican.com/article.cfm?id=darpa-network-challenge-results

8. Burns, J. (2011) "Go Online, Beat a Puzzle and Become a British Spy." New York Times. Accessed: 11 June 2012. http://www.nytimes.com/2011/12/03/world/europe/britains-gchq-uses-online-puzzle-to-recruit-hackers.html?_r=1

9. M-Farm (2012) "M-Farm: About." Accessed: 11 June 2012. http://mfarm.co.ke/about

Building and Running Crowdsourcing Platforms

Regardless of the objective, every crowdsourcing venture shares similarities and necessitates the completion of certain steps. Every time you build, launch, and maintain a crowdsourcing platform, you will need to execute a specific process. This chapter details that process by providing an overview, and then describing how to choose your platform's objective and scope, analyze its target audience and media environment, design its structure and interface, build the technology behind it, market it, measure its success, and learn how to improve it.

Overview of the Process

From a technology standpoint, crowdsourcing platforms are easy to set up and launch. However, maintaining them and ensuring that they are successful are far more difficult. Due to the diffusion and low cost of social media and Web 2.0 technology, almost anyone can build a crowdsourcing platform or hire developers to do so without breaking the bank. Of course, the more complex the platform, the more technology expertise is required and the harder it gets. Still, the hardest parts about designing and maintaining platforms are the fuzzy details and factors that are difficult to make sense of and quantify. These include choosing the right participants with the appropriate access to technology, attracting them despite geopolitical or cultural issues, keeping them interested and motivated over a long period of time, ensuring their participation is proving valuable, and making sure adversaries do not ruin your platform. They also include, in the words of the accidental philosopher Donald Rumsfeld, the "unknown unknowns." In other words, getting the technology behind every platform is a type of science that anyone can master over time; but everything else about the platform is an art form that requires patience, creativity, and intuition about human behavior.

This chapter describes a process that will help you develop and master the art of building and running crowdsourcing platforms. The following is an overview of the process:

1. **Select objective and scope**—Identify which objective and problem you want your platform to accomplish, and decide the size, time period, and nature of your endeavor based on your resources and authorities.

2. **Analyze target audience and media environment**—Determine who you want to use the platform, and analyze their media consumption habits and environment to ensure they can and will participate.

3. **Design the platform**—Determine what the platform should look like from a technology and interface standpoint, and design an incentive structure for the participants.

4. **Build the platform**—Construct the front end, back end, and data tools of the platform using existing technology and through the use of developers and third-party companies.

5. **Market the platform**—Launch and maintain a marketing campaign that appropriately advertises the platform to prospective participants.

6. **Manage the platform**—Create rules, and hire moderators to minimize the risk inherent in crowdsourcing by guarding the community against adversaries, resolving issues, and fostering participation.

7. **Measure the platform's performance**—Create metrics for tracking the platform's success and failure over time, and integrate tools into the platform to collect and analyze the data for the metrics.

8. **Wash, rinse, repeat**—Lick your wounds, learn from the platform's performance, and adapt and relaunch the platform for greater future success.

The following sections describe each step of the process in greater detail. Chapters 9, 10, and 11 teach you how to adapt and add to the process depending on your objective and target audience, and feature case studies that walk you through the process. As you read through this and the subsequent chapters, note that you do not have to execute each step in the process in a specific sequence.

You will find that you will have to do some concurrently, or go back and redo an earlier step depending on the outcome of a later step. Also, be flexible and prepared for unforeseen problems, factors, and hostile audience reactions that force you to redo steps or modify the process.

Select Objective and Scope

Based on your task order or the problem you want to solve, select the objective(s) that fits best. Refine and narrow your problem of interest as much as you can to ensure you select the most appropriate objective.

Refine Problem to Establish Clear Objective

The platforms you build for security issues will accomplish one or a combination of three objectives: collect intelligence, solve problems, and influence populations. If this is your first platform, we advise against combining objectives because it introduces complexity and difficulty. As we describe later, it is better to modify the platform slowly over time to fit new objectives. For example, if your task is to collect information from inhabitants of a rural area about a series of local murders, your objective is to collect intelligence. If your task is to create a prototype algorithm that analyzes Twitter data to identify humanitarian disasters, your objective is to solve a problem. If your task is to persuade dissidents living under a dictatorship to organize and work with your government to overthrow the dictator, your objective is to influence the population. Perhaps you also need to ask the dissidents the best way you can help them overthrow the dictator, in which case the objective is to solve a problem. In most cases involving influence platforms, you will need to combine objectives.

After selecting the objective, continue narrowing and focusing the problem until it is clear and simple or split it up into smaller, simpler problems. Doing so is essential to running a successful crowdsourcing platform. If your target audience is confused about what you want them to do, your platform will fail to generate appropriate outcomes. If you want to collect intelligence about murders in an area, you need to ask participants about specific time periods, locations, and people. If you want to solve a problem as complicated as analyzing Twitter data to identify all types of humanitarian disasters, you need to break up the problem into smaller problems and ask people to analyze Twitter data to identify one type of disaster at a time. Subsequent chapters give more details about how to narrow and define problems for each objective.

Decide the Scope of the Platform

After selecting the objective and refining the problem, define the scope of your effort, which in turn will severely impact everything about your platform.

Several factors comprise the scope, some that are very specific to the problem. A few salient ones are as follows:

- **Need for secrecy**—Determine if you care if anyone can find out about your platform, or if you want to maintain deniability. The level of secrecy and anonymity you desire will greatly impact who your participants will be, how they will interact with you, and what your marketing campaign will look like. If you want to collect information about narcotics smuggling from individuals in areas of Colombia sympathetic to the FARC (Fuerzas Armadas Revolucionarias de Colombia), you probably do not want to openly advertise your platform and intentions. Otherwise your participants may face danger, or you will receive misinformation from FARC sympathizers. In the case of hiding participants' identities, you can allow them to adopt fake personas when interacting with others on the platform.

- **Need to minimize risk**—Risk in crowdsourcing platforms exists in many forms. Recognize what the risks may be and how willing you are to live with them. One of the most salient is the risk that adversarial participants present to other participants and your objective. If your participants are made up of individuals from populations known to be hostile to your government or organization, you will likely need to hire more moderators.

- **Financial resources and manpower**—Budget the money and labor you can commit to the platform. The constraints your resources present will greatly impact your incentive structure, how much you can minimize risk, and the technological sophistication of your platform.

- **Time**—Crowdsourcing usually works best over a longer period of time, especially if you are dealing with hostile or suspicious populations. It takes time to attract participants, win their trust, and convince them to fully help out. If you must accomplish your objective in a short period of time, you will need to rely on more lucrative incentives and amplify your initial marketing push. If you have a longer period of time, you can combine objectives and relax the monetary value of your incentives and the force of your marketing campaign.

Countless other factors exist. As you come across case studies and examples of crowdsourcing, identify and keep a list of factors that may affect your platform.

Analyze the Target Audience and Media Environment

After deciding what you want your platform to do, you need to decide exactly who you want to recruit to use the platform.

The *target audience* is the group of individuals who you expect will use your platform.

The characteristics and numbers that make up the target audience may shift over the lifetime of the platform. So far we have used the word "participants" to describe the target audience. The target audience inhabits a specific media environment.

The *media environment* comprises the types of communication technology available to a target audience, and how the target audience and people around them typically use the technology and influence each other.

Determining the target audience and understanding them and their media environment is essential to the success of your platform. Formulating who comprises the target audience and understanding the audience and their environment will help focus the function and features of your platform, and the marketing campaign around it. Imagine you are a company like Coca-Cola that is trying to sell a product. One of the most important steps for selling a product is identifying who will buy it, how to change it to better fit their needs, and how to advertise it to them. Instead of a product, you are essentially selling a service to a specific group of people. You will not receive money in return, but you will receive information, solutions, and influence.

Determine the Target Audience

Your objective and problem will determine which individuals and groups belong in the target audience. In other words, your objective will determine the characteristics, demographics, and behaviors that define a given individual in the target audience. Figuring out who comprises the target audience is an iterative process. With security issues, your platform likely will focus on a specific physical region such as Southeast India, or a problem affecting a specific population, such as people interested in solving math puzzles. Cast a wide net and choose potential participants based on their location and relevant attributes. For example, if you are collecting intelligence from Southeast India about violent communist groups, at first blush the target audience could be everyone in Southeast India.

Then create a list of characteristics that you would most like your ideal platform participant to have to narrow your target audience. You need people who have access to and regularly use phones or the Internet. Use characteristics on the list to then refine the constitution of your target audience. Thus, instead of everyone in Southeast India, your target audience now becomes 18–40 year olds (an age group that is familiar with communication technology) in Southeast India with phones and access to the Internet. You may determine that another characteristic you would like your target audience to have is that they live in rural areas, because that is where much of the action you are interested in takes place. Your target audience is then refined as 18–40 year olds in rural areas of Southeast India with phones and access to the Internet.

Your goal should be to select a target audience of moderate size. The target audience can be larger only if you have massive resources, the technology behind the platform is simpler, and it is geared toward collecting specific pieces of intelligence from individuals. You do not want a target audience that is too large and is defined only by one or two characteristics because it will dilute your ability to harness them effectively. You will find it difficult to moderate the audience, incentivize them effectively, and keep track of the data they are supplying. If the target audience is too small, you will not have enough diversity within the audience to get novel information and perspectives, and you will be too dependent on only a few people. If you have the resources to run a platform for a longer period of time, you can slowly ramp up the size of the target audience. The most famous social media platforms such as Twitter and Facebook do precisely that.

Another reason for containing the size of the target audience and slowly scaling it up is that expecting a large number of people to instantly join your platform is not realistic. Humans around the world tend to adopt technology and new ways of doing things at rates defined by the technology adoption life cycle. Typically, a small group of individuals in a group called the "innovators"—about 2.5 percent of a population—will be quick to try something new, including a new platform. About 13.5 percent—the "early adopters"—will eventually try it out, followed soon after by 34 percent of the population, the "early majority." The remaining 50 percent—the "late majority" and "laggards"—will slowly come around to trying it out, if ever.[1] See Figure 8.1 for a visual representation of the adoption curve.

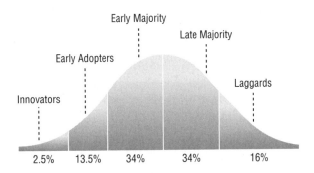

Source: Rogers, E. (1962) *Diffusion of Innovations*. Free Press, New York.

Figure 8.1: Technology adoption life cycle

Consider how people buy Apple's newest product. A very small proportion of individuals line up around stores and wait overnight so they can get the product before everyone else. A few (which includes us) will pre-order it on the Internet and wait two weeks or so for it to arrive, because we want to make sure the product is not a dud and we are too lazy to wait in lines outside a store. A big proportion will wait for the buzz to die down a little and buy it when it is more readily available in stores, and lots of people have given it good reviews. The rest will slowly come around to buying it, if ever. You should be happy if 10 percent of your defined target audience joins your platform and about 5 percent of your defined target audience uses it regularly.

Analyze the Target Audience

After determining what the target audience looks like, you need to analyze them to further refine them and extract insights so you can build a platform they find appealing and useful. This step is extremely important and pivotal to your platform's success. You do not want, for example, to end up creating a crowdsourcing platform accessible only through iPads for the rural populace in Papua, New Guinea who do not have them. If you expect to run your platform for a long time, you will need to routinely re-analyze your target audience and their media environment, and make changes to your platform as appropriate.

To appropriately analyze the target audience you need to uncover information about their lifestyles, media consumption, and social media use. Essentially, you need to find out if the potential target audience:

- Have the knowledge, skills, and/or resources you desire, and if so, what are they exactly?

- Can regularly use communication technology to access the platform, and if so, what is the technology?

- Are willing to interact with you and/or the platform, and if so, how and to what extent?

- Will respond to incentives and thus prove helpful, and if so, what are the incentives?

If some parts of the target audience do not fit any of the preceding criteria, you can discard them and further refine your definition of them. The criteria are fairly broad and the information you need to address them depends on your objective and your guess about the appropriate target audience. Most likely, you will need to find the following specific information about the potential audience:

- Traditional demographics to get an idea of exactly who may be in the audience. Certain age groups, genders, or economic classes may respond to incentives differently or prefer a different-looking platform. Such data includes their age, race, gender, group affiliations, literacy rate, and income. Ideally, you should try to find out the subsequent information for a few major demographic groups, such as age (teens, 20s, 30–50s) and gender (male vs. female).

- Lifestyle information to understand the audience's daily lives and how your platform can integrate into them without disturbing them. Information includes their occupations, hobbies, community participation, and level of material consumption.

- Media consumption to understand what type of media and interaction they prefer and what competition your platform may face. Media refers to traditional media (TV, radios, newspapers, and so on), the Internet (news sites, games), and social media. Relevant data includes how many times a day they consume media and from where; what genre and type of media they prefer; which age groups use it the most; if they use, consume it, or share it with others; which websites they like best; how many hours they spend on the Internet per day on average; and how much they pay for media.

- Technology adoption to see how local cultural and economic factors impact the technology adoption life cycle. Understanding their behavior with all sorts of technology will help you create metrics that appropriately measure what is a good versus poor rate of participation at certain time periods. Relevant information includes sales of new technology, how much money they spend on technology, and their use of social media.

Feel free to look for more or less and different types of information as you see fit. The goal is to choose and understand the target audience well enough to create a platform that appeals to them, and hence works for you.

Analyze the Media Environment

Analyzing the target audience's media environment will further your understanding of not only how the audience may use your platform, but how people around the audience will affect their behavior toward your platform. The people around the audience are not initially part of your audience, but they may become so after some time. The aforementioned criteria and information go a long way toward analyzing the audience's media environment; especially, identifying what sort of media and technology exists in the audience's environment and how they interact with it or use it. See Figure 8.2 for a visual representation of the media environment. The following information will fill in gaps and provide you with information about the people and technologies surrounding the audience:

- Information about the two circles of people that surround the target audience. The people and the audience provide each other with information and influence each other's behavior concerning media consumption and technology use.

  - The first circle consists of people immediately around members of the target audience, such as their family members, friends, classmates, and colleagues. Understanding the audience's first circle can help in numerous ways. For example, if you want to scale up your audience, you can encourage participants to convince their first circle to join. Also, if your platform is controversial, the first circle may steer participants away from participating. It also consists of the media technologies the target audience uses on a daily basis.

■ The second circle consists of institutions, groups, and individuals that guide the audience's behavior, including schools, local governments, popular radio stations, and celebrities. It also consists of all media available in their environment. The second circle may subtly influence the audience to stay away from or to join the platform depending on how they perceive the platform. Identify who they are so you can track what they say about your platform or competing media.

■ The general state of technology in their environment to assess the audience and their culture's relationship to social media, the Internet, and their willingness to try new things. In certain areas, you may need to provide people with phones or access to the Internet in order for your platform to work. Understanding the local relationship to technology and media will help you assess whether you should try and what you should expect from your efforts.

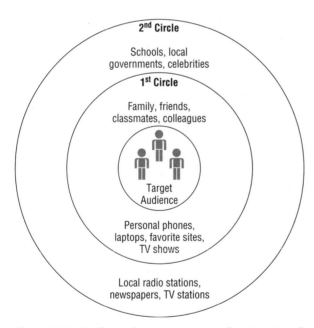

Figure 8.2: Media environment surrounding target audience

Get the Information to Do the Analyses

You may start to feel overwhelmed by the amount of information you need to simply get started with crowdsourcing. However, do not be discouraged. A lot of the information is surprisingly easy to come by, and you can probably make do without the missing information. The following are some of the best and easiest ways to get the appropriate information:

- **Hire subject matter and area experts**—By experts, we mean people who have lived in the locations, know the audience, their culture, and their media environment. We do not mean "pundits" who write lots of articles or tweet all day about the relevant areas without never actually visiting the places. The best way to tell them apart is that the former usually eschew the label "expert," whereas the latter crave it. The real experts can help you craft your platform and maintain it so it is the most appropriate for the audience. We know from personal experience that working on a platform in a remote part of the world without experts generates lots of frustration and wasted effort.

- **Google**—Use the Internet to look up census data, U.N. data sets, various non-governmental organizations data sets, academic research papers, and sociological articles. You will be surprised at how much stuff on the Internet ends up becoming relevant. Make sure to verify the information using some of the tips from Part II of this book.

- **Social media data**—You spent part of this book learning how to collect and analyze social media data, so you might as well use those skills to help build your platform. Your potential audience may talk about their media and technology habits on social media, and the fact that they are using social media provides you with critical information.

- **Crowdsourcing pilot programs**—Simpler crowdsourcing platforms or failed platforms can provide lots of key insights. We explain how to build a simple crowdsourcing platform that employs sending bursts or blasts of texts to collect intelligence in Chapter 9.

Design the Platform

Designing the platform entails determining exactly what the platform will look like, how it will function, how participants will access and use it, and how it will attract the participants. The information you have collected so far and your analysis of the target audience and the media environment will help you make the determinations. This step is the hardest part when it comes to working with crowdsourcing platforms, and you will likely get it wrong more times than you will get it right. It is very much an iterative process and highly dependent on your objective, target audience, resources, and various geopolitical, cultural, and economic factors.

Determine the Platform's Look and Feel

The look and feel of the platform refers to the type of platform, the features available to the participants, and the design of the user interface (UI). Types of platforms are the ones described in Chapter 7 and include standalone websites such as OpenIDEO's or forums, smartphone applications (apps), apps integrated into existing social media platforms, and SMS-based communication networks. The features are the ones detailed in Chapter 2 and include the ability for the participants to chat with each other, share pictures, and friend each other. The UI design includes everything from the colors of a website to the placement of buttons on a smartphone application. Use the findings of your target audience and an honest consideration of your resources to determine the platform's look and feel.

Choose the Correct Type of Platform

The first step is determining the type of platform you will build. Your analysis should have detailed what types of social media platforms, websites, and phone applications your target audience prefers. Unless the media environment is oversaturated with a specific type of platform, build the type of platform that the audience prefers. The audience will adopt it quicker, and it will reduce how many resources you expend trying to teach them how to use it. Thus, if the audience:

- Obsessively uses Facebook, build an app on Facebook. It will lower your development costs and make marketing easier.

- Is very web-savvy and visits lots of websites, build a new standalone website. Many websites for people in third-world countries look awful and are seizure-inducing (lots of annoying, flashing banners). A well-designed and clean website will prove very attractive.

- Uses smartphones a lot, build an app for the smartphone. Generally, the more developed the media environment, the more likely you should build a smartphone app.

- Uses dumb phones and SMS a lot, build an SMS-based network. SMS networks are also helpful when you need to discreetly collect intelligence from individuals or small groups in hostile or rural areas.

- Is made up of different types of people or uses lots of different media, build a mix of platform types. For example, if your target audience includes people from all income classes in Pakistan, you should build a standalone website that users can also access through SMS.

Your budget and the resources available to you will determine your type of platform. Generally, standalone websites require much more money and manpower to build, followed by smartphone apps, existing social media platform apps, and SMS networks. However, do not make decisions solely according to your budget. Whatever type of platform you build has to be familiar and attractive to your audience. Building an SMS network for an audience who prefers complex and feature-full smartphone apps will save you money but prove ineffectual.

Choose Your Platform's Features

Figuring out which features your platform should have is very similar to determining what type of platform you should build. Again, look through data on the target audience and media environment to see what your audience prefers. If the audience tends to prefer platforms with a certain type of feature, make sure to include that feature into your platform. Try to introduce a feature with which the audience is unfamiliar. The novelty of the feature will attract participants and entice them to try out the platform.

However, do not overburden your platform with too many features. If a platform has too many features, the audience may become overwhelmed and stop using it. Simplicity sells. Focus on a few things and do them well. If you must integrate certain features, introduce them piecemeal over a long period of time. Introducing features gradually also enables you to remove features without upsetting the audience too much. Your audience will likely speak up about what kinds of features they want. Make sure to listen to them.

Also, when choosing features, stay true to your objective and make sure the features do not contradict it. If your platform's goal is to only collect intelligence about the movement of terrorist groups in specific parts of Lebanon, you likely do not need to give your audience the ability to friend and communicate with each other. Your audience will likely want anonymity, and the last thing they would want to do is willingly speak with others about the fact that they are providing foreign governments with intelligence about people in their neighborhoods.

Design the User Interface

Your platform must have at least a decent UI to succeed. Few people will willingly use a website or app that has an awful UI. The UI is less important for SMS networks, because all people can do is send texts to each other. For other types of platforms, however, the UI is critical. Again, look through your analysis to see what your audience prefers, paying special attention to their media environment and culture. Culture and personal experience may impact how people view and manipulate objects, shapes, and colors. Study the audience's culture and environment to see what they prefer and expect, and make sure to find out if certain colors or shapes are taboo. Regardless of culture, humans do share some global similarities when accessing interfaces. Check out the references for a list of such similarities, and also differences.[2]

Designing a UI properly is difficult and should not be left to amateurs. Unless you have a background in web or industrial design, do not try doing this step yourself. Hire art or web development students, preferably ones familiar with the target audience's culture, to help you design the UI. As you design the UI, recruit testers to use your platform. A good guideline for UI design is that it should be minimalist, intuitive, and built with the audience in mind. Just because you prefer certain colors or functionalities does not mean your audience will as well.

Determine the Platform's Incentive Structure

The platform may look and function great, but it will be useless if you cannot incentivize your audience to participate. Incentivizing entails encouraging and motivating your audience to sign up, try the platform out, recommend it to others, and use it regularly over a long period of time. An incentive structure organizes the incentives, helps participants understand them, and ensures the participants receive them in a timely manner.

You need incentives for your platform to succeed—there is no free lunch and there is no free platform participant. Well-structured and attractive incentives can also help your platform stand apart from other platforms and gain popularity. They can also encourage your participants to compete with each other and boost their value to you. Those of you involved with human intelligence (HUMINT) collection already understand the power of incentives to recruit and maintain sources. HUMINT officials use the shorthand M.I.C.E. for describing their incentives. M.I.C.E. stands for:

- **Money**—Source needs money to pay off debt or improve quality of life and social status.

- **Ideology**—Source does not agree with her government's way of doing things, or has competing belief systems (social, religious, economic, political).

- **Compromise or Coercion**—Source is susceptible to blackmail or vulnerable and willing to help due to an emotional relationship. It is usually the last resort, and for crowdsourcing the very worst motivator.

- **Ego or Excitement**—Source does not feel valued or is unsatisfied with his reputation or life. He believes he is worth much more than he is currently valued, or thirsts after challenges and adrenaline rushes.[3]

Incentives on crowdsourcing platforms also follow the M.I.C.E. model, although we call them extrinsic and intrinsic incentives.

Choosing Extrinsic and Intrinsic Incentives

Your platform may offer extrinsic, intrinsic, or a combination of both incentives. *Extrinsic incentives* are material items and objects external to a person such as cash, phones, clothes, SMS credits, and toys. They also include services such as the provision of local crop prices and weather forecasts. They are the M in the M.I.C.E. model. The exact nature of the extrinsic incentive will depend heavily on what your target audience likes, prefers, needs, and wants. It is essential to choose incentives that your target audience values. Rewarding free MP3 downloads of the new Iron Maiden album to Tuareg nomads who do not have iPods and have never heard Western heavy metal music will only elicit confusion and disinterest. In contrast, dumb phone ringtones from a local Tuareg rock band such as Tinariwen will resonate with the target audience and leverage technology they already have.

Be creative when coming up with extrinsic incentives. Work with local governments, NGOs, companies, and/or area experts to determine appropriate extrinsic incentives. For example, throughout much of the world where literacy is low and oral traditions persist, new technologies enabling easy recording, replay, and dissemination of local materials may be how you build your platform. Your platform could connect populations (who share a common language that is in danger of dying out) to share security or travel tips across long distances in a remote region. Such a platform could not only provide hard-to-get security tips, but it could map locations, the distribution of the population, and transcribe and create dictionaries (through crowdwork or appropriate language tools). Such an effort would draw not only security-minded organizations, but academics and NGOs (such as UNESCO) as well.[4]

Generally, extrinsic incentives are easy to quantify, measure, inform the target audience about, and provide. They have agreed-upon definitions. Participants can easily understand what winning an hour's worth of credit at the local cyber cafe entails. They are also likely to entice participants in the beginning when the platform is first launched and they do not yet trust you. However, extrinsic incentives can become expensive and lose their appeal over time. People usually like novelty, so over a long period of time you will have to offer a variety of incentives. Also, people may lie or cheat when exchanging information for money and material objects depending on how they acquire the incentives and the oversight they receive.[5] In general, when creating a platform for a long period of time, phase out or minimize the role of extrinsic incentives and replace them with intrinsic incentives.

Intrinsic incentives are internally generated motivations specific to an individual—they are the fuzzy, hard-to-describe things such as pride, a sense of community and belonging, and the feeling of contributing to a valued project and helping out. They are the I, C, and E of the M.I.C.E. model and much more.

Usually, intrinsic incentives are agnostic to a person's culture. Everyone responds to similar intrinsic incentives as long as they are not psychopaths who are motivated by their own set of personal intrinsic incentives.

Intrinsic incentives have enormous potential and power. Most people will respond strongly to them and, if given the opportunity, surpass participation expectations. Because much of intrinsic incentives have to do with social factors, such as maintaining reputation and relationships, their propagation among participants will lead to the development of strong communities on the platform, which in turn will lead to sustained participation. Communities on a platform are the social networks and relationships that participants develop, much like they do in the real world. Once people become part of an online or offline community, they do not want to leave it. People also have an innate tendency to want to be useful to their community. Thus, if their community expands to include you as the moderator and owner of the platform, then even better for you. Also, extrinsic incentives can lead to corruption, but intrinsic incentives have a way of simplifying people's motivations, and ensuring that the participants remain helpful and honest. However, intrinsic incentives are much harder than extrinsic incentives to deliver. You cannot simply tell a 16-year-old Latvian programmer that she will feel wonderful if she participates in helping you to find security gaps in your IT infrastructure. Instead, you have to provide the participants with the environment where they can acquire the incentives. Creating the environment is an art form.

When discussing intrinsic incentives, some people think of the word gamification. *Gamification* is the process of creating a game out of an everyday process. The theory is that people like playing games, in which incentives are delivered through game mechanics such as the earning of points. The theory then continues that by gamifying an everyday process, you can boost a person's willingness to undertake the process. For example, individuals trying to lose weight are more likely to follow their diets if they get points at the end of a day based on what they ate. According to the theory, because individuals really want to earn points they will follow their diets more strictly. Some of the intrinsic incentive delivery methods we describe later have some similarities to such a gamification process. However, the term has become mangled and overused, and is frequently misapplied. It also simplifies and makes light of people's complex motivations. When looking at other crowdsourcing platforms or social media platforms for inspiration on how to create your own incentive structure, be wary of analyses of the platforms done through the lens of gamification. Gamification aficionados often see game mechanics and intrinsic incentives where none really exist. Do not approach structuring intrinsic incentives for your platform as if you were creating a game out of getting participants to complete your objective. Approach it solely as how can you incentivize individuals to do something they would probably want to do anyway. If an individual absolutely does not want to help you, you will not be able to gamify him into doing so.

Overall, both incentive types are useful, albeit for different cases. Extrinsic ones are better for attracting participants when the platform launches, and persuading participants to join and use the platform initially. They are also more appropriate and easier to implement when your objective is to simply collect intelligence and solutions for problems. Intrinsic ones are better for keeping participants interested over a long period of time, and if you need them to do amazing things. They are essential when you need to influence audiences or if you need to encourage participants to work together toward a common goal or solution. Ideally, you should combine both. The best way to combine them is where acquiring one type of incentive allows the participant to acquire the other type.

Delivering the Incentives

Making sure participants can acquire the incentives in a timely manner is essential to keeping participants happy and useful. Delivering extrinsic incentives depends on the target audience's physical, political, and cultural environment. Work with local governments, organizations, and/or area experts to determine the best way for delivering goods to participants. In some cases, discretion may be needed. Delivering services is much easier and should usually be done through the same device with which participants access the platform. Clearly communicate what the reward is, how people can get it, and when people should expect to get it.

You do not deliver intrinsic incentives, per se. Participants acquire them as a result of their behavior on the platform. You must, however, construct the environment to ensure their behaviors can translate to incentives. You have numerous ways to construct the environment, and which you choose will depend on your target audience. Some popular mechanisms for constructing the environment on other platforms include doing the following:

- Allow participants to create a community on the platform and communicate with each other by allowing them to text or direct message each other, form online groups, friend each other, and discuss issues in chat rooms and forums. Implementing this mechanism in platforms that leverage only dumb phone technology and do not exist as websites is markedly more difficult, but not impossible. Try to implement it nonetheless because the platform will then stand out and draw the target audience's attention.

- Implement a leveling (popular in video games such as Warcraft) or virtual badge system (Foursquare, Yelp) that makes participants feel they are earning improvements in knowledge, effectiveness, and status. For example, if a participant provides you with extremely valuable intelligence, reward her publicly with a rare and hard-to-earn gold badge that participants understand only goes to top performers. The boost in the rewarded participant's public status will increase her self-worth, pride, and eagerness to continue to participate in the community and platform.

■ Provide participants with things they can collect. For example, for every puzzle a participant solves, reward him with virtual gold coins. Participants with larger collections will feel as if they are higher in status and more needed by the community.

■ As mentioned before, combine intrinsic and extrinsic rewards in such a way that earning one type of reward boosts the ability to earn the other type. For example, let participants trade in the badges they earned for money. The participants will then work harder to regain the badges and their status in the platform's community. Conversely, publicly congratulate participants who win an extrinsic reward to boost their status and pride.

■ Communicate directly with the participants through community moderators to elicit their feedback, suggestions, and questions. Participants will then feel a sense of ownership concerning the platform, which will increase their desire for the platform to succeed and thus, increase their desire to participate. We discuss the role of moderators later in this chapter.

■ If appropriate, inform participants about how their efforts have helped you complete your objective and/or have helped improve their lives. Like the OpenIDEO platform, get them involved in carrying out any suggestions or solutions they offer.

Look through existing crowdsourcing platforms to identify more mechanisms. Feel free to try different ones, and expect some to fail.

Regardless of the type of incentive, always deliver on your promises. The platform owner and manager's reputation is everything, and failing to deliver incentives on time or lying to participants about what they have won will cause participants hurt feelings and anger. They might even seek retribution against you by, for example, posting about their experience with your platform online for the rest of your target audience and adversaries to see. You may have noticed that word travels extremely fast on the Internet. Also, do not make it too easy for participants to win the rewards. Make them work for it. In return, they will be more eager and thus more useful. It is the same principle as asking a girl out—if you appear desperate and too easy to please, she will either not value you or simply ignore you.

If you expect participation to be high for whatever reason, you can scale back how many rewards you provide and make their bestowment schedule irregular. An incentive or reward's bestowment schedule stipulates when participants can win a reward. For example, participants can answer a question every Friday and win something, which is an example of a regular schedule. Or they can sometimes answer questions on Tuesday to win something, or sometimes on Wednesday, which is an example of an irregular schedule. As is expected, people, like other mammals, can be conditioned to perform actions upon receiving a reward. Ironically, if people expect a reward but are not sure when they will earn it, they will be motivated to perform the action more aggressively and regularly—a phenomenon known as conditioning with a variable schedule of reinforcement. By bestowing rewards irregularly—sometimes immediately rewarding participants and sometimes holding back—you can boost overall participation exponentially.[6] However, use this tactic carefully and only in cases where you are confident the participants trust you, like your platform, and are eager to participate.

Build the Platform

Using the technology to build a crowdsourcing platform is relatively easy, as long as you are not trying to do too much at one time. Building a platform entails creating its components, which roughly are:

- **The front end**—The website or app that participants and moderators see
- **The back end**—The servers that house the website or app and manage the data coming through the platform, and the tools that allow the platform managers to change the platform
- **The data analysis tools**—If applicable, that help you sift through crowdsourced data

Assuming you do not have a web development background, you have three ways to go about building a platform.

The first way is to use and modify existing crowdsourcing platform templates. Increasingly, mostly non-profit organizations are putting up software packages and code online for free so that anyone can use them to create and deploy certain types of platforms. For example, Ushahidi, the Africa-based non-profit, allows anyone to use its templates for creating and deploying crowdmaps. The crowdmaps are ideal for collecting intelligence through SMS and populating them on a map. Anyone can use the crowdmap templates because they are open source and require very little technical skill to use. Some current open source solutions are not quite templates, but rather tools that can still help with deploying and running platforms. These solutions are usually for running SMS-based platforms. FrontlineSMS and RapidSMS are two such free tools that enable anyone to send numerous bursts or mass texts to people and receive and manage their responses. More templates and tools will become available as crowdsourcing grows in popularity. As you may have noticed, the templates and tools are better suited for platforms that collect intelligence as opposed to other objectives.

CROSS-REFERENCE Chapter 9 describes how to use crowdmaps and FrontlineSMS to build an intelligence collection platform.

The second way is to hire in-house or contract developers to build the platforms. If you want to build standalone websites or smartphone applications, you probably need to hire outside help. The developers should help you create the front end, the back end, and any data tools you need. The developers can also help you refine and extend the aforementioned open source templates and tools. We prefer working with developers from the region our target audience inhabits. Local developers will know what their neighbors will like and can steer you away from bad decisions. Also, do not simply hire developers to build the platform initially and then let them disappear. Keep them on retainer, or at least ensure that they are willing to work with you over the long term because platforms will go awry. Web technology is always riddled with bugs.

The third way is to hire or partner with third-party organizations to build and maintain customized crowdsourcing platforms. Increasingly, for-profit companies are starting to offer such services. Most, if not all, of these companies are geared toward helping companies do brand management and marketing. Be wary of such companies because very few deal with security issues or work in the areas you probably find most interesting. Defense contractors in the U.S. are starting to offer services to build and manage crowdsourcing platforms. From our experience, many are simply jumping on the social media bandwagon and promising amazing things, but have little idea of what they are doing. When considering them, make sure to ask about their experience and how many people they have on staff who have built such platforms before. The ideal company will need solid and experienced teams of behavioral experts, area experts, data analysts, and web developers. Very few companies actually have such capabilities because crowdsourcing for security is a relatively new field. Do your due diligence when considering the companies, because hiring the wrong company can lead to a disastrous platform and disastrous consequences. Partnering with experienced non-profit organizations such as OpenIDEO is better in some ways. They are fewer in number, but they have run crowdsourcing platforms before. In OpenIDEO's case, it actually advertises its willingness and preference for partnering with government and other organizations to solve tough societal problems. They will lessen your risk and burden. However, many non-profits are skeptical of people working in the defense and security field. Make sure to approach them cautiously.

Market the Platform

Your platform could be the best designed and constructed in the world, but it will not amount to anything if your target audience does not know about it. You are not Steve Jobs. Regardless of where your target audience lives, you cannot simply build something and expect people to go crazy trying to get in on it. You will have to launch advertising campaigns for your platform, just as you would for any other product or service. In this case, your customer is the target audience. Unfortunately, creating the advertising campaign will not be anything like the TV show *Mad Men* (although, feel free to drink at lunch).

First, decide how much you want and need to advertise your platform. Take the need for secrecy and discretion into account. As we explain in subsequent chapters, often it is better to create platforms that do not make their ultimate objectives clear. For example, if you want to collect microeconomic data to understand instability in certain areas, you may tell your audience that your objective is to create a platform for merchants and farmers to share market price data so they can improve their market strategies. In this case, you would advertise the latter objective and not your ultimate objective. Often, you may not want too many people in an area to know that you are collecting information from individuals in those areas. For example, you could incentivize workers for sex traffickers such as drivers and bodyguards to text you their locations so you can map trafficking ratlines. If word got out that there was an SMS network that was collecting information from such workers, a few sources would probably be put in danger and you may get misinformation. In such cases, crowdsourcing becomes more of a traditional clandestine HUMINT mission, albeit one that relies on social media technology and where word of the network spreads mouth to mouth. Also, take into account how many participants you want on the platform. If you only want 15 users, do not advertise too much. You will have to start turning people away, and people do not like being turned away.

Keep this need for secrecy in mind when naming your platform. Use names that your target audience will understand and knows how to pronounce and spell. Make sure your name is simple and has some indication of what you want your audience to think your platform will do for them. However, your name probably should not reveal your true objective. For example, your objective's platform may be to collect intelligence about how Al-Shabaab activity is affecting economic and thus physical stability in the areas surrounding Mogadishu. However, you may tell your audience that your objective is to collect market prices so you can supply the participants with their area's market prices to boost market transparency and help them set their crops' prices. In such case, name your platform the Somali translation of something like "Open Market" or "Farmer Help." Use common sense and do not name it "Al-Shabaab Tracker."

Apart from secrecy, the media environment also dictates the volume of the advertising campaign. If you are trying to launch a platform in a media-saturated place like France, you have to compete with lots of other activities and media for people's attention. Your advertising campaign will then have to be fairly substantial. If your audience lives in the Andes Mountains and only has access to dumb phones because you provided them, you do not need to advertise that heavily. You will not have to compete with other dumb phone networks because they will not exist. You may, however, have to compete with daily activities that have nothing to do with technology.

After determining the appropriate marketing push, employ a variety of campaigns and ways to advertise your platform. Your advertising campaigns will likely come in waves, depending on your platform's popularity. You will have to launch an initial advertising campaign to get the word out in the weeks leading up to the launch of the platform. After the launch of the platform, you may have to launch smaller advertising campaigns every few weeks to keep participants interested and to attract more participants. Use different methods for each campaign. The methods depend heavily on the media environment. Some examples of methods by media environment type are given in Table 8.1.

Table 8.1: Example Advertising Methods

MEDIA ENVIRONMENT DESCRIPTION	REGION EXAMPLE	ADVERTISING METHOD
Lots of media choices and sophisticated social media technology	U.S., Europe	Use Twitter and Facebook to generate buzz. Use what you learned in Chapter 5 to identify key influencers in social networks and advertise to them to make things go viral.
Much of the country has access to traditional media, and an increasing amount are using social media.	Emerging countries such as India, Thailand, Brazil, South Africa	Advertise through traditional media outlets that have global reach such as al-Jazeera, CNN, BBC, Xinhua; use online social media platforms most popular in those regions.
Little advanced media technology. Only the rich have access to new and even traditional media.	Zones of conflict, developing countries, much of Africa	Put up billboards in markets or on main roads; partner with local NGOs to spread the word; hand out T-shirts and flashlights on the condition that the receiver signs up on the platform.

Apart from external marketing campaigns, you can also advertise through the platform itself. Incentivize participants to recruit others.

Lastly, track mentions of your platform or advertisements in the target audience's media environment to see how much buzz you are creating. If you want lots of people on your platform, your goal should be to get a lot of people in the area of the audience to talk about it. Getting picked up by local media is a good indication that your advertising campaigns are working. Use the metrics we describe later to assess how well your platform is doing, and modulate your advertising campaign as needed.

Manage the Platform

Running a crowdsourcing platform involves dealing with lots of people, many of whom will likely see the world very differently than you. The more features a platform has, the more likely the interactions among participants will lead to disagreements, fights, rule-breaking, and chaos. You need to manage the interactions among the participants and the communities that may appear on your platform. Communities are more likely to appear on platforms with social networking and messaging features, where the objective is to influence or solve complex problems that require working together. If your platform simply collects intelligence from individuals, much of this section probably will not be as relevant. For all other cases, especially when your objective is influence, you will want to foster a sense of community for the participants because it is bound to happen after repeat interactions among participants. Creating a set of rules and hiring competent community moderators or managers to patrol the platform will significantly reduce the risk that antisocial interactions drive away participants and ruin your platform.

The first step for managing the platform is determining what you consider the ideal types of interactions on the platform. If you are running a platform where participants solve math problems, the interactions among participants should not result in political arguments. If you are running an SMS-based platform where participants text you the location of illicit actors, you do not want interactions among the participants. If you are running a platform through which you want to influence participants to denounce extremist activity, the interactions among participants cannot result in language promoting extremist activity. However, do not be too idealistic or strict with what you consider proper interactions. People everywhere frequently like to go off-topic and only sometimes does it produce harm. Providing people with space to interact is essential for creating communities, which could significantly bolster your platform's effectiveness.

Create a set of rules and policies that you want all participants to abide by. They are similar to the rules you agree to abide by but never read when you sign up for platforms like Facebook. The rules should clearly state what you would like the audience to think is the objective of the platform. It should also state what sort of language and behaviors are allowed and, just as importantly, what is not allowed. Read the terms and conditions or rule pages of websites like OpenIDEO or Facebook to get an idea. When participants sign up for the platform, make sure they get a chance to read the rules. You will likely need to work with a translator to make sure it is in language they clearly understand.

Simply reading the rules does not mean participants will necessarily abide by them. However, the rules give moderators the authority and legitimacy to then patrol the community.

Community moderators are key for making sophisticated platforms with lots of social networking and messaging features work. Moderators have numerous roles, including assisting participants, keeping them engaged, securing and protecting them, and regularly updating you with the platform's status. They post on the platform like they are participants similar to the police officers who walk the streets as the people they are charged with protecting. The moderator is an example of how social media has led to the creation of a job that did not exist a few years ago. Because the occupation is new, finding experienced and competent moderators can be difficult. An ideal moderator must be familiar with the Internet and social media, pay attention to detail, have social tact and a desire to work with people, and have the ability to handle lots of stress, awkward situations, and verbal abuse.

Finding moderators is easier if your target audience is Western. If your target audience is in a foreign country or from a different way of life, you must hire and train local moderators who live among the target audience. You will need to hire anywhere from two to five moderators, depending on the sophistication of your platform, the risk you are willing to tolerate, and the number of participants. You can even recruit part-time or full-time moderators from the participants, many of whom will want to help out as the platform becomes more successful. The moderators should work in shifts so that they cover most of the target audience's waking hours. Make your most experienced or talented moderator the lead moderator and put him or her in charge of managing the other moderators and updating you with what is going on with the platform periodically. The moderators should also have access to platform administrator tools, not available to participants, that allow them to warn and ban participants, delete messages, and discuss among each other.

Several books and articles describe how to help train community moderators, a few of which we list in the references.[7] Generally, all moderators should regularly do the following:

- **Answer queries from participants**—Participants will no doubt have questions about how the platform works and how they should behave. The moderators must identify when participants are having problems, acknowledge queries and problems, and provide sound guidance, as needed.

- **Make participants feel important**—Moderators must routinely thank and compliment participants for their ideas, information, and posts. They should also ask participants for advice on improving the platform or other issues. Essentially, the moderators need to constantly treat participants as if they are very important people without seeming too sycophantic.

Participants will consider the goodwill that moderators provide them with as an intrinsic incentive that makes them feel better, and thus spur them to be more active on the platform.

- **Identify and stop trolls and misguided participants**—In Internet parlance, *trolls* are troublemakers and rule-breakers, who sometimes create havoc on social media and online communities for the sake of creating havoc or attention. Often, participants will break the rules because they do not understand or do not agree with them. Moderators must quickly identify and stop trolls and misguided participants. They should reinforce the rules of the platforms and make it clear that rule-breakers face punishments. Otherwise, the platform and the community on it will devolve into chaos. The punishment can include a one-on-one stern talking-to, or even outright banning of the users and their IP address from the platform.

- **Acknowledge criticisms and suggestions**—Your platform will not be perfect and will suffer from several problems. Engaged participants will voice their opinions about the problems. The moderator must listen to appropriate criticisms and suggestions, and inform you of them. Participants often know the best way to make your platform more effective and engaging.

- **Spur participation**—The moderator should serve as a role model for the participants, and frequently ask questions, post their opinions about topics (especially important when your objective is influence), and echo the sentiment and opinions of participants. If participants are engaged and active already, the moderators need not be as active. Ideally, you do not want moderators to act too much like participants.

Measure the Platform's Performance

Regularly measuring your platform's performance is critical to ensuring that your objectives are being met, and for knowing if and when you need to implement changes. There is no one right way to measure performance. You will likely need to create and populate numerous metrics that tell you something about each component of the platform.

Create and Choose Metrics

Traditional information operation metrics and forms are largely unsuitable for crowdsourcing efforts. Instead, you will have to create and select metrics based on your objective, your target audience, and expectations. Use the sample metrics in Table 8.2 and come up with more on your own.

Table 8.2: Sample Metrics for Measuring Crowdsourcing Performance

OBJECTIVE	SAMPLE METRICS
Collecting intelligence	Number of messages over time; Number of corroborating messages; Number of sources; Demographics of most active sources
Solving problems	Number of solutions over time; Number of votes on solutions; Sentiment of comments on solutions; Amount of corroboration over time
Influencing populations	Number of friends each participant has; Number of messages exchanged between participants; Sentiments of posts over time
Any	Number of participants; Number of new participants per day; Amount of time participants spend on site per visit

Set expectations of what you would like to accomplish and make it a habit to regularly update your metrics and compare them with your expectations. By regularly checking the metrics, you can make your expectations more realistic and identify parts of the platform that may need improvement. For example, if you find that participants lose interest after three weeks of using the platform, you can introduce special incentives around the three-week mark to keep the participants interested.

Collect Data to Populate Metrics

The metrics you select are only useful if you can collect data to substantiate them. Three data sources are available. The first is data tools integrated into your platform that measure everything from how many participants you have to what time of day they post. Google Analytics offers a free service that enables you to track usage statistics or how participants are using your website. Smartphone apps and SMS networks are harder to collect data about. However, ask your developers to integrate data collection tools into the app, network, and web page. Integrating data collection tools is easy and will prove very useful. The second source includes everything external to your platform. They can include how many times your platform is mentioned on Twitter or in the local newspaper. Regularly check the newspaper, radio stations, and social media platforms that your target audience frequents to collect this type of data. The third is providing surveys to participants before, during, and after the platform's life. Work with a statistician or someone with a background in quantitative research methods to create and run proper surveys. Ruining surveys with biases and leading questions is very easy and will result in errant data.

Wash, Rinse, Repeat

Do not expect to succeed on your first platform or meet all expectations. Running crowdsourcing platforms is more difficult than it appears. Each time you run one, you will gain new insights for how to run them more efficiently.

Hire outside consultants to do a post-mortem on your platform and identify specific instances where it went wrong or succeeded. Create and maintain a lessons learned chart throughout the life of the platform to ensure you have captured all key insights. However, keep in mind that some of the insights and lessons may be specific to a target audience or situation. There is a burgeoning community of well-meaning individuals who are constantly working on crowdsourcing problems and sharing the lessons they learn on websites such as http://www.crowdsourcing.org/. Consider posting your failure and lessons learned on such sites to look for advice. In an almost post-modern twist to your dilemma, crowdsource the solution to your crowdsourcing problem.

You now have a thorough understanding of the overall process for building a crowdsourcing platform. However, you need to tweak the process to build the platform that will help you meet your objective. Chapter 9 will teach you how to tweak the overall process to build a platform to collect intelligence.

Summary

- Using existing technology to build a crowdsourcing platform is relatively easy; however, ensuring the platform's success is much harder and depends on numerous factors.

- Regardless of the objective, each crowdsourcing platform necessitates the completion of certain steps. Read Chapters 9, 10, and 11 to learn how to tweak the steps according to your objective.

- The overall process for building a crowdsourcing platform is roughly as follows:
  - Select the platform's objective and scope:
    - Refine the problem to establish a clear objective or combination of objectives.
    - Decide the scope of the platform depending on factors such as the need for secrecy, and the overall budget, time, and appetite for risk.
  - Analyze the target audience and media environment:
    - Determine the target audience, who are the people you want to participate on the platform.

- Analyze the target audience to understand how they communicate and what they prefer so your platform is attractive to them.

- Analyze the media environment to see what your platform is up against in terms of other media and how outside forces can influence your participants.

- Get the information to do the analyses from the Internet, social media, research reports, sociological studies, pilot crowdsourcing projects, and area experts.

- Design the platform:

  - Determine the platform's look and feel by choosing the correct type of platform, features available for participants, and intuitive user interface.

  - Determine the platform's incentive structure by integrating a mix of extrinsic and intrinsic incentives into your platform. Doing so will attract participants and keep them active.

- Build the platform:

  - Create a front end that participants will see, a back end that houses the server and data, and data analysis tools to analyze all the incoming data.

  - You can either use existing crowdsourcing platform templates, hire developers, or hire a for-profit crowdsourcing building and managing company.

- Market the platform:

  - Decide how much you want to advertise your platform based on your need for secrecy and the saturation of the audience's media environment.

  - Use a variety and combination of methods including advertising it on the Internet, traditional media, and billboards; also incentivize participants to recruit others.

- Manage the platform:

  - Create a set of rules and policies so participants know how to behave.

  - Hire local community moderators with good social skills to ensure participants abide by the rules, help and listen to participants, shut down troublemakers, and update you on the platform's status.

- Measure the platform's performance:
  - Create and choose metrics that are relevant to your platform and objective.
  - Collect data to populate metrics through tools such as Google Analytics and data tools integrated into the platform that collect user statistics.
- Wash, rinse, repeat:
  - Learn from mistakes you make from your first few platforms.
  - Make the appropriate changes and try again.

Notes

1. Rogers, E. (1962) *Diffusion of Innovations*. Free Press, New York.

2. Johnson, J. (2010) *Designing with the Mind in Mind: Simple Guide to Understanding User Interface Design Rules*. Morgan Kaufmann, Burlington; Norman, D. (1988) *The Design of Everyday Things*. Basic Books, New York; Weinschenk, S. (2011) *100 Things Every Designer Needs to Know About People*. New Riders, Berkeley.

3. Wallace, R., Melton, H.K., and Schlesinger, H.R. (2008) *Spycraft: The Secret History of the CIA's Spytechs from Communism to Al-Qaeda*. Dutton, New York.

4. Rymer, Russ (2012) "Vanishing Voices." Journal of the National Geographic Society. 222 (no. 1).

5. Ariely, D. (2012) *The Honest Truth About Dishonesty: How We Lie to Everyone— Especially Ourselves*. HarperCollins, New York.

6. Ferster, C. and Skinner, B. (1957) *Schedules of Reinforcement*. Appleton-Century-Crofts, New York.

7. Connor, A. (2009) *18 Rules of Community Engagement: A Guide for Building Relationships and Connecting with Customers Online*. Happy About, Silicon Valley; Ng, D. (2011) *Online Community Management for Dummies*. Wiley, Hoboken.

Crowdsourcing Intelligence

Crowdsourcing platforms can help you collect actionable intelligence from the most hostile populations and the most remote areas. The process for building and running crowdsourcing platforms that collect intelligence as opposed to accomplishing other objectives is relatively simple. However, the process can vary significantly depending on the target audience and the type of information you want to collect. This chapter goes over the process by explaining what is possible through crowdsourcing and what is not possible, and shows how intelligence platforms differ from platforms used to accomplish other or mixed objectives. It also walks through how to build and run platforms that collect intelligence for analyzing hard-to-reach populations and helping design other crowdsourcing platforms through SMS, helping law enforcement encourage citizens to identify criminal suspects through smartphones, and helping with crisis response through crowdmap websites.

Understanding the Scope of Crowdsourced Intelligence

Crowdsourced intelligence is intelligence derived specifically through custom crowdsourcing platforms, known as *intelligence collection platforms*, as opposed to from social media in general. It is another form of human intelligence that veers into the territory of signal intelligence. You can apply crowdsourced intelligence to solve a variety of mission sets, ranging from improving disaster relief to identifying and tracking illicit actors and behaviors. Specifically, you can use it to do the types of analyses discussed in Chapter 5 and Chapter 6 of this book, and even the advanced analytics we describe in Chapter 12.

Uniqueness of Crowdsourced Intelligence

Crowdsourced intelligence differs from other types of intelligence in two ways. The first is obviously how you gather it. The second is the form of the data or, simply, what the intelligence looks like. By definition, all crowdsourced intelligence is delivered via different social media technologies. Each technology differs in the type, amount, and format of data it transmits. For instance, Twitter only allows people to share pictures and links, and only 140 characters of text. Thus, the form of the crowdsourced intelligence is heavily dependent on the type of social media technologies you use and the type of platform you build. Table 9.1 lists what form of data you should expect for each type of platform.

Table 9.1: Data Form by Platform Type

PLATFORM TYPE	DATA FORMS
SMS (text-based)	Text, metadata, location
Smartphone application	Text, multimedia, metadata, location
Website	Text, multimedia, metadata, web scripts, feeds, location
Existing social media platform (for example, Facebook)	Text, multimedia, location, feeds

Direct and Indirect Crowdsourced Intelligence

Crowdsourced intelligence comes in two types: direct and indirect. Direct intelligence directly and explicitly tells you about a place, an object, or a person. In other words, the intelligence is direct when a person provides you with information about what he or she sees or you receive data about a place, an object, or a person. On the other hand, intelligence is indirect when you have to sift through acquired data that may seem irrelevant to infer things about a place, an object, or a person.

Direct intelligence is more readily useful but harder to get. It is obvious, tells you exactly what you need to know, and requires less analysis. For example, say you are interested in the movements of an extremist violent group in a certain neighborhood. Individuals in the neighborhood use your crowdsourcing platform to tell you where members of the group live, what churches, restaurants, and meeting places they go to, and when they go there. The intelligence you receive is direct. You may have to compile it and verify it from other sources, but you do not need to do much more analysis on it to figure out the movement of the group in the neighborhood. However, getting such clean and useful intelligence is difficult. Generally, the more direct the intelligence, the more you may have to incentivize people to provide it. People will share critical information with someone they do not know, but it takes rewards or time to convince them to do so. Also, keep in mind that in some cases individuals who provide you with direct intelligence are putting themselves at a greater risk. In the example, say that the individual providing you with the information is actually a member of the group. If the group comes across pieces of very sensitive and complete information about their movements, they may correctly reason that someone from within their group is supplying the information. They may then seek out the mole and punish him or her harshly. However, if they come across information that is indirect and not obviously referencing their movements, the group may have a more difficult time finding out who is supplying the information. Due to the difficulty of acquiring direct intelligence, you should expect to receive it only when the incentives are high enough for potential sources to take the risks, or when the target audience approves of your objective.

In contrast, indirect intelligence is less readily useful but easier to get. You have to infer the information you need from lots of relevant and irrelevant intelligence, which takes time and analytical resources. Using the same example, say you are trying to acquire information about the group's movement through indirect intelligence. You can then ask individuals in the neighborhood about how they feel toward the group. Numerous individuals then tell you that they feel scared when they see several members of the group together. You can then ask individuals in different parts of the neighborhood about how they feel at certain times of the day. If their feelings of insecurity spike at certain times of day and that pattern holds true over a long period of time, you can then infer that the group likely appears at that location at that time of the day. You can then compare the locations of individuals who are experiencing insecurity spikes at different times and map the group's movement. Your assumptions and conclusions may not be completely correct, but you at least get some information about the group's movement. Generally, sources are more likely and willing to give up indirect information. The information they are providing is not as sensitive, and in some cases may even appear completely benign and irrelevant to your ultimate objective. Because the risk to the potential sources is low, the incentives they need to overcome the risk will also likely be low. Due to the relative ease of acquiring indirect intelligence but the difficulty of making sense of it, you should expect to use indirect intelligence when the target audience is unsupportive or scared of your ultimate objective, when you do not have much to incentivize them with, and when you have the time and resources to infer conclusions. In practice, you often need to collect both types and use one to help collect and make sense of the other. Figure 9.1 provides a graphical summary of the differences between direct and indirect intelligence.

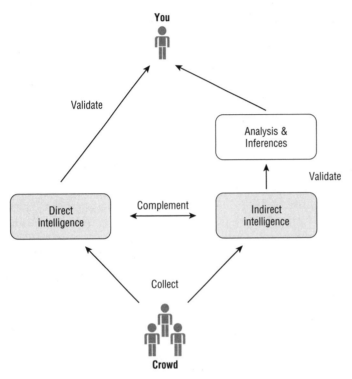

Figure 9.1: Direct and indirect intelligence

Appreciating the Limits of Crowdsourcing Intelligence

Collecting intelligence through crowdsourcing platforms can significantly bolster your missions, but it is not a panacea. It will not always get you the information you need or do it in a cost-effective and efficient manner. Like other intelligence collection methods, it too can fail, produce costly or dangerous embarrassments, and prove useless. It has a few disadvantages that, if not addressed, can limit its utility and power.

Uncooperative Target Audience

The most obvious disadvantage is that the success of every intelligence collection crowdsourcing platform depends heavily on its target audience. Some audiences will simply not cooperate with you or give you the data you need in a timely manner. Understanding the target audience and structuring the platform and incentive structure in a way that appeals to them will significantly increase the likelihood that they cooperate with you. Unfortunately, no platform type or set of incentives can guarantee cooperation. Sometimes, the risk will be too high for potential participants. For example, it is safe to assume that people in Mexico in 2012, in areas that are currently being ravaged by vicious drug cartel violence, will be very unlikely to provide intelligence about drug cartels in their areas. Drug cartels in such areas regularly and brutally kill people who provide sensitive information about them to authorities. Few people will cooperate and want to put themselves and their families in danger. You may still find a few and incentivize them sufficiently, but the chances of incentivizing a lot of people to cooperate are low.

Higher Risk for Participants

Additionally, in some cases the risk is higher for participants to cooperate through crowdsourcing platforms than through more traditional Human Intelligence methods. Unless your target audience consists of only a few people, word can eventually get out that the platform exists. You can take steps to minimize the possibility that adversaries find out about your platform, but you can never eliminate it. Platforms that crowdsource direct intelligence about violent illicit actors from participants living in unstable regions can especially endanger the lives of the participants. Also, if word gets out about the platform and leads to attacks against the participants, then word will probably get out about the attacks. Increased scrutiny can lead to major fallout such as stories about your failed platform and objective on the front page of the *Washington Post* or *Le Monde*. Think about such worst-case scenarios when designing platforms, but do not become paralyzed by them. Risk is not an excuse for inaction. In the case studies, we discuss some ways of helping participants maintain anonymity. In the most dangerous conditions, the best way may be to create a platform that crowdsources only indirect intelligence.

NOTE Notice that a target audience's silence and refusal to cooperate, especially if it is sudden or out of the ordinary, is a form of indirect intelligence that tells you something about the audience and their environment.

Misinformation

Like intelligence collected via traditional HUMINT methods, crowdsourced intelligence may be false. Adversaries may infiltrate your platform and feed you misinformation. Or, individuals who are not affiliated with adversaries but do not know anything about them either may decide to participate simply because they want the extrinsic incentives. They may submit false information that is usually sensational so they can get your attention and win lucrative rewards. Some participants may tell the truth initially, but start to lie over time. Some become addicted to the extrinsic and intrinsic incentives, such as the need to be useful or stay involved, and start to fabricate their information. However, you can minimize the effect of misinformation by having a large and diverse sample of participants. You can then use information from a variety of sources to validate suspicious information. If someone tells you something that contradicts what 200 other people say, it is probably false. On the other hand, one person may know something that others do not. In such cases of extreme outliers, look for third-party, independent verification. Go into the project with the attitude, "if it's too good to be true, it probably is." A healthy skepticism will keep you on your toes.

> **NOTE** An increase in misinformation is also indirect intelligence and a clue that adversaries may have gained access to your platform.

Misinformation not only affects you, but it can also affect other participants and the target audience at large. If your platform allows participants to see submissions from others, an adversarial participant may use the platform to cause confusion and chaos. For instance, in Veracruz, where drug cartel violence is high, the local populace takes to Twitter to inform their communities about violence and possible threats. In the summer of 2011, two Veracruz residents tweeted that drug cartel members were kidnapping children from schools. Parents read the tweet and panicked. Afraid for their children's lives, they rushed out to pull their children from school, generating chaos across the city. The warning, however, was false and the children were safe. However, the panicky chaos among the parents resulted in 26 car accidents.[1]

Misinterpretation

Even if you manage to validate all the crowdsourced intelligence, you may still misinterpret it. The chances of misinterpreting data are especially high when you are dealing with indirect intelligence. Often, the cause for misinterpretation will be mistranslations. Use native translators or very sophisticated automated translation tools when translating incoming intelligence. Also, much of crowdsourced intelligence is text-based. As anyone who has sent a sarcastic e-mail knows, sarcasm is often lost in text. Regardless of claims, no existing natural-language processing tools can accurately detect sarcasm, especially in less popular languages. Misinterpretation may also come about if you do not query your participants properly. If the questions you pose are unclear, participants will interpret them differently and respond incorrectly. The best way to minimize misinterpretations is to hire area experts to help you craft your queries and study the responses.

Hawthorne Effect

Lastly, another disadvantage of crowdsourcing intelligence is related to the *Hawthorne effect*, which is the phenomenon that the behavior of a participant during a study may change because the participant is engaging in the study. In our case, the very act of crowdsourcing intelligence and how you do it may change the nature of the intelligence the participants provide and may even change the participants' environment. For example, if you introduce dumb phones into a community so that you can crowdsource through them, you may fundamentally change how the participants communicate with each other and thus their lives. The ideal way to collect intelligence in most cases is to do so by least disturbing the area in question and the lives of the people involved. However, involvement in a crowdsourcing platform increases the potential for disturbance. In some cases, you may have to provide technology such as cell phones to the target audience so they can participate. Such an introduction of technology can drastically change lifestyles and cultures. Thus, it can affect your target audience analysis and force you to change your platform design.

Also, some intelligence collection platforms offer social networking features that help participants build and change relationships, which can affect the types of people they come across and the sort of information they acquire and share. The effects can be positive or negative for your objective. A participant may make ties with people through the platform who encourage him or her to share information with you. Conversely, the participant may make ties with people who discourage information sharing. Generally, the more technology and social networking features you introduce, the more likely you will affect the lives of the participants and, thus, their ability and willingness to share information with you. In some cases, you may want to minimize the effects, but in some you may want to bolster it. Keep the Hawthorne effect in mind when assessing the target audience before, during, and after the deployment of crowdsourcing platforms.

Tweaking the Process for Intelligence Collection Platforms

Despite the few disadvantages, crowdsourcing platforms still offer a tremendous ability to collect intelligence from seemingly unreachable populations and areas. They are unique platforms useful for accomplishing a specific objective, and thus differ from platforms for other objectives. In general, Chapter 8 describes the process for building and launching them. However, you need to tweak the process and recognize the differences between intelligence collection platforms and crowdsourcing platforms for other objectives.

Usually, intelligence collection platforms are run for shorter periods of time than solution and influence platforms. However, depending on the missions you are supporting, you may need to run intelligence collection platforms for longer periods. Incentivizing people to provide a piece of information does not involve time-consuming activities such as creating social networks and relationships, or even fostering much trust between you and them. As long as you can effectively communicate the fact that people will be safe and get rewarded for the information they provide, people will start providing intelligence. Because intelligence platforms require less time to get going, they require fewer resources to maintain over a longer period of time. You can then save on resources, or use the savings to expand your target audience or make the extrinsic incentives more attractive.

Also, intelligence collection platforms do not require elaborate social networking and messaging features. In some cases, you will not want participants to communicate with each other so you can better protect their identities. Reduced interaction between the participants, and even between the participants and you, reduces the need for moderators. For intelligence platforms that collect indirect intelligence or those that evolve out of influence platforms (as we describe in Chapter 11), you may need to integrate social networking and messaging features.

Finally, we expect that you will use intelligence collection platforms primarily to collect intelligence from rural and poor areas that are hard-to-reach. In these areas, populations are more likely to use dumb phones or access the Internet through cyber cafes. Thus, your platforms will likely be based on SMS networks and websites, as opposed to smartphone applications.

Now that you know where to tweak the process, you can start building and running intelligence collection platforms. In the subsequent sections, we walk through how to build and run several platforms that differ in type, resources budget, target audience, and in the missions they can support. For ease of understanding and comparison, the steps of the walkthroughs follow the structure of the process in Chapter 8.

> **WARNING**   Keep in mind that the subsequent sections are fabricated examples, not paragons of accurate research. We do not have the time and resources to do all the steps thoroughly, especially analyzing the target audience in each example. So we have taken shortcuts and made assumptions when considering what appeals to the target audience. Do not worry about whether we are wrong about the target audience. Instead, focus on how we approach problems and use the technologies.

Collect Intelligence from Hard-to-Reach Areas through SMS

You may need to launch crowdsourcing platforms or other efforts in places where you do not know much about the population. Generally, the more remote the area, the harder it will be to get information about the people there and the more it will cost. Fortunately, SMS technology is becoming ubiquitous, even in the most hard-to-reach and poorest areas. Even if the population there is not already using SMS, you can provide them with dumb phones and they can learn how to use them fairly quickly. Therefore, SMS-based intelligence collection platforms are ideally suited for collecting information about hard-to-reach and relatively unknown populations.

Increasingly, open source technologies such as FrontlineSMS and RapidSMS are making it easier than ever to implement SMS-based intelligence collection platforms, otherwise known as *pilot platforms*. This walkthrough describes how to use SMS technologies to build and deploy a pilot platform to crowdsource intelligence about target audiences for population analysis or for the design and deployment of more elaborate crowdsourcing platforms.

NOTE You also can use the subsequent process for simply collecting intelligence about a specific topic, and not only about the target audience.

Define Objective and Scope

Imagine that you are a member of a Western government and you need to collect information about the target audience in Somalia, a place that is not exactly hospitable to Westerners. You need to collect information about the target audience to aid the design of a long-term crowdsourcing platform that collects commodity price information and opinions from residents in a hostile region of Somalia. You then intend to look at correlations between the prices and the opinions to see if you can use the prices as an indicator of instability and insecurity in the region. Initially, you want to focus on areas that are currently stable so you can collect data to establish a baseline correlation (or lack thereof) between prices and opinions. You also want to see if Somalis are willing to text you information about prices. Your budget is fairly small and its enlargement depends on your initial success. For example, you may have only enough money to purchase and distribute cell phones or to travel to your region of interest. So, you intend to focus on a few stable cities at first with the hopes of expanding to less stable areas later. Gaining success will be easier in the more stable areas and, because this is your first crowdsourcing platform, it is easier to start out in a relatively safer area.

Currently, you need to collect two pieces of information about the target audience. The first is an accurate database of phone numbers in the target region that you can send an SMS message to and ask for information.

> **NOTE** The phrases, "send an SMS to," "send a text to," and "send a text message to" are all equivalent to the phrase, "send an SMS message to."

The second is identifying which of the phone numbers belong to people who are knowledgeable about commodity prices, such as farmers, merchants, and businessmen. With your limited budget in mind, you have the following three options for getting the information:

1. Buy a database of phone numbers from local telephone companies. However, purchasing numbers is costly and difficult unless you have special connections.

2. Use the database of phone numbers from marketing companies that do SMS marketing in the region. Although relatively inexpensive, finding a marketing company that has reach in the region in which you are interested is difficult. Also, through this option you do not get access to the phone numbers because the database of phone numbers is proprietary to the marketing company. The company sends SMS messages to its database of phone numbers on your behalf and you never see the phone numbers.

3. Send an SMS message to a randomly selected phone number to assess its validity. This option is high risk and high reward—it might not work, but you will get access to all the phone numbers. It is relatively inexpensive but requires some patience and ingenuity. It also requires that you either travel to the region or work with someone who lives in the region.

After reviewing your options, you decide to try the third option first because you really want to assemble a list of phone numbers that you can access at any time. Meanwhile, you seek out a marketing company that has access in your region of interest so you can execute the second option later. The first option is too cost-prohibitive. For now, your objective is to crowdsource through SMS technology a list of phone numbers and some basic demographic information about the target audience.

Analyze the Target Audience and Media Environment

To start, you need to analyze the target audience and media environment to see if your plan of random texting to get information will work. Somalia is often depicted in the media as a post-apocalyptic warzone where chaos reigns. In reality, it has a robust and thriving telecommunications sector and is home to a number of mobile and Internet providers. The providers have limitations—most are region specific, do not offer roaming services, and face extortion threats from Al-Shabaab. They mostly provide services in major population centers along the coast and largely ignore the smaller inland cities.

Further research reveals that the largest populations of mobile phone users are in the more stable northern regions of self-declared autonomous Somaliland and Puntland, the tip of the Horn of Africa. These regions have large populations and relative stability and safety from Al-Shabaab, and hence are ideal for your initial crowdsourcing project. Your target audience is thus the population of Puntland and Somaliland. Finding the exact number of Somalis who use mobile phones is difficult—some reports suggest about 10 percent of the population uses mobile phones. However, the regional expert (one of the authors) knows that much of the mobile phone–using population resides in Somaliland and Puntland. Additionally, because telecommunications networks are area-specific and do not offer roaming, many mobile phone users use multiple phone numbers or SIM cards so they can access different telecommunications networks. Also, much of the mobile phone population uses dumb phones. Smartphone adoption is on the rise, but far from becoming the norm. Like in other parts of Africa, the target audience uses phones for not only communicating with each other, but for doing monetary transactions and sending each other SMS credits.

Interestingly, information from other area experts reveals that mobile phone numbers in the region follow a set pattern that enables you to derive a list of possible phone numbers. Mobile providers use a specific prefix in a specific area. By knowing a few prefixes in one area from known phone numbers (found on the Internet), you can figure out which prefixes belong to which mobile provider and which area. You can then generate phone numbers by using the prefix and assigning numbers randomly for the rest of the number. Most numbers might be wrong, but a few will work. For example, if a certain town uses the prefix 242, you know all other numbers in the region must be 242-*XXXX*, where *X* is a random number. You can then create a list of numbers for that area, such as:

- 242-0001
- 242-4242
- 242-5830
- 242-5840

and so on.

Some more research reveals that radio stations are popular in the area, followed by television. Internet usage is sparse and only about 1 percent of the population seems to have access to it. Finally, another key fact is that the target audience routinely comes into contact with non-governmental organizations and other international organizations. The audience and the region in general are heavily dependent on external assistance for projects and are open to working with foreigners to develop their region as a bulwark against the chaos to their south.

In summary, the target audience and media environment analyses reveal the following key insights:

- The primary mode of social media for the target audience is SMS.

- Mobile phone numbers tend to follow a pattern, so you can generate a list of possible numbers.

- The target audience is willing to work with foreigners, as long as they are convinced that their region will benefit as a result of cooperation.

Keep these insights in mind while designing the crowdsourcing capability.

Design the Platform

The first part of designing the platform involves determining exactly what the platform should look like. The second part involves designing the incentive structure, which, in turn, can affect the look of the platform.

Determine the Platform's Look and Feel

The target audience analysis reveals that the crowdsourcing capability should be an SMS-based platform. The audience regularly uses SMS, and other forms of social media are not widespread. Also, the analysis reveals that you can indeed generate random phone number lists and use existing SMS interaction technology to simply ping the audience for information.

After deciding that you need to build an SMS-based platform, you can start determining how the platform should work. First, you need to generate or acquire a list of phone numbers. Then you need to send an SMS message to the phone number asking the participant for information about the price of a certain commodity. You need to provide an incentive for the participant to respond via SMS. You then assemble the responses and determine which phone numbers elicited a response, and how willing the audience is to participate. Because you are initially generating a list of phone numbers from the pattern, do not expect most of your phone numbers to work. You will likely receive a response from non-working phone numbers saying your message could not be delivered.

The features of the platform are extremely limited by the nature of SMS technology and what you are trying to accomplish. Because you are only interested in collecting simple pieces of intelligence from a wide group of people, you do not need to institute sophisticated social networking or messaging features. The only relevant feature is the ability to send text messages between you and the participants.

The dumb phone in the hands of the participant that receives and sends the SMS is only one component of the platform. The other components include the tool that enables you to send SMS messages to multiple people and the data management system that manages, stores, and displays all the information. In practice, the SMS sending tool and the data management system are usually combined into one piece of technology. Figure 9.2 shows the relationship between the dumb phone, the SMS sending technology, and the data management system.

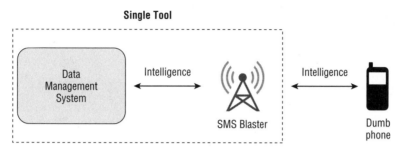

Figure 9.2: Relationship between SMS platform components

The interface for SMS is the text on a participant's phone and the phone's interface for accessing the SMS. As you will see, the other platform component has its own interface, so you do not need to design any interfaces for this platform.

Determine the Platform's Incentive Structure

You are not asking participants for a lot of information or requiring them to dedicate a lot of their time to your platform. Hence, the bar for incentivizing them is low.

The easiest form of incentive is to offer them a few SMS credits for responding. SMS credits function like a gift card at a store, except instead of cashing in gift cards for goods, recipients cash them in to receive free text messages. Typically, an SMS credit recipient receives instructions through a text message asking him to text a specific shortcode (a truncated phone number that is easy to remember) to receive his credit. Upon texting, he is instantly credited with a few free text messages. Because the target audience uses SMS frequently, free text messages are attractive to them. Because SMS is so ubiquitous, purchasing and delivering SMS credits is easy. Contact (usually through its web page) the prominent mobile phone operator in the region and ask if you can purchase bulk SMS credits. By purchasing in bulk, you receive a discount on each SMS credit. Each SMS credit by itself is very inexpensive, sometimes less than a cent, but they can quickly add up. Plan for about a 20 percent response rate when figuring out how many SMS credits you should buy. For example, assume you plan to text 1000 people and offer each 5 free text messages for responding. Out of the 1000 people, you expect about 200 to respond. If you are giving 5 credits, you need to buy 1000 credits. Make sure that you send each participant a text stating clearly that they will receive 5 free SMS credits upon responding.

Apart from the extrinsic incentive of SMS credits, you can also incentivize the audience through their propensity to work with NGOs to improve their communities. In the text message you send them, communicate that you are asking for price information to help their communities coordinate prices and improve market transparency. If you have the time and resources, contact a local NGO and see if you can get its sponsorship. The audience may already be incentivized to participate with the NGO, and so you may not have to incentivize them through extrinsic items.

Build the Platform

Building the platform only involves utilizing one of many existing SMS sending and management tools. You need to set up the tool, acquire the shortcode and SMS credits, and then start sending and receiving texts. For the SMS sending and management tool, we prefer using the open source and free FrontlineSMS (available at `http://www.frontlinesms.com`) and RapidSMS (available at `http://www.rapidsms.org/`). Feel free to try any tool, although we find FrontlineSMS to be the easiest to use. The following steps teach you how to set up FrontlineSMS to "build" your platform:

1. Purchase a GSM modem or dumb phone similar to the type the target audience uses. A GSM modem is essentially a phone without the screen and keyboard. Check out the list available on the FrontlineSMS website here for more information and recommendations: `http://www.frontlinesms.com/the-software/requirements/`. Incidentally, the list is crowdsourced.

2. Purchase or use a simple laptop with a USB port and a serial port, and a cable to connect the phone to the computer via the serial port. If you are using the GSM modem, you will not need the cable, but instead will connect it via the USB port. You do not need access to the Internet.

3. Purchase a SIM card (local to the audience's location) with lots of credits or a robust service plan that can pay for all the texts you send and receive. A SIM card is the little fingernail-sized gold-plated plastic card that you insert into your phone. Insert it into your phone or the GSM modem. You may need to travel to the region to get the card or have a source do it for you. As you see later, having some sort of a physical presence on the ground will be beneficial.

> **NOTE** If you cannot travel or work with someone in the region, you can use services such as Clickatell (available at `www.clickatell.com`) that provide you with a phone number and credits. Check out the FrontlineSMS website and the software help section for more information about using such services. We also briefly go over such services later.

4. Go to `http://www.frontlinesms.com` and download the FrontlineSMS software, which is as of this writing at version 2. Installation is relatively quick and typical of other programs. You do not need to register the software., although it helps the software provider to learn about their users and offer better support if you do. It works on Windows and Apple operating systems, and is available in beta for Linux. The system requirements for the computer are minimal. The software opens in your default browser and performs best with Google Chrome or Firefox.

5. Connect the GSM modem or phone to the computer. Allow any built-in modem management software to install, or open if it is already installed. Enter the PIN, if there is one, when prompted by the software. Once the device is recognized, close the program down.

6. Open FrontlineSMS, and wait for it to auto-detect the attached modem. If this does not work, try some of the steps in the Troubleshooting advice on the FrontlineSMS website: `http://www`
`.frontlinesms.com/user-resources/frequently-asked-questions/`
`how-can-i-troubleshoot-my-frontlinesms-install/`.

7. Test the tool by sending an SMS message to another phone (such as your personal phone or your colleague's phone). To do so, in the home interface, click Quick Message on the top. Enter a short message, click Next, enter the number of the other phone including the country dialing code, click Next, and then click Send. The phone should receive a text. Text back with the other phone. The message should pop up in the Messages section of the software. Keep in mind that it takes about ten seconds to send one message.

8. Because you are hoping the participants will remember your number and respond to it, you should consider purchasing a shortcode (1234 rather than the longer 081234567 number). Shortcodes will be easier for participants to remember and respond to because they are shorter than normal phone numbers. Also, participants will not be able to determine your phone number. Purchasing a shortcode will come at additional cost, and require you to work directly with the mobile operator, or purchase a shortcode from a web-based SMS service such as Clickatell, which is already integrated with FrontlineSMS. You may also want to consider a service such as Clickatell if you are planning to send or receive large numbers of SMS messages, as modems and phones can only deal with 4-8 SMS messages per minute.

After testing and purchasing credits, you can start using the tool to deploy your platform and start sending and receiving texts. You can use and customize FrontlineSMS from this point onwards for other platforms. The walkthrough for our platform continues with the following steps:

9. Identify the prefix patterns from existing phone numbers you find on the Internet for the specific region. Use a spreadsheet program to create a list

of random phone numbers. Save the list as a comma-separated value (CSV) file. The file needs to be formatted in a specific way that is described on the FrontlineSMS website. Click Settings and follow the instructions on the part of the screen that says Import to import the file. An easier method is to simply click Contacts on top of the interface, and start creating and adding numbers. You do not need to fill out all the fields.

10. To start sending the messages, the phone or GSM modem has to be in the region. Set up a computer in the region yourself or have a local partner do it for you. Make sure that you have regular access to power, because power blackouts happen frequently in the region. We recommend you use a laptop in case you need to cope with short-term power outages without losing the device connection. You can also use a service such as Clickatell, which requires steady Internet access. Because you are using a phone or modem, FrontlineSMS does not need the Internet to work. If you cannot travel to the region, you can purchase a roaming package when you purchase your SIM card, much like when you purchase roaming for your phone when you travel. When you do, make sure your SIM card is set up to roam internationally. However, roaming packages tend to be expensive.

11. After inputting all the contacts, click Messages and then click "Create new activity" on the left. You will see a list of activities that you can carry out using FrontlineSMS; for example Announcement, Autoreply, and Poll. To try it out, select Poll. Select a Yes or No question and in the field labeled "Enter question," type **Are you satisfied with the current range of mobile networks? Respond to get 5 SMS credits**. You can try out any question you want as long as it is under 160 characters. Click Next and sort the messages by a keyword if you wish. Click Next, and for the automatic reply option type **Thank you for your response. Text to *XXXXX* to claim your credits**. *XXXXX* refers to the shortcode you receive from the company that sells you SMS credits. Click Next to see the text you will send out. Then select the recipients and send the text.

12. Await the responses. A response means that the phone number is active and the person is willing to speak to you. You have thus narrowed your target audience and can start building your list of phone numbers.

13. Repeat as desired. Once you set up contacts, and information about the messages, you just need to let the software and computer run on its own.

> **NOTE** We suggest you practice multiple types of polls, as well as a simple blast SMS to a few key contacts first, before doing your actual poll. You can then tweak the settings according to your needs, and refine how you collect, respond, export, and then provide the incentive to responders.

If you can work with developers or have a developing background, you can also download and manipulate the source code for FrontlineSMS, which is based on Java, JavaScript, and Groovy (a language platform for Java). Modifying the source code enables you to integrate various analytical tools, tweak the program to your needs, change the format for creating and sending messages, and much more. You can do really creative things with FrontlineSMS.

WARNING   The process for setting up FrontlineSMS may change as the software underlying it changes. Make sure to go to the FrontlineSMS website at www.frontlinesms.com to keep track of the new software and get help for new and existing features.

Market the Platform

The marketing campaign for the platform is inherent in the platform itself. You are marketing it by randomly texting potential participants out of the blue and asking them to participate.

However, you may find that participants do not respond, or you want to expand your platform's reach. The target audience analysis reveals that the audience listens heavily to radio. So, advertise on radio stations throughout the life of the platform. In the advertisements, talk up the fact that participants will not only receive SMS credits, but also gain information about prices. Also, partner with a local NGO or an established local organization. The NGO's workers can spread the word or at least reduce the suspicion people may have about getting texts from nowhere. Your text can simply say, "Sponsored by (*Name of NGO*)."

Manage the Platform

Because the platform does not have social networking or collaborative features, you do not need to hire moderators. You need only one or two people (depending on how many texts you send out) to monitor the FrontlineSMS software and keep track of phone numbers and messages. You also need someone to ensure that you do not run out of SMS credits or credit on your SIM card.

Measure the Platform's Performance

After deploying the platform, start measuring its success rate at finding correct phone numbers and eliciting responses. You can hire developers to integrate analytical tools that measure the performance for you automatically into FrontlineSMS, or you can analyze its performance manually. Example metrics include:

- Number of responses by people
- Number of responses saying "Message could not be sent" because of wrong phone number

- Time and date of responses
- Number of relevant and irrelevant responses
- Number of SMS credits claimed

Wash, Rinse, Repeat

On your initial run of sending texts to participants, you likely will not be very successful. You may find that all the phone numbers you generated are wrong or the pattern finding does not apply to the specific area in which you are interested. You may also find that participants fail to respond, and you may not be sure if they are not responding because the phone number is not valid or because they do not want to respond.

You may need to refine your objective and pick the second option from the list of three you had created earlier. To remind you, the second option is to use the database of phone numbers from marketing companies that do SMS marketing in the region. SMS marketing is typically known as bulk or blast SMS marketing. *Blast SMS marketing* involves sending out massive amounts, or blasts, of text messages to thousands of phone numbers at a time. Each phone number you blast to receives the same text message. Typically, each blast SMS service has a list of thousands of phone numbers in a certain region. For a fee and a cost per SMS sent, they allow anyone to use their service to send out texts to their phone numbers. Some services even allow the recipients to respond to the advertising SMS. The service forwards the response to you. Some blast SMS services such as Clickatell provide tools to customize their interface for your needs and select from a variety of options. They are easy to use, relatively inexpensive, and have reach in the most remote parts of the world. Another major benefit is that they use phone numbers that are valid and updated so you can be sure that your texts are reaching your audience.

If you are interested in using the service, go to www.clickatell.com and select the International site. Then under Products, select either Easy SMS or SMS Gateway depending on which features you require. You can also use Clickatell through FrontlineSMS. Check out their websites for more information.

Collect Intelligence from the Community for Law Enforcement

Facewatch is a smartphone app and website that British police use to help businesses share information about thieves and other criminals. Facewatch enables businesses to share information about crimes with each other and sort through CCTV pictures of potential suspects to aid identification. Through the app, the police collect all reports and effectively crowdsource the identification of possible criminals from local businesses. If, while sorting through CCTV pictures of possible suspects, a business member recognizes someone as being present when a crime occurred, the business member can then instantly report it to the police through the app. Visit Facewatch's website at `http://facewatch .co.uk` to learn more.

Facewatch is an ingenious way of crowdsourcing information about criminal activity targeting local businesses and about the identities of possible suspects. However, it does have a few limitations and causes some legal concerns.[2] One, it is limited to catching petty criminals that affect local businesses and shops and not serial rapists and murderers that terrorize communities. Two, people are poor at identifying possible petty criminal suspects from pictures and they might identify the wrong person. Three, the idea of sharing people's pictures with the suspicion that they are criminals without them knowing it raises concerns about privacy and civil liberties.

CROSS-REFERENCE Chapter 14 addresses privacy and civil liberties concerns involving social media and crowdsourcing in more detail.

This walkthrough explains how to create a smartphone app that, like Facewatch, incentivizes the community to help law enforcement, but with modifications that address Facewatch's limitations. Instead of focusing on petty criminals, this app focuses on catching major criminals such as serial rapists and murderers that affect everyone in the community and not only businesses. The success of the TV show *America's Most Wanted* has shown that people are more adept at submitting information about a few major criminals, rather than lots of petty criminals. Few people take note of petty criminals and can easily become confused about their identities and whether they have seen them, but are less likely to do so with major criminals. Also, major criminals engender the attention and thus submission of more information by the public, which makes it easier for the police to investigate and connect the dots. A few people will always use the opportunity to submit misinformation or get attention, but the police have always had to deal with that. Additionally, by focusing on only a few people, you are not sharing public pictures of thousands of people. Essentially, this app translates the idea of showing a crude drawing of a major criminal's face on TV and asking people to call in with information to the social media world. The following sections walk through the process of creating such an app.

Define Objective and Scope

Imagine you are working on behalf of local law enforcement in a Western city, such as the Houston metropolitan area, and the objective is to help the local police investigate major crimes including serial rape, homicide, the kidnapping of children, and narcotics trafficking. The impetus is to bolster law enforcement at a time of tight budgets, and to encourage community members to help law enforcement.

Crowdsourcing offers the opportunity to crowdsource information from the public about major crimes and missing children, especially at a fast rate when the crime is still fresh. The police already advertise pleas for information on television and newspapers; however, they would like to increase their reach. Reaching more people will increase the likelihood that they will find people with the right information. If police are not dependent on television shows and newspapers to get the word out, they can ask for information whenever they please. By pushing out information on their schedule, the police can ask for help sooner. People with information will then be able to respond sooner, reducing the chance that incorrect memories will degrade the information over time. Also, young people are increasingly spending more time on the Internet and their smartphones, and less time watching television (and especially the local news shows where police usually ask for tips). A way to reach young people through smartphones would likely increase their participation and willingness to help law enforcement. Additionally, digitizing the information coming in can help police quickly store and manage the information. Lastly, you are concerned about making sure that tipsters can protect their identity while submitting information, and are incentivized to participate.

With these considerations in mind, you can further refine your objective. You need to deploy a crowdsourcing capability in your locality that is attractive to the public, including the youth, that incentivizes users to anonymously submit critical information about major crimes. The capability must then store and deliver the data to police, who can use it to further their investigations. With a clear objective in mind, you can continue on and analyze the target audience. Note that information from the target audience analysis could cause you to revisit and modify the objective.

Analyze the Target Audience and Media Environment

The target audience is the people that live in the Houston metropolitan area, and especially the youth. However, that includes nearly 6 million people. Deploying a capability for the first time to such a large number of people is difficult—your message may become diluted, or so many people may participate that your capability gets overwhelmed. So, consider focusing your efforts to perhaps only the city of Houston. The city has 2 million people, which is a large but more manageable number of people.

After choosing the target audience's location, you can analyze their demographics. Some quick research on the Internet reveals that Houston's population is fairly young and diverse, with a significant part being Hispanic. Thus, to reach the widest audience, whatever capability you build should be available in both English and Spanish and appeal to young people.

Analyzing the target audience also involves analyzing their media environment and how they use media. Further research and insight from an area expert (one of us grew up there) reveal that Houston's population is similar to the population of other major American cities. Much of the population has access to the Internet, and smartphone technologies are popular, especially among the youth. However, some parts of Houston are mired in poverty and have less regular access to Internet technologies. Of those who do use the Internet, many use social media including Facebook and Twitter. Analysis of social media use in the United States suggests that 18- to 40-year-olds use social media the most. Also, a significant part of the population and likely much of the youth regularly use smartphone technologies, including the iPhone and Android phones.

Due to the widespread use of Internet and social media, Houston's media environment is saturated. People there consume media in numerous ways and are constantly being bombarded with commercials about new ways to spend their time and resources. In a given day, people living in Houston can watch cable television, access Facebook on their iPhones, and read numerous newspapers. Getting their attention will be difficult in such an oversaturated media environment. Also, they will have to be incentivized in some way to replace one form of media use with your capability.

In summary, the target audience and media environment analyses reveal the following key insights:

- Much of the target audience is young and Internet-savvy.
- A significant part of the target audience regularly speaks Spanish.
- Smartphones are very popular among the target audience.
- Getting the target audience's attention will not be easy.

Keep these insights in mind while designing the crowdsourcing capability.

Design the Platform

The first part of designing the platform involves determining exactly what the platform should look like. The second part involves designing the incentive structure, which, in turn, can affect the look of the platform.

Determine the Platform's Look and Feel

The target audience analysis reveals that the crowdsourcing capability should be a smartphone application like the apps available in the Apple and Android app stores. Much of the target audience regularly uses smartphones. Also, because smartphone applications are very popular, the audience will likely respond approvingly to a smartphone app as opposed to simply another website.

After deciding that you need to build a smartphone app, you can start determining what the app should do and, specifically, which features it should have. The app should allow law enforcement to push out information about a crime, such as the photo of a suspect, the last known whereabouts of a missing child, and other details to participants who have downloaded and installed the app. The participants should then be able to consume the pushed information and respond to it with tips. In response, the participants should receive some type of extrinsic and/or intrinsic incentive, especially if their tip proves useful. Participants should also be able to share the app and the police's requests with others. Figure 9.3 represents an overview of the app.

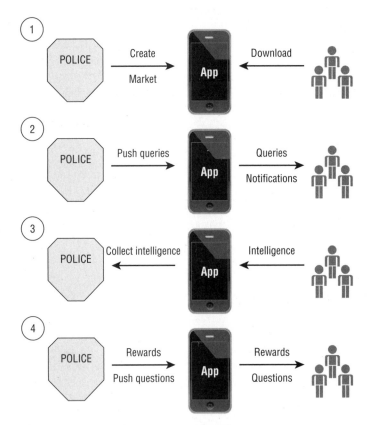

Figure 9.3: Law enforcement app overview

The features will be heavily dependent on how you would like the participants to use the app in a way that best helps your objective but also keeps participants interested. The following list describes some of the features you can implement and the reasoning behind them:

- **Messaging between police and participants**—The most obvious feature, the ability to send messages between the participants and police, is pivotal. Police can push a message to participants about the crime or the suspect.

The participants can then respond with whatever tips they may have. The messages can include all sorts of multimedia, including pictures, text, and video. The police can also message only a single participant. For example, if a participant submits useful information that leads to a breakthrough in the investigation, the police can send that individual a thank-you message for his or her efforts.

- **Notifications**—Notifications are the messages you receive when you are not using your smartphone that remind you that you have mail, or need to make a play in Words with Friends, or have a new text message. Participants who download the smartphone app have the option of turning on notifications for the app. With notifications on, when police push information about the crime, participants will receive a small reminder alerting them that police are requesting new information.

- **Location**—Many smartphone applications ask the users for permission to track their physical location. If the platform asks participants for their location, which they can always decline to do, you can track where they are located. By analyzing the location of participants you can determine whether your platform is especially popular in some parts of the city, or completely absent in other parts. Also, you can use a participant's location to validate the tips. Say that a series of related crimes happen in the south part of the city. A participant then submits information about the crimes, suggesting that he or she is near the crime while the information is being submitted. However, the location may reveal that the participant is actually in the north part of the city. You can then figure out that the participant is likely lying or, at best, not telling the complete truth.

- **User accounts**—After installing the app, each participant has to create a user account. Participants must specify a username, which the app will recommend is not the participant's real name. Participants will then also have the option of submitting information about their age, gender, and race to understand what parts of the audience are using the app. Participants will also have the option of creating a password for the app.

- **Social sharing**—To ensure that the largest number of people possible hear about the police's requests, the app will enable participants to share information with people in their contact lists. The participants will have the option of sharing the requested information with anyone else through a text message or an e-mail. The shared message will also contain instructions for the recipient to either download the app, or call the police tipline. For example, a participant may see the picture of someone and think he recognizes it, but is unsure. He may feel that a family member might have a better idea, and so he can immediately message the picture and instructions to that family member. The family member can then check out the picture and respond to either the participant or directly to the police.

The app that participants use is only one component of the platform. The other components include the data management system that handles all the data and the website that enables the police to access the crowdsourced intelligence. The data management system should generally allow for the delivery and storage of all messages and metadata about the messages. The data management system should also ensure that it routinely deletes information about participants and does not store any information that personally identifies them, according to legal and privacy obligations that the police face. Figure 9.4 shows the relationship between the app, the data management system, and the website.

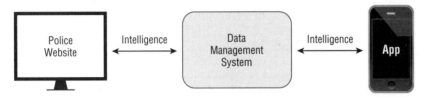

Figure 9.4: Relationship between app platform components

The website that police access on their computers should have at least the following features:

- **Messages**—All the communication including the text and media shared between the police and the participants must appear on the website. The messages can be organized by case. Police users can click on a case and then see all the messages and information pertaining to the case, including the usernames of the participants who submitted the messages. Police users should then be able to click on the username and submit a message directly and only to that participant.

- **Updates**—The police user should be able to post new case information on the site and then push it through the message feature onto the smartphone apps.

- **Sharing**—Police users can create accounts for themselves and share the interface with other members of the police force, including analysts.

After outlining which features the app and the police website should have, you could start designing the graphical user interface (GUI) of the app and the website. However, we recommend thinking about the incentive structure first, because that can affect the features available on the app and, thus, how the app should display the features.

Determine the Platform's Incentive Structure

Looking at prior ways of incentivizing the general population to submit information to police regarding crimes is a good starting point for determining your incentive structure. Usually, law enforcement, community organizations, and families of victims offer cash rewards for information. The cash rewards depend on the seriousness of the crime and the need for new information.

Cash rewards are important extrinsic incentives that routinely encourage participation and are easy to implement for the app. Small cash rewards in the range of a few hundred dollars are likely adequate for incentivizing people. In the case of very serious crimes or missing children where time is of the essence, the police can increase the amount of the cash reward by a few hundred dollars. Delivering the cash reward is also a simple endeavor. The website on which the police access the incoming messages stores each message and the name of the person who submits it. If a message proves useful, the police can then use the app to communicate with the participant who submitted it. Through the app, the police can tell the participant how to collect the reward—most likely by calling a phone number and providing his name and address, or coming to the police station with his phone to prove that he was the one with the username.

Intrinsic incentives also come into play—specifically, the pleasure people gain when they feel they are contributing to their community and helping their neighbors. The app enables people to be useful, and the police can routinely send thank-you messages to participants through the app and let them know they were helpful. Even in cases where the information was not especially helpful, the police can still send messages to participants now and then thanking them for trying to help. The message can say something like, "Thank you for the information. We appreciate your service to your community." In the case of crimes or events where the likelihood of repercussions to the informant is nonexistent, the police can even publicly thank the informant. Public thanks and kudos are a strong intrinsic incentive.

Determine the Platform's Look and Feel, Redux

The incentive structure does not impact the design and structure of the app or the website. Thus, you do not have to reassess ideas for the GUI and can continue as planned.

You can design the GUI in countless ways. Whichever way you choose, it has to ensure that participants and police can access the features of the platform in an intuitive way. Figure 9.5 shows one example of how the app's GUI could look, or in other words, what the app could look like to a participant. It shows the different windows, screens, or interfaces that participants can access in the app.

Figure 9.6 shows one example of how the GUI of the website that police use to access the information could look.

NOTE   When you are actually designing platforms, make sure to work with developers and graphic designers before settling on a design. More likely than not, you will have to go back and make changes in the process of development.

Figure 9.5: Example GUI for app

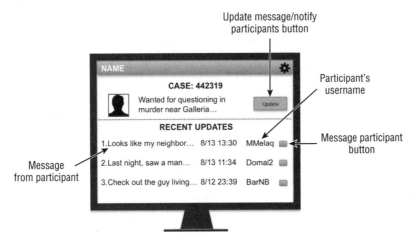

Figure 9.6: Example GUI for police website

Build the Platform

Building the components of the platform is a simple technology problem that requires contracting out work to developers. You can also use services such as AppMakr (www.appmakr.com) and Magmito (www.magmito.com) that help you build and deploy smartphone apps. We prefer going to developers rather than doing it ourselves because they can ensure that the software behind the platform is secure and that we get all the desired features without cutting corners.

Ideally, you should work with a team of developers that work together on all of the components of the platform, rather than farming out different components to different developers. With the latter strategy, piecing the platform components together can become difficult.

Providing the developers with example GUI graphics and a list of the features you need significantly increases the chance that the end product fits your desires.

Market the Platform

Because the target audience's media environment is saturated, getting the audience's attention and getting them interested in the app will require a robust marketing effort. The effort should consist of an initial marketing push and a sustained marketing effort throughout the app's existence.

The initial marketing push should introduce the app to people and encourage them to sign up and try it out. The most important step for the initial marketing push is naming the app. You do not want to pick something too cheesy, nor something that obscures what the app does. For lack of a better idea, we will go with "CrimeSpotter." After naming the app, list it in the Apple and Google app stores. Listing it in the app stores involves going through an approval process, which may take some time and require modifications to the app.

Most of the target audience regularly consumes traditional media. So, talk about the app on television news shows, and place advertisements on television, radio, and in magazines and newspapers. Contact Apple and Google and encourage them to help you market the app, because doing so would improve their public perception. Also, because much of the target audience regularly uses the Internet, advertise on the Internet. Launch a website that explains, in simple terms, what the app does and why people should use it. Run ads on Facebook targeted toward young people living in Houston. Contact celebrities and encourage them to tout the ad on television and at concerts.

The sustained marketing effort includes regularly sending messages to participants through the app that encourage them to tell their friends about it. You do not want to send messages too regularly, otherwise you will annoy them—once a month may be enough. Also, analyze who is signing up for the app based on the demographic information you are collecting through the app and use it to tweak the marketing effort. If you find that only females are signing up, start advertising in magazines for men such as *Men's Health*. If the participation rate follows the technology adoption curve and your participation rate is high, you do not need to advertise as much.

Manage the Platform

Because the app does not have social networking or collaborative features, moderating the platform will not require many resources. Dedicate a few analysts or police officers to monitor the police website to ensure people are submitting relevant information. If you find that you are receiving only spam and nonsense, you may want to shut down the app. Also, have the dedicated analysts or officers message out reminders and thanks to participants.

Measure the Platform's Performance

After launching the app, start collecting metrics for its performance. Of course, you will want to think about what metrics to use before you even commission its design and building. The data management system component of the platform should house some performance tools that measure statistics about the app's usage. You can also acquire data from Apple and Google about the app. Example metrics include:

- Download rate of the app over time, compared with the schedule of marketing pushes
- Number of incoming messages, compared with other ways of getting tips
- Number of successful tips
- Number of cash rewards given out
- Time and day people submit information, to assess when participants are most active and when notifications should be sent out
- Demographic data about who is using the app
- Stories in the media about the app and participants' assessments of it

Wash, Rinse, Repeat

Undoubtedly, your platform will fall short in some ways. Participants may demand certain features, or you may need to tweak the marketing efforts, or even further refine your target audience. Use the performance data to identify areas that you need to improve. You may even consider hosting a focus group a few months into the app's existence to talk with participants about what they do and do not like about the app. Use the results of the focus group as a guideline, not commands. Sometimes people do not know what they are talking about and may suggest very stupid things.

While writing this, we came up with a few ways of improving the app through its subsequent iterations and updates:

- One major flaw jumped out immediately—with the existing app, participants cannot look at past messages. You never know when they might remember something or stumble onto the information you need. You will need to integrate an option into the app that enables participants to browse past messages.

- Create a companion website for the target audience that enables people without a smartphone to participate.

- Coordinate the sending of messages with television and radio advertisements to ensure that participants know a new message is up.

- Drastically increase a reward every now and then to keep participants interested and excited over the long term.

- Enable participants to upload videos through the app, and even turn their smartphone into a live video camera that the police can view in case a crime is occurring near the participant.

Collect Intelligence to Bolster Disaster Relief

Natural disasters and humanitarian crises are events that require crowdsourcing information from affected victims. Without on-the-ground information about the crisis and its effects, relief workers and community members are helpless. Responders and relief organizations use the crowdsourced information to identify areas of distress and coordinate supplies. News organizations and community members use the information to share warnings about road closures and locations of shelters, and raise awareness about the crisis.

However, not all information is useful. The best and most useful information is the type that is timely and valid. During or immediately after a crisis, responders need information as soon as possible so they can coordinate their efforts and reach people in need quickly. For example, responders who find out days after a tornado that a baby is missing will not be able to help the baby, who will likely have died since. Crowdsourcing relevant information through social media offers the ability to significantly improve the timeliness of the information. Also, information is only good if it is true and verifiable. People take advantage of crises to commit crimes against victims and responders, and wreak havoc.[3] They may send information asking for help, but instead set traps to kidnap relief workers. The ability to validate incoming information can go a long way toward ensuring that relief efforts are not diverted toward false and possibly dangerous ends. Social media technologies offer the ability to cross-validate incoming information and quickly employ others to validate questionable information.

Crowdmaps are websites where people can submit information that is then displayed on an interactive map, similar to how Google Maps displays information about stores and tourist attractions on its maps. Crowdmaps are ideal for quickly capturing a lot of reports and pictures during times of crises and displaying that information on a map. Numerous individuals and groups have used crowdmaps to track disasters and coordinate disaster relief. Some have helped first responders coordinate disaster relief and identify victims. However, the vast majority are either rarely used, ignored, or not shared with the proper authorities because of numerous reasons. This walkthrough describes how to successfully implement a crowdmap-based crowdsourcing intelligence platform to collect intelligence during crises to bolster disaster relief and document problems. The following sections walk through the process of designing, creating, deploying, and maintaining a crowdmap.

Define Objective and Scope

Imagine you are charged with helping coordinate disaster relief in Haiti, a few months before the hurricane season is expected to start there. Your main task is to collect information about the hurricane and its effects from affected Haitians and provide the information to disaster responders so they can better plan their actions. A crowdmap is the ideal crowdsourcing platform for collecting and managing intelligence during crises.

Considering past crowdmap deployments for the purpose of disaster relief in Haiti and other places can help further refine the objective and its scope. Although some crowdmaps prove enormously useful to the victims and responders, most crowdmaps fail because no one knows about them. If people do not know that a crowdmap exists, they will not submit reports to it. Responders also need to know about the crowdmaps. Crowdmaps that are popular with the affected population will receive and host a lot of information. However, if responders do not use the information, the crowdmaps become a simple exercise in documenting damage and problems. Therefore, your crowdmap deployment must feature a significant marketing effort. Additionally, popularizing a crowdmap and populating it with lots of information is not enough. False and nonsensical information can significantly harm, or at the very least prove useless to, responders. A successful crowdmap deployment must manage and make sense of the crowdsourced information, especially if responders will use it to plan their actions.

With these considerations in mind, you can further refine and restate your objective. You need to deploy a well-known crowdsourcing platform in Haiti during disasters that collects reports from the affected population about problems they face and the help they need, manages and prioritizes the information, and then pushes it to responders quickly for their use.

Analyze the Target Audience and Media Environment

The region you are interested in largely determines the target audience for the platform. Your target audience is obviously the population of Haiti, which has about 10 million people. The number of people is far too large to deal with for an initial crowdsourcing deployment, so you will have to further refine the target audience.

The easiest option is to pick a major city and focus on the population there. Populations in major cities tend to have the most advanced technologies and are more likely to use social media technologies and participate in crowdsourcing. Haiti's capital city, Port-au-Prince, seems ideal because it is one of the most advanced cities in Haiti. It has suffered significant damage in past crises and so will likely suffer the consequences of future earthquakes and hurricanes. Also, it has almost 1 million people. The number of people is still quite large, but much fewer than 1 million will likely even have the ability to participate in the platform. Keep in mind that a significant portion of Port-au-Prince's population does not have access to social media technologies. Indeed, research shows only 35 percent of Haiti's population uses dumb phones. Compared to other countries, the number is small, but large enough for the platform's purpose. Therefore, you can select the population of Port-au-Prince as the target audience for the platform.

The target audience's media environment is heavily dependent on traditional media technologies. Haiti has numerous television and radio stations. Overall, radio remains the most popular source of media for Haitians. Only about 10 percent of Haitians have access to the Internet. However, access to mobile technology is rapidly growing. Haiti is also deploying 3G networks, which will further spur use of social media technologies. Also, the Haitian diaspora has a significant influence on Haiti's way of life, and thus the media environment. The diaspora has even become involved in past crowdmap deployments in Haiti. It is unclear from the analysis how many Haitians know about crowdmaps, but we expect they will participate if they find out about them. Disaster response in Haiti suffers from significant problems, resulting in the loss of hundreds of thousands of Haitian lives. Thus, it is safe to assume that the target audience will welcome ways of improving disaster response.

In summary, the target audience and media environment analyses reveal the following key insights:

- A significant portion of the target audience regularly uses dumb phones and is likely familiar with SMS services.

- Traditional media dominates Haiti's media environment, and radio is the best way of reaching people.

- The target audience is already incentivized to try out tools that will improve disaster response.

Keep these insights in mind while designing the crowdsourcing capability.

Design the Platform

The first part of designing the platform involves determining exactly what the platform should look like. The second part involves designing the incentive structure, which in this case will likely not affect the look of the platform due to the nature of the crowdsourcing technologies in question.

Determine the Platform's Look and Feel

The target audience analysis reveals that the crowdsourcing capability should be based on SMS technology. The platform should allow the target audience to submit SMS messages to a centralized data management system detailing the help they need and where they are. The system should then take the information, and through either automated tools or human labor, clean up, verify, translate, and prioritize the pleas for help. Responders should then be able to look at the information and use it to plan their actions, and even update the crowdmap or contact the person who submitted the information. Figure 9.7 represents an overview of the platform.

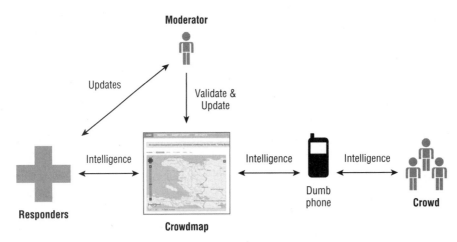

Figure 9.7: Disaster relief platform overview

The platform has two components. The first is the SMS capability that allows the target audience to submit information to the platform. The second is the crowdmap, which stores, manages, and displays the crowdsourced information. The platform is relatively simple and has the following few features:

■ **Messaging**—Obviously, participants should be able to send a text message to the platform with details about where they are and what help they need.

■ **Location**—The amount of location information you receive depends heavily on the settings of the participants' cell phones, the policies of the local telecommunications providers, and other technological items. Typically, the location is estimated by analyzing which cell towers the message bounced off of on its way to the crowdmap. The location you receive may not be exact, but it will good enough. Remind the participants to specify where they are in the body of the text message.

- **Social sharing**—To improve relief coordination, the collected messages must be shared with the responders. The platform will enable all responders or coordinators to immediately see what type of help people need, where they are located, and when they need the help. The coordinators should also be able to quickly share the information with others organizations or persons.

A simple set of features is a clue that the user interface for the platform will also be relatively simple. The user interface for SMS is only text on a person's phone. You do not need to design any graphics. Numerous user interface options exist for the crowdmap. You can design one from scratch, adapt existing ones, or use a template with minimal changes. Assuming available resources and time are low, you should opt for doing the least amount of work possible. Fortunately, Ushahidi provides easy-to-use crowdmap templates with the desired features for free. The template determines what the interface will look like. Thus, unlike other platforms, you have to do almost no work in regards to designing the look and feel of the platform. Obviously, more custom and expensive options offer more features, but for our purposes, time, and budget, Ushahidi's crowdmaps will do.

Determine the Platform's Incentive Structure

Haitians have suffered massively due to disasters, which is an unfortunate fact that significantly simplifies your platform's incentive structure. One of the strongest intrinsic incentives people have is the need to feel secure and to be free from harm. The need for security is so strong that you do not need to consider other incentives. If deployed and used correctly, the disaster relief platform can considerably reduce Haitians' insecurity and likelihood of harm during disasters.

However, it takes effort to convince the target audience that the platform will indeed help them. If the target audience believes the platform will not help them, they will not use it. A convincing marketing campaign is essential for articulating the incentive for the audience. Also, an incentive is only as good as its delivery. Even if you convince the audience that your platform will help them, if you then fail to help them through the platform, you will not be able to deploy another platform there again. Even during a disaster, word will spread among the affected communities about the failures and accomplishments of the platform. Make sure the platform works, otherwise the effect of the intrinsic incentive will disappear and the participation rate will plummet.

Build the Platform

Building the platform involves creating and deploying a crowdmap, and syncing it with an SMS management and blasting tool such as FrontlineSMS or

Clickatell. The process is fairly easy and does not require much technological skill. The following steps describe the process:

1. Go to www.crowdmap.com and click the big red button that says Sign Up For Free. In the next window, fill out the form and create an account and a crowdmap. The map address should be something that is easy to remember and spell. We have created a crowdmap containing fabricated data with the acronym of this book's title. You can check it out at usmfgs .crowdmap.com.

2. After you have finished filling out the required forms, your browser will load the crowdmap website. On the top-right corner of the window, click your account name, and in the drop-down menu, select Your Dashboard. The dashboard contains the modifiable settings and options to customize the crowdmap.

3. Near the top right, click Settings. Fill out the form as you wish. Use your mouse to hover over the ? symbols next to each form header if you are confused or need more information. Make sure to fill out a "site message" and "submit report message" that respectively clearly explain what your crowdmap does and what you want participants to contribute to it.

4. A lot of options are available in the settings form. For example, the Private Deployment setting enables you to limit who can see your crowdmap. If integrity of information is important or you want to keep outsiders from guessing the identities of the participants, you may want to make it a private deployment. You will likely want to keep most of the default options.

5. Make sure to click the Save Settings button at the top or bottom of the page.

6. Near the top of the settings page, you will see several tabs as shown in Figure 9.8. For this case, you will need to go through the Map and the SMS tabs. The other tabs enable you to set options to collect information through e-mail, Facebook, and smartphones. According to the target audience analysis, Haitians are not likely to communicate through those methods, so you do not need to set them up. However, you may need to for other cases.

7. Go to the Map tab and select the correct options. In most cases, simply keep the default options. However, you should change the Default Location to Haiti or use the map to select a part of Haiti, and select Yes under Map Timeline. By enabling the timeline, you can see when the reports are being submitted. Again, click Save Settings.

You will now need to set up the SMS component of the platform. You can use FrontlineSMS to do so, but it is tricky to use for this case so we prefer using Clickatell:

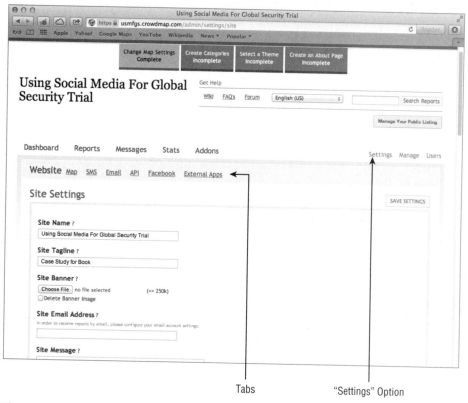

Figure 9.8: Screenshot of crowdmap dashboard settings

8. Open a new browser window and go to www.clickatell.com. Sign up for an international account that enables you to send and receive SMS to and from Haiti. Make sure to buy enough credits to pay for all the incoming SMS. Estimating how many you need is difficult, but fortunately you can easily buy new credits. Keep track of the Clickatell account through the disaster and crowdmap deployment to ensure you do not run out of credits. For now, buy enough credits to send and receive 2000 texts. Also purchase a shortcode that is easy to remember.

9. After setting up the Clickatell account, go back to the browser window with the crowdmap settings. Instead of clicking the SMS tab, click the Addons tab, which should be above it. The Addons tab features several options and third-party plug-ins that you can use to further customize your crowdmap. For your purposes now, enable the Clickatell option, which should be the second addon listed. After selecting the Clickatell option, make sure to click the button above it that says Activate.

10. After activating you should see that the row that said Clickatell now says Settings next to it. Click Settings and fill out the form in the subsequent window.

11. Click Settings again in the options on the far right, and then click the SMS tab. Fill in the shortcode for the phone number or any other phone numbers you may want to use.

12. Next, click Manage on the far right. The window will now enable you to edit the categories, which are the buckets into which you will categorize the incoming texts. Relevant categories can include Medical Help, Road Closures, and Food Shortage.

13. You have now gone through a sufficient amount of the settings and are ready to deploy the platform. Submit a report under the Reports tab to ensure the crowdmap works. After ensuring that the crowdmap works, you can set additional options to customize the crowdmap to your heart's content. You will find that you will need to come back to the dashboard and frequently tweak the options to get it exactly how you want it. The big red boxes on the top of the page guide you through the setup process and remind you what settings you really should go through.

WARNING The process for setting up the crowdmap may change as the software underlying it changes. Make sure to go to Ushahidi's website at www.ushahidi.com to keep track of the new software and get help for new and existing features.

Market the Platform

Crowdmaps succeed only if people know about them, and so you need to put a lot of resources into marketing the platform. Ideally, you want to routinely advertise the platform over the course of many months and even years till it becomes common knowledge among Haitians. The target audience's media environment is heavily dependent on traditional media. Advertise the platform on radio and on television. Make a jingle out of the shortcode so it becomes memorable. Consider that almost everyone in the United States knows to dial 911 in the case of emergencies. Similarly, everyone in Port-au-Prince should know to text to shortcode *XXXXX* during a disaster when they need help. The name of the platform might as well be the shortcode because it is the shortcode that is the most important piece of the platform. If the audience does not know it, they and the responders will not be able to use the platform.

To ensure such ubiquity of your message, you will likely need to partner with Haitian organizations. Contact the Haitian government, the Red Cross, and other NGOs and convince them to market your platform. They can help tell key influencers in communities about your platform and print and distribute flyers. Also, consider contacting Digicell, the largest provider of mobile services in Haiti. Digicell can help market the platform and shortcode, which in turn will make its product, the mobile phone, look more useful and attractive to its potential customers.

You can also use blast SMS to market the platform. While building the crowdmap, you had to sign up for Clickatell, which you can also use to send text messages to Haitians. Every few weeks, blast SMS reminders about the platform to the target audience to slowly build up the number of people who know about it.

Also, consider running drills to both market and test the platform. Work with NGOs and local government offices in Port-au-Prince to stage moderate-sized drills where you simulate a disaster and ask a small portion of the target audience to role-play as disaster victims and use the platform. The drills will help the audience appreciate what the platform does, and it will generate buzz and raise the audience's interest.

Manage the Platform

Moderators will play a significant role in managing the crowdmap and coordinating with responders. They will categorize, validate, translate, and push the information. You will likely need to hire at least six moderators to manage the platform during a crisis. The moderators should know English, French, and/ or Haitian Creole, which are the most commonly used languages among the target audience. The moderators should work in shifts, with at least two working together at the same time. The following list describes the most important of the moderators' duties:

- Categorize the incoming text messages into the categories you delineated when setting up the crowdmap.

- Validate or approve messages by cross-referencing them and seeing if they make sense according to what is generally happening on the ground.

- Send alerts to responders about messages that ask for immediate assistance.

- Translate incoming messages by themselves or through the use of other tools.

- Manage the crowdmap and SMS credits settings to ensure everything is working fine and they have enough credits to receive texts.

- Update the crowdmap with information they pick up from other sources, and if certain issues are resolved by responders.

If you cannot find moderators with all of the appropriate language skills, or if they are being overwhelmed with messages that need to be translated, then you can use crowd labor to translate. Chapter 10 describes how to use crowd labor to solve problems such as the translation of language containing slang, abbreviations, and idioms.

Fortunately, Ushahidi's crowdmap software already features all the moderating tools you need. Make sure to train the moderators on the crowdmaps. Drills are ideal for training and testing the moderators. The moderators will spend the majority of their time in the Reports section of the crowdmap dashboard. See Figure 9.9 for a screenshot of the Reports section. The Reports section provides moderators with the tools to track incoming reports, and validate and approve them. Moderators can also click on each individual report and edit them to add more information. Moderators can also go to the Messages section where they can classify messages as reports and even send messages.

Figure 9.9: Screenshot of crowdmap Reports section

Measure the Platform's Performance

After deploying the crowdmap, collect the metrics to measure the platform's performance. You likely noticed as you set up the crowdmap that it features several tools to collect and make sense of the data. Use these and other tools, and moderators to assess the platform's performance. Example metrics include:

- Number of texts received
- Number of different phone numbers texting in
- Number of victims identified compared to past disasters
- Number of victims helped compared to past disasters
- Increase in response time compared to past disasters

Wash, Rinse, Repeat

The success of the crowdmap depends heavily on the marketing push and how much of the target audience knows that the crowdmap actually exists. Do not be surprised if only a few participants text in during your first crowdmap deployment. You may need to sustain your marketing campaign for a long period of time before the target audience realizes that they need to text in to a specific shortcode to get help. Getting buy-in from the local government may be critical.

Also, we addressed only a few of the features that crowdmaps offer. So far, we have restricted how Haitians can send messages to the platform to only SMS. For future deployments, you may need to expand the modes of communication to include e-mail and Twitter. Increasing the ways participants can communicate with you leads to an increase in the intelligence you receive. To compensate for the increase, you will need to hire more moderators or employ crowdsourcing to help with some of the problems you may face.

Chapter 10 focuses on building crowdsourcing platforms to solve problems, including the translation of hard-to-understand languages and much more.

Summary

- Crowdsourced intelligence is the information you collect from crowdsourcing platforms known as intelligence collection platforms.
- The type of intelligence you receive is dependent on the form of social media participants use to submit the intelligence. For example, if collecting intelligence through SMS, the intelligence will be in text format.
- Direct intelligence tells you about a place, an object, or a person, and other than validation and sorting, does not require additional analysis.
- Indirect intelligence tells you about the things surrounding a place, an object, or a person, and requires analyses and correlations with other intelligence to derive insights about the place, object, or person.

- Intelligence collection platforms suffer from a few limitations:
  - The target audience may be uncooperative because they do not want to help or they are afraid to participate.
  - Participants may face certain risks due to the somewhat open nature of social media communication.
  - Participants may send you incorrect information, either intentionally or by accident.
  - You may misinterpret data and draw wrong conclusions from it.
  - The platform may change the behavior of the target audience, which may impact what kind of intelligence you can get.
- Compared to other types of crowdsourcing platforms, intelligence collection platforms are typically run for shorter periods of time, require less elaborate incentive structures and social networking features, and are primarily deployed in hard-to-reach areas where SMS use is high.
- You can use intelligence collection platforms to collect information about the target audience from hard-to-reach areas through SMS networks.
- You can use intelligence collection platforms to collect information about crimes from the community through a smartphone application.
- You can use intelligence collection platforms during disasters to collect information from affected victims through a crowdmap and SMS network.

Notes

1. Burnett, J. (2011) "Mexican Drug Cartels Now Menace Social Media." NPR. Accessed: 18 August 2012. http://www.npr.org/2011/09/23/140745739/mexican-drug-cartels-now-menace-social-media?sc=tw&cc=share

2. Badger, E. (2012) "How the Cutting Edge in Crowdsourced Crime Fighting Could Do More Harm Than Good." *The Atlantic Cities.* Accessed: 18 August 2012. http://www.theatlanticcities.com/technology/2012/07/how-cutting-edge-crowdsourced-crime-fighting-could-do-more-harm-good/2626/

3. Jordan, M. & Gauthier-Villars, D. (2010) "Kidnapped Aid Workers Released in Haiti." *Wall Street Journal.* Accessed: 18 August 2012. http://online.wsj.com/article/SB10001424052748704349304575116011173049380.html

Crowdsourcing Solutions

Through crowdsourcing platforms, you can leverage populations worldwide to help you solve problems and complete tasks. The process for building and running crowdsourcing platforms is technologically simple, but requires the visceral ability to incentivize and foster collaboration between different types of people. The process also increases in complexity along with the complexity of the problem or task you want the crowd to solve. This chapter goes over the process by explaining what is possible through crowdsourcing, two ways of approaching crowdsourcing solutions, what is not possible, and how solution platforms differ from other types of platforms. It also walks through how to build and run platforms that leverage the crowd to translate obscure languages and to identify antagonistic actors on video footage.

Understanding the Scope of Crowdsourced Solutions

Crowdsourced solutions are solutions derived specifically through custom crowdsourcing platforms known as solution platforms. They differ from other, more traditional forms of solving problems or completing tasks in the way the problem is solved and the people who solve the problem. Traditional forms involve specifying the individuals or groups that will solve the problem, and compensating them for their work based on a predetermined rate. The specified individuals or groups may collaborate with one or two other groups. Usually, the party contracting out the work knows the identity of the workers and specifies, or at least knows, which tools and methods the workers will use. In contrast, when crowdsourcing solutions, the party contracting out the work does not usually specify the individuals or groups that will solve the problem, does not always know their identity, and does not specify or know the methods they will use. These features give rise to the creativity and flexibility that traditional forms of solving problems typically lack. Also, solution platforms differ from traditional forms in that how you formulate problems and the actual platform design can differ wildly. You have a limited number of ways to perform traditional contract work, but many different ways to crowdsource solutions. The following two sections expand on this feature.

Formulating the Right Type of Problem

Solution platforms can help you solve and complete a variety of problems and tasks. Possible problems or tasks can include translating a pidgin language that computer translators do not understand, creating complex computer algorithms for cameras so they can identify people behaving suspiciously, solving tedious but essential math problems, forecasting the likelihood that a certain event will take place, finding the right person for a job opening, and much more. In some cases, the line between solutions and intelligence is blurred. If you consider solutions to simply be unknown intelligence, solution platforms can help you solve the problem of finding that extremely elusive piece of intelligence.

> **NOTE** From now on, we do not make a distinction between problems and tasks. When we refer to problems, we also refer to tasks. So, if we say solution platforms can solve problems, we also imply that solution platforms can complete a task.

When designing solution platforms, focusing on exactly how you define the problem for the crowd is key. If you do not properly formulate the problem, you will receive either wrong solutions or solutions that do not solve the problem the way you want it solved. Differentiating the problems into three types can help you think about whether you have properly formulated the problem you intend to put to the crowd.

The first type is what we call *objective problems* and they have only one correct answer and usually one solution. The answers are falsifiable and they have clear right and wrong answers. In some cases, they are simply intelligence collection problems. Example problems include:

- Who is the current prime minister of Zimbabwe?
- What is the American English translation of "que pase un buen dia"?

The second type is what we call *subjective problems* and they may have more than one answer or, in other words, more than one solution. They tend to be much more complex than objective problems and are open to interpretation. They do not necessarily have right or wrong answers, but simply answers that are better than others depending on a number of factors. Example problems include:

- What is an algorithm underlying a natural language processing tool that can detect sarcasm in a tweet?
- What is a design of a rugged hybrid-vehicle chassis that is durable and inexpensive to manufacture?

The third type is what we call *mixed problems*, which have features of both the objective and subjective types. Consider the types not as independent categories but as a spectrum, with objective problems taking up one end, subjective problems taking up the other end, and mixed problems somewhere in the middle. These middle, mixed problems usually have a right or wrong answer, but many ways of finding that answer. Example problems include:

- What will be the annual murder rate in Caracas for 2013?
- What is an algorithm underlying a natural language processing tool that can, in near real-time and with an 80 percent accuracy rate, detect sarcasm in a tweet?

You may have noticed that a problem's categorization depends on how exactly you formulate the problem and how exact you want the answer to be—the boundaries on the solutions. By boundaries we mean factors that define and limit what solution you want, which problem it should answer, and how it should work. They include the solution's accuracy rate, what place or time period you want the solution to consider, or the amount of resources required to create the solution. Generally, the more boundaries you put on a problem, the more you push it toward the objective part of the spectrum. Subjective problems have few boundaries and no right or wrong answer, only answers that are better than others according to certain criteria. Mixed problems are essentially subjective problems with well-defined boundaries and some answers that may be right or wrong, and some answers that are simply better than others. Objective problems are essentially subjective problems with very strict boundaries and a falsifiable, right or wrong answer. Strict boundaries tend to lead to falsifiable answers because the more restrictions you put on how someone may solve a problem, the fewer ways the person can solve it. Note that when we say there is only one way to solve the problem, we mean that there is only one solution that solves the problem. For example, many ways exist to figure out the identity of the current prime minister of Zimbabwe, but only one solution solves the problem of finding the identity of the prime minister. In contrast, many solutions or computer programs can, for example, find sarcasm in language. A subjective problem usually has countless solutions, whereas an objective problem usually has only one. Figure 10.1 graphically summarizes the relationship and differences between the different parts of the problem type spectrum.

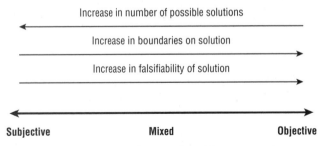

Increase in number of possible solutions

Increase in boundaries on solution

Increase in falsifiability of solution

Subjective   Mixed   Objective

Figure 10.1: Spectrum of types of problems

Keep the problem types in mind when designing your platform. They do not reflect hard-and-fast rules, and you are not required to typify problems. In some cases, the types will not apply or make sense. The types of problems are simply guidelines that help you formulate your problem more precisely. If you neglect to put strict boundaries on your question, the crowd will tend to see it as a more subjective question, and so the kinds of solutions you get may differ greatly from what you would like. To better appreciate this point, consider the following example.

AN EXAMPLE OF TYPIFYING AND FORMULATING A PROBLEM

Say you want a computer program that can detect the physical location of future placements of improvised explosive devices (IEDs) in a given city. You decide to crowdsource and put the following problem to the crowd: "Design and create a functional computer program that automatically detects the physical location of future placements of IEDs in any city."

Your problem formulation indicates that the problem is of a very subjective type. There is no one right way to answer the problem—there may be hundreds of ways of designing a computer program that can predict placements of IEDs. Also, you do not specify the boundaries of the problem. For example, you do not indicate how accurate you want the solution to be. Some computer programs might detect IED placements with a 99 percent accuracy rate but take months to output an answer, whereas other computer programs might detect with a 70 percent accuracy rate but take only minutes to answer.

Because many ways exist to solve the problem and you do not define boundaries such as the expected accuracy of the program or how long it should take, you will receive a wide variety of solutions. Some will solve the problem with an accuracy rate of 65 percent, and some with an accuracy rate of 80 percent. If you want a wide variety of solutions and do not care about a given solution's accuracy rate, then the solutions you receive are fine.

> However, if you do want boundaries such as solutions that have at least an 80 percent accuracy rate, you need to push the problem more toward the objective part of the spectrum and reformulate it. Note that the problem is still somewhat subjective, but by endowing it with more objective characteristics and reformulating it, you bound the solution and change what kinds of solutions you receive. Your problem now becomes: "Design and create a functional computer program that automatically detects, with an 80 percent accuracy rate, the physical location of future placements of IEDs in any city." The problem becomes more of a mixed type of problem.
>
> You will now receive computer programs that have at least an 80 percent accuracy rate. However, the programs may now take days or weeks to output when you want a program that outputs an answer in hours. You can then further bound the solution by reformulating the problem as: "Design and create a functional computer program that takes less than four hours to automatically detect, with an 80 percent accuracy rate, the physical location of future placements of IEDs in any city." Then the solutions you receive will be programs that have an 80 percent accuracy rate and also output an answer in less than four hours.

Formulating the Right Crowdsourcing Approach

The type of problem is not the only feature that affects and defines your solution platform. The way you want the crowd to solve the problem also affects and defines it. The way, or what we call the approach, helps define the look and features of your solution platform, the identity of your target audience, and the intensity of your marketing campaign—in other words, the design of your platform. Similar to how thinking about the type of problem can help you formulate the problem, thinking about the type of approach can help you formulate the actual platform. Think of determining the approach as determining how you should fulfill some of the steps of the process that we detailed in Chapter 8. To aid understanding, we separate the approach into three types. In some cases, some approach types are better at solving certain types of problems than other approach types.[1]

The first approach involves focusing more on leveraging the wisdom of the crowd and is usually best for solving problems that fall near the objective end of the spectrum. The focus is not on crowdsourcing from the "right" people, experts, or niche communities. Instead, it is on asking a large, diverse, and independent group of people what they think the answer is to a specific problem. As described in Chapter 7, leveraging the wisdom of the crowd involves averaging the responses of lots of people. Under the right conditions, the average of the responses is more accurate than the response of any given individual, including experts. However, getting the conditions right is not always easy. Utilizing the wisdom of the crowd approach requires understanding the right conditions as they relate to your platform and how you can bring them about. The following list describes the conditions and their impacts on your platform:[2]

- The problem must be clear and near the objective end of the spectrum. Clarifying and simplifying the problem ensures that all the platform participants, regardless of their background, understand what response you expect from them. A simple problem usually requires a simple response, which makes it easier for the responder. Generally, your question should start with phrases such as, "Who is," "When did," "What is the likelihood that," and "What is the translation of."

- The participants must be diverse. The greater the diversity, the more likely different insights and information are brought to bear on a problem, increasing the likelihood that you reach the correct answer. By diverse, we mean they should have different ways of looking at the world and different pieces of information. To achieve this type of diversity, you should recruit participants who are diverse in other ways, such as their cultural background, education level, and their political leaning. In practical terms, your target audience must be heterogeneous, numerically sizeable, and geographically distributed over a large area.

- The participants must be independent and refrain from biasing the responses of others. People inherently tend to conform and change their considerations of things to match that of their peers.[3] Participants should not have their responses subjected to the whims of their peers, because then most participants will change their response to match that of others. Also, keeping participants independent actually increases the likelihood they will come up with something creative. Brainstorming and working in groups is all the rage in at least corporate America, but studies show that brainstorming and group work actually reduce creativity and effectiveness.[4] Most people work better when they are given a problem, they can go away in a quiet spot to think about and work on it, and then come to the group with a rough draft of the solution. Do not get caught up in the pop-psychology babble about always forcing people to work as a team, and instead let people be hermits. They will be much more productive and creative. Thus, your platform should have minimal social networking and collaboration features.

- Information about the problem must be widely available. A large number of participants cannot bring information to bear on a specific problem if they cannot access that information. The ideal problems for the wisdom of the crowd approach are the ones that virtually anyone can think about. Thanks to the Internet and social media, the information is usually easy to get even if it is obscure. However, some cases of information paucity still exist. For example, there is no point in asking a large group of people on the Internet exactly which military personnel in North Korea have the most influence over Kim Jung-Un, because very few people have access to that sort of information. Thus, ensure that your problem is not asking something impossible to answer or too obscure.

- Recruit persons who are well informed and who you would traditionally go to for an answer to such a problem to help sift through the responses. Sometimes you cannot literally average out a response to the problem from all the participants' responses. In some cases, there may be a lot of prevalent misinformation that badly obscures the participants' responses. In such cases, it is always handy to have a subject matter expert who can help guide how you should structure the platform, what kinds of problems you should ask, and what sorts of responses you should expect. Do not let the expert just outright disqualify certain responses because he or she disagrees with them, and ignore any predictions he or she makes with absolute confidence. Take the expert's advice only as guidelines. Or, ask a crowd of experts and compare it with responses of other crowds. Use your judgment and intuition when using experts. Of course, it is a good idea to always keep in mind that sometimes crowds can be terribly wrong, ignorant, and dumb.[5]

WARNING   Someone calling themselves an expert does not make them an expert. Test and check the background of experts to make sure they know what they are talking about before you recruit them in any way to help you.

Table 10.1 summarizes the conditions under which the wisdom of the crowd approach works best and how they affect your platform.

The second approach involves moving away from leveraging a very large group of people, and instead focusing on leveraging a few select niche communities or uniquely knowledgeable individuals. We call it the niche approach. Crowdsourcing is not only about farming out tasks and problems to large groups of people. It is also about reaching the right people you may never be able to employ under traditional circumstances. Some problems may be too complex or obscure and only a few individuals or groups may have the resources and information to solve them. For example, say you want to crowdsource a sophisticated computer algorithm that uses Bayesian belief networks to automatically identify the spread of a virus in a community based on the appearance of symptoms in that community. Most people will not have the knowledge, ability, or interest in solving the problem. Your efforts would be more fruitful if you focused your target audience on people in universities, healthcare consulting companies, and research hospitals, who do have the wherewithal to offer solutions. Or, you may need to translate a text from a very obscure language. You could ask everyone on the Internet to do it, but your marketing campaign would be enormous. You would be better off identifying the few people who do know the language—for example, the members of a forum dedicated to talking about obscure languages—and incentivize them to participate.

Table 10.1: Wisdom of the Crowd Approach Conditions

CONDITION	EXPLANATION	EFFECT ON PLATFORM
Problem is clear and objective.	Clearly define the problem and put boundaries on the solution.	Participants understand exactly what they need to do and how they need to do it.
Participants come from diverse backgrounds.	More diverse participants will result in you receiving a greater diversity of information and expertise.	The average of the participants' answers will be more representative of the actual answer.
Participants are independent and do not talk to each other too much.	Participants should be kept from biasing each other's responses through peer pressure.	Keeping participants independent will ensure that the need to conform does not bias the responses you receive.
Problem is not too obscure.	If a problem is too obscure or about a secret topic, information will not be available to the participants to reason about it.	The lack of information will reduce the diversity of the information available to the participants and reduce the likelihood that you will receive the correct answer.
In some cases, recruit experts to sift through the answers.	Subject matter experts can help identify widespread misinformation and help you guide the participants and formulate the problem.	Too much easily accessible misinformation about the problem can bias the participants' responses. You can also compare the responses between the expert and other crowds.

The niche approach has a significantly lower marketing effort than the wisdom of the crowd approach and it involves more complex and obscure problems. It also, in some cases, requires more collaboration between participants. Often, problems are so complex that certain people from all over the world need to come together to share their insights and solutions. In this case, your platform should feature social networking and collaboration tools that allow participants to come together organically to solve the complex problem. Usually, these people will have strong opinions about their efforts and may have solved a piece of the problem, and so will be less affected by the views of others. Collaboration then becomes more about stitching together different pieces of the solution.

The third approach, as you may have guessed, is the mixed approach, and one that you will use more often than not. Like the problem types, think of the approach types as a spectrum. Some problems will have components that are simple to solve and some that are very difficult to solve. The former will require a wisdom of the crowd approach and the latter will require the niche approach. In some cases you will need to re-create the wisdom of the crowd approach within a niche approach. For example, say you want to know the location of a stolen antique. Only some people in the world care about antiques, but those who do may be very knowledgeable about the location of antiques, where they might end up, who might steal them, and so on. Your target audience, then, is the niche community of people interested in antiques, but you can still use elements of the wisdom of the crowd approach to ensure you get a response that is representative of the antique crowd and, you hope, the actual location of the stolen antique. If you employ the third approach, you will need to undertake a smaller marketing campaign than you would with the wisdom of the crowd approach. However, you will need to implement some social networking and collaboration features into the platform. In summary, the wisdom of the crowd approach has a bigger and wider target audience and marketing campaign, but fewer social collaboration features in the platform. The mixed approach has a moderate size of each, with some differences depending on the case. The niche approach has a smaller and more focused target audience and marketing campaign, but more social collaboration features. Figure 10.2 graphically summarizes the relationship and differences between the different parts of the approach type spectrum.

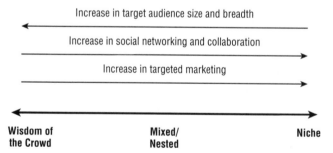

Figure 10.2: Spectrum of approach types

Keep the approach types in mind when designing your platform. Like the problem types, the approach types do not reflect hard-and-fast rules. They are guidelines that clue you into the social features of your platform, the span of your marketing campaign, and the identity of your target audience. Also, you do not need to take our word for it. We devised these rules after reading diverse literature on the wisdom of the crowd phenomenon and creativity. Check the references for more information.

Appreciating the Limits of Crowdsourcing Solutions

Solution platforms are very powerful and cost-effective ways of completing mundane and obscure tasks, and solving seemingly impossible problems. However, they cannot help you solve all problems. In some cases, they can and will return inaccurate solutions. Understanding the limitations will help you understand where and how solution platforms can go wrong, and what you can do to mitigate complications.

Unsolvable Problem

Not every problem has a solution, and not every task can be completed. Some problems simply may be too difficult or complex for anyone, let alone crowds on the Internet, to solve. Some problems do require traditional forms of problem solving. They require special equipment and a dedication of manpower and resources that you cannot incentivize platform participants to match. Do not put problems to the crowd that require an enormous amount of resources, unless you are willing to incentivize them effectively and lucratively. If the problem does not require special resources but is simply very difficult, you might as well bring it to the crowd because you do not know which problems really are unsolvable. In some cases, the problem may have a solution, but you may not be able to reach the individual or group who can solve it. Finding the right participant involves conducting an intelligent marketing campaign and defining the target audience properly. Still, in some cases you may never be able to find the right person. But you will not know unless you try, so you might as well try.

Incorrect Solutions

A lot of the responses you receive will be junk, especially if you do not formulate your problem clearly and do not institute features in the platform that effectively pre-test the solutions. Some solutions may be correct in some areas but wrong in others. You should expect to receive incorrect solutions, and should have a plan in place to sift through the selections and pick the ones you think are the most accurate and effective. The plan depends heavily on the nature of your problem and wants.

Adversarial Participants

Participants sign on to solve problems for a variety of reasons. Most want to help solve the problem, but a few have malicious reasons or may adopt malicious reasons if they feel scorned. Adversaries can purposefully torpedo your platform using a variety of methods, although the chance of them doing so is low. The more likely threat is that of a few participants on platforms geared more toward the niche approach that aggressively criticize other participants and generally wreck any forms of collaboration. Moderators that effectively patrol the platform are the most effective defense against them.

Political Fallout

Sometimes the ends do not justify the means. Occasionally politicians, corporate heads, and public relations departments do not want their organizations using crowdsourcing to solve problems. For example, after the 9/11 terrorist attacks, the U.S. Defense Advanced Research Projects Agency (DARPA) tried to create a prediction market, a website that crowdsourced people's perception of when the next terrorist attack would occur. If people guessed right, they could win money. However, some politicians complained that it seemed the U.S. government was encouraging people to gamble on the basis of terrorist attacks and lost human lives. The platform was soon shut down. To mitigate such fallout, you should frame the problem in a more politically correct way or change the incentive structure. Instead of collecting direct intelligence, collect indirect intelligence. Similarly, collect solutions to problems that appear more politically correct, but in turn can help you solve less politically correct problems. Or, instead of paying people money, incentivize them through other ways. Tell them you are paying them to serve as patriotic analysts that predict terrorist attacks, rather than gamblers betting on terror. The U.S. government's Intelligence Advance Research Projects Agency apparently learned the lessons from DARPA's prediction market, and is now trying out a new terrorism prediction market that does not let people profit off their gambles.[6]

Lastly, sometimes an organization may prohibit you from bringing a problem to the public. A defense laboratory may not want to reveal it is working on a specific project, or a company assessing risks in a certain region of the world may not want to reveal to its competitors that it is looking to expand to that region. Keep such considerations in mind so you do not unwittingly reveal a costly secret.

Tweaking the Process for Solution Platforms

Despite the limitations, solution platforms can still greatly help you and your organization. They, of course, differ from other types of crowdsourcing platforms. Because of these differences, you need to tweak the process from Chapter 8 somewhat and adapt the approaches to them.

The most obvious is that the way you formulate problems matters immensely with solution platforms. They matter with other platforms as well, but exactly how you phrase the problem and what details you give, or how you bound the solution, can greatly affect the responses you receive. With intelligence collection platforms, if you put out a slightly misshapen problem to the participants, you can still receive useful indirect intelligence. However, a misshapen problem for a solution platform can result in useless solutions. For example, asking participants to come up with an algorithm that detects sarcasm in tweets written in the English language is very different from asking participants to come up with an algorithm that detects sarcasm in tweets, without specifying which language.

Also, the level of social networking and collaboration features you integrate into the platform affect the level of moderation you need. They depend highly on which approach you want to take. With the wisdom of the crowd approach, you should integrate fewer social collaboration features, which will require fewer moderators. With the niche approach, you should integrate more, which will require more moderators to ensure that the participants play nice. With the mixed or nested (wisdom of the crowd within niche) approach, you will need a moderate amount.

The type of approach will also affect how narrow you go with your target audience and what your marketing campaign will look like. With the wisdom of the crowd approach, you need to reach a wider and more diverse range of participants and so will need a marketing campaign that can reach a diverse number of people. With the niche approach, you need to reach niche communities and specific groups and so will need a more targeted and focused marketing campaign that reaches those people. With the mixed approach, you may need both.

Now that you know where to tweak the process, you can start building and running solution collection platforms. In the subsequent sections, we walk through how to build and run several platforms that differ in the missions they can support, and the type, resources budget, and target audience. For ease of understanding and comparison, the steps of the walkthroughs follow the structure of the process in Chapter 8.

WARNING Keep in mind that the subsequent sections are fabricated examples, not paragons of accurate research. We do not have the time and resources to do all the steps thoroughly, especially analyzing the target audience in each example. So we have taken shortcuts and made assumptions when considering what appeals to the target audience. Do not worry about whether we are wrong about the target audience. Instead, focus on how we approach problems and use the technologies.

Crowdsourcing Translations during Disaster Relief

In Chapter 9, we walked through designing a crowdsourcing platform that enabled responders to collect information during disasters from affected victims about what type of help they need, triage the information, and then respond immediately. Part of triaging the information involves translating incoming texts. By translating, we mean everything from literally translating words and phrases from one language into another and making sense of idioms, sarcasm, slang, and abbreviations.

Companies like Google and Microsoft (through its Bing service) offer a variety of translation services, each of which has strengths and weaknesses. Integrating their services, some of which are free, into a crowdmap or other crowdsourcing platforms is relatively easy because the services usually function as APIs. You simply send a phrase or word to their API and it sends back the translated version. In Chapter 6, we discussed several other services that also attempted to make sense of idioms, slang, and other elements of speech that foreigners may not understand.

The problem with these services is that they are focused on translating and making sense of popular languages such as English, Mandarin Chinese, French, and Spanish. Machine translation works well with popular languages because there is so much of it in text format, such as books to use to train the translators, and because there is a greater demand for them. Increasingly, machine translation services are starting to focus on more obscure languages, but they still have a long way to go. They are often inaccurate and unable to translate large parts of a less popular language's vocabulary. They are not ideal for translating messages from victims during disasters because they will likely fail to translate the messages properly. Poor translation leads to poor information, which in turn leads to responders being unable to find out which people need help and help them.

For now, the only option available to you for translating incoming messages during a disaster in a place like Haiti is to use people, who are very good at translating and making sense of language. This walkthrough explains how to create a capability that uses existing tools and platforms to crowdsource translation. Crowdsourcing translation is a form of crowd labor that is much more efficient and relevant for this situation than hiring full-time translators. Hiring full-time or even part-time translators takes resources and immense planning. You have to guess well before the disaster how many translators you will need and when you will need them. You also have to pay them a salary. In contrast, crowd labor enables you to quickly surge the number of translators, and in many cases you do not have to pay them. Through crowd labor, you can also get help from native communities that know the language and vernacular very well, as opposed to traditional, non-native translators who only know a more artificial and academic form of the language. The following sections walk through the process of creating such a capability.

Define Objective and Scope

Continuing with the disaster relief walkthrough in Chapter 9, imagine you have set up and deployed a crowdmap to collect and manage text messages from victims of a disaster in Haiti. (We got the idea for this walkthrough example from a real crowdsourcing effort that we reference again later. Read the corresponding reference in the note to learn more.)[7] You will need to instantaneously translate and make sense of the incoming texts and push them to responders, some of whom speak only English. Basic research tells you that Haitians primarily speak French and Haitian Creole, which is an amalgam of French and various African languages. Also, because participants will be communicating through text messages, which limit texts to 160 characters, you expect the texts to contain many abbreviations and linguistic shortcuts. You also expect them to use slang and idioms. Lastly, because they will be texting at a very stressful time while possibly facing danger, you expect the texts to have many misspellings and errors.

No existing natural-language processing tool or machine translator can help you make sense of the incoming texts in an automatic manner. The best they can do is identify the language of the text, but integrating those tools into the crowdmap requires technical development. Ideally, you would like to use real people to translate and make sense of the texts, but you have already used up your manpower resources. You do have a number of moderators, some of whom can help you translate the texts, but you need more help.

With these considerations in mind, you can formulate your objective. You need to create a capability that can take the texts flowing into the crowdmap and send them to a crowdsourcing platform where participants can translate the texts. The participants then send the texts back to the crowdmap, where it is displayed for the responders to use. Additionally, you need to be able to stand up this capability quickly. You also want this process to work smoothly and quickly, and you do not have much financial or manpower resources to dedicate to it.

Analyze Target Audience and Media Environment

Because your requirements for an ideal platform participant are important, you should use them to figure out who belongs in your target audience. The target audience for the translating capability is not the Haitians suffering from the disaster, but rather people away from the disaster who can translate French and Haitian Creole to English. You also need people who understand the nuances, idioms, and slangs of the Haitian language. The target audience also needs to have access to the Internet so they can download texts from the crowdmap and send the translated ones back.

One possible group is Haitians living in parts of Haiti that are not affected by the disaster. However, your previous target audience analysis shows that most Haitians do not have access to the Internet. You could get them to help using SMS, but then you have to pay the cost of the SMS and it slows down the process. Also, if victims are sending texts full of abbreviations because they do not have space left, the person translating it over SMS will also use the abbreviation to save space. Due to the complications, you eliminate this group from your target audience considerations.

Another group is the Haitian diaspora living in the United States, which consists of at least one million people. Much of the diaspora has extensive contacts with relatives living in Haiti, so they are caught up with the culture and language. Also, many in the diaspora likely have access to the Internet and will likely be willing to help their relatives in Haiti during a disaster. The media environment in the United States is, of course, over-saturated. The media environment for the Haitian diaspora is somewhat limited by their preferences but still very similar to that of other Americans. Young members of the diaspora use Facebook and Twitter, whereas older members watch television and read newspapers. A cursory search on Facebook shows that many people in the diaspora form social media groups with the intention of connecting diaspora members in the United States. They also form groups dedicated to helping Haiti. Indeed, this target audience has helped past crowdmap deployments in Haiti with translating Haitian text messages, so the chance they will do so again is fairly high.[7]

In summary, the target audience and media environment analyses reveal the following key insights:

- The Haitian diaspora in the United States and similar countries such as Canada are the ideal target audience. They understand the language, have regular access to the Internet, and are willing to help.

- Many of them are active on social media such as Facebook, but also consume traditional media.

- The target audience is inherently incentivized to participate because they want to help their relatives in Haiti.

Keep these insights in mind while designing the crowdsourcing capability.

Design the Platform

The first part of designing the platform involves determining exactly what the platform should look like. The second part involves designing the incentive structure, which, in turn, can affect the look of the platform.

Determine the Platform's Look and Feel

The target audience analysis reveals that the crowdsourcing platform should be based on social media technologies because the target audience actively uses social media. The platform should enable crowdmap moderators to submit texts that need translation to participants. The participants should then translate the texts and send them back to the moderators. Figure 10.3 shows a graphical overview of the platform. Note that the problem type falls near the objective part of the spectrum and the approach type falls between the mixed and niche part of the spectrum.

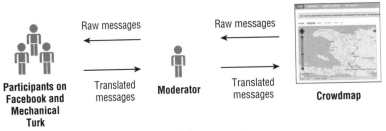

Figure 10.3: Crowd translation platform overview

The platform really has only one component. It is the piece of virtual real estate where the participants will receive the texts, translate them, and send them back out. In all, the platform is relatively simple and has the following features:

- **Messaging**—Obviously, participants need to receive and send the texts that need translation.

- **Task Tracker**—The platform should have a capability that enables you or your moderator to keep track of which texts have been translated and who is doing the translation.

You do not need to design the interface for the platform because platforms with your desired features already exist. Ideally, you should create your own platform, but for now you can simply use one of the existing platforms. By using existing platforms, you will save resources because you will not need to build a new platform from scratch. You will also save time because you can put an existing platform to use much quicker than you can create a new one. Amazon's Mechanical Turk and Facebook are good existing platforms to use. Other platforms provide further customization options, but you do not have time to fiddle with those options now. Mechanical Turk is better suited for when the incoming flow of texts is not too great and you are willing to dedicate manpower and a little bit of time to be organized. Facebook is more ideal for when you desperately need help and are willing to sacrifice order for a quick turnaround. When you have more time you can also create tools that automatically use Mechanical Turk or Facebook to recruit participants and get the translations done. But for now, you will need to settle with using moderators to do most of the unglamorous coordination work.

Determine the Platform's Incentive Structure

The target audience is very involved with Haiti and has a history of helping their relatives. Parts of the diaspora will be willing to participate due to their intrinsic motivation to help people from their homeland. You need only to make it clear to the participants that their efforts are going toward helping Haitians. The great thing about crowdmaps is that you can share them on the Internet.

If needed, you can show the participants the crowdmap filling up with reports in real time, and you can also show the crowdmap receiving updates from responders saying they are taking care of victims.

Some parts of the target audience and others who you may not have initially considered as part of the target audience but still have the language skills to qualify may need extrinsic incentives. If the rate of participation is low, you can introduce small amounts of cash as incentives for participants to translate texts for you. Most likely, though, you will not need the extrinsic incentives. Based on past disasters, diaspora and others are willing to spare some time and resources to help out disaster victims as long as they know that their help is needed.

Build the Platform

For the crowd translation capability, building the platform entails using existing social media platforms. The platforms are Facebook and Mechanical Turk, and they differ greatly in how you use them. In essence, Facebook enables you to crowdsource translation of individual texts more quickly without using extrinsic incentives, whereas Mechanical Turk enables you to translate texts in batches, but more slowly and usually by using extrinsic incentives. You should use both platforms just in case you find more willing participants on one than on the other. Usually, you will find more participants for such general crowd labor on Facebook because more people know about Facebook. We walk through how to use each platform. The following steps describe how to use Facebook:

1. Go to www.facebook.com and create a Facebook account. Do not use your personal Facebook account, but instead create a new one that represents your organization or effort. (We assume you know how to use Facebook. If you do not, check out Facebook's help guide.) Enable the option in your settings to receive a notification, either through e-mail or text, every time someone comments on your post.

2. On Facebook, search for groups or pages that represent the Haitian diaspora in the United States. (Facebook is seemingly switching its groups to pages, hence we use both terms interchangeably.) Use words such as "Haitian." Look for groups that have thousands of members—the more, the better. You can also create your own public group or page for the effort. For example, create a page for "Helping Haitian Disaster Relief." If you are creating a group, make sure to market its existence and invite people to it. Generally, creating and marketing a page to a community to which you have no connections is very difficult. Ask Haitian organizations to help you.

3. After finding or creating the group/page, introduce yourself and what you intend to do. Specify that you will be posting the text of messages from victims on the page's wall that need to be translated. You will then

welcome anyone to comment on the message with the translation. If you are using someone else's page, make sure to get permission from the creator of the page first. Ideally, the creator of that page should introduce you to the rest of the group.

4. During a crisis, send a message to members of the page to log on and await texts that need translation.

5. Have your moderator monitor incoming messages to the crowdmap. The moderator should then post any messages that need to be translated onto the Facebook wall. (It is implicit in the directions that you need to train the moderators and give them access to the Facebook account.) The moderator simply needs to look at incoming reports on the crowdmap and see which ones do not make sense. She then copies the text of the report and pastes it on the Facebook wall as a post, asking someone in the group to translate it.

6. Anyone can then comment on the post with the translated version of the text message contained in the moderator's post. The moderator then needs to check the notifications or monitor the page.

7. The moderator then copies the translation and replaces the text of the relevant report in the crowdmap by entering the crowdmap's dashboard and clicking Reports.

8. The moderator can keep track of which messages have been translated by looking at the wall of the page.

You now have a simple way of getting people on Facebook to translate the texts for you. As you set up the Facebook capability, you should also set up the Mechanical Turk capability when you need to translate many texts at a time. You can also use Mechanical Turk to translate only one text at a time, although it is not as efficient. The following steps describe how to use Mechanical Turk to translate a one-time batch of texts:

1. Go to www.mturk.com and click Get Started on the right side of the home page, under the column that says Get Results, to become a requester. Follow the instructions to fill out the form and create an account. Do not use your personal Amazon account but instead create a new one.

2. After signing into your new account, click Get Started under the header Work Distribution Made Easy to start a new project.

3. In Mechanical Turk you pay workers to complete a task. You can pay them anything from zero to hundreds of dollars per task. If you are paying your workers, you need to add funds to your account. On the top of the page, click Account Settings and follow the directions to fund your account. You want to put enough in now so you do not have to worry about it later.

4. After funding the project, click the Create tab at the top of the screen under Amazon's logo.

5. In the new screen, under the tabs to the far right, you will see small-sized text that says "Create HITs individually." Click that text. (HIT stands for human intelligence task.)

6. Follow the instructions to create the HIT. Fill out the form as you wish. Name it something like "Helping Haiti Disaster Relief by Translating Text Messages from Haiti Disaster Victims." Notice that you need to go through a lot of options to fully customize and create your HIT. We will now quickly go through how you should customize some of the options. Generally you want to give them a couple of hours to complete a task. You do not want to limit the number of workers who can access your tasks, so reduce the qualifications required of the workers to the minimal thresholds. Remove all additional qualifications unless you want to specifically target a particular location. You can pay the workers anything from zero to hundreds of dollars. Start with zero and then ramp it up if the participation rate is too low. If you want to ensure that translations are done right, you can have more than one worker work on a translation and get them to cross-verify.

7. In the same page, fill out the basic directions and what you want the workers to see when they open the task. In the box that says Provide Detailed Instructions, say something like "In the box below, write the translation for each sentence. Separate the sentences by the number of the message you are translating." Then paste in the text messages from the crowdmap that you want translated and separate them out by numbers or however you want. Choose Free Text Answer as the answer format.

8. Click Preview, make sure it looks like you want it to, and then post the HIT to the Mechanical Turk marketplace.

9. You can then use the Manage tab to edit and manage your projects. You can also view your results, which include the translations. The moderators can then edit the reports in the crowdmap with the translations. Generally, it is a good idea for each report to contain the original text and the translation in case there is confusion or mistranslation.

10. Create new individual HITs for each batch of text messages that you need translated. Keep in mind that workers will usually search for HITs to complete at times that they are awake. So if you post something at 2 a.m. their time on a Wednesday, do not expect too many people to answer immediately.

We have showed you only a very simple capability to translate the texts. When you actually do deploy this sort of capability, you will want to create the capability for text to download automatically from the crowdmap and upload to Mechanical Turk or post to Facebook. Developers can easily help you implement it. Explore the Mechanical Turk platform to see how else you can use it. Go through the section that says Applications where third-party organizations can help you to easily implement and deploy more sophisticated translation capabilities.

Market the Platform

Marketing the platform to the target audience is not difficult because of the nature of the message and the rich media environment in which the target audience lives. You are not convincing people to buy a new product or take part in a risky and suspicious endeavor. You are simply asking them to help you help their relatives, friends, and countrymen. Previous pleas for help, everything from crowd-translating Haiti texts to donating money to the Red Cross, elicit massive amounts of participation.

The media environment consists of all sorts of media technologies, and you should use all of them in different phases of the marketing campaigns. Before there is a disaster, you need to spread awareness of what you intend to do with a low-key but somewhat consistent marketing effort. Advertise on Facebook and in newspapers and magazines that the Haitian diaspora reads. In the advertisements, explain what it is you intend to do and how you would like them to help. Tell them specifically that they need to sign on to Facebook and join a certain group, or sign on to Mechanical Turk and expect to find a certain task. Because you can create a group or page on Facebook whenever you like, getting people to join the group is a preferable option. On the group page, you can then advertise Mechanical Turk to them. You can make sure your initial marketing push is working by counting how many people join the group and when.

During hurricane season or in the run up to a disaster, increase your marketing campaign with a few bursts. Place ads on social media and news sites to once again remind people that their help may be needed. If you are part of a government, you do not need to pass the legitimacy test in people's eyes. If the U.S. government came to someone for help, the person would likely comply. However, if you are a company or a non-profit, perhaps working on behalf of a government agency, you should look to partnering with Non-governmental organizations that most people trust and admire, such as Doctors Without Borders or the Red Cross. Partners can also help you spread the word about your efforts.

When a disaster does happen, you will need to once again ramp up your marketing campaign. Much of the Haitian diaspora in the United States live in New York and Florida. Take out television advertisements for those markets urging people to sign on and help. Only take out such advertisements if your marketing efforts so far have not been very fruitful. If you already have ten thousand people signed on to your Facebook group, all you need to do is send them a message through Facebook at the time of the disaster. You do not need that many participants to help unless you are running an extremely massive crowdmap operation. In such a case, you will need to implement tools that automatically process data instead of only relying on moderators to transfer messages between the crowdmap and Facebook and Mechanical Turk. Finally, after the disaster passes, make sure to send a message through Facebook or Mechanical Turk thanking people for their efforts. Give them a few anecdotes about how their efforts helped. If Haiti's history with disasters is any guess, you will need their participation again.

Manage the Platform

Depending on the number of participants and the size of the crowdmap operation, you may need anywhere from five to ten moderators for both the crowd translation and the crowdmap. Make sure to train the moderators and run them through drills. During the disaster, they should not be asking you for the password to the Facebook account. Also, give them the opportunity to play around on Facebook and Mechanical Turk and become familiar with the numerous options both sites offer. The moderators need not speak French and Haitian Creole, but it is beneficial if they do. They can then double-check some randomly selected messages to make sure participants are translating them correctly. They do need to be social-media savvy and comfortable with multitasking.

Not including their duties with the crowdmap, which we explained in Chapter 9, the moderators will have the following duties concerning the crowd-translation platform:

- Identify messages on the crowdmap that need translation.
- Ensure that the Facebook and Mechanical Turk platforms are working and updated frequently.
- Post messages that need translation on Facebook and Mechanical Turk.
- Monitor the platforms to ensure translation is being done and at an acceptable standard. If not, educate the participants about what they need to do differently.
- Thank the participants for their help regularly.
- On Facebook, message members of related groups to remind them to participate.
- Make sure the fund with which to pay Mechanical Turk is full. Keep track of the participation rate on Mechanical Turk, and if it is low, modify the payment structure to incentivize more participants.
- Update the crowdmap with the translated messages.

If you implement development tools into Mechanical Turk, Facebook, and the crowdmap, your moderators' duties may change. For example, they may not need to post messages from and to the crowdmap, but they will have to ensure that any automated message-posting tools are working correctly. They will need to open up and maintain lines of communication with developers in case of problems.

Measure the Platform's Performance

Facebook and Mechanical Turk enable you to collect performance data easily during and after the disaster. Depending on privacy settings on your page or the page of another group that you are using, you can see all the posts and comments ever posted on the page. You can then go back and see who translated which messages. Mechanical Turk provides several tools and a dashboard with which you can track which participants completed which translation tasks, and other relevant data. Use such tools and the moderators' overall assessments to measure the platform's performance. Example metrics include:

- Number of messages successfully translated
- Number of messages translated incorrectly
- Number of participants who signed on to a group
- Number of participants who actually translated a message
- Peak time when participants were most active
- Average time to translate a posted message

Wash, Rinse, Repeat

The process we detailed so far is not very sophisticated, and for good reason. One benefit of using social media data and technologies is to do things that you can do traditionally, such as translating, through much more inexpensive methods. Also, social media enables you to improve and execute spontaneously, and modulate the scale of your effort as it transpires. If you need more translators and you need to boost participation, you can post tasks on the Mechanical Turk platform and pay people to complete them. However, you will find that simply leveraging people through Facebook is enough.

In some cases, though, you will need a much more sophisticated effort. If your crowdmap is receiving hundreds of text messages an hour and they all need translating, your moderators cannot keep posting messages back and forth between the crowdmap and Facebook. You will need to hire developers to build you relatively simple tools that post the messages automatically, and sift through the messages automatically looking for ones that need translation.

Many of these tools are language-agnostic and so you can use them for other crowdmaps in very different places. You will still have to find and incentivize the target audience, but your job will become slightly easier. Also, you need to implement more formal tools and processes to verify the text messages and their translations.

Another more sophisticated tool you can implement is machine-learning language processing tools that essentially learn Haitian Creole and other languages over time. They basically look at how people read and translate certain words and phrases, and then they learn from those people and change how they read and translate those same words and phrases. Eventually, the machine-learning language processing tools can replace your need to crowd-translate entirely. Crowd-translation platforms then become tools to teach computers how to translate less popular languages. So the next time a disaster comes to Haiti, you will not need to recruit and incentivize as many participants. The machine will pick up the slack. Finally, think about eventually building your own crowd-translation platform. With your own platform, you can better control privacy settings and limit who sees what information and for how long. With your own platform or not, and the machine-learning translation tools, you can then translate other types of texts including other types of intelligence.

Crowdsource Tools to Identify Antagonistic Actors in Video Feeds

Solution platforms are ideal for crowdsourcing responses to complicated, scientific problems. In Chapter 7, we described how governments have used solution platforms to crowdsource the solutions to everything from designing computer programs that make sense of shredded documents to unmanned aerial vehicle schematics. The sponsoring organizations then use the crowdsourced solutions as starting points for developing much more robust and operational tools. The organizations also receive kudos from their colleagues and the public for using a relatively inexpensive method for coming up with a solution that would have cost much more if done through traditional means.

Like many other technologies, social media not only enables the solving of complex problems, it also creates new problems to solve. One problem is the need for governments, analysts, and security officials to make sense of the gargantuan amount of video that is now available on the Internet. The amount increases when you include videos from other sources such as closed-circuit television, security cameras, and cameras belonging to apprehended individuals. The majority of the videos serve no purpose; however, some video clips offer revealing insights about security events and suspects. Specifically, some video clips such as the ones taken at the London Tube before and during the July 2005 attacks in London show the suspects in action.[8] Also, YouTube videos and news video feeds during the Arab Spring show the actions of pro-Mubarak forces infiltrating the anti-Mubarak protests to cause chaos and incite violence.[9] Suspects and other antagonistic actors, who intend to cause harm or infiltrate peaceful crowds, behave differently than peaceful people around them. For example, their position or gait may be different from everyone else around them or they may make many physically imposing movements. Some tools can identify and discriminate between different types of behavior on the individual and group level, so some tools can also theoretically identify antagonistic behavior and thus individuals.[10]

Identifying antagonistic individuals who are behaving strangely in video feeds of otherwise peaceful settings can help security officials preempt the antagonistic individuals before they commit harm. Officials can then keep an eye on them to make sure they do not cause problems or to make sure they are not persons already thought to be suspicious. However, few if any tools can detect antagonistic individuals and behavior on video quickly and with great accuracy. Also, some tools that can do so cannot process the large amounts of video that are now available. Solution platforms provide the ability to crowd-source processes and tools that can process large amounts of video feeds to detect antagonistic individuals quickly and accurately. The following sections walk through the process of creating such a platform.

Define Objective and Scope

Imagine that a domestic law enforcement force tasks you with creating a tool that can detect antagonistic individuals on real-time video feeds and immediately notify security officials. You have a moderate-sized budget but a lack of ideas and a need to get started quickly. Overall, you expect that coming up with a robust and operational solution will take time. However, you need to jumpstart the process and need to crowdsource ideas and prototype tools off of which you can build.

You have done some research on your task and have acquired a decent-sized archive of videos of antagonistic individuals and normal, peaceful individuals in numerous contexts and settings. You can crowdsource tools and test them against this archive of videos to see which ones look promising. By testing the tool on different types of videos, you can also ensure that the tool can work against any other video, even ones that are not in your archive. You realize this problem is a difficult one and so you are open to all considerations and ideas. Because the project is at such an early phase, you also do not have to abide by security restrictions and can accept solutions from all over the world, barring a few special exceptions.

With these considerations in mind, you can formulate your objective. You need to create a platform that crowdsources the capability to identify different antagonistic individuals in different videos quickly and accurately. The capability must work on numerous videos subsequently. After identifying antagonistic individuals, the capability or tool should then somehow tag the individual on the video and send a notification. Note that because you are not wedded to any solution set and are open to any idea, the objective does not state exactly how the capability, or in other words, the tool, needs to work. The boundaries to the solution for this problem are limited to the capability's performance and not its makeup.

Analyze Target Audience and Media Environment

Because you are not bound by idea type, need for secrecy, and region, almost anyone can make up part of your target audience. The problem you are putting out to the crowd is a very difficult one that requires expertise in a number of disciplines. A group trying to solve the problem will need some background in at least behavioral science, video processing, and computer programming.

Anyone could become part of your target audience; however, not everyone will. You need to use some factors to limit your target audience, because advertising to and accommodating everyone is not realistic or cost-effective. Most people around the world will either not care about solving the problem, or will not have the resources, expertise, and time to do it. At a minimum, your target audience needs to have access to the Internet to participate in the platform. They also need to have some level of formal or informal technical expertise or education so they can begin tackling the problem. Also, only a small subset of the world's population will be interested in the problem and dedicate their free time to figuring out how to detect strange-behaving people in videos. Based on examining the types of people who talk about and participate in similar crowdsourcing platforms, you can stereotype a little and expect that most of your participants will tend to be geeks, scientists, entrepreneurs, young people interested in such topics, and older people with disposable time. Looking at other platforms also tells you that they incentivize such people through cash, their interest in solving a problem that they find appealing, and even bragging rights. Thus, you can refine your target audience to include people globally interested in behavioral, security, and video technology topics who have disposable time and regular access to computers and the Internet.

It is easy to imagine the media environment for such a target audience; at least it is for us, because we fit into it. Your target audience's media environment is rich and over-saturated. They likely use Facebook and Twitter regularly, and frequent websites dedicated to scientific and technology topics such as WIRED and Scientific American. They also likely frequent sites, blogs, and forums that specifically talk about video technology and human behavior.

In summary, the target audience and media environment analyses reveal the following key insights:

■ The target audience is made up of well-connected and tech-savvy people from around the world.

■ Their media environment is very rich and skews toward new media content, such as Facebook and websites that talk about technology and science.

■ Based on their participation in similar platforms, the target audience is incentivized through extrinsic items such as cash, and intrinsic items such as their interest in the problem and willingness to compete against like-minded individuals.

Keep these insights in mind while designing the crowdsourcing capability.

Design the Platform

The first part of designing the platform involves determining exactly what the platform should look like, which will matter a great deal in this platform because you will design it from scratch. The second part involves designing the incentive structure, which, in turn, can affect the look of the platform.

Determine the Platform's Look and Feel

The crowdsourcing platform should be a website for a number of reasons. One, everyone around the world can access a website easily and without the need of special devices such as smartphones. Two, websites provide you the space and tools to feature a variety of content including the videos you want your participants to process. Three, websites are easy to advertise and link to from other sites and platforms.

The platform will have a simple overall process that is made up of many component steps. Initially, participants will register on the platform either as individual participants or as teams. You will then post ten or so short, different looking videos from different environments, most with antagonistic individuals in them and some without. These videos are known as the training videos. You will know who the antagonistic individuals are in all the videos concerned. The participants will then develop a video processing capability and test it on the training videos. After a certain time period, so that participants have the time to develop a tool, you will then release a completely new video and invite participants to quickly process it and send you a note identifying the antagonistic individuals in the video, and saying so if none are in the video. You will score the participants based on how quickly and accurately they identified and notified you of the antagonistic individuals. This completely new video is known as the test video. Over the lifetime of the platform, at, say, a specific time each week, you will release several new test videos and aggregate the participants' scores over all the videos. Figure 10.4 graphically represents the platform overview.

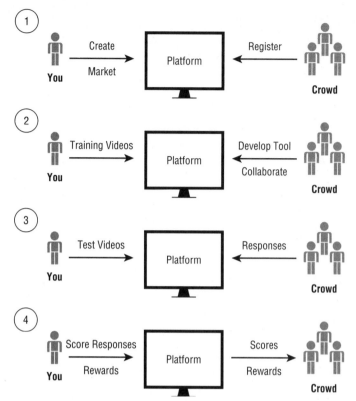

Figure 10.4: Video processing platform overview

Clearly state exactly what you want the participants to do and fully describe how you will score their tools. On the website, create a page dedicated to explaining instructions, providing samples, and answering frequently asked questions. Note that the problem type falls near the subjective part of the spectrum with a few boundaries, and the approach type falls near the mixed part of the spectrum.

The platform is made up of three components. The first is the website that participants will access to interface with you and your videos. The second is the data management system and servers that will host the videos and the website, and store participant information. The third is the back-end web interface that enables you to keep track of the participants and their scores, and upload videos. In all, the platform will have the following features:

- **Messages**—Participants can send messages to each other on the platform through a forum interface so they can collaborate on ideas and find potential partners. Participants and platform moderators should also be able to message each other with submissions, questions, and comments.

- **Video archive**—Participants can download the training videos and the test video easily from the platform. The servers hosting the videos must be able to take on a substantial amount of traffic.

- **User accounts**—Participants can create accounts for themselves (including their teams). Participants must specify a team name and have the option of submitting demographic information about themselves. To safeguard privacy, encourage the participants to pick names for themselves or their teams that mask their true identity.

- **Notifications**—Moderators should be able to send notifications to the participants by posting on the platform and by sending e-mails to the participants about the posting of new test videos. The notifications should come far in advance of the posting of the test video so participants have the time to prepare and fix their schedule.

The website interface has no set look. Check out existing government platforms using the links we provided in Chapter 7 to see examples of what your interface should look like. Overall, the website should not be overly flashy or have lots of colors and banners. You want the participants to navigate the website easily, not get seizures. The most important thing about the website is making sure that participants can access the videos easily and submit responses to you. The back-end interface that you and your moderators access should provide the following features:

- **Messages**—You and the moderators should be able to easily send messages, e-mails, and notifications to the participants.

- **Tracking system**—Keeping track of the participants' scores is essential to the platform. A digital tracking system integrated into the platform will make sure you do not make any mistakes. If need be, it also enables you to then show the participants their scores.

You do not need to create a completely separate interface for your moderator controls. You can simply integrate them into the website that participants use, but make sure you integrate passwords to protect participants and outsiders from accessing the moderators' tools.

Determine the Platform's Incentive Structure

The first step in creating an incentive structure is to examine the incentive structure of other similar platforms. Our research shows that the majority of the platforms, at least the most successful ones, tend to offer moderate-sized cash prizes. Smaller challenges feature cash rewards worth somewhere in the hundreds or thousands of U.S. dollars, whereas bigger, more comprehensive challenges feature rewards worth tens of thousands of dollars. Cash rewards are an ideal incentive to offer target audiences that are wide and made up of people with different backgrounds. However, the size of the cash rewards may change depending on the region in which your target audience mostly resides. Generally, the more money a member of the target audience has in general, the more with which you need to incentivize them. Past platform participation information suggests that most of our target audience resides in the West, where cash reward sizes are generally larger than they are in less developed areas. Almost everyone wants money and will expend effort to get it. Also, providing the cash reward is easy because you can simply mail out checks. Overall, consider providing the participants with the top three aggregate scores at the end of the platform with a major cash prize worth tens of thousands of U.S. dollars. Depending on the tools you receive, you can also hand out smaller cash prizes at your discretion to participants who you feel were the most creative or innovative.

Some past platforms also use intrinsic incentives. Participants like to compete with each other, especially when it comes to solving a complex problem. Successful participants feel accomplished and can brag to others about their skill. You can intensify the drive to compete by letting participants know how their colleagues are doing and how they are faring in comparison. You will have to reconsider your design so far to integrate such a feature.

Some incentives combine extrinsic and intrinsic motivators. For example, you can offer the participants with the highest score at the end of the platform the opportunity to continue working on their tools with others in a more traditional contractor setting. The winning participants will receive compensation for continuing work on the tool and perhaps eventually converting it into a business, and they will feel good about building something tangible and long-lasting from their initial contribution that goes on to help secure the world.

Assuming you will provide the large and small cash rewards and the opportunity for the participant with the highest score to work long-term on the project, clearly state on the website what the prizes are and how participants can win and collect them.

Determine the Platform's Look and Feel, Redux

To provide participants with an incentive to compete with each other and boost their efforts, you need to make it obvious to the participants how their efforts compare with others. A leaderboard is a simple feature that fulfills the delivery of the intrinsic incentive and that you can integrate into the platform easily. A leaderboard is a ranked list of perhaps the top five or the top ten participants at a given time in the competition. Remember that you are scoring the participants based on the accuracy and speed of their tools in regard to the test videos. You are also keeping track of the scores and updating them regularly after you verify the participants' response with what you know to be the correct answer. You can then reveal the top five or ten scores and the names of the participants (teams) with the top scores at all times through a leaderboard. Some of the participants with the top scores will likely take to the forums to brag about their video processing prowess, which in turn will motivate others to try harder. See Figure 10.5 for a graphical example of a leaderboard.

Rank	Participant(s)	Overall Score	Accuracy Score	Quickness Score
	Leaderboard: Week of March 4th 2013 5 Test Videos Remaining			
1	Video 534	185	95	90
2	DaneWar	184	87	97
3	TXCA Team	167	81	86
4	UofK Team	164	71	93
5	BruceBruce	156	76	80

Figure 10.5: Leaderboard example

Build the Platform

The video processing platform is relatively easy to build and deploy but requires some developmental expertise. Do not use existing website templates such as WordPress to build the website because you need to account for significant security and privacy concerns, especially because you are sending out cash rewards to certain participants. The fewer features you implement, such as the forums and leaderboard, the easier it is to build and maintain the website. Work with a development team that can help you design, build, deploy, and maintain the website.

Also, ask the developers to integrate tools into the platform that enable you and the moderators to upload videos quickly and easily, and download and track participant responses. The website should also update the leaderboard automatically with the rankings at all times.

Market the Platform

The marketing effort should consist of an initial marketing push that starts a few weeks before the launch of the platform, and depending on the participation rate, a few marketing bursts soon after the platform's launch. Unlike for other platforms, you will want to focus most of your marketing energy on the initial campaign. The platform has a definite end point and participants win a cash prize depending on the scores they aggregate over the lifetime of the platform. Participants who engage with the platform well after the release of a few test videos will be at a disadvantage in terms of aggregating scores and winning the major cash prize and the opportunity to work on their tool long-term. Thus, you should concentrate most of your efforts to making sure participants sign up at the beginning. However, if your participation rate is low, you may need to advertise a little after the platform's launch. Check out past platform participation rates to determine a realistic participation rate.

Because the target audience is tech-savvy and spread around the world, you will need to focus your initial marketing campaign at media that reflect the target audience's key interests. Of course, their key interests are aligned with your platform's topic, as it should be for all target audiences you pick. A few weeks before the platform launches, start advertising on sites, such as WIRED and Scientific American, that the target audience tends to frequent. Contact news organizations and urge them to write about the platform. Also, advertise on social media, and target the ads at Facebook users who list technology topics as their interests and on Twitter hashtags that have to do with technology and science. Additionally, find a few forums or websites dedicated to video processing and visual behavioral recognition and advertise there. Ideally, you will want to have a presence on such forums well before you start your advertising campaigns. You will want to post regularly on such forums and show you care about the topic to gain the forum community's trust. Eventually, you will want to subtly state information about the platform without overdoing it. No one likes being spammed at a site that they visit frequently. The strength of the marketing campaign should increase in intensity as the platform launch date nears to create buzz and get the participants excited. Also, ramping up the advertising will remind the participants who already intend to participate that the platform will launch soon and that they need to clear up time in their schedule to work on the tool.

If participation rates are low, release an infrequent burst of ads at the aforementioned sites. As participants sign up on the platform, try to collect demographic information about them. You can then understand exactly who your target audience is and where you should focus your marketing. If you have already released half of your test videos and participation rates are low, do not bother advertising any more. It is too late for participants to join, create a tool, and then start aggregating scores. Your platform may be a failure; however, you can always deploy it again.

Lastly, make sure to e-mail the participants regularly about the release of upcoming test videos. You will especially want to e-mail them during the time period between the training and test videos when participants are developing their tools. You will want to make sure that they do not forget, and remain engaged at that critical time.

Manage the Platform

The platform will have a few social messaging features, such as the forum, that will require moderation. However, because such features are not the focus of the platform, you will not need too many moderators. Expect to hire one to two moderators depending on the number of participants and the extent to which the posting of videos and aggregating of participants' responses is automated. The moderators will have the following roles and duties:

- Monitor the forum to make sure participants are abiding by the rules and refraining from picking fights with each other.
- Answer all participant questions about the platform and rules.
- Explain the rules to participants.
- Make sure participants' responses are collected and scored properly.
- Ensure that the platform is working properly, including the uploading of videos and the leaderboard.
- Inform participants that they have won and make sure they get their rewards in a timely manner.

Measure the Platform's Performance

Use the tools integrated into the platform and other web analytical services such as Google Analytics to measure the platform's performance, which includes the participation levels on the platform and the success of the participants in regards to creating a useful tool. Example metrics include:

- Number of participants registered on the platform
- The scores of the participants and how close they are to perfect scores
- Time between releasing test videos and receiving responses
- Number of participants per team
- Number of page visits
- Number of video downloads

Wash, Rinse, Repeat

If any parts of your platform fail or cause confusion, it will be the parts that deal with the scoring and the nature of the participants' responses. You will find that what you thought of as intuitive, the participants might think of as confusing—hence, the need for moderators to interact with the participants and learn their insights. You may want to consider releasing the test videos on an irregular schedule. As we discussed in Chapter 8, an irregular schedule can increase the participants' interest and eagerness to participate. However, keep in mind that an irregular schedule could backfire because it may upset the participants' lives too much.

Now that you know how to design and deploy crowdsourcing platforms to collect intelligence and solve problems, you can start creating crowdsourcing platforms to achieve the relatively harder objective of influencing populations. Chapter 11 will describe how to build crowdsourcing platforms to influence populations.

Summary

- Crowdsourced solutions are the solutions to problems and tasks you collect from crowdsourcing platforms known as solution platforms.

- A limited number of ways to traditionally contract out work exist, but you have many different ways to crowdsource solutions.

- Thinking about the type of problem you want solved can help you formulate the problem. Solution platforms can help you solve three types of problems:

  - Objective problems that have a right or wrong answer and usually only one method of coming up with the answer

  - Subjective problems that have no right or wrong answer and numerous methods of coming up with the answer, with some being better than others according to some criteria

  - Mixed problems that may have a right or wrong answer and numerous methods of coming up with the answer, with some being better than others according to some criteria

- Thinking about which approach you want to use or how you want to solve the problem can help you define your platform's look and features, the identity of your target audience, and the intensity and focus of your marketing campaign. Solution platforms employ three types of approaches:

  - The wisdom of the crowd approach involves asking a large, heterogeneous target audience the answer to objective-type problems, and thus requires a large marketing campaign but a platform with few social networking features.

  - The niche approach involves asking a small, specialized target audience the answer to mixed- or subjective-type problems, and thus requires a focused marketing campaign and a platform with social networking features.

  - The mixed or nested approach involves asking both types of target audience or a heterogeneous version of a specialized audience the answer to mixed- or subjective-type problems, and thus requires a moderately sized and focused marketing campaign and a platform with some social networking features, depending on the case.

- Solution platforms suffer from a few limitations:
  - Some problems are too difficult for crowds to solve.
  - Participants may provide incorrect solutions.
  - Adversarial participants may bias other participants and wreck collaboration.
  - Problems stated politically incorrectly may engender scorn from politicians, corporate heads, and public relations departments.

- Compared to other types of platforms, everything about a solution platform is highly dependent on the type of problem you want to solve and the approach you want to take to do it. Also, the success of every solution platform is completely dependent on how clearly you state the problem to the crowd.

- You can use solution platforms to crowd-translate text messages from affected victims during disasters.

- You can use solution platforms to crowdsource tools to identify antagonistic actors in video feeds.

Notes

1. Lanier, J. (2010) *You Are Not a Gadget: A Manifesto.* Knopf, New York; Leonhardt, D. (2012) "When the Crowd Isn't Wise." *New York Times.* Accessed: 27 August 2012. http://www.nytimes.com/2012/07/08/sunday-review/when-the-crowd-isnt-wise.html

2. Surowiecki, J. (2005) *The Wisdom of Crowds.* Anchor, New York.

3. Asch, S.E. (1995) "Opinions and Social Pressure." *Scientific American,* 193, pg. 31-35.

4. Cain, S. (2012) "The Rise of the New Groupthink." *New York Times.* Accessed: 27 August 2012. http://www.nytimes.com/2012/01/15/opinion/sunday/the-rise-of-the-new-groupthink.html?pagewanted=all

5. McKay, C. (2009) *Extraordinary Popular Delusions and the Madness of Crowds.* Wilder, Radford.

6. Dilanian, K. (2012) "US Intelligence Tests Crowd-Sourcing Against Its Experts." *Stars and Stripes.* Accessed: 27 August 2012. http://www.stripes.com/news/us/us-intelligence-tests-crowd-sourcing-against-its-experts-1.186464

7. Meier, P. (2010) "Ushahidi and the Unprecedented Role of SMS in Disaster Response." Ushahidi Blog. Accessed: 27 August

2012. `http://blog.ushahidi.com/index.php/2010/02/23/ushahidi-the-unprecedented-role-of-sms-in-disaster-response/`

8. (2008) "Jury Sees 7/7 Bombing CCTV Images." BBC News. Accessed: 27 August 2012. `http://news.bbc.co.uk/2/hi/uk_news/7377649.stm`

9. Kirkpatrick, D. and Fahim, K. (2011) "Mubarak's Allies and Foes Clash in Egypt." *New York Times*. Accessed: 27 August 2012. `http://www.nytimes.com/2011/02/03/world/middleeast/03egypt.html?_r=1&pagewanted=1&hp`

10. For examples of such tools, check out the New York University Movement Lab at `movement.nyu.edu`.

CHAPTER 11

Influencing Crowds

Crowdsourcing platforms provide a safe space where you can discreetly persuade populations to adopt new viewpoints and change their behavior. Although the influence process is slow and fragile, it confers enormous power and advantage. Through crowdsourcing platforms, you can spur populations to undertake actions and help you complete seemingly unachievable security objectives. This chapter explicates the process by describing what is possible, how you can make it possible, what is not possible, and how influence platforms differ from other types of platforms. It also walks through how to build and run an influence platform to collect intelligence on the ties between extremists and government officials by getting participants to talk about their daily lives and then submit intelligence about corruption in their government.

Understanding the Scope of Influencing through Crowdsourcing

Influencing through crowdsourcing platforms is the act of persuading populations to adopt certain ideas and/or undertake certain behaviors. Such platforms, known as *influence platforms*, differ from traditional types of influence operations in a number of ways. Influence platforms enable you to take advantage of the two-way communication that is integral to social media in ways that other influence operations cannot. The most apparent difference is that on influence platforms you work closely with the participants to engender influence. You do not inundate them with information through endless flyer drops and radio commercials, and try to hammer a viewpoint or data into their heads. Instead, with influence platforms, you slowly persuade participants to come up with ideas and change their behaviors by making them believe that they are the ones promoting the changes. Influence is a more subtle and powerful form of incentivizing. It is especially relevant at times when material incentives do not work or when people are reluctant to accept any type of incentives from you. Think of influencing as convincing people to let them be incentivized to think or act. You can influence others to do almost anything you would like them to do, although such overwhelming success is hard to achieve. Realistically, you can use influence populations to counter extremist propaganda, provide intelligence, coalesce against a violent regime, and adopt a more favorable attitude toward issues that are important to you. Keep in mind that building and deploying influence platforms is more of an art than a science. It requires an understanding of human nature and behavior to get it right, and such understanding is hard to teach.

Delineating Influence Goals

Influencing participants on your platform entails accomplishing two goals. The first is changing a participant's way of thinking. Every person uses a form of mental heuristics called *frames* to make sense of the enormous amount of information available in the world. Frames are the filters through which a person processes information. Generally, people only allow information to filter through that validates their frames and how they already perceive the world, while discarding other types of information. For example, the frames of political partisans are usually very robust and ingrained. They routinely ignore arguments and data that poke holes in their political theories, producing the headache-inducing shouting matches prevalent on television shows about politics. Changing a person's way of thinking and viewing the world necessitates introducing or changing his or her frames—a very difficult task. Unsurprisingly, frames are resistant to information that is trying to undo them. The task is made easier if you do not make it obvious that you are trying to introduce or change a person's frames. Also, peer or societal pressure heavily influences frames. Sometimes, a person is hesitant to indulge in a certain way of thinking or express himself as he really wishes because of societal pressure. Lifting that repression is a function of changing the pressure the person faces. Overall, working with frames involves either providing participants with new frames, modifying their existing frames, or enabling them to express repressed frames.

The second goal is motivating the participants to change their behavior and execute a specific action. Accomplishing the second goal necessitates accomplishing the first one. A person's behavior is heavily dependent on the frames he or she utilizes to make sense of the world. Information affects behavior, which in turn affects the type of information a person will seek out. As with frames, a person may resist undertaking an action because either he does not think he should, and/or he wishes to do it but his society does not condone it. We have already discussed incentivizing people to undertake actions and change their behavior in terms of participating in platforms. However, we are now discussing incentivizing people to perhaps take part in action that goes beyond simply participating in crowdsourcing platforms. The amount of behavior change required is higher, and thus the quality and level of incentives required are also higher. Fortunately, measuring change in a person's behavior is much easier than measuring change in his or her way of thinking. Anyone can see a person's actions, but no one can see the thoughts in his head. For your influence platform, strive to accomplish the second goal. Overall, changing a person's behavior involves either modifying his way of thinking and then incentivizing him to act, and/or enabling him to undertake repressed acts. See Figure 11.1 for a graphical representation of the relationship between information, frames, and behavior. Frames, behavior, and their interplay are complex and fascinating topics that we cannot do full justice to in only a few paragraphs. You should check out the notes for accessible material that can help you appreciate the topics more.[1]

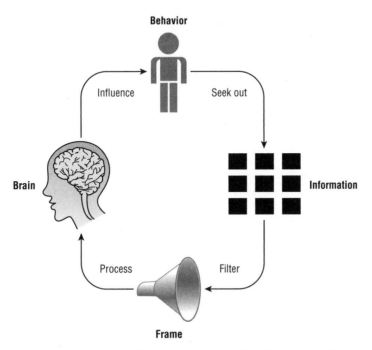

Figure 11.1: Relationship between information, frames, and behavior

Grasping How Influence Happens

Identifying and amplifying the most influential items can help you focus your efforts to achieve maximum effect and influence. Your methods must contain those items if you want to achieve influence. Picking out the most influential items is not at all an easy task. People and the things around them are constantly influencing each other. As people, we like to believe that we possess a unitary, consistent set of views; however, the reality is much more complicated. Our minds are a cacophony of impulses and stimulations that are constantly competing with each other to shape our thoughts and actions.[2] Various items can impact the cacophony and influence us, most of which function at a level out of sight of our conscious awareness. We now describe the most salient and relevant items.[1, 2, 3]

As you may have noticed when arguing with someone, rational, logical arguments containing lots of objective facts are rarely one of the influential items. Do not expect much success by laying out, for example, arguments about why your target audience should believe your government and not jihadists about the true goal of your government's foreign policy. Such arguments contain information that our frames usually filter out. Suppressing our frames long enough to process and consider new and conflicting information is difficult and requires dedicated mental effort. We are not suggesting that you cannot use rational arguments to persuade others. We are simply saying that doing so is difficult, especially when dealing with critical security issues, and that easier ways exist to go about it.

Lots of items can subtly persuade and influence others, and the best methods employ a variety of them. One item is repetition. Constantly repeating a piece of information makes it more likely that a person will remember it and consider it to be true, regardless of its veracity. Consider how politicians are constantly repeating talking points. Whatever message you are delivering through your platform must be repeated, in lots of different ways, to ensure the point gets across. Another item is getting people to believe they came up with the ideas you want them to adopt. In many cultures, if you overtly tell them to do something or think a certain way, they will likely resist. Also regardless of culture, if you are a member of a group that a person considers suspicious, then the person is also likely to resist your ideas and commands. However, if you can make people claim ownership of the idea and think they are the ones who came up with the idea to think a certain way or do a certain thing, they are much more likely to go along. Good salesmen use this trick all the time. They subtly seed ideas and wait for you to adopt them as your own. Then when you communicate the idea to them, they say that it is a fantastic idea. You then go along and spend money on something you did not want to buy initially. The reason the idea ownership trick works is because people tend to value things they think they have created more than the creations of others. If you think you came up with an idea, you are more likely to value it, and hence follow through with it. Other items also relate to how the information is delivered. You are more likely to claim ownership of an idea or simply be persuaded by it if it comes from a credible source and incites interest in you. These items do not betray common sense. You are not likely to believe something a crook tells you. Also, you are not likely to listen to others if they are boring and droll. Thus, your influence platform must feature interesting media and material. You must also develop trust between yourself and your participants because if they do not trust you, they will not participate or may rebel against you. Perhaps the most influential item is social influence, also known as peer pressure or a person's culture.

> **NOTE** In this chapter, we use the word "culture" as a catch-all term that describes a person's surroundings, immediate and extended social network, traditions, rituals, and general knowledge.

In most cases, the society a person inhabits, whether it be a country or a small group, strongly influences how that person thinks and acts. In Chapter 10, we briefly discussed how most of us have a tendency to conform to match our peers and social network. We are unlikely to engage in actions and ideas that people around us do not engage in. Culture also delineates actions and ideas that are taboo, and either discourages people from indulging in them or compels people to suppress them. Apart from urging conformity and identifying taboos, our surroundings also impact the frames we structure. Cultures construct traditions and myths through repetitive rituals. The rituals, whether they are actions or ways of thinking, help construct and reinforce frames in people's minds. Simply put, our family, friends, and community teach us how to view the world, and few of us really depart from that viewpoint. A few, in every culture, have a tendency to be non-conformist and adopt new frames. They, in turn, influence their surroundings, which in turn influence the culture and other people. Your influence platform should take advantage of the power of social influence and of people who tend to be non-conformist.

Process of Influencing Others

Social media is ideal for influencing others for a number of reasons. As we already discussed, you need to provide interesting and repetitive information to your participants. Crowdsourcing platforms can feature all types of interesting media, such as pictures and videos, and there is no limit to how many times you can deliver a piece of information to someone. Also, because crowdsourcing platforms can increase the rate of communication between you and your audience, it increases the likelihood that your audience will become familiar with you and come to trust you. Using crowdsourcing platforms to get people to claim ownership of an idea and propagate influence through their social networks is more difficult and requires the completion of certain steps. The remainder of this section first presents a conceptual overview of the necessary steps, and then presents details about what the conceptual steps mean in the real world. The section focuses on how to seed ideas into your platform's participatory audience and then get them to take ownership of it and execute it. It also focuses on how to propagate influence through the audience's social network and shift their perspective on what they consider to be valid viewpoints and actions, and taboos. A walkthrough section then goes through the steps in greater practical detail.

Conceptual Overview of Influence Process

The first and most critical step is determining exactly where your audience is now and where you want them to be, in terms of ways of thinking or willingness to perform an act. You need to determine the starting point, the intermediate points, and the end point. For example, you may want your audience to provide you with intelligence about drug smugglers in their area. However, for a number of reasons, the audience may be unwilling to provide the intelligence. You then know that you need to take the audience from being unwilling to provide intelligence, to becoming willing, to then actually providing the intelligence. The overall process of getting people to move from the starting to the end point is similar to helping people navigate a dense forest.

Consider a forest such as the one represented in Figure 11.2. To the left of the forest is the starting point, where the participants are at the start of your platform. To the right of the forest is the end point. Notice that numerous end points represent the numerous ways to exit a forest. Some of the exits and end points are counterproductive and some are harmless. Continuing with the previous example, you can try to take your participants on a journey through your process, but they may end up at end points such as becoming more unwilling to provide you with intelligence, or becoming willing to provide only intelligence about anything other than local drug smugglers.

You can guide your participants from the starting point to your desired end point through the numerous pathways in the forest. You do not always know which path the participants are taking or which end point they are likely to come out of because you cannot always see them through the dense foliage, similar to how you cannot see inside a participant's head and know for sure what she is thinking while she is participating in your platform. As your participants choose and traverse the mental paths, you should nudge them on to the paths that will lead to your end point. If they veer too far off the correct set of paths, they will go on wrong paths, and end up at the wrong end points.

Use a variety of nudges known as *cognitive inserts* to guide your participants. Cognitive inserts can be pieces of information, events such as games, and actions from the platform moderators that nudge your participants and the people around them to adopt new ways of thinking. Through cognitive inserts you can seed ideas, and reward people who gravitate to the idea and then urge their peers to adopt it as their own. Cognitive inserts can affect individuals and groups, and as we discussed before, the group can also affect each participant's behavior through social influence.

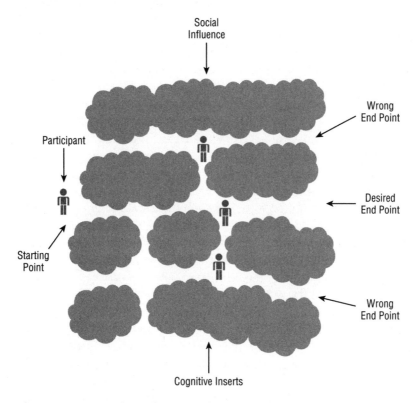

Figure 11.2: Metaphorical representation of influence process

Real-World Implications of Influence Process

The first step in determining your audience and their mental state vis-à-vis your ultimate objective is critical. If you get this step wrong, you will surely fail. Pick a target audience whose members are at least somewhat open to your ideas or at least willing and able to listen to you because they are either disenfranchised or are in need of a thing or certain rights. If the audience is outright hostile to you, they will not listen to you no matter what. Also, if members of the audience are physically located in a very chaotic place such as a war zone, they likely will not have the time or resources to engage with you. In most cases, they will be too busy trying to survive and will pay you little heed unless you help them survive. Of course, you can take advantage of such desperate situations, but they usually can become unstable and unsafe very quickly. Lastly, the audience cannot be located in a place ruled by a regime that is so hostile to you that they will immediately shut down any efforts you launch and threaten the lives of participants, unless you can guarantee their and your anonymity. Thus, overall, pick an audience whose members have enough time and resources to engage with you, and are willing to at least engage with you because they are unhappy with their current situation.

Guiding your audience along a path first means picking a path for them and then enticing them to follow along. In most cases, your ultimate objective will not be attractive to them. For example, if you want an audience in a rural area to provide you with intelligence on local drug smugglers, they may be unwilling to do so because of the dangers associated with it or because they do not trust you to protect their anonymity. Instead, start with an intermediate objective that will appear benign and attractive to them so you can get their attention and get them engaged. For example, to attract the audience in a rural area, you can offer them an SMS service that they can ping to get weather forecast information. Rural farmers would appreciate such information, and so will be willing to participate.

Further, guiding them along the right path and to the right end point involves slowly introducing your ultimate objective to them. However, couch it in terms that they will understand and feel some affinity to. There is no right way to do this, because it depends heavily on the audience and your objective. One way is to align your ultimate objective to an old cultural norm or tradition that the audience held dear and is now being oppressed by their current regime or situation. For example, the rural farmers may have had a weekly tradition where they gathered together with their families in the open at night, but are now afraid to do so because of the looming threat of violence brought by the drug smugglers. Engage with the audience and bring memories of such traditions back to them. Convince them that they can regain their tradition if they help defeat the drug smugglers, which involves providing you with intelligence about them. Of course, the process from engaging with them about an old tradition and then making them act is not as easy as we make it seem. It will take time and more intermediate objectives. First, you may need to simply query them about how they would like to improve their lives. Doubtless, one participant will eventually mention the need to increase security in his area. Reward and praise that participant, and make sure the other participants see that. The participants will then likely move toward the rewarded participant's viewpoint so they can also bask in the reward and praise. Ideas elicited from the participants are then reseeded in the community, but in such a way that they seem attractive and powerful. Reward and praise other participants who then recommend starting a neighborhood watch program and providing intelligence about the drug smugglers in their area. Another way to describe this process is to pick a small grievance that the audience has that is indicative of a larger underlying societal problem. Then poke at the grievance and focus on it till it drives the audience to act to solve the grievance and eventually the underlying problem. You should realize that in almost all cases, an influence platform is a crowd-sourcing platform with numerous and often mixed objectives.

Appreciating the Limits of Influencing Crowds

Influence platforms can significantly affect how populations around the world help you, even when they hold unfavorable views of you and your mission at the outset. However, successfully running influence platforms is difficult. Although certainly not impossible, changing people's minds is difficult. Getting them to perform an act that may be dangerous or taboo in their culture is even harder. Influence platforms also suffer from other limitations, which you should recognize and mitigate to achieve success.

Unrealistic Expectations

Influencing people in small ways is hard enough; trying to get them to drastically change their thought processes or their willingness to perform major actions is harder. Influencing primarily through social media is even harder. Do not set unrealistic expectations and expect amazing feats from the participants on your platform. Do not be surprised if individuals in dangerous and oppressive regions hesitate to provide you with intelligence about criminal entities around them, regardless of how much they come to trust you. Pick your target audiences wisely and look for some indications that the target audience is willing to be influenced. Build and deploy influence platforms in places with a lot of young people who are unhappy with their current situation. They are more likely to act against their culture's wishes and are more open to persuasion.

Adversarial Participants

In previous chapters, we have discussed how adversarial participants can ruin your intelligence collection and solution platforms and subvert your mission. Their impact is greater on influence platforms. Your ability to influence people depends heavily on your ability to persuade their social network to change their viewpoints. Adversarial participants who denounce you on your platform or call on others on the platform to resist you will coalesce support around existing practices and ruin your ability to change them. Platform moderators will play a key role in identifying adversarial participants and either persuading them to reverse their intentions or outright stopping them from causing too many problems.

Political Fallout

As with adversarial participants, political fallout plays an immense role in influence platforms. Although you should not lie about your intentions to participants, you also do not want to tell them bluntly that you intend to influence them. Telling a person that you are about to persuade him usually does not help when you are trying to persuade him. Overt persuasion especially does not work when the person comes from a completely different culture and is suspicious of you. Political fallout will likely reveal your ulterior intentions to your participants, thereby compromising your platform.

Unknown Unknowns

Although all social media platforms have some sort of influence component inherent to them, few are launched with influence as the ultimate objective. Many similar platforms, sites, and other media operations are obvious about their intentions, and so likely are not very effective. Lots of things can go wrong with influence platforms because they primarily feature human behavior and thoughts, which are chaotic and mysterious. As with other platforms, be wary and on guard. With influence platforms, you need to be especially on guard because the smallest problem can have a ripple effect that then disrupts the community you are building on your platform. Once disarray spreads, your platform will fail. Make sure to hire talented and dedicated moderators, who can identify and deal with problems quickly as they emerge.

Tweaking the Process for Influence Platforms

Despite the limitations and difficulties, influence platforms are unrivaled in their potential. Their potential derives from their uniqueness, which sets them apart from other types of platforms. You need to tweak the process from Chapter 8 somewhat and adapt it to fit the conceptual process we discussed before.

Although not mandatory in some other platforms, you absolutely must spend a lot of time and resources formulating your ultimate and intermediate objectives with influence platforms. Often, you will need to tweak your objectives over the lifetime of the platform. You may find that the participants are willing to help you with your ultimate objective from the outset or that they require more time and convincing. Formulating the objectives properly requires conducting a lot of target audience analysis. You need to understand their grievances, their history of cooperation and engagement with you, and the nature of the threats they face on a daily basis.

The influence platform must have a lot of social networking and messaging features. Influencing people involves seeding ideas into their social networks and encouraging their peers to change along with them. Participants must have the opportunity and space to communicate with each other so they can influence each other. The platform must also have lots of other features and preferably multimedia to get the participants' interest. Of course, participants who can message and network with each other can also send each other messages that are counterproductive for you. Hence, you need moderators to engage with the participants constantly and urge, not force, them to think and act the way you want them to think and act. Because of the inherent complexity of influence platforms, more things can go wrong, and so you need to keep close watch of everything.

The moderators must also help you keep track of the platform's success along with other performance measuring tools. Expect to reform your platform as you go along to better suit the needs of the participants. To reform it correctly, you will need lots of information about what the participants think about the platform, how they use it, and how they want it to change. Overall, everything about influence platforms is more intense and complex. Expect to dedicate a lot more manpower, time, and resources with influence platforms than you would with other platforms.

Now that you know where to tweak the process, you can start building and running influence platforms. In the subsequent section, we walk through how to build and run an influence platform. For ease of understanding and comparison, the steps of the walkthrough follow the structure of the process in Chapter 8. To aid understanding and to keep the walkthrough accessible and brief, we will simplify many concepts. Do not take the simplifications and assumptions in the walkthrough as evidence against the severe complexity of designing and running influence platforms. Some parts may seem unrealistic, but do not fret too much. Consider the walkthrough as an example of what is possible through crowdsourcing platforms, given a decent amount of luck and skill.

> **WARNING** Keep in mind that the subsequent sections are fabricated examples, not paragons of accurate research. We do not have the time and resources to do all the steps thoroughly, especially analyzing the target audience in each example. So we have taken shortcuts and made assumptions when considering what appeals to the target audience. Do not worry whether we are wrong about the target audience. Instead, focus on how we approach problems and use the technologies.

Influencing to Collect Intelligence on Corrupt Officials

Imagine you are a member of a government tasked with finding out if members of a certain foreign government, such as local officials, are either helping or have a friendly relationship with violent extremists who wish to hurt your government.

> **NOTE** Unlike in the other walkthroughs, for this walkthrough we will not name a specific country because we do not want it to seem as if we are encouraging influence operations against a certain country.

You, of course, cannot simply ask the foreign government about the issue because it will not want to admit that its officials are behaving questionably. Also, you may not have many sources on the ground that both have the relevant information and are willing to give it to you. You also do not want to make it obvious to the foreign officials that you are trying to collect intelligence about them. If they find out, they might change their behavior or protect their questionable relationships. You can incentivize the general public of the foreign country to provide you with intelligence about local officials. In some cases, they may have the best information because they are likely to see with whom local officials meet and talk. However, the general public may be reluctant to help. They could be either suspicious of your motives or scared that you will not protect their identity and cause them harm. Still, you may be able to influence the public to overcome their reluctance and help you. We now walk through the process of creating a capability to influence the public.

Define Objectives and Scope

Before you can start mapping out all the intermediate objectives, you need to take stock of where you stand at the beginning and formulate your ultimate objective. Your ultimate objective is to collect intelligence from the general population about the relationships their local government officials have with violent extremists. Currently, members of the population are reluctant to help you and you need to influence them to help them overcome their reluctance. You need to get the population from the starting point of reluctance to the end point of providing you with the intelligence you desire. Successfully taking them on that journey entails accomplishing a few intermediate objectives. To identify the intermediate objectives, you will need to find out more about your target audience.

Analyze Target Audience and the Media Environment

The target audience includes members of the general public in the country of interest who have some information about their local officials. Assume that the general public of the country is made up of people from virtually all walks of life. Some are affluent, more are from the middle class, and the majority of them are somewhat deprived and living in rural areas. You can assume from the trends in other countries that the affluent have reliable daily Internet access through personal computers, the middle class have somewhat less reliable daily access through personal computers and cyber cafes, and the poor have only sporadic access through cyber cafes, but tend to use a lot of SMS. The country, as a whole, still relies a lot on traditional media including televisions and newspapers. However, the youth across the income classes are quickly adopting social media and are fairly web-savvy. They know how to get around the Internet and are eager to consume more of it, especially parts of the Internet that feature rich media. Unfortunately, few functioning and well-designed sites on the Internet are targeted toward the audience, so the youth do not always have an attractive place on the Internet to express themselves and build relationships with others. Because you intend to crowdsource using the Internet, your target audience should be the youth and others who have at least some access to the Internet.

The public, in general, is not exactly happy with their government for a number of reasons. Looking at opinion polls and regional studies, you find that one of the biggest grievances people have with their government is that it is corrupt. Some, especially the young, more affluent, and more educated, are also somewhat worried about the possible relationship between the violent extremists and their government. They also hold unfavorable views of your government and are suspicious of its motives. However, they do have a history of engaging with charity and non-governmental organizations from your country and generally appreciate the help.

In summary, the target audience and media environment analyses reveal the following key insights:

- The target audience is made up of young people and others who have some access to the Internet, and who are generally web-savvy. They are eager to seek out more interesting places on the Internet where they can share their experiences, especially places that are designed with them in mind.

- Most are disillusioned with their government. They are reluctant to help you but are at least open to talking to you or partner Non-governmental organizations, as long as you can offer them some help to prove your trustworthiness.

- Most are concerned and fed up with corruption in their government, and some are concerned with the relationship between their officials and violent extremists.

These insights can help you formulate intermediate objectives.

Define Objectives and Scope, Redux

You can leverage the target audience's grievance with corrupt officials to influence them to meet your ultimate objective. They are likely to want to do something to identify and stop corruption, which is not that far from your problem of identifying and stopping links with extremism. If you can persuade the target audience to act on corruption, you can then likely persuade some to act on extremism. You can also use the fact that the young and the web-savvy part of the audience are always eager to seek out new and interesting platforms on the Internet where they can express themselves and consume interesting media. You can now start to lay out your influence plan.

The starting point is that members of the audience are reluctant to help you, but are willing to engage with you if can help them overcome their grievances somehow. They do not care about your ultimate objectives, but they do care about their main grievance, which is the corruption in their government. Some of them are also looking for interesting sites on the Internet that are designed with them in mind. However, before you can get them to do anything for you, you have to do something for them and prove your trustworthiness.

The *first intermediate objective* (*IMO-1*) is to get the audience to simply engage with you by creating a well-designed platform where participants can share stories about their lives with each other. IMO-1 will attract parts of the audience who are willing to communicate with each other and you, and are interested in participating in crowdsourcing platforms. The platform can focus on small parts of their daily lives and ways they can improve it. The platform will motivate the participants to constantly share information with you, even if the information is not directly relevant to you at first. Because the information is not that sensitive or interesting to you, participants will be less reluctant to begin sharing with you. Also, the platform will spur the creation of a social network among the participants, to whom you can seed ideas and leverage.

The *second intermediate objective* (*IMO-2*) is to get platform participants to share stories about corruption. Over time, some participants will become more comfortable with sharing information with you, and undoubtedly some of the information will involve serious subjects such as corruption. You can also pointedly ask information about serious subjects and get participants to open up to you about them.

The *third intermediate objective* (*IMO-3*) is to get the participants to provide detailed information about corruption, including names of the people involved. Note that guiding the participants from IMO-2 to IMO-3 is harder than we make it seem. To get the participants to IMO-3, you have to persuade them to act on their dissatisfaction with corruption and trust you with very sensitive information. You have to convince them that you have their best interests in mind, can do something positive for them with the information they are providing you, and can protect their identities.

The *ultimate objective* (*UO*) is to get the participants to provide detailed information about corrupt and other officials who are involved with extremists in any way. By the time you accomplish IMO-3, some participants will be comfortable naming names and will have built enough of a trust with you to give you even more sensitive information. Some participants who will help you will realize that their grievances with their government are ultimately rooted in deep societal and governmental problems that also give rise to the grievance of ties between officials and extremists. Spurred by the need to solve the deep problems, they will eventually become motivated to provide information about all sorts of problems. However, many, if not the majority, of participants will not help with the UO. Still, you only need some help and any intelligence is better than none. Figure 11.3 summarizes the objectives.

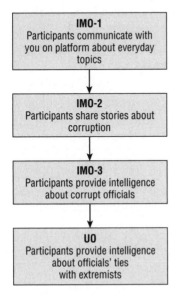

Figure 11.3: Summary of objectives

Design the Platform

Influence platforms are much more complex than other platforms, and so it is more difficult to separate out the design of an influence platform's components. To aid understanding and to illustrate the relationships between different parts of the platform, we will integrate the look and feel part and the incentive structure part together. We will also describe the moderators' duties. The platform will evolve over time as each objective is accomplished. Thus, the design of the platform will also need to evolve over time. To match this evolution, we will separate the descriptions of the design of the platform by each objective. Overall, the platform will have three components. The first will be the front-end interface that the participants see, the data management system and server that host the website and corresponding data, and an administrator interface that you and/or your moderators will use. In reality, the administrator and front-end interfaces will be built into the same website.

Designing for IMO-1

The target audience analysis reveals that the platform should be a website with lots of attractive and well-designed features. At first, it should attract participants and provide them with a space where they can interact with each other and you and/or your moderators. Inspired by websites such as OpenIDEO, Facebook, and forums, the website will feature social networking elements that allow participants to chat with each other. The moderator should also regularly post questions and query participants about their thoughts on various subjects. Remember that at this point, the goal is to simply deploy a website that gets people to interact with each other. It should not be too complicated.

The participants will be able to access the following four parts of the platform:

- Web pages with information about how to behave on the platform, how to use the platform, frequently asked questions, and the objective of the platform (something like "Building a Community Online")

- The user account page

- The public messaging forum

- The query wall, with separate walls (web pages) for each query

The first part is fairly self-explanatory. Be clear and concise when drafting the rules and behaviors, and do not post dishonest information about your intentions. Again, you do not have to post everything, but do not lie about who you are or what you are up to. As we describe in the "Market the Platform" section later, you will likely need to partner with an NGO. The subsequent list describes the other three parts and the features the platform will have:

NOTE We have described some of these features many times before in previous chapters, so we will keep the descriptions short this time.

- **User accounts**—All participants can create a user account, which they can use to identify themselves and track other people. All usernames should, of course, mask their true identity. Participants will be able to access their own user account pages where they can see all the posts they have made and send private messages to the moderator. To register for a user account, participants have to submit some basic demographic information. Try, but do not expect, to always succeed at getting participants to submit more sensitive personal information. Make sure you explain to the participants exactly what information you are collecting and do not ever make it public.

- **Messaging**—Like in forums, the participants can start topics or threads and post messages or comments, and engage with each other. Moderators can also post messages to the participants and vice versa. All the messages between participants will be viewed publicly. Messages between the moderators and individual participants may also be done through a private messaging system. Also, the user account page will feature private messages between the participant and moderators, and enable participants to respond to moderators.

- **Public messaging forum**—All participants will message each other in two separate portions of the site. The first will be the public messaging forum that will have a bulletin board forum-type interface where participants can openly chat with each other about virtually any topic. They can start threads to pose questions and respond as they wish. The public forum will enable participants to engage with each other and the moderators, and develop the sense of community on the platform.

- **Regular queries/query wall**—The second messaging portion of the site is the queries section where participants will respond to specific queries and post comments on a Facebook wall–type interface. Every week or so, the moderator will post a question or query about a fairly pedestrian topic such as "Tell us about your school and what you find so interesting about it." Each query will have a special separate wall or page that participants can access through the platform, where they can then respond and see and approve of the responses of each other. All conversations about the queries will happen on the relevant query's page, although participants should be free to discuss issues around the queries in the public forum. A separate query section will compel the participants to focus on the query and not get sidetracked by unrelated conversations. The queries will also make the platform stand out from other sites and provide a theme for the platform, such as asking the youth what they think about certain issues. Participants will then join, knowing that they are supposed to express themselves in a certain way.

- **Approves**—As on Facebook, the participants can like or approve of another participant's comment in the query section. An "approve" counter will publicly keep track of the number of "approves" a comment receives.

- **Tokens (Intrinsic Incentives)**—For each response to a query, participants will receive some sort of token. Moderators may also reward participants with tokens for good behavior (for example, being courteous to other participants or posting a lot of information) so as to point out to other participants how they should act on the platform. The number of "approves" a response gets will also lead to a participant receiving a predetermined amount of tokens. The moderators should also simply praise participants regularly for being involved.

- **Leaderboard**—This displays who has the most tokens and is the most active on the platform. The leaderboard will elicit competition between the participants and give a few participants something to brag and feel good about.

At first, provide participants with virtual instead of real, material incentives to ensure that the focus remains on building trust and a sense of community on the platform. You want the participants to engage for intrinsic reasons and not to simply earn some money or thing. Involving extrinsic incentives this early may result in participants engaging for the wrong reasons, and possibly even lying or gaming the platform to simply earn some money.

Design for IMO-2

At the point of IMO-2, the platform should have a solid core of participants who are regularly communicating and responding to queries. They will be few in number. A bigger portion of participants will be either new to the platform or on the precipice of engaging more. For IMO-2, the platform should roll out new features that pique the interest of participants, make it appear as though the platform is going to be around for a while, and get participants talking about serious subjects including corruption. Introduce and improve on the following features:

- **User accounts**—Participants can upload a picture (not a personal picture) as an avatar. Users can also start friending each other and receiving notifications on the user account page when a friend comments on their messages in the forum or query sections.

- **Queries**—Start posting queries that touch on serious subjects such as corruption, security, education, and community issues. Ask participants for suggestions on how they can improve problems in those subject areas. For example, ask "What are some improvements you would like to see in your local community?" Or "Are you happy with your local government? Why or why not?" Keep in mind that adversaries may be monitoring your site and even spying on the participants, so do not make the queries too pointed. Immediately identify a participant who posts responses—for example, saying that corruption is a problem—that help you achieve IMO-2. The moderator should then praise that participant or give him tokens. Others will then implicitly recognize what the "right" answers are and start to say similar things because they also want the tokens and praise. However, do not be too obvious, because participants will recognize that you are trying to social-engineer them.

Throughout the course of the platform, the moderators should ask participants for suggestions on how they would like to improve the platform. Implement some of the suggestions so that the participants feel a sense of ownership of the platform and that you are willing to listen to them. They will appreciate it and consequently become more involved.

Design for IMO-3

At the point of IMO-3, you should have at least some participants who are willing to talk about corruption. Reiterate that their identities are protected and encourage them and others to talk more.

WARNING   Protecting their identities should not be an empty promise. Make sure to implement strict privacy and identity protection tools into your platform so that adversaries cannot find out the identities of the participants. Some of the participants may be putting themselves in jeopardy because of their responses, and you should respect them for taking the risk.

Keep introducing new features into the platform. Also, the moderators should start asking more pointed questions about how the participants would like to solve the problem of corruption. If a participant mentions something along the lines of "I wish we had a place to report corrupt people," then recognize the response and urge others to echo it, thereby building a consensus around the idea. If no one mentions it or anything close to it, the moderator should post the idea as simply a comment to a participant's comment. If the participants are adamantly against it, you likely have not built enough trust with them and you will have to try again later. It may take months to get the participants to IMO-3.

You can also enact the "special query or challenge" feature, where participants can respond with ideas to win material prizes and the chance to enact their ideas. The special query or challenge will pose a real-world problem to participants and ask them for solutions. Essentially, you will convert part of your platform into a solution platform. The material prize will get the participants' attention and help emphasize the importance of the challenge. One of the special queries will, of course, be asking participants to come up with a way to identify and report corrupt officials anonymously. Make sure to launch other special queries in other areas. For example, ask participants for a way to improve water quality in their area. You cannot make it too obvious that you are only interested in corrupt officials. Guide the participants to the "correct" response, which is a crowdsourcing capability where participants can send in sensitive information about a corrupt official.

After some time and enough participants are interested in the idea, launch a capability to do just that. It is as if you say, "You came up with the idea, you talked about the idea, you wanted the idea, so now here it is." You can either deploy a crowdmap, a separate website, or an SMS platform where participants can submit information anonymously. The anonymous part is very important. It will communicate to participants that you intend to protect their identities. You may need to partner with an NGO or anti-corruption group (or create your own) that may actually do something beneficial with the information. The participants will also appreciate that their information is coming in handy and creating positive change.

Also, make sure to keep the new capability separate from the existing platform. It should be a spin-off, not an extension. You can discreetly put a link somewhere on the platform but do not advertise it too loudly. Participants will talk offline and you will attract unwanted outside attention. Some participants will not want to be involved, but they would like to stay a part of the community that already exists. You do not want to push them out and make it seem as if you really only cared about the capability to report the corrupt official. You can give tokens to participants who sign on to the spin-off to motivate others. Finally, make sure to spin off other ideas and websites. Someone may recommend creating a website that collects charity donations to fund school supplies for poor children. Say that is a great idea and build it with them. The resulting increase in communication and trust between you (or the moderators) and the participants will surprise you, and maybe even warm your heart.

Design for UO

The process for getting participants from IMO-2 to IMO-3 is the same as getting them from IMO-3 to UO. Encourage the participants to start talking about the problems of extremists and their relationship with their government. Tread lightly on the topic because it can inflame personally held beliefs and lead to arguments between participants. Moderators must be on guard to make sure everyone is behaving courteously. As with the issue of corrupt officials, incentivize and praise participants who say what you want them to say—we need a way to identify the officials involved with extremists. Post special queries for which the ideal response is another spin-off capability where participants can submit intelligence about extremist ties anonymously. Then create the spin-off capability. Do not create too many spin-offs at this point, otherwise you will confuse participants and they will, in turn, not take the spin-offs seriously. A handful should be enough. Also, do not convert one spin-off into another or mix them. Keep things simple and consistent to avoid confusion.

If the participants are not eager to start talking about extremists, then wait and try again in the future. Do keep in mind that there is no guarantee that your platform will work. Hopefully, you will have enough participants interested. You many need only a few because perhaps only a few have the information you want.

Keep the original platform going as you collect intelligence through the spin-off. If you are lucky and talented enough, you may be able to keep the platform going for years and use it as a prime spot to ask participants to legitimately solve problems or provide intelligence. Over time, you will also likely change their views or how they talk about certain topics and what information they consider. You can also leverage the community emerging on the platform as a way to coalesce support around various causes, such as improving women's rights or countering oppressive autocratic regimes. The possibilities are endless.

Build the Platform

Influence platforms are usually complicated and involve a lot of moving parts. You will need to hire developers to help you develop and build the platform. You will also need them to develop various privacy tools to protect the identity of the participants and data collection tools so you can measure the platform's performance. Keep the developers around throughout the lifetime of the platform, at least on retainer. You need them for general maintenance and to introduce new features into the platform.

You will also need to hire designers and area experts—people who really know your audience—to help you design a platform and ways of interacting with the participants. One of the selling points of your platform to participants is that the platform is attractive. You need designers to help make it attractive.

Market the Platform

You want to make sure that at any time you have a decent number of participants on the platform. No one wants to join and be part of a platform that has only five other participants. The exact number will depend on how much information you want to collect and the population size of the audience. If participation rates fall or are not where you would like them to be, you will need to release a burst of advertising to get people's attention again. The pace, intensity, and frequency of the marketing campaign will depend heavily on circumstances.

You will likely need to partner with an NGO doing charity work in the region or similar organizations to help participants overcome their reluctance. Some may be turned off by your UO, so you will need to explain what you are trying to do with some finesse. Again, do not be dishonest. If they find out, word will get out and you might not be able to launch your platform in the area. On the platform, you also do not want to make it obvious exactly which office you represent. If you are working on behalf of the British government, then say so, but you do not have to necessarily say which office. Work with the area expert to figure out what to say.

Depending on the circumstances, you may also need to target your advertising to only parts of the audience that you know will participate. You may want to keep adversaries from finding out or creating a lot of buzz because it might get the wrong people interested in your platform. In this case, focus on advertising on Internet sites and platforms frequented by the targeted part of the audience. Also, you may need to implement IP blocking and other mechanisms, such as making people provide their phone area codes when signing up, to make sure that people outside of the region do not sign up. Be cautious with implementing blocking tools, especially with IP blocking. Tools to mask IP are widely available and easy to use.

Moderate the Platform

In previous sections we briefly touched on some of the roles that the moderators will play. Moderators are essential to your platform. If you do not have good moderators, you will fail. You will need to hire numerous moderators to ensure that at least someone is keeping an eye on the platform at all times. Ideally, the moderators should have a familiarity with the audience's culture, way of life, and language.

Expect the moderators to participate heavily in the platform. Their duties will include:

- Enforcing the rules of the platform and making sure everyone abides by them.

- Identifying and dealing with troublemakers and adversarial participants. Initially, the moderators should reach out to them through private messaging and urge them to change their behaviors. In extreme cases or after repeat violations, the moderators can ban adversarial participants. Make sure they do not abuse the power to ban people. The platform is supposed to be a community where free expression is encouraged, so you do not want to seem too heavy-handed and oppressive. Allow some participants to post statements contradicting your objective and viewpoints. It will spark arguments that the moderators can then influence, and it will seem a lot more authentic and genuine to participants.

- Encouraging conversation and guiding it to appropriate ends. The moderators should expect to ask and answer questions, praise participants, change the topic of conversation, and much more. If the level of communication within the platform is low, the moderators should increase their participation. If the level of communication is high and your objectives are being met, the moderators should be less involved.

- Helping participants as needed and taking their suggestions. People like being listened to and looked after, and that fact is no different on the Internet.

- Keeping watch over the platform in general and making sure everything works without glitches and bugs. Moderators should tell you and your developers immediately if something is wrong with the technical aspects of the platform. Few people will put up with a broken website.

Measure the Platform's Performance

Use the various data tools to measure the platform's performance and ensure your influence platform is succeeding in accomplishing all your objectives. Example metrics include:

- Number of participants on the platform over time
- Age and gender of participants
- Number of posts or comments per participant
- Number of messages participants submit on spin-off
- Time to each intermediate objective

Wash, Rinse, Repeat

Undoubtedly, your influence platform will need lots of reforms as time goes on. You will need to introduce new features and fix others that you thought might work but are proving unpopular. Assess your platform's performance periodically and read through the suggestions of participants to come up with reforms. If participants are not advancing to the next objective, you may need to make drastic changes. You can also try providing new material incentives on a regular basis instead of mostly relying on intrinsic incentives. You may need to offer material incentives at the beginning to get people to join the platform. Additionally, you can try to get the participants to interact with each other through more interesting media such as pictures or video. For example, you can post queries and ask participants to respond by uploading pictures. Lastly, try deploying a similar platform elsewhere and compare the results. A comparison of the successes and failures of both platforms may reveal insights about problems with each platform.

Influence platforms are complex and an advanced way of using social media technologies. However, many more advanced and impressive uses exist. Chapter 12 discusses some of these uses and how you can perform more advanced analyses on social media data.

Summary

- Influencing through crowdsourcing entails persuading people to adopt a specific idea and accomplish a specific behavior based on their interactions on a crowdsourcing platform known as an influence platform.
- Influencing is a more subtle and powerful way of incentivizing someone to do something.

- Influencing involves completing the following two goals:
  - The first goal is changing how a person thinks, which involves subtly modifying the mental shortcuts or frames he or she uses to make sense of the world.
  - The second goal is changing a person's behavior, which involves accomplishing the first goal and helping him or her overcome hesitation to perform a certain act.
- The following can influence a person's thought processes and behavior:
  - Repeating a piece of information will make it more likely that a person will remember that information and consider it to be true regardless of its actual veracity.
  - Making a person believe he came up with the idea you want him to adopt, because people value things and thoughts more if they believe they created it.
  - Delivering information to a person in an interesting and exciting way.
  - Building trust between you and the person you want to influence will make it more likely he will listen to you.
  - Peer pressure and a person's culture significantly help a person make sense of and act in the world.
- Influencing populations through influence platforms is the process of guiding your audience regarding your ultimate objective from where they are today to where you want them to be by way of getting them to complete multiple intermediate objectives. You guide them through cognitive inserts (games, information, other ways of interacting with them) and by leveraging the interactions between all the participants on the platform.
- To effectively influence an audience, its members must be unhappy with their situation or current lives in some way and have the time, resources, and willingness to at least engage with you.
- The intermediate objective must in some way help resolve the problem that is causing them consternation.
- Constantly reward and praise participants who approach your ultimate objective so that you can also persuade other participants to act similarly.
- Influence platforms suffer from a few limitations:
  - Influencing populations through social media is difficult and will fail if you have unrealistic expectations of your influence platform.
  - Adversarial participants can ruin your ability to leverage social influence on a platform to your ends.

- ■ Overt acts of influence or lying about your ultimate objective can destroy the trust between you and the participants.

  - ■ Influence platforms are very complex, and so even the smallest thing going wrong can have severe consequences.

- ■ Compared to other types of platforms, influence platforms are much more complex and heavily dependent on how well you define your objectives and understand your audience. They also require significantly greater social networking and messaging features. Also, the quality of your moderators will determine your platform's success.

- ■ You can use influence platforms to get participants to provide intelligence about the ties between extremists and government officials by first getting them to talk to you about their daily lives and then getting them to provide intelligence about corruption in their government.

Notes

1. Lakoff, G. and Johnson, M. (1980) *Metaphors We Live By*. University of Chicago, Chicago; Luntz, F. (2007) *Words That Work*: *It's Not What You Say*, *It's What People Hear*. Hyperion, New York; Romm, J. (2012) *Language Intelligence*: *Lessons on Persuasion From Jesus, Shakespeare, Lincoln, and Lady Gaga*. CreateSpace, North Charleston.

2. Hood, B. (2012) *The Self Illusion*: *How the Social Brain Creates Identity*. Oxford, New York.

3. Adams, B., Sartori, J. and Waldherr, S. (2007) *Military Influence Operations*: *Review of Relevant Scientific Literature*. Defence Research and Development Canada, Ontario. Accessed: 15 September 2012. http://www.dtic.mil/dtic/tr/fulltext/u2/a477201.pdf

Broadening Your Horizon

In This Part

Social media technologies and data offer more for global security than we can possibly cover in one book. However, we can give you a taste of what else is out there and prepare you to go forward and break new ground while respecting old norms. In Part IV, we introduce you to bleeding-edge ways of analyzing and using social media data. We also describe how you can use crowdsourcing techniques to deliver educational and health services in hard-to-reach areas critical to security. We end with a discussion about privacy, and explore how you can use your newfound knowledge without infringing on basic human rights. We also teach those who are conscious of privacy and using social media to secure their communities about how they can protect themselves and their cause.

CHAPTER 12

Advanced and Emerging Analytical Methodologies

So far we have covered only a few methodologies for analyzing social media and related data. Numerous other methodologies exist, many of which are complex and only now starting to be modified for and applied to social media data. This chapter briefly reviews a few advanced and emerging analytical methodologies you may come across and eventually need in your work. It first introduces and then describes the three methodologies of cluster analysis, geo-spatial network analysis, and agent modeling.

Expanding the Scope of Analysis

You can analyze social media and related data using a variety of analytical methodologies. Some are readily applicable to social media data and thus are used by analysts today—we covered some of them in Chapters 5 and 6. Many more methodologies exist and they differ in their applicability and relevance. Some of these methodologies tend to be harder to use because they are complex or require more advanced technical training. Some also require the type and size of data that is only now becoming available. Undoubtedly, as more people start to analyze social media data, the variety and number of relevant and applicable analytical methodologies will grow.

In this chapter, we briefly review three advanced and emerging analytical methodologies that are becoming increasingly applicable and relevant for analyzing or using social media data. Analysts have been using the three methodologies for quite some time in other fields and for other types of data. They differ in their complexity or difficulty, how they use social media data, and what types of questions they can help you answer. Cluster analysis, geo-spatial network analysis, and agent modeling were introduced briefly at the end of Chapter 3, and we explore them in this chapter in the order of how difficult they are to implement, starting with the least difficult. We measure difficulty in terms of the available software tools, resources, and technical skill it takes to use the methodology. Unlike with the methodologies in Chapters 5 and 6, we do not get into great detail about how you can use all the methodologies. However, we do point out resources and prepare you to at least understand the relevance of these methodologies to your mission sets. Based on our descriptions alone, you may be able to implement the first two methodologies. The last one, however, takes considerably more technical skill and familiarity with the science of data modeling. Expect to come across these methodologies more in the future. Understanding the content in this chapter will prepare you to learn and use these tools and review studies that use them.

Cluster Analysis

Cluster analysis is the process of assigning a population of items to a group or cluster according to their similarities, defined by a single or set of specific attributes. You can cluster or group virtually anything including types of data, hi5 accounts, people in a city, political parties, and analytical methodologies. Also, you can cluster them by almost any attribute. We clustered the analytical methodologies in this book according to the attributes of ease of implementation, relevance, and applicability. The methodologies in Chapters 5 and 6 are easier to implement, and more directly relevant and applicable to social media data. The ones in this chapter are somewhat less related on all three counts.

Essentially, cluster analysis helps you answer the question: "How can I separate a large number of people or things into different groups or clusters?" By using cluster analysis, you can focus your resources and analysis only on the groups of people or things that interest you the most. If you are faced with analyzing a large number of blogs and wish you could focus only on the blogs that, for example, mentioned certain topics, then cluster analysis can help you. Or if you are faced with marketing a crowdsourcing platform to a large number of people and wish you could focus only on the people who, for example, are young and Internet-savvy, then cluster analysis can help you.

The Process of Clustering

You can cluster things in a number of ways, and the best way depends on the question you want to solve. As long as you have at least two of something in a population, you can separate the population into clusters. You can separate a population of items into a number of different clusters. The clusters can also have subsidiary clusters, thereby producing a hierarchy of clusters. Some of the clusters can even overlap. Consider a simplistic example to make sure you understand the concept behind clustering and the process of clustering. Say you have a population of shapes, as depicted in Figure 12.1.

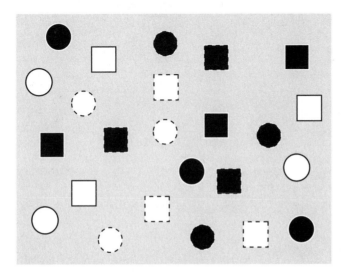

Figure 12.1: Population of shapes

Notice that some of the shapes have outlines made up of jagged dotted lines, whereas others have smooth straight lines. Some have a black outline and are filled with white, whereas others do not have a black outline and are filled with white. Some are circles and some are squares. You can cluster the shapes in a number of different ways. You can cluster them by the type of outline they have or by their shape type. Say you choose to cluster them by the type of outline. You can then further cluster each existing cluster by the color with which they are filled. You now have hierarchical clusters. You can then also cluster by shape type and create a cluster for shapes that are squares and a separate cluster for shapes that are circles. Notice that some of the shapes that are together in one cluster set (by shape type) may be separate in another cluster set (by outline type). In this case, the shapes belong to more than one cluster and are said to be overlapping. Figure 12.2 shows these different cluster sets.

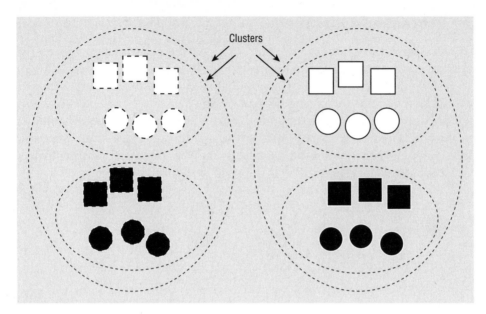

Figure 12.2: Hierarchical cluster sets

We have barely touched the surface of how you can cluster a population of items and what attributes you can use to define the clusters. We will not even get into the process of soft or fuzzy clustering, which takes place when an item is said to only kind of belong in one cluster.

Also, note that there is no objectively correct way to cluster. Like network analysis, cluster analysis involves applying one or a combination of several algorithms to a data set. Each algorithm clusters a data set differently, even if they are clustering according to the same attribute. Network analysis only provides you with an estimation of the importance of the node to the network. Similarly, cluster analysis only provides you with an estimation of the relationship and closeness of a node to other nodes. Different tools use different algorithms that will give you different results, and no one tool or algorithm is necessarily more correct. Some tools, however, are more appropriate for certain situations or types of data. When you search for cluster analytics online, you are likely to come across clustering by a simple formula of mathematical distance. We describe this process in an example later.

Many cluster analytical tools exist, but only a few are relevant for social media data. Many existing tools focus on clustering people or other potential nodes in a network (such as individual blogs in a network of blogs that link to each other) according to their position and status in the network. In other words, the tools cluster nodes in a network according to attributes such as their centrality in the network or the number of links they have with other nodes. In fact, NodeXL features cluster analysis tools that cluster according to a node's relationship to the network to which the node belongs. NodeXL version 1.0.1.224 enables users to use three different clustering algorithms on their social media data. Expect for tools to emerge that cluster, for example, social media users by the type of words they tend to use, their behavior on a social media site, or their sentiment toward certain topics.

The Relevance of Clustering

Clustering has a wide variety of applications, and analysts have used it in other fields for years. Analysts have used it for grouping genes according to their expression patterns, customers according to various marketing segments, and crime hot spots according to their history of crime. It can also help you solve security problems related to social media in a number of ways. The most salient is that clustering can help you further understand social networks and relationships between people. You can use clustering to:

- Separate Twitter users who make up a sprawling social network into small groups. You can then better focus your efforts and conduct social network analysis only on the most relevant groups instead of the entire network.

- Identify the subgroups of a target audience to which you should market your crowdsourcing platform, and then direct your marketing campaign only at them.

- Separate a large amount of user-generated social media content into groups by their time of creation so you can analyze only the most recent content.

At first, focus on clustering people rather than things or pieces of data because the act of clustering people is usually easier to grasp. Work on clustering people by several attributes including their age, behavior on social media, likes and dislikes, position in a social network, and even the news sites they usually tweet/retweet. If you are still unsure about how clustering works and how you can use it, consider the following example, which clusters by a formula of mathematical distance. Also consider the references for more resources.[1]

CLUSTERING TARGET AUDIENCE EXAMPLE

Imagine you are deploying a solutions platform to crowdsource algorithms that process and decipher antagonistic behavior on video feeds, such as the platform we described in a walkthrough in Chapter 10. You need to market the platform to your target audience, who are primarily tech-savvy geeks and connected enough to spread the word to others. However, only a few members of the audience have the free time to work on your platform, and fewer have a large social network and can help you get the word out. Because your marketing resources are finite, you need to target only members of the target audience who are the most likely to use your platform and tell the most people

Continued

CLUSTERING TARGET AUDIENCE EXAMPLE (*continued*)

about it on your behalf. You would like to cluster members of your target audience into a group that is likely to participate on your platform and has a big network (which we will call "Cluster Yes") and a group that is not as likely to participate and has a small network (which we will call "Cluster No"). Your marketing resources may increase in the future so you would like to keep track of both groups, in case you have the resources to market to Cluster No later.

You can use a number of different methods to gauge a person's free time and social network. For the sake of simplicity, assume you decide to measure a person's free time by his or her age. You assume that people in their 20s and 30s have more time to work on your project than people aged 40 and up because older people are more likely to have families and more job responsibilities. You also assume that you can gauge a person's social network prowess by the amount of people following him or her on Twitter. You have the required information (ages and Twitter followers) for a thousand people who you believe belong in your target audience.

To begin clustering the thousand people into two groups using a simple mathematical distance formula, you need to first create two seeds or pick two seeds from the target audience, one for each group. A seed represents the person who typifies the group. So, the seed or person who ideally represents Cluster Yes is a person who is aged 30 and has 30 followers on Twitter. The person who ideally represents Cluster No is aged 50 and has 10 followers on Twitter. You now need to place the other audience members into the two clusters.

You start with a member of your target audience who is aged 33 and has 12 followers on Twitter (call this person "Person Three"). Person Three is in the right age group but has a tiny social network. You need to determine the cluster to which she belongs. For mathematical reasons we will not get into here, simply taking the difference between a person's age and number of followers with that of the seeds will not work.

Instead, first take the difference between the age of Person Three and the age of the seed from Cluster A. Then, take the differences between the number of followers of Person Three and the number of followers of the seed from Cluster A. Square the differences and take their sum (we will call the sum "Sum A"). Then, repeat the process but with the seed from Cluster B. Take the difference between the age of Person Three and the age of the seed from Cluster B, and the difference between the number of followers of Person Three and the number of followers of the seed from Cluster B. Square the differences and take their sum (we will call the sum "Sum B"). Table 12.1 shows the calculations.

Table 12.1: Clustering Calculations

CLUSTER A CALCULATIONS			
	Person Three	Cluster A Seed	Difference	Difference Squared
Age	33	30	3	9
Number of followers	12	30	-18	324
Sum	—	—	—	333
CLUSTER B CALCULATIONS			
Age	33	50	-17	289
Number of followers	12	10	2	4
Sum	—	—	—	293

Finally, compare Sum A and Sum B. The smaller the sum, the closer the person is mathematically to the seed. In this case, Person Three has a smaller Sum B (293) than Sum A (333), and so belongs in Cluster B. Person Three is in the right age group but her serious lack of Twitter followers indicates she is not an ideal person to whom you should market.

However, the cluster process is not yet finished, even for Person Three. Every time you place all people in a cluster, you need to take the average of every person's age and the number of followers in that cluster to come up with a new seed that accurately represents the average person in that cluster. You need to do this process for both clusters. You then need to kick all the people out of the clusters, and then recalculate which cluster they belong to and reassign them. You need to continue to do this process until you reach a steady state where no matter how many times you recalculate and reassign, people end up in the same cluster. Clearly, you need to use a computerized statistical tool such as NodeXL's clustering tools to cluster efficiently.

Geo-Spatial Network Analysis

Chapter 5 described how to conduct social network analysis. As you may recall, social network analysis is only one type of network analysis. You can perform network analysis on virtually any complex system where discrete entities are linked to each other. For example, you can conduct network analysis on a network of blogs that link to each other to find the most influential blog. You can even conduct network analysis on infrastructures such as oil pipelines to find parts of the pipelines that are the most essential to the functioning of the complete pipeline system. In such a system, the points of intersections of pipelines are the nodes and the pipelines are the links between the nodes. You can also use it on subway systems to find the stations that are the most important to the proper and timely function of the entire system. In such a system, the subway stations are the nodes and the lines connecting stations to each other are the links. Some research, some of which we conducted, suggests that some terrorists may even be picking which stations to attack based on the stations' network measures such as their betweenness centrality.[2] By identifying the stations with the most centrality or importance, the terrorists can maximize the damage they cause to the entire subway system and hence the feeling of terror in the victims' community. Law enforcement can use the same tools to identify the most critical subway stations and deploy resources accordingly. City planners can also use the tools to design subway systems where a few stations do not become so critical to the entire system that their elimination would totally disrupt the entire subway system.

Because of easy access to network analysis tools, analysts are expanding the systems to which they apply network analysis and are broadening the types of questions they are trying to answer with it. All sorts of insights are tumbling out and answering questions in unexpected ways. The proliferation and easy availability of social media data is adding to this golden age of network analysis. One interesting and relevant insight is that the likelihood a group will commit violence internally or against another group appears related to how it is linked with other groups by virtue of being next to them on a physical space.

The Process of Geo-Spatial Network Analysis

In a geo-spatial population system, each group or population of people is a node, and if they share a physical boundary with each other they are linked to each other. How you define what constitutes a certain group depends on various demographic and regional factors, and the level of analysis in which you are interested. Using this way of considering nodes and links, you can create a geo-spatial network map of any distributions of populations in a region. To aid understanding, consider Figure 12.3, which shows a geo-spatial network map of the central European countries. You will see that the Germany node is linked to the Czech Republic node because it shares a physical boundary with the Czech

Republic. However, the Germany node does not share a link with the Hungary node because Germany does not share a physical boundary with Hungary.

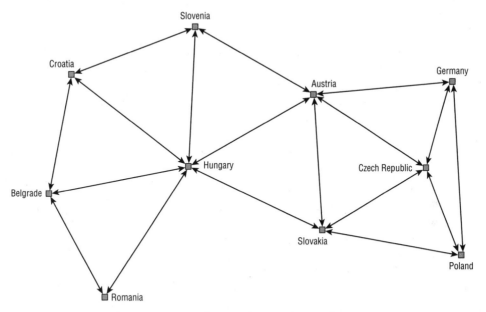

Figure 12.3: Example of a geo-spatial network map of Central Europe

After mapping out the geo-spatial network map of the groups in a region, you can then conduct network analysis on the map. The network analysis will reveal that groups (nodes) with the highest measure of centrality will be more likely to engage in internal or civil war with members of their own group and less likely to engage in external conflict with members of other groups, regardless of other variables. A pilot study using this method found that an African country is more likely to engage in civil war and less likely to engage in external conflict if it has high measures of centrality.[3] Although much more work and many more studies need to be done to verify the validity of this conclusion, the insight seems promising. If you need more details to understand this concept, check the book's website for a related study we are completing.

The Relevance of Geo-Spatial Network Analysis

Geo-spatial network analysis is relevant to social media because social media provides the venue through which you can collect data to forecast the type and likelihood of conflict that might take place in an area. You can crowdsource information about where certain groups and populations are located and whom they share boundaries with to do geo-spatial network analysis. Incorrect or incomplete data can seriously hamper your ability to do network analysis, and crowdsourcing enables you to collect timely and detailed data.

Crowdsourcing also enables you to collect data about nomadic groups and shifting boundaries with a level of accuracy and detail that traditional census data collection methods cannot match. You can then use the crowdsourced data to conduct geo-spatial network analysis and get an idea about where groups are located and how the location of the groups will impact the type of conflict in which they are likely to engage. Think of the analysis as another way to forecast the likelihood and type of conflict, and another way to understand why certain conflicts occur. Using network analysis in this way is especially relevant in cases where you do not have other information that can help you forecast and understand conflict.

Overall, it is not completely clear why a group that shares boundaries with lots of other groups is more likely to engage in internal conflict, while a group that shares few boundaries with other groups is more likely to engage in external conflict. However, remember that human and group behavior is often counter-intuitive and heavily influenced by seemingly unimportant factors. Consider the following example for a more thorough understanding.

GEO-SPATIAL NETWORK ANALYSIS EXAMPLE

Imagine you need to determine the likelihood that certain clans will engage in external or internal conflict in a certain region. You do not have much information about the clans and the reasons why they may engage in any conflict. You do have a general sense of the number of people in each clan and where they are distributed across the region. However, you do not have detailed information about exactly where the clans are at a specific moment in time and with whom they are sharing physical boundaries.

Say you create an SMS crowdsourcing capability, such as the one we described in the first walkthrough in Chapter 9. The capability simply sends SMS messages to people distributed across the region, asking about their clan affiliation and location. Over time, you build up a database of enough samples of people with information about what clan they belong to and their location. You can then create a topographical map of the clan distribution in the region. For illustrative purposes, say you create a map as shown in Figure 12.4. The map tells you the clans, where they are physically located, and with whom they share boundaries. (For simplicity's sake, we will label each clan with only a letter from the alphabet.)

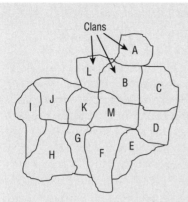

Figure 12.4: Example map showing clan distribution

You can then use the population distribution map to create a geo-spatial network map for analysis. Treat each clan as a node and each boundary between clans as a link between them. Then use UCINET, NodeXL, or your network analysis software of choice to create a network map as shown in Figure 12.5.

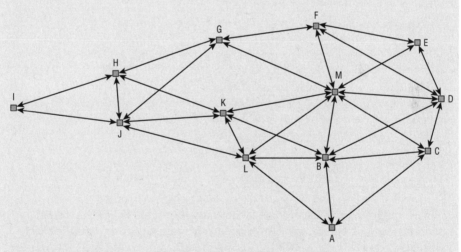

Figure 12.5: Example geo-spatial network map of clans

NOTE We posted the UCINET data file, `geo_spatial.##h`, we used to do the analysis in this example on the website.

Continued

GEO-SPATIAL NETWORK ANALYSIS EXAMPLE (*continued*)

You can now conduct network analysis on your geo-spatial network data set. Different algorithms produce different results, and we are not sure yet exactly which algorithm will give you the best result. However, past research and experience suggests that UCINET's algorithm for betweenness centrality may provide the best results. You simply need to run the betweenness centrality algorithm on the data set. We posted our results in Table 12.2, in descending order of betweenness centrality ranking. The clans at the top have the highest centrality rankings, and the ones at the bottom have the lowest.

Table 12.2: Centrality Rankings of Clans

RANKING	CLAN
1	M
2	K
3	G
4	J
5	L
6	B
7	H
8	D
9	F
10	C
11	A
12	E
13	I

The results indicate Clans M and K are more likely to engage in internal conflict, whereas Clans E and I are more likely to engage in external conflict with other clans.

Geo-spatial network analysis and social network analysis on their own are powerful tools. The real fun starts when you combine the different networks and layer them on top of each other. In other words, you create a social network map of all the people you are interested in, and then layer them on top of a geo-spatial network map of where they are located. Although we have not done the research, we expect that such layering and cross-analysis between the two maps might produce some interesting insights about how social networks and physical locations influence each other and the tendency to engage in conflict.

Also, note that clustering can also help you determine how you define what constitutes a group. You then reach a point where you are combining different types of analytical methodologies and crowdsourced data to produce a powerful and elegant way to forecast and understand conflict.

Agent Modeling

The universe of social media comprising the people who use it, how they use it, and what they create on it, is a highly complex, inter-related, and dynamic system. Countless factors and variables go into influencing people's behavior, which in turn influences the type of data they create on social media, which influences their behavior. Trying to understand people's behavior on and because of social media is difficult to do. Trying to forecast how people might behave in the near future because of the influence of social media in certain scenarios is even harder. Fortunately, emerging and existing computational modeling tools can help you model, forecast, and make sense of people's behavior vis-à-vis social media.

Agent modeling or *agent-based modeling* is a type of computational modeling where you can simulate the mental and physical behaviors of any discrete, autonomous entity or agent to better understand and forecast the entity's behavior. Simply put, agent modeling enables you to virtually model any (single or numerous) person, group, or thing based on a variety of data sources including social media. Once you can virtually model a person, group, or thing, you can program the virtual model to behave in specific ways, and watch as it interacts with other entities and reacts to virtual situations and environments. You can then identify how the behavior of the entities changes over time. Agent modeling is used in a variety of fields such as economics, biology, and ecology to model and forecast everything from the interactions between wolves and sheep to the shifting biases of intelligence analysts to the behavior of companies on a stock market. Numerous types of agent modeling tools exist and they differ greatly in how they model entities, how many and what type of entities they model, how they let the entities behave, what data they use to model the entities, what types of environments they place the entities in, and what they output. Regardless, the entities you model must be discrete and decentralized actors.[4]

Agent modeling may seem difficult to understand at first, but it is actually fairly intuitive and elegant. The operational details are difficult to fully grasp, but the overall concept is not. We encourage you to read the subsequent sections with an open mind so you can fully grasp the concept of agent modeling. We are big fans of certain types of agent modeling and use it in our work to solve seemingly intractable problems. We hope you will also.

The Relevance of Agent Modeling

To aid understanding, we discuss the relevance of agent modeling to you and social media before we delve into how it works. Understanding the relevance of agent modeling will spur you to think about how you can use it as you learn how it works. You may want to read this section again when you get to the end to fully grasp the concepts discussed.

Agent modeling can you help you model and forecast, for example:

- How a specific social network on a social media platform will grow and evolve into the future
- The behavior of rioters (groups and individuals), their physical location and likelihood to engage in violence, and how information on social media is influencing them
- How participants on your crowdsourcing platform will respond to specific influence injects

Numerous other applications exist. Some, as the aforementioned, are directly relevant to the interaction between social media and people who use it. Other security applications are more indirectly relevant and may use social media simply as one of many data sources or even not at all. In a lot of cases, the more data you use to inform and program the agents, the more accurate and precise the model will be. Also, many existing agent modeling applications simply build models of people or events and then do not update them with real-world information. You can now process real-time social media feeds and constantly input them into your agent application to build a more realistic and accurate model.[5] Other security applications that may not involve social media as heavily may include modeling and forecasting:

- The placement of IEDs along a certain road
- The logistics of transferring a unit and its equipment to a certain location
- The behavior of people evacuating a building

More advanced applications of agent modeling, which we work on, involve using it to tease out patterns in all sorts of data including social media. In such cases, agent modeling tools can identify how the emergence of a set of data points tells you that a specific behavior or event is about to take place or has taken place.[6] For example, say that the tool downloads public information from sites known to be popular among violent extremist groups and information about the purchase of sensitive and hazardous materials in certain cities. The tool can then identify that a person used the same credit card to purchase certain types of dangerous chemicals from different stores. The tool can also identify that a person visited an online forum where he discussed purchasing the chemicals to make a bomb, and that on another site, a person with a similar username as the person on the other forum made threats to members of a religious group at around the same time as the other actions. The tool can then autonomously connect the dots and send a warning to law enforcement and the religious group that a person in their locality may be making such a bomb to attack them. Such an overwhelming tool is not yet fully operational, but we hope to make it so very soon.

NOTE Visit the website to learn more about this advanced type of data pattern analytics and other interesting agent modeling applications.

The Process of Agent Modeling

Agent modeling may sound too good to be true, and in some cases it is. You need to understand which type of agent modeling to use and when to use it. We primarily discuss a subset of agent modeling known as *multi-agent modeling* or *multi-agent systems*. (Different types of multi-agent systems exist, but we will not get into them here.) In a multi-agent system, numerous agents, following a few simple rules of behavior, interact with each other and their environment. The product of their repeated interactions is a change in the makeup or behavior of agents and an overall solution to a problem. For example, say you are mapping the social network of human traffickers across Europe by monitoring their cell phone usage. You may like to know how the social network of traffickers will evolve over time and how it will change in response to police action against certain parts of the network. You can model the traffickers as agents and watch how their interactions and social network evolve over time and how it changes in response to police action. You can then get an idea of, for example, what the network will look like three months from now (which agents form links and relationships with other agents), or how the network will adapt if you cripple a part of it.

Right about now, you probably would like to ask us the following two sets of questions:

- How do you train the agents to behave as traffickers and how do you make sure they are behaving realistically? If you program agents to behave like traffickers, then you are assuming you know about the behavior of traffickers. Then is the model not based on a bunch of assumptions that could be very wrong?

▪ Human behavior is extremely complex and if you tried to program an agent to behave like a human, you would have to program hundreds and thousands of rules of behavior and variables. To get around this problem, you give the agents only a few rules of behavior. However, how can a few agents following a few simple rules tell us something about complex behavior?

Understanding the questions and their answers is critical to understanding agent modeling. The answers lie in the concepts of swarm intelligence and genetic algorithms.

Swarm Intelligence

The type of agent modeling we prefer is a data-driven, bottom-up method that has its roots in induction. In other words, the agents produce results without you telling the agents what the results should be. This bottom-up approach is similar to the concept of *swarm intelligence*, which is the collective behavior of a system of numerous discrete, decentralized actors. Swarm intelligence explains how you can train agents with only a few simple rules but then watch them interact and produce complex, system-wide behavior, also known as emergent intelligence.[7]

Swarm intelligence derives its name from the fact that swarms of birds and ants are able to engage in amazing complex behavior even when each bird or ant is relatively dumb. Understanding how swarm intelligence works in nature will help you understand how it works in agent modeling. Consider how ants successfully forage for food at a large scale, given the fact that each ant by itself has little intelligence. Say you have an ant colony and a few sites containing food surround it. Some of the sites have a lot of food and some have little. Figure 12.6 shows a schematic of the ant colony and the distribution of food sites. The ants have to figure out a way to find the food, tell other ants about it, and carry the food back to the colony.

Each ant follows only a few simple rules, much like how agents in most agent modeling circumstances follow only a few simple rules. The rules are:

▪ Move stochastically or randomly around the ant colony looking for food.

▪ Upon finding food, carry it back to the ant colony.

- Drop chemical pheromones, which evaporate over time, while walking.
- Move toward the direction with pheromones, or in other words, be attracted to pheromones.

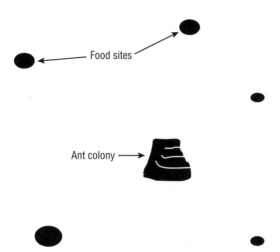

Figure 12.6: Ant colony and food site distribution

With these rules in mind, consider what happens over time as the ants move out from the colony. First, the ants wander around looking for food. Eventually, a few ants stumble upon the food, pick it up, and carry it home. These ants now know the location of the food. As they pick up the food and carry it home, they drop pheromones on the trail from the colony to the food. Other ants stumble onto the pheromones and start following the trail of the ants that discovered the food. They then stumble onto the food, and also start dropping phero-mones on the trail from the food source to the colony. Eventually, the amount of pheromones on the trail from the food source to the colony grows and more ants become attracted to it. Eventually though, the food runs out. However, another trail to another food source starts growing in pheromone intensity. Ants then become interested in that trail. Meanwhile, the pheromones of ants that moved around randomly without finding food quickly evaporate because they are not walking the same paths due to the lack of food. Over time, the ants stumble onto all the food sources and successfully forage for food. Figure 12.7 illustrates this swarm behavior.

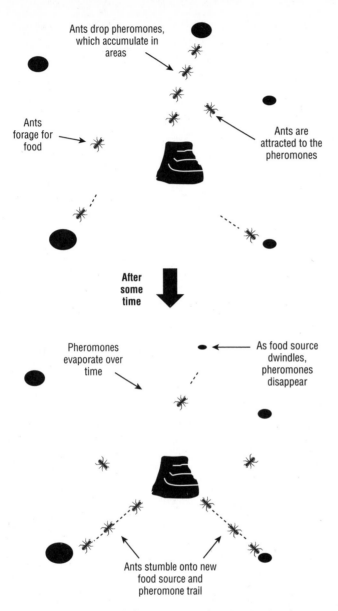

Ants drop pheromones, which accumulate in areas

Ants forage for food

Ants are attracted to the pheromones

After some time

Pheromones evaporate over time

As food source dwindles, pheromones disappear

Ants stumble onto new food source and pheromone trail

Figure 12.7: Swarm behavior of ants foraging for food

A few dumb ants knowing only a few rules interacting with each other can exhibit impressive emergent intelligence. Similarly, a few agents knowing only a few rules interacting with each other can produce complex system-wide behavior that impacts them and their environment. In the case of the trafficker network example, you would simply program a few rules into the traffickers and let them interact and form links with each other, somewhat randomly. The somewhat random part takes into account the fact that human behavior can often seem random and unexplained. The interactions will affect the traffickers and the traffickers will affect the interactions in untold ways, producing behavior you might not expect. You will need to use some past data to provide the trafficker agents with the few rules of how to interact and make links with other trafficker agents. To make sure that you are providing them with the right few rules and that the trafficker agents are behaving realistically, you may need to introduce a genetic algorithmic component into your agent model.

Genetic Algorithms

Genetic algorithms are processes and rules based on the phenomena of evolution and natural selection that enable computers to evolve agents that resemble the entities you are trying to model.[8] Think of the computer in which you are creating your agent model as a planet. Virtual agents live in the computer planet in their virtual environments. You would like to fashion agents to resemble the entities you are trying to model. Initially, the agents do not have much of a personality and do not know how to behave with each other and their environment. Following our example from before, you need the agents to behave like traffickers and form a social network with other trafficker agents. You provide them with a few rules of behavior and modify their environment to fit that of the traffickers. The environment could be anything from the virtual representation of the physical infrastructure of a city, to the virtual representation of a social environment with virtual obstacles that make it difficult for some agents to interact with other agents.

So far you have agents with some intelligence and a tendency to act somewhat randomly and explore on their own, and an environment. However, you cannot be sure that the agents really behave like traffickers. You may have programmed them incorrectly and likely neglected to take into account some behaviors that significantly define the behavior of traffickers. Ideally, you would like the agents to figure out on their own exactly how to behave so that your prejudices, biases, and lack of knowledge do not sway them and ruin your agent model. Fortunately, your agents can somewhat figure out how to act on their own through the process of genetic algorithmic computing.

Before we continue, we need to refresh your biology knowledge and your understanding of natural selection. During reproduction, the genetic code of organisms often mutates and produces a few organisms with different characteristics and abilities. Some of the mutations improve the organism's ability to succeed in life (reproduce), some hamper it, and some have no effect. Over time, organisms compete with one another for resources and mating partners.

Organisms with beneficial mutations are more likely to win the competition and produce more offspring, which propagates the mutation through the ages. Other organisms tend to lose the competition. In essence, nature selects against the losing organisms. Instead, nature selects for organisms that have evolved the correct characteristics and behaviors for them to succeed, which is to reproduce at that time in their environment.

Genetic algorithmic computing follows this same process. You provide the agents with a few behaviors initially, but then you let the agents experiment, mutate, and evolve. Some agents begin exhibiting behavior patterns that help them succeed in their environment, and others evolve behaviors that hurt them. Instead of defining success as the ability of agents to reproduce, you can define success as how close the agents come to resemble the traffickers (how close the agents' networks look like the traffickers' networks) at some point in time. Specifically, you map out what the traffickers' social network looks like at different periods of time. Say that you have information about the traffickers' social network going back ten years from 2003 to 2013. You do not have perfect information about exactly what the network looked like at any point of time during that decade, but you do have a significant amount of information about what the network looked like at points throughout the decade. You then start your computer planet and agents at virtual year 2003. You program the agents to behave as you think traffickers probably behave and form the social network the real traffickers had in 2003. The key is that you create multiple iterations of the computer planet with multiple populations of the trafficker agents. You then let the agents in the planets evolve. After some time, the computer planets reach the virtual year of 2006. At that point, in some planets the agents' networks will look like what the real traffickers' network looked like in the real 2006. In other words, some agents will succeed and accurately resemble the real traffickers. You select the agents that do resemble the real traffickers and destroy the other planets and agents.

You then again let the agents evolve some more. Again you stop the clock at the virtual year 2009 and see which agents' networks resemble that of the real traffickers' network in the real 2009. You again select for the agents that best resemble the real traffickers, and repeat the process. Eventually, you will end up with agents that evolved in such a way that they end up behaving and forming networks like the real traffickers in the real year 2013. You can then let the agents evolve into the future to see how the traffickers might act in the future. Or, you can examine how the agents behaved and how their behaviors look different than when you initially programmed them to try to figure out how the real traffickers actually behave. Figure 12.8 illustrates this process.

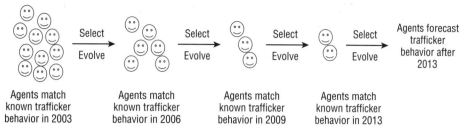

Figure 12.8: Genetic algorithm process

You may need to reread the preceding sections a few times to fully understand the power of agent modeling and how it can help you. Admittedly, it took us some time to understand it fully but we are glad we did. Check out the references for more information, some of which is technical but some of which explains the subjects we touched upon in layman terms. In the appendix, we also list some websites and software solutions that can help you build simple and complex agent modeling capabilities. Some such as George Mason University's MASON application (available at `http://cs.gmu.edu/~eclab/projects/mason/`) or Northwestern University's NETLOGO application (`http://ccl.northwestern.edu/netlogo/`) are relatively easy to use and require little technical knowledge. Others are significantly harder and require specialized technical expertise.

Agent modeling, geo-spatial network analysis, and cluster analysis are impressive and powerful tools that can help your mission sets in exciting ways. However, always keep in mind that no analytical methodology is perfect. They all have their limitations and none can yet accurately and precisely model the world and all the intricate, complex beings and things that exist in it. Keep an open and skeptical mind as you research and use the methodologies we covered in this book. You will also need to keep an open and skeptical mind for Chapter 13, where we explore how you can use crowdsourcing to solve problems of health and education that are increasingly tied up with issues of security.

Summary

- Many analytical methodologies, some of which are quite complex, use and analyze social media data. Over time, they will grow in their number, applicability, power, and relevance.

- Cluster analysis is a method of assigning discrete entities into clusters or groups according to certain criteria.

- Cluster analysis can help you categorize people, data, and things so you can better focus your efforts and understand your populations of interest.

- Geo-spatial network analysis enables you to analyze the distribution of groups of people over a region to derive the likelihood a specific group will engage in internal or external conflict.

- Crowdsourcing enables you to collect detailed data about groups of people, especially nomadic people, thereby improving your geo-spatial network analysis.

- Agent modeling is the process of modeling the behavior of any discrete, decentralized entities to understand and forecast their behavior.

- You can use agent modeling to model the past, present, and future behavior of entities ranging from rioters to the movement of warfighters to social networks on social media.

- Many sophisticated agent modeling systems are based on the concepts of swarm intelligence and genetic algorithmic computing, which explain how virtual agents can evolve over time to produce and explain complex behavior.

- No analytical methodology, regardless of its complexity and power, can perfectly explain and forecast the world and human behavior.

Notes

1. Everitt, B., et al. (2011) *Cluster Analysis*. Wiley, United Kingdom; Romesburg, C. (2004) *Cluster Analysis for Researchers*. Lulu Press, North Carolina.

2. Jordán, F. (2008) "Predicting Target Selection by Terrorists: A Network Analysis of the 2005 London Underground Attacks." *International Journal of Critical Infrastructure* 4: 206-214; Gupta R. (2012) *Utilizing Network Analysis to Identify Critical Vulnerability Points in Infrastructure and Explain Terrorist Target Selection*. Georgetown University Security Studies Program, UMI Dissertation Publishing.

3. Johnson, D. and Jordán, F. (2007) "The Web of War: A Network Analysis of the Spread of Civil Wars in Africa" Annual Meeting of the American Political Science Association, Chicago.

4. Parunak, H.V.D., Savit, R., and Riolo, R. L. (1998) "Agent-Based Modeling vs. Equation-Based Modeling: A Case Study and Users' Guide." *Multi-Agent Systems and Agent-Based Simulation*, 1534: 277-283; Epstein, J (2006) *Generative Social Science: Studies in Agent-Based Computational Modeling*. Princeton University Press, Princeton, NJ; Railsback, S. (2011) *Agent-Based and*

Individual-Based Modeling: *A Practical Introduction*. Princeton University Press, Princeton, NJ.

5. Parunak, H.V.D., Brueckner, S., Gupta, R., and Brooks, H. (2012) "Dynamically Tracking the Real World in a CSS Model." Annual Computational Social Science Society of the Americas Conference, Santa Fe, NM.

6. Parunak, H.V.D., et al. (2009) "Stigmergic Modeling of Hierarchical Task Networks." Proceedings of the Tenth International Workshop on Multi-Agent Based Simulation, 98–109.

7. Parunak, H.V.D. (1997) "'Go to the Ant': Engineering Principles from Natural Agent Systems." *Annals of Operations Research*, 75: 69–101.

8. Mitchell, M. (2011) *Complexity*: *A Guided Tour*. Oxford University Press, Oxford, UK.

CHAPTER 13

Delivering Services through Crowdsourcing

The spread of social media and other technologies continues to empower non-state actors and increase the connections between seemingly disparate populations. Accelerated connectivity is producing conditions where poor standards of living and oppressive lifestyles in one part of the world can produce ideologies and epidemics that can cause catastrophe in other parts. The norms and arguments that define global security are shifting with the realities of contemporary global connectivity. Thus, in some cases, the provision of adequate education and health services is becoming critical to ensuring security and stability. The link between health and security is even more pronounced and apparent. Today, social media technologies can enable the provision of such services in areas where they are critical to ensuring security but are nonexistent or crippled for various reasons. This chapter explores how you can use social media to deliver educational and health services in remote parts of the world.

Delivering Education

Inadequate access to education, especially for girls in rural areas, can severely damage a population's health and security.[1] Major powers such as the United States consider increasing global access to mainstream education important to maintaining global security and are, therefore, undertaking efforts to build schools and provide school materials in poor, dangerous, and denied areas.

Also, they wish to push back against education that poor children in some areas typically receive, which can be incomplete, in dangerous conditions, and more focused on inoculating children with a certain ideology. However, such efforts are hard to sustain over the long term because they are expensive and difficult to execute.[2] Emerging countries such as Indonesia also wish to increase access to education to their rural and poor populations to sustain their development. They are dedicating enormous parts of the economy to providing educational services, but still do not have the resources to deliver education to their entire population in a traditional manner, which requires school buildings, teachers, and books.[3]

Fortunately, social media technologies can provide educational services to denied populations in an innovative and cost-effective manner. As we discussed in Chapter 2, the use of mobile phones and SMS technology is widespread in even the most rural areas. In the following sections, we discuss two methods by which you can leverage this existing mobile phone use, inexpensive tablet computers, and crowdsourcing mechanisms to deliver education to children in the most remote areas. Delivering education through social media also enables you to collect intelligence about the perceptions of local populations. We address the side-benefits of a social media–based education provision later. However, before we detail the two methods, we need to explore some new research and considerations that will help you structure an education provision through social media.

Understanding How People Learn

In the past decade, academics and non-governmental organizations have tried novel ways of educating children in urban and rural areas using a variety of technologies. Their efforts have illustrated how cheap and readily available social media technologies can provide education, and illuminated the conditions under which children and people, in general, learn best. (From now on, we refer to children as opposed to all people because the findings are more pronounced in children due to of the elasticity of their brains; however, they still relate to all people, including adults.) Some of their findings are surprising, counterintuitive, and go against traditional notions and methods of education. You need to understand their key findings so you know which methods work best and what results you should expect. We do not get into detail about the findings or how they came about—this is not a chapter about education. We only summarize the findings so you can use social media effectively and in a way that is aligned with human behavior. You may find that some of the insights about how people learn may help you better structure influence platforms with other objectives. The key findings are that children learn better when:[4]

- They are placed in groups of four to five and encouraged to learn educational material together. Children do not need sustained individual attention from teachers. Instead, when in groups, children can teach each other and help each other comprehend difficult or complex parts of the material even in a language they do not fully understand.

- They can go at their own pace and choose subjects that interest them. Everyone learns different information at different rates. Also, they are more likely to pay attention and expend the mental effort to learn something if it interests rather than bores them.

- Information is delivered through metaphors and stories. As discussed in Chapter 11, people do not always pay attention to rational arguments and objective facts. Metaphors and stories possess emotional content that attracts attention and utilizes shortcuts to deliver complicated information, which makes it more likely that an individual will remember and adopt the information.

- Moderators, who are not necessarily full-time, trained teachers encourage children and praise their learning. The encouragement can be as simple as leaving a message saying they are doing a good job.

- The educational material is directly relevant to the children's daily lives. Children are more likely to educate themselves, and their families are more likely to let them, if it is apparent that the material they are learning will teach them vital skills that will boost their family's income. The time anyone spends on education is time they do not spend working and supporting their family. Thus, the immediate economic utility of education must be apparent.

- Rote memorization of facts is replaced by interactive material that focuses more on problem solving and teaching the perceptions, frames, and viewpoints a person can use to make sense of the world. In the age of Google, human brains need not waste effort remembering facts that the Internet can recall for them in a moment's notice. Instead, they need to focus on using the facts and other information creatively to produce an innovative solution to a problem. This is as relevant in the design offices of Apple as it is in the farmlands of Indonesia.

- Gaming elements, some of which we explored throughout Part III of the book, are integrated into the educational material and are used to deliver the material. Integrating gaming elements in education can involve creating a simple math game that children can play on dumb phones that, for example, gives them points for getting multiplication questions right. In certain cases, especially when children are involved, gaming elements can introduce competition and motivate children to work harder to beat their peers. Games also enable you to quantify and track a child's performance over time. Additionally, just as children are more willing to take medicine if it is packaged as a sweet candy, they are more willing to learn material if it is packaged as an educational game. Another benefit of games is that children are willing to play them over and over again. As we discussed in Chapter 11, repetition improves information adoption. Lastly, in some cases, children can actually play a part in creating educational games. Creating such games improves the children's retention of the educational material. By enabling children to create games, you also end up crowdsourcing educational material and games that you can then provide to others.

Another key finding, and one that is most relevant to you, is that technology can play a significant positive role in delivering educational services. Specifically, existing and emerging social media technologies can help deliver educational material, track progress, and modulate coursework as required. Next, we describe the two methods by which you can use social media technologies to deliver education in denied areas. Many more methods exist, but these are the easiest to implement today. The first method is relatively more complex and expensive to implement but more comprehensive, and the second is simpler and cheaper but not as powerful. Still, both methods are much cheaper and, in cases involving poor, hard-to-reach populations, more effective than the traditional education method of building schools, printing and distributing textbooks, and employing full-time teachers.

Building crowdsourcing platforms to deliver services involves following the same process we detailed in Chapter 8. You can even label the platforms to deliver educational and health services that we describe in this chapter as service platforms. However, to focus on the most distinguishing elements of the platforms and to keep from being repetitive, we will not describe the service platforms in the same structure and format as we described the other platforms in Part III. Instead of going over the process of analyzing the target audience or marketing the platform, we simply focus on how you can design the platform. Assume for both methods that the target audience is a small population of young children in a rural and poor village in a large, developing country such as Indonesia where dumb phone use is widespread although not ubiquitous.

NOTE When actually implementing a service platform, you still need to go through the entire process of designing, building, and deploying a platform. You still need to focus your objective, analyze your target audience, design every element of the platform including its interface and incentive structure, market the platform, hire and train moderators, track the platform's performance, and refine the platform over time.

Delivering Education through Tablets and Mobile Phones (First Method)

The first method involves providing inexpensive tablets and dumb phones to children in the area to deliver educational content and track overall and individual performance. Before we detail the design of the platform, we first describe the tablets and mobile phones involved.

Overview of the Tablets and Phones

We briefly covered the different types of tablet computers in Chapter 2. Most popular tablets such as the iPad or Kindle are expensive and provide numerous features, some of which are quite complex and powerful. The tablets we refer to in this section are much more inexpensive and have fewer features, although they still are impressive machines. Such tablets include the UbiSlate tablets (known as Aakash tablets in India) that are priced at around $35–$60 USD and currently are being supplied to Indian schoolchildren. UbiSlate tablets come in two types: the UbiSlate7 and the UbiSlate7+. We focus on the latter tablet, which has slightly more features. (Check the website at www.ubislate.com for the most updated price and feature information.)

The tablets run Google's Android operating system and feature a sufficient amount of memory and power. They enable users to log on to the Internet through either Wi-Fi or cell network connectivity much like an iPad with 3G connectivity or an iPhone. The tablets have a built-in battery that users can charge using a variety of methods, including small, portable solar kits. The tablets are built using special material that makes them durable and able to withstand abuse by children. In all, the tablets are not that different from more powerful Android tablets widely available in the West. Users can use UbiSlate tablets to surf the Internet, play games, read documents, take pictures, make phone calls, watch videos, and listen to music.

The mobile phones are typical dumb phones, the kind that most Westerners used before the advent of the iPhone and smartphones. The dumb phones typically used in developing countries are manufactured by Nokia and enable the user to make and receive phone calls, send text messages, and play a few simple games. Some dumb phones also feature the ability to surf the Internet using a special browser. Dumb phones are fairly inexpensive and widely available in almost every part of the world. Our target audience may have a few dumb phones, which they usually charge by paying a person in their village who possesses a charging station, also known as reliable electricity.

The Process of Using the Tablets and Phones

The tablets and phones both possess certain content and enable the participant, who in this case is a child, to receive educational services. Assume the target audience consists of fifty children, all part of a small village with some access to electricity. A few families may possess dumb phones, but generally the use of social media technology is low.

You need to build a service platform made up of tablets, phones, and a back-end system that manages the data. The overall process is that groups of children use the tablets together to review and learn educational material. They then use the phones individually to take tests and receive feedback. The children also use the tablets and phones to create and share educational content with their peers. The back-end system tracks how the children use the tablets and phones, the content on the devices, and the performance and feedback of each child.

First, you need to purchase five tablets and load them with educational content. Each tablet focuses on a specific subject such as math or biology. Educational content can include anything from screenshots of textbooks, to videos of lectures, to simple applications and games that help children learn some basic concept. Free repositories of such content already exist—examples include Khan Academy (`http://www.khanacademy.org`) and PhD Gaming (`http://www.phdgaming.com`). You can update the information on the tablets remotely because they will have Internet connectivity through the cell network. To enable Internet access for the tablets, you need to purchase and install a prepaid SIM card in each tablet so they can access the local cell network.

Designate either a local village person or a person from your organization as the moderator for the village. If the person is a member of the community, you may need to incentivize him by providing him with a dumb phone to use. The moderator will take care of the tablets and oversee the program for you. Give the tablets to the moderator, along with an ability to charge the tablets. In some cases, providing the moderator with the ability to charge things might be incentive enough.

The moderator is primarily responsible for maintaining and storing the tablets and handing them to groups of four to five children. The tablets rotate through multiple groups over the course of a week or day. The children access the educational content on the tablets as they wish, albeit with a little structure and help from the moderators. As we discussed in the education findings, children are remarkable at teaching themselves and each other various subjects, often regardless of the difficulty of the content. The children can also use the tablets to create educational content including games and quizzes, which you can collect through the tablet's Internet connectivity. You can also program the tablets to collect information about exactly which group is accessing the tablet at a given time, what they are doing with it, and how they are using it. After group time, the children return the tablet to the moderator.

The children then use the dumb phones as their individual learning station. Some families in the area likely have dumb phones, but you may need to provide others with one. Each family thus possesses a dumb phone with ample incentive to maintain it and ensure that their children can use it. You can tell the families that they are allowed to use the phones for other things only if they ensure that their children get to use it for two hours a day. Equip each phone with simple educational content, including simple games, and a prepaid SIM card that connects the phone to the cell network. When the phone has access to the cell network, you can also enable it to remotely download new and updated content and games.

The children use the phone to review some of the content they learned during group tablet time at their own pace. They also use the phone to respond to blast SMS quizzes that test their retention of the content. See Figure 13.1 for a picture of an example SMS quiz.

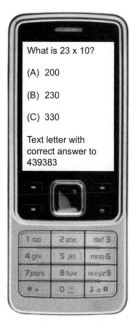

Figure 13.1: SMS quiz example

Remember that you can track which child is using which tablet and for what. You can also track which phone belongs to which child's family and how they are using it. You can program both the tablet and phone to regularly and automatically upload information and usage metrics to your data management system. Using the same connectivity, you can also frequently update the tablets and phones and the content on it. The moderator also needs to keep track of who is using what device. Because you can track which child is using which tablet and phone, you can make sure that the child receives an SMS quiz to her phone that pertains to what she reviewed on the tablet. The data management system can track the child's response and thus also track her performance and educational content retention. Moderators and volunteers from around the world can also text message the child every once in a while and provide her with encouragement and solicit feedback. For cases where families have multiple children, you can either provide multiple phones or simply ask each child to respond with their name. Your moderator can also ensure that each device is collecting information about the correct child. The information you collect does not have to be perfect or that individualized. You simply need an idea about how children in the village are doing overall and whether the trends of retention and performance are positive. Lastly, the children can also use the phones to text each other questions and create games that they share with their peers. The moderator can reward the children for creating and sharing games and content. You may need to integrate services such as GroupSMS (`http://www.grouptext.info`) that enable users to mass text a group of people. This way, the group of children who review a tablet together can also send each other text messages about what they have reviewed or quiz each other without bothering the other groups. See Figure 13.2 for a graphical overview of this method.

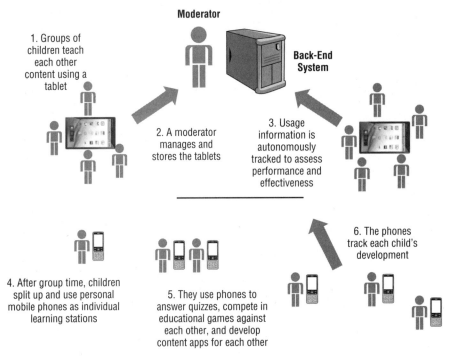

Figure 13.2: Tablet and phone method overview

Over time, as the method grows in acceptance and popularity, you likely need to scale up your efforts to more villages. Because you are crowdsourcing content and games from children throughout, you can then send the same content and games to other children. In this way, your educational content will become refined and more relevant and applicable to your target audience. The children will start teaching the other children digitally in the most austere parts of the world for a fraction of the cost and effort without requiring school buildings, outdated textbooks, or full-time teachers.

Delivering Education through Mobile Phones Only (Second Method)

The first method involves purchasing and distributing both tablets and phones, which can get expensive and, in some cases, may be hard to manage. The second method reduces the cost and complexity involved by distributing only dumb phones to children to deliver educational content and test their performance. The second method is similar to the first method in many ways, but the focus is solely on the phones.

You still need to designate a moderator for the village, and purchase the same type of dumb phones with prepaid SIM cards. The key difference is that you need to preload the phones with more educational content. You may need to provide the moderator with books or a single tablet that he can regularly distribute and use to supplement the content.

Each child's family receives a phone that the child uses as an individual learning station. Depending on conditions on the ground, the moderator provides books or a single tablet to rotating groups of children. The groups of children also review the content on their phones together. The children then receive blast SMS quizzes on their phones and encouragement from the moderator and volunteers, and send out responses, feedback, and share content with others. The data management system and the moderator track the performance of each child by regularly and automatically collecting various usage metrics from the phone. See Figure 13.3 for a graphical overview of this method.

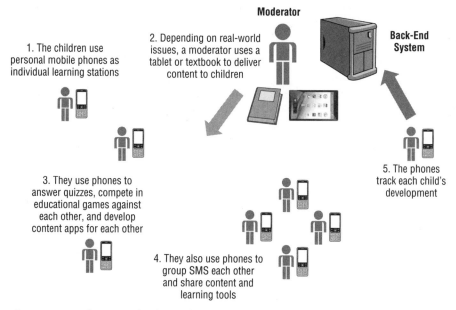

Figure 13.3: Phone method overview

Compared to the first method, the amount of content you deliver to children will be smaller through the second method. You also need to be more creative about how you package the content for a device with a small interface, memory, and processing power. Still, the second method provides educational content and tracks overall performance much more effectively than the lack of any educational service or a haphazard and infrequent one. Unlike schools that often shut down and reopen, with the second method, the children will at least always interact with updated educational content.

Side-Benefits of Delivering Education

A service platform not only enables you to deliver humanitarian services, but it also enables you to use the platform as an intelligence collection, solution, or influence platform. The social media technologies and crowdsourcing techniques involved in service platforms are the same as in other platforms. A participant with a dumb phone can use it to educate himself, provide you with intelligence and solutions, or engage with others about their views and willingness to engage in certain behaviors. By providing phones to families, you are also expanding the size and diversity of your target audience. You can even encourage or mandate the adults in the family to use the phones for regularly providing you with intelligence about illicit activity in their region. Also, take note that when you are providing education to children, you are also influencing them and their families. The content they learn can significantly alter how they view the world. You are also improving their views of you because you are openly helping them by providing them with a critical service that will improve their lives. Additionally, asking children to create and distribute educational games that their peers will like is no different from asking participants to submit solutions to complex problems.

As you become more experienced with crowdsourcing, expect to deploy platforms with multiple diverse objectives. Doing so will incentivize the target audience to participate and can help obscure more sensitive objectives. Use one type of platform, such as a service platform, to incentivize participants to participate in another type of platform, such as the intelligence collection platform. Meanwhile, you need not advertise that you want participants to join a platform to provide you with intelligence. You can simply advertise that you are encouraging participants to join so they can receive a service, and only then make it known that a condition of receiving the service is also providing intelligence.

You can also use one service platform to deliver multiple services, including health services as we describe next. By using the same technology for multiple purposes, you are saving enormous amounts of money and making it easy for the target audience to engage with you on a number of levels, help themselves, and help you.

Delivering Health

When we refer to delivering health services, we do not primarily mean delivering medicine, although social media can help amplify medicine delivery efforts. Instead, we refer to delivering health-related services such as the ability to diagnose individual disorders based on symptoms, collect aggregate information about health problems in an area to track epidemics, and provide updated and critical health and safety information to populations.

The link between health and security is more obvious and immediate than between education and security. Because of this link and other reasons, a significant amount of money and effort has been spent on delivering health services through social media technologies. A number of organizations have deployed health services platforms, also known as mobile health or mHealth projects and applications. The platforms typically deliver two types of services. The first type helps users figure out what ails them and provides a diagnosis. The second type collects and aggregates medical information about many users for various purposes. Some combine the two types.

However, many such platforms are unsustainable for various reasons, stymied by regulations, or not applicable for poorer and more denied populations. They typically focus on expanding health services in the Western world. They require their users to have Internet access through either computers or their smartphones. Although such health services may not appear directly relevant to your needs, you still need to know about them. You can adapt the services for access via dumb phones, and as smartphones and Internet access become more widely available, many developing regions will gain the ability to access similar services. If you can deliver such services, you will drastically improve the health of the populations and prevent catastrophic epidemics. In the subsequent sections, we review some of the platforms by their type and briefly describe how you can adapt them to deliver basic health services to denied areas and improve the health and security of populations globally.

Diagnosing Health Problems

Virtual diagnostic platforms or applications are becoming widespread because they are relatively easy to make and deploy. A popular example of a diagnostic service is WebMD's symptom checker, which is available at `http://symptoms.webmd.com`. When first accessing the service, a user plugs in some basic demographic information about herself such as her age. The user then identifies various symptoms from which she might be suffering. As the user selects symptoms from the list, the service reasons about what ailments the user may be suffering from and presents them in a list. As the user picks and refines her symptoms, the list of ailments decreases until only a few remain. Finally, the service presents the user with the ailment she likely suffers from according to the information she provided, and also provides information about her ailment. The user then has an idea of how and why she is sick and what she needs to do about it.

Other virtual symptom checker and diagnostic services also exist. An Android application and website named Symcat, available at `http://symcat.com`, works similarly. Different diagnostic services primarily differ in the algorithms they use to figure out a diagnosis for the user, and the data they use to train their algorithms.

Problems with Existing Diagnostic Services

Diagnostic services are mostly available in the Western world for Western populations, and they are not always applicable for populations in developing regions. They create algorithms based on data collected in Western hospitals about Western populations, and thus are more adept at understanding the symptoms and diagnosing the ailments that people in rich, developed countries typically suffer. Also, they design the interface of their applications in such a way that the applications only work on computers and smartphones. For example, WebMD's symptom checker enables users to click on parts of a diagram of a body to indicate where on the body they are suffering pain or discomfort. A user with a dumb phone that has only SMS messaging capability cannot use such an interface.

Lastly, assessing the accuracy and precision of diagnostic services is difficult, which is not a critical issue for most Western diagnostic service users. Many people who use such services likely do it for ailments that are not very serious, like colds and the flu. If they do it and find out they have something more serious, they have the option of going to a doctor to get a proper diagnosis. People in developing regions are regularly threatened by much more serious diseases such as malaria and do not always have the option of going to a doctor to get an accurate diagnosis and treatment. A mobile diagnostic service would be a significant help for people in areas denied of traditional diagnostic services. Upon learning of his condition, a person in rural Africa may not be able to visit a clinic, but he may be able to still acquire generic drugs or take some simple precautions that could save his life or prevent the spread of his disease. Fortunately, adapting such applications for dumb phones and less wealthy populations is not difficult.

Adapting a Diagnostic Service for Denied Areas

We are currently designing and hope to soon deploy a symptom checker and diagnostic service that populations in developing regions can access through their dumb phones and SMS. You can deploy a similar service, albeit with a little effort. The service has three parts: the algorithms, the data management system, and the SMS interface.

First, create the algorithms that can understand the symptoms and demographic information of people in a developing region, and use that information to diagnose them. Creating and refining the algorithms is arguably the most difficult and technologically intensive part. Various data modeling tools and methodologies can help you create and train the algorithms to ensure they can adequately diagnose a person based on their symptoms and demographic information, including their location (some ailments are more likely to occur in certain areas). You will likely need to work with healthcare and data modeling organizations to create the appropriate algorithm.

After creating the algorithms, you need to create a robust data management system that houses the data you collect from users, runs the algorithm on the data, and then sends the user the diagnosis. The system is the lynchpin of the service platform and helps you coordinate and combine the different parts of the platform.

The third and final part involves enabling people in denied areas to interact with your data management system and submit data to it so it can process it and respond back with a diagnosis. Essentially, the user sends an SMS message to the system, via a shortcode, containing her symptoms in a specific format. The system responds automatically with a text message asking for more information. After the user has submitted enough information, the system texts back a diagnosis to the user. The service can also suggest pharmaceutical advice and coordinate delivery of drugs, if appropriate. Figure 13.4 provides a graphical representation of the diagnostic service process.

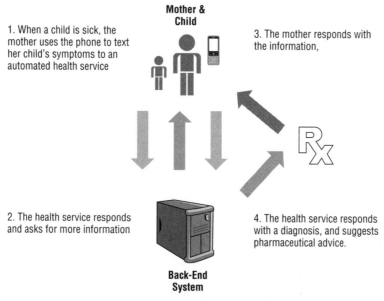

Mother & Child

1. When a child is sick, the mother uses the phone to text her child's symptoms to an automated health service

3. The mother responds with the information,

2. The health service responds and asks for more information

4. The health service responds with a diagnosis, and suggests pharmaceutical advice.

Back-End System

Figure 13.4: Diagnostic service for denied areas' process

Ideally, you need to create the algorithms in such a way that they can offer diagnoses by using only a little bit of user-submitted information. People in developing regions likely do not want to spend a lot of money sending text messages to your service platform. One way to improve the diagnostic process and collect more information from users without compelling them to send more text messages is to use physical diagnostic tools. Various organizations are working on small tools that you can connect to dumb phones and smartphones that can, for example, measure blood sugar levels.[5] You may be able to partner with an non-governmental organization in an area, who sends out a facilitator armed with a physical mobile diagnostic tool that regularly measures some critical information about people in the area. The facilitator can then provide the information to the user who texts it to your system.

You may have noticed that you are simply collecting a form of intelligence from people in denied areas. As discussed at the end of the education section, you can use the information you collect for a variety of reasons. You can use it to refine and improve your algorithms and to track the spread of disease in an area. The next section briefly describes how you can collect intelligence about various health indicators and analyze it to identify and track epidemics and other health events of concern.

Collecting Health Information

Numerous service platforms collect the health information of people for various purposes. They collect information using different methods and for different purposes. Many collect aggregate information about a population to track the spread of epidemics, which we focus on here. You can also easily collect information from populations in denied areas to figure out if they are suffering from diseases, how those diseases are spreading over time, and if you need to be concerned about it.

Existing Health Information Collection Services

One of the most popular examples of such a service is Google Flu Trends, which you can access at `http://google.org/flutrends/`. Google Flu Trends uses an ingenious but simple method of semantic analysis to figure out how flu is spreading over time in various countries around the world. Google simply keeps track of how many times and when a person in a certain area uses Google's search engine to search for terms related to flu and influenza. Google assumes that people will search for information about the flu if they have the flu. If a lot of people in an area are searching for information about the flu, then lots of people in the area likely have the flu, and so the flu is spreading. Google counts the number of times people in an area search for flu-related terms and figures out if, at a given moment in time, a lot of people in a specific area are searching for things related to the flu. Google can then figure out where and at what rate the flu is spreading at any given time. According to studies cited on its website, Google Flu Trends is fairly accurate.

Other services collect much more detailed and personal information about a person's health. They actively seek out people and ask them about their health. They either ask the person and/or store the information using social media technologies. Many such services focus on collecting health information in hard-to-reach, rural, and poor areas. A quick search on the Internet will easily reveal several.

We have already covered some of the technologies and platforms these organizations use to collect data. For instance, the FrontlineSMS software community released a version of its software now known as Medic Mobile (`http://medicmobile.org`) and previously known as FrontlineSMS:Medic. Medic Mobile's website features several tools that anyone can download and use to collect health information. Another example of a technology that we have covered and is relevant to collect health information is crowdmaps. You can see an example of a crowdmap that encourages people to text in information about health and other related items at `https://smsinaction.crowdmap.com`.

Unfortunately, for various reasons either much of the information these services collect goes unused or the services do not collect enough information for it to be useful. One reason is that the organizations and individuals behind the services simply do not know what to do with the information. The organizations collecting the data are typically non-profits that are either wary about turning over their data to companies and governments or are willing to share the data but do not have the right contacts. Another reason is that the various organizations do not coordinate data collection and so end up repeating a few projects. They either collect data about one area over and over again or they only collect data about one item. Some even haphazardly collect data without paying attention to consistency and reliability. Assessing the validity of their data is difficult.

Two other reasons have to do with the problem of approaching issues in poor regions with the same mindset as approaching issues in Western, developed regions. The first reason concerns the issue of privacy. People in the West typically are wary about sharing personal health information with others, especially organizations that they do not know. Although many Westerners do not have access to health services, many in the West still have the luxury of being picky about with whom they share data. People in poor regions that are likely rampant with disease do not have that luxury, and so are not as concerned about privacy. In many cases, they are willing to share information with others as long as it can help them and their families. Some organizations are understandably but needlessly too concerned about privacy in such regions. Thus, they collect incomplete data that is not useful. The second reason concerns the issue of regulations. Western government organizations stipulate exactly how health services should function, including health information collection, and often for good reason. However, some do not seem to realize that such regulations do not exist in other parts of the world and that they can try out things they would not be allowed to try in the West. They artificially limit the types of services they launch and the type of data they collect. Of course, some will abuse the lack of regulations and cause problems. However, we see it as a blessing in disguise that enables you and others to deliver health services in ingenious ways to areas that desperately need them.

Adapting Health Information Collection Services

With knowledge about what types of services exist and their problems, you can easily adapt and create new services to collect information about people's health around the world. You can then create an epidemic tracker and early-warning system. You can also use the same mobile health information collection tools to collect health data from forward deployed units.

You can easily adapt existing health information collection services to serve your needs. The easiest way is to combine and analyze various health data sources to create your own version of Google Flu Trends that looks at trends of other health problems. You can create a semantic analysis tool that, for example, counts how many times people in a certain location tweet or text about a certain illness or symptom. You can then figure out if a disease is prevalent and spreading in a certain area. Creating such a tool is relatively simple.

To get the data, you need to search the Internet for existing data sources and build your own intelligence collection platform. First, search the Internet, news sites, and the Medic Mobile site for services that provide data about people's health issues. Also check out data feeds from the World Health Organization's website (`http://www.who.int/research/`). Although news and data feeds will be slightly delayed over those gleaned from social media or SMS, they offer important validation for the other data you collect via social media and your own intelligence collection platform. Also, consider partnering with local organizations that regularly collect health data from local populations. By combining the various sources, not only will your accuracy be higher, but your practice at using the different technologies will improve as well.

If enough data does not exist for your region, you may need to create an intelligence platform. The platform should incentivize participants to periodically submit information about their health. We already discussed one such incentive—provide them with an ability to diagnose their ailment. You can create your own platforms using a variety of methods, many of which we discussed in previous chapters. We encourage you to use a combination. Ideally, you should use the types of tools available at Medic Mobile to create a local or directed version of your own platform just to test it out in its entirety. The tools are free other than the cost of text messages, and a broad support community exists to assist in fixing bugs and other issues you might have along the way for your first iteration. Once you've ensured that you can get everything to work, you can use that same deployment for medical use as well as other uses.

After acquiring the data, build a simple semantic analysis tool such as the one we described before to analyze mentions of symptoms. Of course, this is easier said than done. In practice, properly creating appropriate analytical tools will be somewhat difficult and require creativity. You have lots of ways to analyze the health data to track the spread of disease. You can do spatial analysis to see the spread of disease over physical space, and therefore can simply plot the mention of symptoms on a map (such as with Ushahidi's crowdmaps). You can also do temporal analysis to see the spread of disease over time by using a simple spreadsheet program that tracks the mention of a symptom along with when it was written. Better yet, you can combine the two types of analyses and create a tool that shows the spread of disease over space and time. Some tools will do this for you, such as Google Earth, ARCGIS, and even crowdmaps. Ideally, you should design your own interface for the most flexibility and analytical power. Real-time information feeding into such a system could easily be the most advanced platform for looking at diseases in the past and in real time. To take it to the next level, you could even use software such as the type created by Recorded Future (available at `https://www.recordedfuture.com`) that attempt to extract "future events" from the Internet. Simply put, they take a tweet that says "Cholera will hit Zimbabwe in two weeks," reason that cholera may occur in Zimbabwe in two weeks, and then map it temporally.

To create an even more robust system, you could bring in past data and do comparisons to your real-time data. You can then test the validity of your analytics. You can also compare the health information you collect with information that measures the existence of other events such as famines, food shortages, and migration. You can then identify correlations between seemingly disparate events and forecast the spread of epidemics with much more fidelity. All this may sound impossible, but it is not beyond the current technical capabilities. It only requires coordination, motivation, and some ingenuity.

As you read this chapter, you may have concerns about the implications of collecting and using information that people typically consider private. Chapter 14 considers the implications of privacy, and how you can use the techniques without infringing on people's privacy and right to freely express themselves.

Summary

- You can use social media technologies and crowdsourcing techniques to deliver humanitarian and other services that are integral to security.
- Social media can inexpensively and effectively provide educational services to populations in denied areas.
- Through a combination of inexpensive tablet devices and dumb phones, you can provide education to young people in rural, poor areas.

- You can use crowdsourcing platforms that provide education to complete other objectives such as collect intelligence.

- You can use crowdsourcing techniques to collect information from participants about their symptoms, and use the symptoms to provide them with a diagnosis, all through text messages.

- You can also use crowdsourcing techniques to collect information about the health of populations in remote areas to track epidemics over space and time.

Notes

1. Oxfam International (2011) *High Stakes: Girl's Education in Afghanistan.* Accessed: 3 October 2012. `http://www.oxfam.org/sites/www.oxfam.org/files/afghanistan-girls-education-022411.pdf`

2. Winthrop, R. and Graff, C. (2010) *Beyond Madrasas.* Brookings Institution. Accessed: 4 October 2012. `http://www.brookings.edu/~/media/research/files/papers/2010/6/pakistan%20education%20winthrop/06_pakistan_education_winthrop.pdf`; United Nations (2010) *Millennium Development Goals.* United Nations Summit. Accessed: 4 October 2012. `http://www.un.org/millenniumgoals/pdf/MDG_FS_2_EN.pdf`

3. ACDP Indonesia (2010) *2010-2014 Ministry of National Education Strategic Plan.* Accessed: 3 October 2012. `http://www.acdp-indonesia.org/files/attach/MoNE_Strategic_Plan_2010-2014.pdf`

4. Gee, J. P. (2007) *What Video Games Have to Teach Us About Learning and Literacy.* Palgrave Macmillan, New York; Mitra, S. (2010) "The Child-Driven Education." TED. Accessed: 3 October 2012. `http://www.ted.com/talks/sugata_mitra_the_child_driven_education.html`; Robinson, K. (2011) *Out of Minds: Learning to be Creative.* Courier Westford, MA, USA.

5. Bettex, M. (2010) "In the World: Health Care in the Palm of a Hand." *MIT News.* Accessed: 4 October 2012. `http://web.mit.edu/newsoffice/2010/itw-sana-0927.html`

CHAPTER 14

Protecting Privacy and Yourself

Using social media for global security effectively requires that you use it ethically and legally. As you apply the techniques in this book, you will face circumstances where you come across information that someone considers sensitive and private, or use technologies in a way that may threaten people's privacy and freedom of expression. This chapter presents guidelines and tools that help you navigate such circumstances and use social media without infringing and jeopardizing the privacy, rights, and laws of others. It starts with a discussion about why you should care about privacy norms and laws globally, regardless of your authorities, objectives, or views. It then presents a list of guidelines and tips you should consider while using the techniques in this book with concern for people's rights and privacy. Undoubtedly, some will use the techniques without care for privacy and free speech or even abuse it for ill purposes. Thus, this chapter ends with a list of tips and tools for people who want to protect their information and identities from the abuse of the techniques found in this book and elsewhere.

Considering Privacy and Free Speech

Issues concerning people's privacy and their freedom to use the Internet and social media as they please are complex and messy. Organizations, populations, and governments differ widely on how best to handle such issues, and countless factors shape their preferences and views. Regardless of your views, you need to recognize that issues of privacy and free speech seriously influence the techniques you can or should use today and tomorrow. We have a specific viewpoint—that privacy and free speech are paramount and must be protected—and although we would like you to, we do not expect you to agree with us. This is not a book about the ethics of privacy and free speech, but about doing certain things effectively.

Reasons to Consider Privacy and Free Speech

If you want to analyze social media data and deploy crowdsourcing platforms effectively, you must consider and abide by concerns of privacy and free speech. In the past few years, numerous news stories have highlighted how law enforcement and government use of social media is clashing against laws, norms, and concerns related to privacy and free speech. For example, numerous American police departments have faced lawsuits, denunciations from politicians, and criticism from citizens for how they use social media data to identify and catch alleged criminals involved with the Occupy Wall Street protests.[1] The U.S. military has also come under criticism for its use of social media in information and influence operations, and sparked discussions about whether they may be harming people's rights and freedoms.[2] In many cases, the criticisms and lawsuits have stopped abuse and boneheaded programs, but they are also leaving well-intentioned and competent organizations confused and meek about using cutting-edge technologies. Additionally, continued ignorance or scoffing of concerns about privacy and free speech will eventually alienate populations, whose help you need to provide security in a new world where non-state actors are more powerful, knowledgeable, and influential than ever before.

Apart from influencing your ability to do things, you should pay attention to privacy and free speech because they are essential to the existence and proper functioning of the technologies this book is about. The Internet has given rise to and driven the adoption of incredible technologies such as Twitter and smartphones because it is a hotbed of creativity and interaction. The ability of people to protect their identities and freely express themselves online has generated and sustained much of the creativity on the Internet. If your actions threaten the free speech and anonymity available on the Internet, you erode the very things that make the Internet and social media interesting, useful, and powerful.

Appreciating the Complexity Involved

Despite their influence on effectiveness, we understand that issues of privacy and free speech are much more complicated. In some cases, you may need to infringe on someone's rights for good, such as to catch a murderer or find a missing child. During disasters, you do not care so much about victims' privacy as you do about finding out who they are, where they are, and how you can help them.

In other cases, an organization may use the techniques in this book combined with a disregard for free speech to identify and jail dissenters. In even more complicated cases, well-intentioned organizations may go overboard and abuse their authority with poor results. To add to the confusion, policy makers and politicians have barely begun to address related issues. Norms and ethics concerning social media use for security are still emerging. Due to the globalization inherent in the Internet and the ease with which people can interact with each other, the norms and ethics concerning social media use will start to converge globally. The Internet ignores boundaries and connects people and converges their thoughts and ideals. However, clear laws and universal norms will still take years to emerge. Mark Zuckerberg, the founder of Facebook, infamously said that the age of privacy is over and that Facebook is simply reflecting the changes that society is undergoing. He believed the changes are that people have gotten more comfortable sharing things and are less concerned with traditional notions of privacy.[3] We think that his comments may accurately describe the situation now. However, eventually the pendulum will swing back and people will become much more concerned with privacy after they start realizing the negative consequences of sharing too much online.

Lastly, we realize that your objectives and reasons for learning about social media and security influence how you consider issues of privacy and free speech. If you are working on behalf of a government, you need to know how you can protect your organization and your citizenry. If you are an individual concerned about your privacy or afraid of backlash from an oppressive regime, you need to know how you can protect yourself.

Due to the complexity involved, we present only a few guidelines about how you can navigate issues of privacy and free speech in general terms. Also, we split the subsequent sections in two to better address the issues from differing viewpoints and intentions. The first section is relevant for organizations that want to analyze social media data and deploy crowdsourcing platforms. The second section is relevant for individuals who want to protect their identities, privacy, and speech.

WARNING   We are not lawyers, and we are more familiar with American laws and norms. Check with a lawyer in your region of interest for proper legal advice and to keep abreast of changing laws and norms.

Acting Legally and Ethically

The following guidelines and tips are for those who will be analyzing social media data and/or building and deploying crowdsourcing platforms. We strongly urge you to follow the information in the subsequent sections so you can accomplish your objectives effectively without running into legal or ethical problems.

You should approach the information using two frames of thought. First, consider the information in terms of whether an action or behavior is legal in any jurisdiction in which you are involved. Laws concerning using social media data and technologies differ widely and will likely change soon, but some trends do exist, which we point out. Second, consider the information in terms of whether you believe an action is ethical. We do not intend to be preachy, but you may not have the luxury of abiding by only yours, your organization's, or your country's ethical code. Ethics and norms concerning use of social media data and technologies are changing and differ widely. However, as described earlier, norms and ethics concerning the Internet seem to ignore boundaries and converge into universal norms that you may have no choice but to follow. With these two frames in mind, consider the following guidelines and tips.

Analyze Non-Personal Open Source Intelligence

Open source intelligence is data that is freely available for the public and does not have a covert or secret classification. Although some debate exists about exactly what constitutes open source intelligence, examples include news stories, public tweets, public census information, and articles on Wikipedia. Usually, you can use open source intelligence as you wish, especially when it does not contain sensitive information that personally identifies someone.

All of the techniques we showed you in regards to analyzing data involved analyzing open source intelligence. You also use the techniques to analyze aggregate data and uncover large trends, such as famines and safety conditions, that have little to do with the identities and privacy of people. In some cases, you may care about where a few tweets are coming from but you usually do not care who is sending them, and you do not store or try to uncover that information. Keep in mind that social network analysis is an exception because you are using open source intelligence to track sensitive information about specific people and their social networks.

If you are using publicly available, open source intelligence that does not deal with personal, sensitive information about certain people in your analysis, you are probably fine. Simply put, if you are downloading tweets about a topic from a lot of people without caring about the identities of those people, you are likely fine; if you are downloading tweets only from a specific individual and tracking the tweets of that person, you may be setting yourself up for trouble. Open source intelligence is available for the public to use for a variety of purposes. However, some exceptions and restrictions do exist.

Follow Rules of Social Media Data Sources

Simply because data is available for free or publicly does not mean it does not come with restrictions about how you can use it. If you are downloading social media data from social media companies, you must follow their rules.

For example, if you are downloading and storing tweets for analysis, you are technically downloading data that Twitter owns, so you need to abide by Twitter's rules and restrictions. The rules and restrictions are usually commonsensical and what you would expect. According to Twitter's web page, Twitter currently forbids anyone to store non-public Twitter content without explicit permission from a Twitter end user. In other words, you cannot hack into a private Twitter account where only people who the Twitter user authorized can see the tweets, download the tweets, and store them.

Always check the developer rules and regulations of any platform from which you are downloading data. Most major platforms, including Twitter and Facebook, clearly state exactly how you can use their data and exactly what constitutes their data as opposed to private data that no one can use. The rules and regulations may change at any moment, so check them periodically.

In some cases, you can bypass the rules and regulations by subpoenaing the social media companies for the data. In the U.S., police departments have successfully subpoenaed Twitter for tweets concerning protests.[1] Most social media companies understandably do not like being subpoenaed and will resist turning over information about their users to you unless you have a very good reason. These companies depend on their users for their success, and they need to protect them as best they can. Laws and norms concerning subpoenaing social media data are still very unclear, but are emerging.

Do Not Involve Children

Do not analyze data concerning children or knowingly recruit them to participate in your crowdsourcing platform. Several companies and countries strongly discourage organizations and individuals from using data about children under the age of 13. In some cases, government agencies might be able to collect data about children but they are the exception.

In the U.S., a law called the Children's Online Privacy Protection Act, or COPPA, stipulates that websites must notify and obtain consent from parents before collecting, using, or disclosing personal information about children. Even web services that are solely about children's interests cannot skirt the rules. Recently, the U.S. Federal Trade Commission fined an organization that managed websites dedicated to pop musicians, including Justin Bieber.[4] Simply put, stay away from children under the age of 13.

Identify Extra Restrictions

Usually, militaries and intelligence agencies are given much more leeway with data that originates from overseas or is about citizens of other countries. However, they face extra restrictions when dealing with data that originates from their home countries or is about their citizens. In the U.S., military and some intelligence agencies are not allowed to collect, store, or disseminate information collected on U.S. citizens or citizens from allied countries. The globalization inherent in the Internet adds to the confusion. Most major social media platforms are based in the U.S., and so U.S. law governs them, but some may be based abroad.

Identify restrictions that apply specifically to you, and try to decipher which country the data you are interested in is actually from. Also, U.S. and allied military organizations are typically not allowed to have participants on their influence platforms who are U.S. citizens. When running a crowdsourcing platform, make an effort to understand where your participants are from and whether they are allowed to be on your platform.

Do Not Store People's Personal Information

This guideline relates to the open source intelligence one and reiterates the fact that you should not store or collect personal and sensitive information about individuals unless you need to and have explicit authority. If you collect and store personal information about individuals, you create the possibility that someone may hack into your system and steal and leak the information. If you are going to store personal information, take special steps to guard the information from hackers.

Help Your Participants Protect Themselves

If you are deploying a crowdsourcing platform, implement tools and techniques that help protect the participants' identities from each other and outsiders. Some of the tools, which we describe later, enable participants to hide exactly where they are texting or visiting a website from or what their phone number is if they are texting to you. In some cases you can keep information about them, but you need to make sure that other participants cannot see their personal information. For example, if you are building a website-based intelligence collection platform, you likely do not want the participants' real identities revealed to each other in case they face threats from adversaries posing as participants. You may also not want the participants to reveal too much personal information to you for liability or other reasons. You need to then train your moderators to identify instances in which your participants post sensitive information that reveals their identities, such as their real name or address. The moderators should immediately delete the information and inform the participants of their mistake.

Use your judgment to determine when you need to help your participants remain anonymous. For example, if you are deploying a crowdmap to aid with disaster relief, you likely want people to text in with information that helps you identify them so you or others can help them. On the other hand, in certain dangerous areas, you may want to keep malicious actors from accessing the crowdmap, viewing personal information, and taking advantage of victims.

Solicit Professional Help When Possible

Because laws vary widely from country to country, you should get professional legal help whenever you are launching a major social media project. Online behaviors or online speech that may seem normal and banal to you may be criminal elsewhere. You could jeopardize participants on your platform without knowing it, or download and disseminate information that can get you in trouble later. For example, in Vietnam, citizens are forbidden to post material online that is critical of the government. Three prominent Vietnamese bloggers who posted articles opposing the government received prison sentences of almost a decade each.[5]

Also, consult with area experts before launching a platform targeted at a specific population. In some cases, local governments may be wary of your efforts or even find it threatening enough to shut it down and harass any participants who signed up. In some cases, if a government sponsors a social media platform, you may need to be extra careful about how you use data from that platform.

Value Privacy and Strive for a Good Reputation

Make it part of your objective to act legally and ethically. If you do not, you likely will infringe on a law or norm and face problems. If you use data illegally or deploy crowdsourcing platforms without protecting your participants, word will spread about your misdeeds and incompetence. You may face a backlash, such as angering entire target audiences that will severely impact your ability to build and deploy similar platforms. Or, NGOs and others will hesitate to partner with you or even supply you with data that you may need. If you are a government agency and you misuse social media and identity data, you will anger the public and face a political backlash that could severely curtail your abilities.

This guideline goes back to our tips in Part III of the book about being as honest and transparent as possible about your intentions regarding your crowdsourcing platforms. People do not like being tricked or lied to, and they especially do not like having their personal information and identities misused. If they find out you are being inauthentic or careless, you may suffer in the long term. A recent troubling trend that highlights the points we are trying to make involves military agencies creating fake social media accounts and pretending to be someone they are not in hopes of joining the online social networks of persons or communities of interest. They hope to trick people into engaging with them online and providing them with vital information. Gauging their success is difficult, but the fact that their schemes and intentions are being plastered all over the Internet provides a clue. Also, in some cases, pretending to be someone you are not may be illegal on certain social media platforms.[2]

As a rule, people on social media are a lot smarter than you think, and they have little problem figuring out who you are and what you are up to. If you do not respect their intelligence and privacy, they will not respect yours.

Imagine and Prepare for the Worst-Case Scenario

For many involved in the security world, the worst-case scenario is when your operational plans leak for everyone to see. Anytime you are embarking on a major analytical or crowdsourcing platform that involves sensitive information, imagine how you will appear if your plans or intentions are leaked. If you believe you will appear as incompetent, malicious, or willing to engage in questionable behavior, you should probably change your plans. This especially holds true when designing and deploying a crowdsourcing platform. When you crowdsource, you involve a lot of people in your plans. Therefore, the chances increase that someone will find out something you do not want them to about your platform and leak it.

When you deal with sensitive information or engage in sensitive operations, something may always go wrong. You should be prepared for when it does, because it probably will.

Be Aware of Changes in Laws and Norms

The number of laws that deal with social media data and crowdsourcing platforms will drastically increase in the next few years. Many of the laws will be confusing and contradictory, and some will directly affect your operations. You need to keep aware of changes in laws and norms, and identify any meaningful trends.

We listed only a few guidelines but many more exist. Read the news, scour the Internet, check out the resources in Table 14.1 at the end of this chapter, and consult with professionals for more information.

Protecting Your Identity and Speech

The following guidelines and tips are for those who are concerned that the content they create on social media will be used in ways they do not approve of, or in ways that hurt them or someone they know. Such people include individuals in the West who are rightfully concerned about privacy and their rights to say what they want on the Internet without it being used to undermine them or threaten their civil liberties. It also includes individuals for whom what they say on the Internet is a matter of life and death, specifically protestors and activists fighting oppressive regimes. The subsequent sections focus on teaching you how you can protect your identity and yourself from the social network analysis tactics or other tactics that you find threatening.

At this point, you may have the important criticism that we will end up teaching criminals, terrorists, and violent rioters how to bypass the very techniques we have been teaching to help you stop them. Although your intention is understandable, the criticism itself is misguided for several reasons. One, most of the techniques in this book do not involve dealing with people's privacy and personal data. They either involve collecting and analyzing aggregate, personally non-specific data, or they involve getting people to work with you on their own volition through crowdsourcing platforms. Thus, teaching people to protect their identities will not have an impact on most of your work. It may even help, specifically in cases where you would like your crowdsourcing participants to protect themselves. The one exception is social network analysis. However, you often need minimal personal information to conduct online social network analysis. Besides, you should gather other information that will help you build a much more robust social network map that takes into account offline relationships. Two, many malicious actors already protect themselves in fairly impressive ways. The ones who do not are usually not as smart, technologically savvy, or do not have the resources and time as others, which describes a large population of malicious actors. Three, we believe that people have an obligation and a right to protect themselves, which, in turn, will improve overall security. The more law-abiding or "good" people can protect themselves, the less likely malicious actors such as identity thieves and oppressive regimes will take advantage of them. Four, improving security is a cat-and-mouse game that requires people to come up with new and better ways of doing things. We hope this book gives you some ideas and tips to innovate and evolve techniques that can defeat the protection techniques malicious actors may use.

The criticism also may not be as relevant because protecting your identity and your social media content is actually fairly easy to do and somewhat inevitable. Many people already do it and as people become more familiar with social media, they will realize the benefits and techniques to protect themselves. Although protecting yourself is not that difficult, it does require you to be sensible about it.

Part of the sensibility involves realizing that social media monitoring by government agencies and others is not as evil or intrusive as you might think. There will be abuses of power, but unless you are an activist fighting an oppressive regime, governments and others are not interested in who you are or what you are saying. We hate to break it to you, but you probably are not as important or interesting as you may think you are. You should probably be more concerned about identity thieves and overzealous marketing agencies that use your social media data to spam you. Still, protecting privacy and free speech is important and you should do your part by considering the following guidelines and tips.

WARNING The following sections only pertain to techniques that involve protecting yourself on social media and crowdsourcing platforms, and from the techniques in this book and in other similar publications. They do not address protecting yourself on the Internet in general, which you should definitely consider. Lots of widely available resources cover that type of information, including http://www.us-cert.gov/cas/tips/.

Set Basic Security Settings

Every trustworthy social media platform you sign up for and use will feature several security settings that help you protect yourself and the content you create. Always make sure to go through your account and privacy settings on any social media site you frequent to make sure only people you are comfortable with can access your data. Many social media sites do not allow others to use your content in any way if you choose the correct security settings.

Another part of going through your security settings is making sure you do not use simple passwords. Also, do not use the same e-mail address and password for multiple platforms. When you link your accounts in this way, a person who hacks into one account will instantly have the e-mail and password to hack into your other accounts.

Do Not Post Sensitive Information

If you do not post sensitive and personal information about yourself on the Internet, people will not be able to find it on the Internet. Sensitive information includes your birthdate and address. Others can use sensitive information about you to not only gain access to your accounts, but also to learn how to pretend to be you and gain access to your online social network.

Be Wary of Enabling Location Services

Many applications and sites request that you enable them to access the information on your phone and computer that tells them your physical location at any given time. Most applications are harmless and use your location to provide you with better, more customized service. For example, the smartphone application Yelp asks you for your location so it can instantly tell you which restaurants are around you.

Although most uses are harmless, be selective about who you provide with your location information. For example, if you provide Twitter your location and do not set appropriate security settings, others can figure out the location from which you are tweeting. They can then use that information to track your physical movements. If you do not receive an appreciable reward or service for enabling sites to access your location information, then do not let them.

Use Technologies That Anonymize You

Most people, especially in the West, do not have to worry too much about whether others know their identity. However, people living in oppressive regimes do have to protect their identity and make themselves appear anonymous when using social media services. If you believe you need to anonymize yourself, use one or a combination of several anonymizing tools.

Some of the most popular anonymizing tools either hide your Internet protocol (IP) address or provide you with a fake one. Every device that accesses the Internet has an IP address, which functions as a way to identify the device. Many websites and applications track your IP address. Your Internet service provider (ISP) provides you with the IP address. Usually, the ISP will provide you with a dynamic IP address that changes over time and switches from user to user. However, the ISPs keep track of who uses which IP at what time in case they are asked about it later by law enforcement.

Figuring out what your IP is at any time is not difficult. You likely leave lots of clues all over the Internet about you and your IP. Many sites do not dedicate a lot of resources to hiding the IP addresses of people who visit them. Some services such as IP2LocationTM (available at `www.ip2location.com`) let you figure out the physical location from which an IP address originates. The location they provide is not exact—depending on the country and city, they may locate you to a region in the city. However, governments can usually subpoena ISPs for IP addresses and then find out exactly who you are and where you are located.

Tor is one of the most popular ways to anonymize your IP address and identity. Tor is a free service (available at `www.torproject.org`) that was invented so that dissidents could anonymously post politically sensitive information online without revealing their identity. In simplistic terms, Tor takes the information coming out of your device, bounces it around the world through several other devices, and then finally delivers it to the site to which you want to submit the information. The site only sees the IP address of the last device through which your information went and never knows your actual IP address. You can use Tor in Nigeria to visit a forum, and the forum will think that your IP address originates from Poland. In theory, someone can map out all the devices your information bounced around through; however, in reality, it is close to impossible.

New technologies also adapt Tor and other anonymization tools so they work on mobile devices. For example, Covert Browser (available at `www.covertbrowser.com`) encrypts and reroutes data you send through your mobile devices. You can also use much less technologically sophisticated methods to protect yourself when using mobile devices. When using dumb phones, make sure to buy a prepaid SIM card and use it to send sensitive text messages. Others will find it difficult to track who bought a prepaid SIM card and who is using the phone.

Another form of anonymization technology makes it difficult for others to keep track of and analyze any content you post on social media. In Chapter 6, we discussed language analysis tools that help determine the authorship of a piece of text. Anonymouth (available at `https://psal.cs.drexel.edu/index.php/Main_Page`) is a tool that does the opposite by helping you avoid detection and confound authorship detection tools.

Use Social Media Platforms That Hide Your Identity

Instead of using tools like Tor to hide your identity when using social media platforms, you can simply use certain social media platforms that automatically hide your identity for you. Vibe is an example of a social media platform that lets users send messages anonymously, which expire after a selected amount of time, from their mobile devices to other users in a selected physical radius. People have used Vibe to coordinate protests and send each other sensitive information. The messages expire and are not stored like they are on Twitter or Facebook, so others cannot download them if they are not at a certain location at a certain time. The makers of such platforms also rarely cooperate with subpoenas or release sensitive information. Of course, such platforms can be hacked, but others constantly pop up.

Identify Who Is Behind What and Why

Before using a technology, try to figure out the identity and intentions of the organization behind it. In the majority of cases, the identity and intentions are completely harmless and of no concern to you. However, if something seems suspicious, you should investigate. Do not sign up for crowdsourcing platforms without knowing who is behind them and what they will do with any data you generate on the platform. In special cases, you should also keep track of who is creating the devices you are using. For example, Huawei is a Chinese company that makes affordable smartphones for populations in developing countries. Some are suspicious of Huawei and allege that the Chinese government may be putting software on the phones that can spy on their users.[6] Major American companies that make smartphones such as Apple and Google have also come under criticism for keeping track of their users without informing them.[7]

Use Common Sense and Be Reasonable

Probably the most important tip is to use common sense when using public social media platforms and be reasonable about your expectations. Social media platforms are about letting others see what you are posting and, to some extent, who you are. If you choose to participate in social media, you also choose to give up some of your privacy. Facebook is currently free for anyone to sign up and use. It does not charge you money, but it does expect you to give up a part of your privacy and identity. Any data you share openly on Facebook becomes the property of Facebook, and it can use it as it sees fit.

Also be sensible about what technologies and techniques can help you maintain your privacy. A recent trend has emerged where people post the following as a status update on Facebook to protect their data:

> *For those of you who do not understand the reasoning behind this posting, Facebook is now a publicly traded entity. Unless you state otherwise, anyone can infringe on your right to privacy once you post to this site. It is recommended that you and other members post a similar notice as this, or you may copy and paste this version. If you do not post such a statement once, then you are indirectly...allowing public use of items such as your photos and the information contained in your status updates.*

> *PRIVACY NOTICE: Warning — any person and/or institution and/or Agent and/or Agency of any governmental structure including but not limited to the United States Federal Government also using or monitoring /using this website or any of its associated websites, you do NOT have my permission to utilize any of my profile information nor any of the content contained herein including, but not limited to my photos, and /or the comments made about my photos or any other "picture" art posted on my profile.*

> *You are hereby notified that you are strictly prohibited from disclosing, copying, distributing, disseminating, or taking any other action against me with regard to this profile and the contents herein. The foregoing prohibitions also apply to your employee, agent, student or any personnel under your direction or control.*

> *The contents of this profile are private and legally privileged and confidential information, and the violation of my personal privacy is punishable by law. UCC 1-103 1-308 ALL RIGHTS RESERVED WITHOUT PREJUDICE*

The preceding message has so many inaccuracies and is so useless we do not even know where to begin.[8] The key point is that such messages do not do anything. Just because you post this as your status update does not mean you gain any form of protection at all. Also, as explained earlier, Facebook does not own all your data. It only owns some data (technically it licenses it without giving you any royalties) and can use it in limited ways, depending on your privacy settings and other factors. Instead of wasting time posting such messages, simply follow the aforementioned guidelines and, except in the most dangerous cases, you should be fine.

Again, we listed only a few guidelines and tips. Whether you are a government organization or a concerned citizen, check out the resources listed in Table 14.1 for more information.

Table 14.1: Resources with More Information Regarding Social Media and Privacy

RESOURCE	LINK
Privacy Rights Clearinghouse	`https://www.privacyrights.org`
American Civil Liberties Union	`http://www.aclu.org/`
Reputation.com	`http://www.reputation.com/ reputationwatch/articles/ top-five-social-media-privacy-concerns-2012`
Electronic Privacy Information Center	`http://epic.org/privacy/privacy_resources_ faq.html`
MobileActive.org How-To's	`http://mobileactive.org/search/ apachesolr_search/?filters=type%3Ahowto`
Safer Mobile	`https://safermobile.org`
ACLUNC dotRights	`http://dotrights.org/`

You are now prepared to use social media data and technologies to maintain and improve global security. More so, you can now do it ethically, legally, and effectively. We touched on only a few techniques and technologies. Our intention was to give you an idea of what you could do, not dictate what you should do. Many more techniques and technologies exist, and we encourage you to find, create, tweak, and share them.

Summary

- Issues concerning using social media for security while respecting people's privacy, identity, and right to free expression are complex and messy.

- Using social media effectively requires being concerned about protecting people's privacy and free speech.

  - Misuse of social media data and technologies can result in lawsuits and widespread criticism, which will impact your ability to complete your mission.

  - Misuse of social media may alienate populations whose help you need.

  - Rampant abuse of people's privacy and free speech online will harm the proliferation and power of the Internet.

- Even though ethics and norms concerning such issues are still emerging, you should pay attention to them now.

- Issues of protecting privacy and free speech concern organizations that use social media to improve security and individuals who want to protect themselves from abusive regimes.

- You can protect your organization, and analyze social media data and deploy crowdsourcing platforms ethically and legally by:

  - Analyzing open source intelligence that does not contain people's personal information that can help identify them.

  - Following the rules and regulations of your social media data sources.

  - Not involving children under the age of 13.

  - Abiding by special restrictions relevant to you that typically apply to military and intelligence organizations.

  - Not storing people's personal information unless you have permission or authority to do so.

  - Helping your crowdsourcing participants protect their identities.

  - Soliciting professional legal and area-specific help whenever possible.

  - Valuing privacy and maintaining a good reputation concerning privacy protection issues.

  - Imagining and preparing for the worst-case scenario.

  - Being aware of changes in laws and norms.

- Individuals protecting themselves from the techniques in this book will not impact most organizations' abilities to use the techniques to complete their objectives.

  - Most of the techniques in this book do not involve dealing with people's privacy and personal data.

  - The savviest malicious actors already know how to bypass the techniques that involve using their personal data.

  - Individuals who can protect themselves from malicious actors will increase overall security.

  - Improving security is a cat-and-mouse game that requires you to improve on our techniques.

- As a private citizen, you can protect your identity, privacy, and information by:

  - Setting basic security settings on any social media site you use.

  - Not posting sensitive information online.

  - Being wary about when you let others know your location.

  - Using software tools that anonymize you online, such as Tor.

- Using social media platforms that automatically hide your identity and data.

- Identifying the persons or organizations behind the sites or tools you use, and their intentions.

- Using common sense and being reasonable about your expectations when using social media.

Notes

1. Kravets, D. (2012) "Twitter Reluctantly Coughs Up Occupy Protestor's Data." WIRED. Accessed: 14 October 2012. `http://www.wired.com/threatlevel/2012/09/twitter-occupy-data/`

2. Fielding, N. and Cobain, I. (2011) "Revealed: US Spy Operation that Manipulates Social Media." The Guardian. Accessed: 14 October 2012. `http://www.guardian.co.uk/technology/2011/mar/17/us-spy-operation-social-networks`

3. Kirkpatrick, M. (2010) "Facebook's Zuckerberg Says the Age of Privacy Is Over." ReadWriteWeb. Accessed: 14 October 2012. `http://www.readwriteweb.com/archives/facebooks_zuckerberg_says_the_age_of_privacy_is_ov.php`

4. Singer, N. (2012) "Fan Sites Settle Children's Privacy Charges." New York Times. Accessed: 14 October 2012. `http://www.nytimes.com/2012/10/04/technology/fan-sites-for-pop-stars-settle-childrens-privacy-charges.html?smid=pl-share`

5. Hookway, J. (2012) "Vietnam Convicts 3 Bloggers Over Posts." Wall Street Journal. Accessed: 14 October 2012. `http://online.wsj.com/article/SB10000872396390444358804578015383720801250.html`

6. Engleman, E. (2012) "Huawei, ZTE Provide Opening for China Spying, Report Says." Businesweek. Accessed: 14 October 2012. `http://www.businessweek.com/news/2012-10-07/huawei-zte-provide-opening-for-china-spying-report-says`

7. Newman, J. (2011) "Phone Location Tracking: Google Defends, Apple Stays Mum." PCWorld. Accessed: 14 October 2012. `http://www.pcworld.com/article/226156/phone_location_tracking_google_defends_apple_doesnt_comment.html`

8. Ngak, C. (2012) "Viral 'Facebook Privacy Notice' Is a Hoax." CBS News. Accessed: 14 October 2012. `http://www.cbsnews.com/8301-501465_162-57447801-501465/viral-facebook-privacy-notice-is-a-hoax/`

Extra Information and Resources

Throughout the book we gave several examples of existing social media platforms and software tools. However, we barely scratched the surface of what is available. In this appendix, we list several more platforms and tools that you may find useful and point you to resources where you can get even more information.

Social Media Platforms

Hundreds of social media platforms exist, a few of which we list in Table A.1. This list is barely exhaustive but should help illustrate the diversity of social media platforms. For more information, check out the source that we used to fill out Table A.1. The source is, of course, one of the most popular crowd-sourcing platforms in the world, Wikipedia (`http://en.wikipedia.org/wiki/List_of_social_networking_websites`).

Table A.1: Social Media Platforms

PLATFORM	DESCRIPTION / SUBJECT
AsianAvenue	Asian American networking
aSmallWorld	European social elite
BIGADDA	Indian networking
Blip.no	Norwegian networking
Busuu	Language learning
CafeMom	Mothers
CaringBridge	Connects families during a health event
Cloob	Iranian networking
CozyCot	East and Southeast Asian women
Cyworld	South Korea networking
douban	Chinese reviews
FledgeWing	University students interested in entrepreneurship
Fotolog	Photoblogging
GovLoop	People in and around government
Grono.net	Poland networking
Ibibo	Talent in India
Jiepang	Location-based networking for Chinese
LAGbook	Africa-based networking
LaiBhaari	Marathi networking
mixi	Japanese
OUTeverywhere	LGBT community
Plurk	Microblogging in Taiwan
Raptr	Video games
ScienceStage	For scientists
Skoob	Brazilian
Sonico.com	Networking—Spanish and Portuguese
Spaces	Russian mobile phone users
Taringa!	Argentinian
Vkontakte	Networking for Polish and former Soviets
Vampirefreaks.com	Gothic subculture

Wakoopa	Software and games
WAYN	Travel
XING	Business in West-Central Europe
Xt3	Catholic networking
Zoo.gr	Greek
Zooppa	Creative talent

Software Tools

The number of relevant software tools available is too long to list. In Table A.2, we list some that we use frequently.

Table A.2: Software Tools

SOFTWARE	ORGANIZATION	URL
Big Sheet	IBM jStart	`http://www-01.ibm.com/software/ebusiness/jstart/bigsheets/`
R	R Foundation	`http://erzuli.ss.uci.edu/R.stuff/`
Gephi	Gephi Consortium	`http://gephi.org/`
Analysts Notebook	IBM i2	`http://www.i2group.com/us/products/analysis-product-line/ibm-i2-analysts-notebook`
Palantir	Palantir Technologies	`http://www.palantir.com/`
Pajek	Creative Commons	`http://pajek.imfm.si/doku.php`
Mathematica	Wolfram Research	`http://www.wolfram.com/mathematica/`
ORA	CMU CASOS	`http://www.casos.cs.cmu.edu/projects/ora/`
Netminer	Cyram Inc	`http://www.netminer.com/index.php`
Visone	Universität Konstanz	`http://visone.info/index.html`
NetworkX: Python	Los Alamos National Lab	`http://math.lanl.gov/Research/Highlights/networkx.shtml`

For information about social media monitoring capabilities, check out the list at `http://wiki.kenburbary.com/`.

Index